FINALLY STATEHOOD!

FINALLY STATEHOOD!

UTAH'S STRUGGLES, 1849–1896

Edward Leo Lyman

SIGNATURE BOOKS | 2019 | SALT LAKE CITY

Jacket design by Ron Stucki

www.signaturebooks.com

Finally Statehood! was printed on acid-free paper and composed, printed, and bound in the United States of America.

LIBRARY OF CONGRESS CATALOGING-IN-PUBLICATION DATA

Names:	Lyman, Edward Leo, 1942– author.
Title:	Finally statehood! : Utah's struggles, 1849–1896 / Edward Leo Lyman.
Description:	Salt Lake City : Signature Books, 2019. | Includes bibliographical references and index. | Summary: "Utah's quest for statehood lasted longer, involved more political intrigue, and garnered more national attention than any other US territory. While Utahns-especially the Mormon population-hoped statehood would grant them increased political autonomy, the several decades of refusal by church leadership to denounce polygamy stalled even the most carefully executed political schemes. Even without the albatross of polygamy, the territory presented a unique set of challenges. Lingering distrust toward the federal government blurred the lines separating church and state. LDS leaders considered themselves anointed by God to lead the government. Officials sent from Washington to dilute Mormon control found themselves in hostile, dangerous terrain. Aware of the complexity of this fifty-year struggle, historian Edward Leo Lyman carefully traces the key figures, events, and cultural shifts leading to Utah's admission to the Union. Utilizing an abundance of careful research, Finally Statehood! is a unique attempt to understand the state's history on both a local and national level, with each political roadblock, religious conflict, and earnest attempt at compromise meticulously examined under the vantage of time"—Provided by publisher.
Identifiers:	LCCN 2019028193 (print) | LCCN 2019028194 (ebook) | ISBN 9781560852735 (hardback) | ISBN 9781560853725 (ebook)
Subjects:	LCSH: Statehood (American politics) | Utah—History—19th century.
Classification:	LCC F826 .L948 2019 (print) | LCC F826 (ebook) | DDC 979.2/02—dc23

LC record available at https://lccn.loc.gov/2019028193
LC ebook record available at https://lccn.loc.gov/2019028194

CONTENTS

PREFACE

When the Latter-day Saints located in the Great Basin in 1847, they had already established an important priority of mainly governing themselves. When Mexican Alta California, an area comprising seven later states, was annexed into the United States in 1848, the LDS people had no choice but to accept territorial status. But they immediately aimed at the greater degree of autonomy through statehood. This proved to be a long process taking forty-six years and involving six petitions to the US Congress, as well as many drafts of proposed state constitutions, debated in conventions and ratified by the citizens. A persistent irritant during this period was the appointment of outsiders to territorial offices. The outsiders often viewed Latter-day Saints as heretics and traitors who needed to be watched over and contained. Certainly one major reason for desiring home rule was to be able to more fully establish the new system of plural marriage practiced by the LDS people. But it did not help that Church leaders, in their sermons, and members of the territorial legislature in speeches and memorials to Congress, went out of their way to antagonize US officials—president, cabinet members, and congressional representatives—with threats and ridicule. Noted American historian Howard R. Lamar summarized the problem succinctly: "Nowhere else had the federal government ever faced the problem of turning a desert frontier theocracy into a standard democratic American state." Latter-day Saints violated virtually every norm, politically, economically and socially, and at times did not appear to want to join the union as much as to leave it.[1]

1. Campbell, "Government Beginnings," 153–56; Lamar, *Far Southwest*, 409.

Some historians have suggested that LDS people had every reason to be wary of the government because of past experiences in the Midwest, where mainly state and local officials had often been their enemies.[2] Because of that, Brigham Young and others thereafter distrusted and opposed American political leaders at every turn. On the other hand, the Latter-day Saint claim to have been the victims of unprovoked opposition in Ohio in 1834-37, the 1838 Mormon War in Missouri, and the 1844-46 conflict in Illinois is due to what other historians identify as the "myth of persecuted innocence."[3] Latter-day Saints were not pacifists and were certainly not fans of American republican democracy. There were Church-sponsored Danites who sometimes persecuted apostates and anti-Mormons. Their task, as they saw it, was to build the City of God, to bring about the second coming of Jesus Christ and his millennial reign. They went about this in the way some European leaders had occasionally achieved religious rule centuries earlier through military conquest and arbitrary legal statutes.

If polygamy was usually cited in Washington, DC, as the reason Utah should not be granted statehood, the theocratic structure of the territory loomed just as large an impediment. Under Brigham Young, Church leaders, believing they represented God on earth and carried the divine mandate for real-world power, left little for the electorate to decide. The hierarchy determined who would run for office, and those men appeared on the ballots unopposed. Voters were asked to simply ratify an approved ticket. Dissent was frowned upon, outsiders were marginalized. LDS leaders believed they were serving as a wall against the dilution of God's law through secular appropriation and human error, and those who disagreed with this aim were regarded as antagonists. Thus many observers, among them congressmen, judges, and newspaper editors, believed that rule by the LDS Church was incompatible with the American system of government. Many, particularly those allied in Utah Territory with

---

2. Walker et al., *Massacre at Mountain Meadows,* 19.
3. Hallwas and Launius, *Cultures in Conflict,* 300.

the *Salt Lake Tribune* worked diligently for the eradication of the religious hierarchy from domination of Utah politics.[4]

Conflict over polygamy illustrated the inherent tension between the structure of the regional theocracy and representative government. For LDS leaders there could be no going back on a commandment from God, and they therefore engaged in a persistent, even heroic, struggle for what they fervently believed was a divinely mandated order. Yet while many church leaders were in hiding from US marshals "on the underground," men with but one wife, many from the recently matured younger generation, took over the reins of civil government locally and territorially through provisions of the Edmunds Act of 1882. A not-often-recognized large number of these men had never personally advocated "celestial marriage" and demonstrably desired to be able to make their own decisions in political and business affairs. They regarded the outside world—those of other faiths—with less hostility and assumed they might interact collegially without compromising their own faith.

This book breaks new ground in showing the political strategies formulated at Washington, DC, involving LDS-sponsored lobbyists and federal officials, coordinated with high Church officials at Salt Lake City. Having thirty years ago recounted the final steps toward statehood, this time I reach back earlier to previous attempts at rapprochement and the reasons they failed. Of major value is the correspondence between George Q. Cannon and Brigham Young, along with the diaries, official papers, and accounts of other government, news-media, business, and lesser Church personalities. Even congressional debates and insights from opposing parties illuminate the account. In order to emphasize these previously under-explored avenues of inquiry, I have skimmed over parts of the story that have been treated in full elsewhere, such as the doctrinal explication for

4. Clements, *Dubois*, quoted in *Political Deliverance*, 38–39n42, admitted that although he and his allies aimed at political domination, they understood how the emotion-laden issue of polygamy made it easier to arouse national public opinion against LDS Church rulers.

polygamy and statutory interpretations of it.[5] Suffice it to say that those on either side of the question believed they had the foundation of Christian morality on their side, making the clash longer and more bitter than it otherwise may have been. The well-developed LDS lobby networks several times made public announcements that plural marriage would be abandoned. These were intended by the Church hierarchy to be no more than strategic retreats until resumption might become more feasible through the political independence of statehood. But what these leaders did not anticipate was that many of their own people took the announcements at face value and themselves refused to support anything that appeared to be retrocession regarding legitimate public promises. To some, this included the Woodruff manifesto of 1890. Many do not understand that this was simply a public announcement, after several earlier Church decisions prohibiting the contracting of further plural marriages within the United States at that time. It had become absolutely necessary because of the *Davis v. Beason* US Supreme Court decision literally taking American citizenship away from all believing LDS members, including non-polygamists, in Idaho, and expected to soon be applied throughout the nation. Threatened confiscation of Church temples was another major consideration under this change of policy.

In a related dramatic aspect of the time, a now little-known James G. Blaine, who was one of the most popular political figures of the era, acted as the patron saint of Utah by interceding to halt legislation threatening the Church. This was partly in opposition to policies recently advocated by his party rival, President Ulysses S. Grant. An alliance between Blaine and his former LDS friend in Congress and now counselor to LDS President Woodruff, George Q. Cannon, brought about a major easing of tensions and new friendship between Church members and the Republican Party. It was an important step toward eventual statehood. From the beginning of his presidential regime, Woodruff was markedly less militant

5. For more, see Linford, "Mormons and the Law"; Firmage and Mangrum, *Zion in the Courts*; Gordon, *Mormon Question*.

in defense of plural marriage than his predecessor and more realistic in recognizing the realities of the changed circumstances of the consistently watchful federal government. He was also much more open to allowing his people to assimilate more completely into the American nation than either of the previous two Church presidents. He was inspired, but also realistic, certainly more so in his approach to interacting with other Americans than John Taylor and Brigham Young had been.

The author's interest in these subjects was long ago spurred by the mentoring and encouragement of the late Leonard J. Arrington and his former student, my professor, Thomas G. Alexander. Both have always been crusaders for honesty and objectivity in writing Latter-day Saint history, a great example to my generation and those thereafter. The staff of what is now the LDS Church and Family History Library and Archives has been helpful to this writer in locating and utilizing documents. The recently retired Church Historian and Recorder Steven E. Snow and his assistant Reid L. Neilson have been helpful with current citations of old manuscript collections.[6] I have relied on Kathleen Broeder and her staff at the Dixie State University Library special collections and Dianne Aldrich in charge of the interlibrary loan department of the same facility for many favors and requests, for which I am most grateful. The renowned editor of Mormon topics Lavina Fielding Anderson appreciably improved much of this book. My wife, Brenda, has supported me in every way with enthusiasm and

6. There is no guarantee that some of the documents utilized herein will be available to researchers at any given time. Access to some material seems to come and go at the otherwise unrivaled Church History Library, according to policies set by officials who are not directly in charge of the collections. It may be of use to those with a special interest in the topic to know that I have placed my research notes, including typescripts of many documents, and some printed material in the E. L. Lyman Papers at Southern Utah University's Sharratt Library Special Collections in Cedar City, Utah. Copies of the much longer original version of the manuscript are available there and at Dixie State University Special Collections and the Utah State Historical Society. Similarly, Scott G. Kenney, a longtime scholar of related subjects, placed his papers at the Marriott Library Special Collections, University of Utah, including a good number of photocopies of documents I only thought to make typescripts of, especially for material cited in chapters 5–8 of this work.

interest through the entire process. I am also most appreciative of editor Ron Priddis and his staff at Signature Books for their help trimming down the length of the manuscript and editorial suggestions, assisting with photographs, the wonderful design, checking for typographical errors, and indexing.

1

A DECADE OF STUBBORN FUTILITY

1847–57

The United States Constitution takes only sixty words to detail how a state can become a member of the union.[1] Like other parts of the new nation when the country was founded, the means of becoming a state would be expanded through trial and error. Residents of a territory could draft a proposed governing document and send it to Congress for consideration. Congress could pass an enabling act, legislation detailing how a territory might obtain statehood, including abolishing slavery, or in the case of Utah the abandonment of polygamy.

Latter-day Saints took steps early on to make their new settlement of what they called Deseret a state rather than a territory, and were almost immediately rebuffed. Efforts to secure the political independence that would come with statehood was traumatic for givers and takers. The missteps, the theocratic obstacles, and the offish nature of the Mormons themselves predisposed Congress against granting self-rule. It started with the people of the Great Basin founding their own government, reluctantly pursuing territorial status via an intermediary, and treating federal officials with hostility.

In today's strong national government, statehood might seem a strange way to guarantee political freedom. But in the nineteenth century, territorial status meant oversight from officials from Washington circles who were usually not drawn from among the area's

1. U.S. Const. art. IV, § 3, cl. 1.

own residents. When LDS people trekked into the Salt Lake Valley, it was before telegraph poles had reached across the prairies, before rails and steam engines had brought people overland. Washington, DC, was on the other side of the world, for all it meant to the day-to-day lives of the settlers. Statehood, and statehood alone, would grant them the kind of semi-autonomy they sought.

The arrival of the LDS leadership in July 1847 was to confirm that the Salt Lake Valley was the right place to settle, to plant a flag, so to speak (not the American flag), but they were not yet to remain. They assigned members of the previously organized Council of Fifty to oversee the outpost's operations and the ranking members of the leadership returned to the Omaha, Nebraska, area. It was not until 1848 that Brigham Young and other senior officials returned to the Great Basin for good and the Council of Fifty "organized itself into a legislature."[2] This legislature was Utah's first government, called the Kingdom of God. Clearly, this would not be just another state or territory.[3]

It was actually Mexican territory, but not for long. The 1848 Treaty of Guadalupe Hidalgo ceded huge swaths of land to the U.S., including the Great Basin, and forced Latter-day Saints to seek an affiliation with the United States. Congress responded by sitting on its hands. Enter a prominent friend of the exiled Latter-day Saints, Pennsylvania political operative Thomas L. Kane. From his first contact with LDS leaders, he agreed with their aim of self-government. Due to his efforts, they were able to utilize way stations on Indian lands across the prairies for their people to obtain fresh supplies while journeying to the Rocky Mountains. Kane's intervention constituted what one historian characterized as a "public relations campaign designed to shape a pro-Mormon government policy." He was also the one who proposed that Brigham Young seek territorial status as a stepping stone to statehood.[4]

The Pennsylvanian presented his territorial plan to President James K. Polk in February 1848 and made it clear that Young and

2. Rogers, *Council of Fifty*, chapter 4.
3. Hansen, *Quest for Empire*, 123–30; Morgan, "State of Deseret," 79.
4. Walker, "Thomas L. Kane," 105–06.

his people were willing to accept it. Polk was sympathetic: popular sovereignty was widely accepted within the Democratic Party. Even so, the US president failed to push through the necessary legislation. To spur him on, LDS leaders generated a petition with more than 2,000 signatures attached to it. It included a request for local Church members to be given the main positions of power and influence, headed by Brigham Young as territorial governor. John M. Bernhisel, a soft-spoken, fifty-year-old LDS physician, was selected to deliver the petition as the Church's representative.[5]

By the fall of Polk's last year in office, 1848, Kane saw the shifting winds and the growing reluctance to grant autonomy to settlers of the Great Basin. He withdrew Utah's pending request for territorial government, fearing that if they pushed on, two territorial governments would emerge, one official and filled with federal appointees from Washington and another a shadow government led by LDS leaders. His worries proved prescient: Utah would repeatedly clash with territorial officials over a period of fifty years and would maintain an unofficial parallel government.[6] Kane's and Bernhisel's efforts were the first short-lived attempt at setting up any kind of government in the new western empire.

The Council of Fifty ruled, albeit quietly, from Great Salt Lake City. Their decisions were made privately, then shared over the pulpit through announcements from Brigham Young and others.[7] Many of their decisions focused on practical matters such as land allotment and control of wild animals. On March 4, 1849, the council called for a convention to draft a constitution for an area covering what is now the greater part of three states and portions of another six for an entity they proposed be named Deseret. The council was organizing

5. Bernhisel reported he arrived in Washington in late 1849 and "mingled freely with the members of congress." Journal History, Mar. 21, 1850.

6. Walker, "Thomas L. Kane," 100, 101n42–45, 108, 110–11. The Council of Fifty functioned behind the scenes, but it drew more attention from Church members than the edicts of the territorial government. See Grow, *Liberty,* 86; Hansen, *Quest for Empire*, 11, 65–66.

7. Arrington, *Great Basin Kingdom*, 31–32; Rogers, *Council of Fifty*, chapter four; Manuscript History of the Church, Mar. 1849, 29. This supposed "ghost government" faded in effectiveness over time.

things "until the congress of the United States should otherwise provide by law." There was never a convention, or talk of organizing one, and the constitution was ultimately drafted in secret, a "façade to mask the establishment of the Political Kingdom of God," according to historian Eugene E. Campbell. Several historians have since drawn attention to questionable aspects of the process by which this first bid for statehood was organized.[8]

The priority in the minds of Church leaders was the millennial kingdom to rule the world under the direction of Jesus Christ. This would be alluded to by Brigham Young when he called on followers to remember Joseph Smith's prediction that the kingdom of God would "prevail over all our enemies." In mid-January 1863, Young told legislators that the time would come when "we shall ... give laws to the nations of the earth."[9] The repeated problem in obtaining statehood was this allegiance to a future millennial government intended to triumph over any secular system of governance. Being part of the United States was seen as a necessary evil rather than a privilege, and so the tension between the long-term goals of the Church and the more mundane requirements of Washington turned on the belief that the men in the desert were political emissaries of God, not just spiritual guides for the Church. This predisposed them to resist earthly authority outside their own ranks.

The constitution the Council of Fifty secretly drafted in March 1849 for a "provisional state government" borrowed from older state constitutions, particularly Iowa's, with deviations to remove any separation between church and state. Nor was there an allowance for decision making by the electorate. Church authorities assumed that by virtue of their stature, they possessed the right to make decisions for the good of the people. When the Latter-day Saints were in Missouri and Illinois prior to their migration to the West, they had

8. Campbell, "Government Beginnings," 153–57; Hansen, *Quest for Empire*, 129–30, 136; Crawley, "Constitution of the State of Deseret," 9–12; Poll, review of Morgan's *State of Deseret*, 3–4.

9. Journal History, Jan. 19, 1863; Hansen, *Quest for Empire*, 52, 54–57, 61–65; Campbell, *Establishing Zion*, 135–38.

already, according to outside observers, shown an un-American tendency toward autocracy, and that inclination continued.[10]

Eventually the leadership concluded to create what historian David Bigler termed "a new nation-state of their own without the approval of congress." By doing so, they did not endear themselves to Washington. Nevertheless, the government outlined by the Council of Fifty for the State of Deseret quietly went into effect without federal approval.[11] When notice of it was made by Senators Stephen A. Douglas and Truman Smith, they conceded that it was alright for the time being, since Brigham Young was already in control of the Great Basin. His ascendancy after the death of the Church founder had, in fact, come at the expense of both the Council of Fifty and the Quorum of Twelve Apostles.[12] In the spring of 1846 in Iowa, Young became frustrated with the established system of how the Church was governed and began to make unilateral decisions, superseding those of the Quorum of the Twelve. Later he would tell his people that they should obey him unquestioningly. It would not happen overnight, but in December 1847 the other apostles gave in to his coaxing and agreed to a new Church presidency with Young at the head, and Heber C. Kimball and Willard Richards as counselors, two men who were capable but would not dominate the president. In the first years in the Great Basin, the ecclesiastical leaders shared administrative responsibilities with the Council of Fifty as it evolved into a shadow government led by Young. The council was careful not to challenge Young's authority, mostly rubberstamping his proposals.[13]

One of the notable features of the proposed State of Deseret was the landmass it sought to control, extending from the Rocky Mountains to the Sierra Nevada and southward two-thirds of the way to Mexico through Arizona, jogging to the southwest to include San

10. Jensen, "Mormon Theory of Church and State"; Caldwell, "Mormon Conception of Individual Rights."

11. Bigler, *Forgotten Kingdom*, 45–47; Journal History, Mar. 21, 1850.

12. Bennett, *We'll Find the Place*, 71; Bitton, "Mormons in Texas," 5–6; Bennett, "A Samaritan Has Passed By," 8–12.

13. Bergera, *Conflict in the Quorum*, 53–83; Bennett, *Mormons at the Missouri*, 205; *Wilford Woodruff's Journal*, 3:283; Quinn, *Mormon Hierarchy: Origins of Power*, 247; Lyman, *Political Deliverance*, 303.

Diego and Los Angeles.[14] This geographical extravagance alone was enough to assure that the petitioners would be rebuffed by Congress.

Two days after the Council of Fifty accepted the constitution, penned by a few of its members, the government convened. Young's biographer Leonard J. Arrington rightly observed that this "began a nine-year period when the reins of political and ecclesiastical authority were united under Brigham's leadership." In the eyes of his followers, he personified the inspired government, and neither he nor they had much concern for what the world outside of the Salt Lake Valley thought of that. As Arrington explained, Young held the United States officials in "contempt" and was disinclined to compromise with them. His opinion was "seldom tempered by political expediency."[15] He felt the same way about any outsider. His disdain of any "Gentile" came to cloud his political judgement.

God would see to it that statehood was achieved, as he told territorial delegate John Bernhisel in June 1856: "I trust that when our application is fairly before them it will be favorably considered and acted upon. The Lord will control all for our good." As time marched on, however, and the federal government failed to meet Young's expectations, he "had little alternative but to accept the continuing territorial arrangement and unloose occasional hyperbolic bombast," which only produced additional animosity and delay. When Almon W. Babbitt left Great Salt Lake City in July 1849 with the proposed constitution, he was told to seek full-fledged membership in the union of states, not territorial status.[16] An unseasoned diplomat, Babbitt was an unfortunate choice to accompany the document to Washington, as Thomas Kane immediately recognized and Brigham Young soon acknowledged, due to his lack of tact and manners, the opposite of Bernhisel. He made the senators suspect that the constitution was a smokescreen and not a good-faith gesture, but intended only to conceal the theocratic supervision of the region.

---

14. Morgan, *State of Deseret*, 65–100. The proposed state would comprise about one-fifth of the contiguous United States.

15. Arrington, *American Moses*, xvi, 224, 232.

16. Arrington, 46–47, 238; Morgan, *State of Deseret*, 116, 117, 122. Bernhisel was also still representing the Saints in Washington.

At the same time, Babbitt was blindsided by William Smith, the erratic brother of Joseph Smith who was now living in Kentucky and sent his own memorial to Congress alerting them to his suspicion that Young and other LDS leaders had sworn an oath to avenge the blood of Joseph and Hyrum Smith (true) by toppling the U.S. government (false).[17] What's more, LDS aspirations fell victim to the sectional conflict between the North and South, even though it was still a full decade before the Civil War. For a time, the tension over slavery was placated by the Compromise of 1850 that, among other things, created a much reduced Utah Territory, about half the size of the proposed footprint of Deseret. As Ronald W. Walker stated, the compromise ended the hope that the LDS Church would control a grand western empire complete with seaports. What riled Church leaders even more was the fact that Washington had called all the shots. The terms had not been negotiated as much as dictated.[18]

Before General Zachary Taylor, of the recent Mexican–American War, became involved in a successful race for the US presidency in 1848, he predicted that slavery in the territories would become the "gravest [problem] the nation had ever faced." The topic arose when Pennsylvania Democrat David Wilmot suggested that slavery not be allowed in any part of the territory acquired from Mexico. It never became law, but the idea of it enraged southern politicians. Taylor could see, as he settled into the presidency, that the best solution would be for him to declare statehood for California (in which he proposed to include the LDS region as well), and southerners would be unable to object if the new state decided on its own to disallow slavery, without violating the sacred canon of states' rights. The problem would be peacefully resolved.

Upon entering office early in 1849, Zachary Taylor dispatched former Georgia congressman Thomas B. King to California to ask federal officials and miners to initiate a statehood effort. Although it was not explicitly stated, the understanding at the time was that a

17. *House Miscellaneous Document* 43 (31–1), 1850; Clayton, *Intimate Chronicle*, 223; Bernhisel to Young, Sept. 10, Dec. 31, 1849, Young Office Files.

18. Walker, "Thomas L. Kane," 100–119; Young to Bernhisel, Sept. 10, 1850, Young Office Files.

territory needed to have 60,000 inhabitants before it could be considered for admission as a state.[19] The president was careful not to appear to be interfering, but when his sentiments became known a movement quickly materialized. Historians have noted the irony that two slave owners, Taylor and King, were the ones who sought to shepherd California into the union as a free state.[20] They were reconciled to the belief that it was necessary for the sake of national reconciliation. This was the effort that culminated in the Compromise of 1850. Almost unknown later, this was preceded by another behind-the-scenes effort to attach the Mormon empire to California.

As John M. Bernhisel traveled east toward Washington, he encountered John Wilson, newly appointed federal Indian agent for the region the U.S. had acquired from Mexico. Bernhisel detected in Wilson a possible ally. A week after arriving in the Salt Lake Valley in August 1849, Wilson met with the First Presidency and assured them that President Taylor was "friendly disposed" and "fully appreciated [their] situation," probably a reference to their desire for self-government. If they entered into an alliance with politicians in California as one large state, Wilson suggested, that would help alleviate the trouble they otherwise anticipated through congressional debate involving slavery in the territories.[21] The president had "proposed a plan of making the whole territory [California and Deseret] into one state, leaving it in the power of the people to say whether it shall be a slave or a free state," which would remove a major bone of contention from Congress. Also, the Great Basin did not yet possess sufficient population to be considered independently. This was the most generous offer Washington had made thus far, but LDS leaders did not immediately detect its advantages.

Young disclosed to apostle Amasa M. Lyman, who was living in California, that he had thought it over and was inclined to favor the approach. If southern slave holders like Taylor and Wilson were "willing to make a sacrifice for the public good," against the interests

19. The Northwest Ordinance of 1787 stated this explicitly.

20. Smith, *Presidencies of Zachary Taylor*, 94, 103; Hamilton, *Prologue to Conflict*, 17.

21. Culmer, "General John Wilson," 321–26; Brigham Young to Amasa M. Lyman, Sept. 6, 1849, in Journal History; also Lyman, "Larger than Texas," 27–28.

of their southern cohorts, then the Saints ought to follow in tow, he believed. If elements on the Pacific Coast connected to "southern influence" could be neutralized, in part by the opinion of the added LDS population, the intended result would be realized. He was willing to pull for a free state, even though there were a few prominent slave owners among the Latter-day Saints.[22] Young understood that this was the primary reason the settlers of the Great Basin were being invited to join the statehood attempt. He explained to Lyman the hope "that by our influence we should be enabled to counter balance that of the slave holders" and their sympathizers who were plentiful in some areas of the West.

The Church president confessed that when the proposal was broached, he and his counselors "rejected altogether the idea of any amalgamation whatever with the government on the coast." This came from the mistaken belief that Deseret might still be admitted on its own, even though its small population might disqualify it. The Zachary Taylor initiative was the most viable alternative, as the Church authorities realized, once they understood that their independent effort was faltering.[23]

From its inception, the Taylor–Wilson plan anticipated a temporary union of the eastern and western slopes of the Sierra Nevada, the eastern inland area being allowed to split off as early as 1851, they were told. Young discounted the vastly superior population of California, arguing that it mostly comprised gold seekers and few families, much of the population transient, whereas Utah's population of 15,000 was expected to grow to over 75,000 by 1851, he said. The growth of the Great Salt Lake area was impressive, but he was also overly optimistic. The population would not reach 75,000 for another three decades. Thinking that 1851 would arrive soon enough, before "the yoke will be broken," he decided that "while government is using us to save the nation, we are using them to save ourselves." He cautioned Lyman that "there must be no doubt of our

22. Bringhurst, *Saints, Slaves, and Blacks*, appendix C, lists ten LDS slave owners, including apostle Charles C. Rich, Provo mayor Abraham O. Smoot, and legislator William H. Hooper.

23. Journal History, Mar. 21, 1850.

being a [separate] state at the commencement of '51, without any further action of Congress."[24]

He erroneously assumed that LDS leaders in California had time to negotiate with the politicians on the West Coast before any action would be taken. He designated Lyman and J. W. Pickett to assist Wilson in traveling west and pitching the US president's suggestion at the constitutional convention that was anticipated. Pickett was an attorney, a former Latter-day Saint who had married Agnes Coolbrith Smith, the widow of Joseph Smith's brother Don Carlos, and had moved to San Francisco. Unknown to the traveling party, the convention had already been convened in early September in Monterey. All along they assumed they would have a role in the formation of the state. Young had cautioned Lyman against letting the Californians take a dominant position, stating that "no man in all our councils will consent for a moment to wear a broken yoke," meaning an unequal position. If it looked like it, the LDS lobbyists were to break off their participation and tell Congress to keep Deseret out of the alliance. Young thought the delegates could make good use of the *California Star*, one of the first newspapers in the region, founded by Samuel Brannan, who had led LDS immigrants to California in 1846 on a ship that had sailed from the East Coast around Cape Horn (Patagonia).[25]

While there is no evidence that Zachary Taylor and his advisors favored Young's wish that Deseret include part of California's southern coast, Young pressed for that outcome. He instructed Lyman to ascertain if the people of Los Angeles and San Diego were "as favorable" to the Mormon presence as they had been earlier when the Mormon Battalion arrived there after the Mexican–American War.[26] If the same sentiment prevailed, Lyman should "find no difficulty in securing our proposed boundary." Young encouraged Lyman to exert "a religious influence over the people and government," to gain as much support in the region as possible. He candidly disclosed his

24. Young to Lyman, Sept. 6, 1849; also Lyman, *Amasa Mason Lyman*, 168–92.
25. Lyman had a good relationship with Brannan, even if Brigham Young did not.
26. Lyman, "Larger than Texas," 18–23.

ambition "to inhabit that country as well as this and [receive] our share of good [land] in common with the great whole."[27]

John Wilson and his wife and family left Salt Lake City under military escort in the fall of 1849, led by Bvt. Captain R. M. Morris. The entire way the self-important Wilson quarreled with Morris until finally striking out on his own against Morris's orders. When a storm hit the Sierra Nevada in December, Wilson had to leave his law books and other baggage behind as they struggled through snowdrifts, taking twice as long as it had taken Amasa Lyman the previous spring to reach his destination. The *Alta California* in San Francisco announced Wilson's arrival in mid-December with a report of his treatment of Captain Morris, an uncomplimentary tale that would have undermined his effectiveness as a lobbyist.[28] In any case, the late timing had already thwarted their intent to influence the outcome of the constitutional convention.

Already six months earlier, General Bennett Riley heard that the US Congress had adjourned without providing so much as a territorial organization for California. Determined to rectify that, on June 3, 1849, the military governor called for a constitutional convention in Monterey in the fall, the same month Brigham Young dictated his instructions for apostle Lyman. While Riley had no authority to establish a civilian government, he knew President Taylor would not mind the action, especially because he made sure that of the forty-eight delegates elected, only eleven came from the southern portion of the proposed state. When the proceedings commenced in early September, Wilson was still in the early part of his ninety-day journey, and Lyman would probably not receive Young's missive until October. That meant that there were no LDS representatives at the convention. It is unfortunate because there had been a controversy over whether the southern half of California should even be included in the state. The hottest national question about slavery was hardly mentioned before the delegates voted overwhelmingly to

27. Young to Lyman, Sept. 6, 1849. This could not be considered a serious goal until the Church founded San Bernardino in 1851 (see Lyman, *San Bernardino*).

28. *Alta California*, Dec. 15, 1849; Culmer, "General John Wilson," 317–19.

exclude the "peculiar institution" from the state.[29] What stimulated the greatest discussion was where the eastern boundary should be. Some believed it should embrace the entire tract of land Mexico had held as Alta California, which would include present-day Arizona, Nevada, New Mexico, Utah, and western Colorado. Others argued that only areas represented at the convention should be included. As the discussion progressed, delegates changed their minds, alternately becoming upset with each other to the point that the proceedings nearly broke up over the question of boundaries.[30]

The day was won by a committee assigned to consider the matter, when it offered the conclusion that if the Mormon people had wished their area to be included, they would have sent delegates. Little did they know the effort Wilson was making, trudging through the snow in the Sierra Nevada. If the LDS delegates had attended, it seems likely the proposal for a larger California would have been adopted.[31] A month after adjournment, about the time Brigham Young's letter reached Amasa Lyman, Peter H. Burnett was elected first governor of the proposed coastal state. On December 15, 1849, the legislature held its first session at San Jose, despite not yet having legal status since Congress had not yet recognized it.[32]

While the legislature was engaged in its inaugural duties, John Wilson and Amasa Lyman arrived. They met with Governor Burnett on January 8, 1850, to present an unusual petition. The citizens of "East California" had, in fact, sent delegates, they explained, "with instructions to have the Salt Lake region included for the time being." Since they had not been able to reach the Pacific Coast until after the convention had concluded its work, they requested that Burnett call a new convention to consider forming a single state out of "all the territory acquired from Mexico." The petition suggested the advantage of considering the "final settlement of the vexed question of slavery" for the whole region. While Latter-day Saints had

29. *Alta California*, Sept. 20, 1849; Brown, *Report of the Debates*, 446.

30. Rawls and Bean, *California*, 108; Rice et al., *Elusive Eden*, 206–07.

31. *Alta California*, Oct. 1, 1849.

32. Browne, *Debates in the Convention of California*, 443–49. Burnett was a former attorney who had assisted Joseph Smith in 1838 in Missouri.

not specifically excluded slavery themselves, they announced themselves as being anti-slavery due to the instructions they had received to take that position.[33]

Wilson and Lyman candidly disclosed that they would want to eventually separate from California, and that the Mormon people had pushed for their own state to include "all the territory east and south of the Sierra Nevada," the obvious "natural boundary dividing West California from East California." The western section had the superior "right of access to the Pacific Ocean," extending for miles northward, so it would only be fair to allow their neighbor the harbors of San Diego, Los Angeles, and San Pedro, and that "a boundary line should be agreed on" now to facilitate separation later, they argued.[34]

Burnett was not averse to airing this in a written message to the legislature, but he added a personal note that in his opinion the two communities were "too far apart" in their views, like Texas and Maine, he offered as a comparison. The lawmakers agreed. They did not need to be prompted either, since the question had consumed so much of their energy months earlier. Their sympathy and good will toward the LDS people was different than associating their statehood attempt with the emotion-charged controversy involving the Mormons. Some of the delegates were more sympathetic than others. A few wondered if the new applicants had their eye on California's gold fields.[35]

The tone and volume of press coverage the issue attracted must have informed Brigham Young and his associates at the outset that their movement had been launched too late. If Zachary Taylor had been more committed, he could have dispatched an emissary at the same time he sent T. B. King to California. Even Wilson's slow pace in reaching Salt Lake City in late August 1849 and not conferring

---

33. According to the Compromise of 1850, Utah and New Mexico could choose to favor slavery or not when they became states. Hittell, *History of California,* 2:802–04; Bancroft, *History of California*, 4:325–26.

34. *Alta California*, Dec. 15, 1849; also *Journal of the Senate of the State of California*, 129, 429–51; *Journal of the Proceedings of the House*, 766–71.

35. *Alta California*, Feb. 9, 1850.

with the LDS leaders until around the first of September indicates a degree of indifference. In retrospect, it was impractical to expect Californians to adjust their plans for the benefit of the people of "East California." Nothing offered by the Mormons would have been to the benefit of the Golden State. The delegation from the area around the Great Salt Lake was looking for concessions with little to give in return. Even when they received President Taylor's proposal through his emissary, it took LDS leaders some time to realize its value and respond to it.[36] It may have been just an idea President Zachary Taylor had of how to deal with the Latter-day Saints, because he did not want to see the Church gain either territorial status or statehood on its own.

Before California rejected the proposal in February 1850, President Taylor concluded that it might even impede the area's choice to become a free state. In his annual message to Congress on January 23, 1850, he suggested that no harm would come from leaving the Great Basin alone for now, without a government: "No material inconvenience will result from the want of a government established by Congress over the part of the territory which lies eastward of the state of California."[37] LDS leaders were discouraged by the turn of events, but still assumed they had a chance at territorial status with access to the ocean until their congressional delegate, John Bernhisel, told them otherwise. The Church's most sympathetic supporters in Congress, Senators Stephen Douglas of Illinois and Truman Smith of Connecticut, were not "disposed to give the Mormons any territory on the coast."[38]

Bernhisel knew that Douglas and Smith were in favor of allowing Deseret to elect its own officers for a provisional government. However, there had been no real progress toward that goal. Smith agreed to introduce Bernhisel to Zachary Taylor, the president known as Old Rough and Ready. Bernhisel found him "rough enough, though he does not appear very ready; he is an exceedingly

36. Whitney, *History of Utah*, 1:407–10.
37. Richardson, ed., *Compilation of Messages*, 6:2564–68.
38. Journal History, Mar. 21, 1850; Barrett, "Dr. John M. Bernhisel," 155–59.

plain man in the fullest sense of the term," a "strictly honest" man who appeared out of his element as chief executive, Bernhisel surmised. The delegate was disappointed to hear Taylor confess that the matter was out of his hands. The deduction Bernhisel made was that Taylor was "somewhat prejudiced against us" as a result of the "slanderous reports in circulation" from William Smith and others about Brigham Young running "a theocracy," which was true enough but not helpful.[39]

Senator Douglas was the most important Democrat involved in assimilating former Mexican lands, along with Whig Senator Henry Clay of Kentucky, the main sponsor of the Compromise of 1850. Bernhisel reported that Douglas disliked Deseret as a name (he preferred Utah) and was opposed to the proposed state's gigantic size. Claiming sympathy for the people of the region, Douglas argued that the Church would have more "peace and quiet" if the state's boundaries did not extend to the Pacific Coast. He predicted that when other people moved in, the all-too-familiar pattern of conflict between the Mormons and their neighbors would erupt and the inland region would do better as a friendly neighbor establishing trade and travel.

In subsequent days and in letters that followed in March 1850, Bernhisel ascertained that there was no chance for the region to be admitted as a state, although there was support for its acceptance as a territory. This would not be welcome news to Young, so Bernhisel attempted to sweeten this information by adding that there would be funds available for the provisional government. Smith, who was reputedly the closest legislator to President Taylor, promised to introduce legislation to that effect. Those plans fell apart when Taylor died in July.[40]

The leaders of the LDS Church accepted these developments with the stoicism to which they were conditioned by their previous experience with the federal government. They still had one

39. Bernhisel to Young, Mar. 5, 1850; Bernhisel to First Presidency, Mar. 15, 21, 1850, both in the Journal History.

40. Journal History, Mar. 21, 25, 27, 1850.

last hope for statehood and for a part of the Pacific Coast. Apostle Charles C. Rich, who had replaced Amasa Lyman to run Church affairs in California, wrote that month to Young that the "inhabitants in the south part of this state are more and more dissatisfied with the proceedings of the north part." If Congress did not admit it as a state, "the south [of California] will no doubt go against being attached to the north and will petition for a separate territory or [be] attached to Deseret." Hoping against California's imminent admission, Rich expressed belief that Zachary Taylor's plan might yet come to pass.[41]

There was a movement among the Hispanic population of the southern half of Alta California to remain separate. The reason was illustrated two years later in a statement by the second governor of the state, John McDougal, about the property taxes received that year for six ranching counties (the "cow counties") of Southern California, amounting to $42,000 from a population of only 6,000. The twelve mining counties in the north, with a population of at least 120,000, had paid half that much, in part due to the fact that the state had exempted many of the mining claims from taxation.[42] Because the twelve mining counties had four-fifths of the legislative representatives, the southern counties could not expect a fair shake.

That was rendered irrelevant when the US Congress admitted California to the union as part of the Compromise of 1850 and accepted the boundaries proposed at the constitutional convention. Utah was designated a territory. The Latter-day Saints had no choice but to accept this. They were left with an advantage in Washington, DC, because of Thomas Kane, who was on friendly terms with Millard Fillmore, the vice president until Taylor's death and now suddenly chief executive of the United States. Fillmore offered Kane the governorship of Utah. Kane declined the offer because of his unpredictable health.[43] At a crucial juncture soon after, as President Fillmore was determining what his approach to Utah would be,

41. Charles C. Rich to First Presidency, Oct. 2, 1850, Journal History.

42. Rawls and Bean, *California: An Interpretive History*, 126.

43. Walker, "Thomas L. Kane," 115; Barrett, "Dr. John M. Bernhisel," 143–67; Grow, *Liberty*, 86.

he asked Kane for an appraisal of Brigham Young. Kane's glowing endorsement "fully satisfied" Fillmore, according to Kane's account. The president decided to appoint Young and other Latter-day Saints to most of the territorial positions.

That intention was undermined by the clumsy Babbitt in trying to secure appointments for personal friends, at which Fillmore changed his mind and looked to tried-and-true party loyalists for half of the eight available positions, leaving the other half for Latter-day Saints. The LDS positions went to Young as governor, former Texas Ranger and LDS missionary Seth M. Blair as US attorney, LDS bishop Joseph L. Heywood as federal marshal, and judicial leader Zerubbabel Snow as an associate justice. The non-Mormon appointees included newspaper editor Broughton D. Harris as territorial secretary, former US congressman Joseph Buffington as chief justice, Washington attorney Perry C. Brocchus as an associate justice, and Washington justice of the peace Henry Day as the Indian agent. Bernhisel apologized to Young that the appointees were not all "from our number" and assured him that Fillmore had otherwise chosen people who were "friendly disposed" toward the Latter-day Saints.[44]

When Young heard how nearly they had come to gaining full control of the territorial government, he probably resented the way Babbitt had bumbled the assignment.[45] It set the tone for years of constant conflict with non-LDS territorial officials, which would define the relationship between the LDS Church and the US government. Bernhisel observed that "the appointing power has been far more liberal to us than it has ever been to any other territory," attempting to soften the blow.[46] This was true, and the encouragement they received from Polk and Fillmore predisposed Church leaders to expect more of the same in the future, even suggesting in late 1856 and early 1857, through the territorial legislature, that only

44. Walker, "Thomas L. Kane," 115–17; Bernhisel to Young, Oct. 2, Nov. 9, 1850, Journal History. Apostle Orson Hyde was later considered for a position, but the US Senate favored non-Mormon Leonidas Shaver (Barrett, "Dr. John M. Bernhisel," 95).

45. Turner, *Brigham Young*, 200–01, shows Young's disillusionment with Babbitt.

46. Bigler, *Forgotten Kingdom*, 59; also Cooley, "Carpetbag Rule," 115–21; Alexander, "Conflict and Fraud," 119–25; Walker, "Thomas L. Kane," 118.

Latter-day Saints should be appointed to government positions in the Great Basin. This presumptuousness generated an unprecedented outpouring of antagonism toward Utah and contributed to President James Buchanan's decision to send the US Army to Salt Lake City to compel submission to federal officials. The unsophisticated attempt, to that juncture, to gain self-rule provides context for the Utah War. Howard R. Lamar wrote that Fillmore's selection of four non-LDS officials set the stage for "bitter battles with federal appointees for control of Utah government," persisting almost a half century.[47]

The conflict was not inevitable. It began on February 3, 1851, when Daniel H. Wells administered the oath of office to Brigham Young. Instead of waiting for the arrival of federally appointed Chief Justice Lemuel Brandenbury (Buffington had declined the position) and others, Young began performing the duties of all the appointees. Conscious of normal protocol, the federal officials were right to interpret it as an infringement of their responsibilities. For example, in the spring of 1851, Young ordered a census that should have been administered by the territorial secretary. He ruled that elections could be run by local non-US citizens. Secretary Harris said he arrived to find that Young had expended federal funds to pay Church debts. The officials' stay was short—less than two months—before they packed up in September and left in disgust, Harris refusing to hand over the $24,000 Congress had appropriated for operating the government.[48] Indian agent Henry Day arrived to find people already appointed to positions in Indian Affairs and Brigham Young already in full control of matters related to that important area of the government. The three-member territorial judiciary consisting of Brandenbury, Snow, and Brocchus found that the legislature had selected probate judges and justices of the peace from a pool of candidates consisting of LDS bishops and other Church officials. The judges and JPs were "handling the cases usually handled by federal courts," the men of the supreme court noted, and the untrained decisions rendered by these LDS judges lacked any apparent benefit

47. Lamar, *Far Southwest*, 328–29.
48. Arrington, *American Moses*, 227–30.

of custom or precedent.[49] This was not resolved until passage of the Poland Act in the early 1870s.

After that bristly beginning, neither Brigham Young nor the appointees made any movement toward rapprochement. The non-LDS men publicly commented on the offenses that had been committed against their offices and rendered critical views of the situation. They sent a steady stream of letters to Washington explaining the insults and offenses in etiquette. All four of the indignant outside appointees who had arrived in the summer of 1851 left in the fall, taking the territorial seal with them.[50] Chief among them was Judge Brocchus, who had not hidden his ambition to become the territorial delegate to Congress. Within weeks of arriving, when Young invited him to speak at the September Church conference on Temple Square, the judge took the occasion to comment on the still-secret practice of plural marriage and to reprimand Young for having said that Zachary Taylor was in hell and deserved to be there. Young was astonished that the judge would say such things in a Church meeting where he was invited to speak as a guest and in defiance of Young's grip on control of both church and state, especially after Young had come to the judge's aid when he had been ill in August to make sure the judge received the best possible care.[51]

After the speech, Young tried to reach a compromise with the judge on several issues, a fact that is not widely known.[52] In the stream of letters between the two, Young was patient and accommodating, but he played to his LDS audience by publishing his correspondence. When the federal appointees abandoned their posts and traveled to Washington, three of them, Brandenbury, Harris, and Day, lodged complaints and retreated to their respective states. Brocchus stayed in Washington to beat the drum of military necessity to put down the insurgence in the West. It was fortunate

49. Campbell, "Government Beginnings," 161–63; Bigler, *Forgotten Kingdom*, 51, 58; Roberts, *Comprehensive History*, 3:501.

50. Boreman, "Crusade against Theocracy," 11–12; Alexander, "Utah Federal Courts," 25–78; Allen, "Unusual Jurisdiction," 133–39.

51. Turner, *Brigham Young*, 88, 90, suggests that Brocchus "inflamed the controversy with his speech" as an excuse to leave.

52. Ronald W. Walker to Leo Lyman, July 15, 2010.

for the Latter-day Saints that people looked dimly on desertion. The four men became known as the "runaway officials" or "flying officers," the press finding out they had less than stellar reputations in other areas, as well, so that their complaints about Utah created little real stir.[53] The problem was that when Washington replaced them, the replacements received the same treatment in Salt Lake City and reacted the same way, by leaving their posts or reporting back to Washington that the region was in a state of revolt. The same pattern would repeat itself over the next six years: officials would arrive; their authority would be undermined; they would hear of threats against their lives; and they would report back to Washington on the disloyalty and low state of morality in their desert outpost, including details about men having multiple wives. Gradually bills would be introduced in Congress aimed at remedying the Utah problem.

John Bernhisel offered Governor Young some advice in July 1851. If the governor had followed it, it could have prevented an unfortunate subsequent chain of events. The delegate warned that any further provocation could result in Young's removal from office. "No pains nor effort [should] be spared to cultivate the most friendly relation between the new appointees and the authorities and people of Utah," Bernhisel advised. "In order to attain and maintain so desirable a state of things, it may frequently become requisite to exercise great patience and forbearance—to 'stoop to conquer' as the play says." This fell on deaf ears. Haunted by the past, especially the Mormon War in Missouri, Young could not bring himself to demonstrate the forbearance Bernhisel desired.[54]

Babbitt had earlier advised Young not to insist on the continued existence of the State of Deseret, but Young consistently used it when signing his name as governor of Deseret. In a public discourse in June 1853, over a year and a half after the departure of the first four federal officials and long after their replacements had arrived, he affirmed: "I am and will be governor, and no power can hinder it, until the Lord

53. Journal History, Sept. 20, 25, 1851; Lamar, *Far Southwest*, 328–29. Congress soon passed a law requiring that officials remain at their posts until excused.

54. Campbell, *Establishing Zion*, 219.

Almighty says 'Brigham, you need not be governor any longer' and then I am willing to yield to another governor."[55] A year and a half later, in February 1855, he returned to the subject by acknowledging that the US president had authority to replace him, but asserted that this would not happen if God wished otherwise. "No other power can prevent" him continuing in office, he said, if it were so fated.[56] This tempering of the rhetoric failed to reassure those watching from Washington that he would go quietly if asked to leave.

Young did not care, because he was fiercely committed to the idea that Jesus Christ's return was imminent. That made him disinclined to be a political chess player or to suffer fools gladly. He would make overtures, and there were times when it did seem that he wanted compromise in order to achieve peace. On the other hand, he was easily offended, considered himself a victim, and was convinced there was a conspiracy to deprive him and his people of their rights. Therefore he appointed his own trusted associates to government positions, some of them still serving as officials in the illegal government operating alongside the territorial apparatus. To those involved in the organization of the State of Deseret and the intertwined structure of the Church, there was not anything out of order in this. So Judge Zerubbabel Snow took on cases in all three district courts before the territorial supreme court was properly reconstituted, on authority of the already existing government. To understand the dynamics of this conflict, it is essential to see, as Arrington stated, that Young's political authority was "religious rather than secular." Without anything like ordinary self-appraisal or reflection, he believed he need defer only to God, which is why he had little interest in what outsiders thought of his reign.[57]

This created a catch–22: it was vital that the territory achieve statehood for the sake of political independence, but Young acted as

55. Brigham Young, "Where the Wicked Go," *Journal of Discourses*, June 19, 1853, 1:187.

56. Arrington, *American Moses*, 245–46. Brigham Young, "The Priesthood of Satan," *Journal of Discourses*, Feb. 18, 1855, 2:183.

57. Young's "explanations have the ring of a self-satisfied but misunderstood man, slightly on the defensive, ready to see opposition and persecution in little things, but sure of his rightness and confident of his power," wrote Arrington, *American Moses*, 230.

if they already enjoyed that privilege, making it harder for Congress to grant it to them. Consider the next attempt to persuade Congress. In August 1852 the territorial legislature dispatched a memorial requesting an enabling act setting out the steps the territory needed to take before assuming "her place beside her elder sisters in the great federal union." A few weeks later, Brigham Young authorized apostle Orson Pratt to acknowledge in public for the first time that members of the Church were indeed practicing polygamy as part of their religion. If Congress had been at all favorably disposed toward the territory's aspiration for statehood, this confession chilled its receptivity, as did the intensity with which the Church defended its marital anomaly over the ensuing forty years. Despite that reality, the territory sent new memorials to Congress in 1853, 1854, and 1855,[58] oblivious to the national mood, and always accompanied by the proposed 1849 constitution for the State of Deseret. The territory gradually became more aware of normal diplomatic procedures, yet its petitions received less heed than the less sophisticated previous communications.

The resistance on the part of the US Congress to the territory's overtures generated intense frustration in Utah. A *Deseret News* editorial in the spring of 1855, after the failure of the fourth memorial attempt at statehood, noted that the settlers had mostly come from the eastern states and were the country's political offspring. "What should be done by the parent government?" The newspaper's reply was to "knock off the shackles," not just in Utah but in any territory when they "petition for it, and present a proper state constitution." The U.S. should "admit them into the union as states" without regard for "the number of their population."[59]

In 1856 Utah mounted a more concerted effort by convening a real convention, the first to be held publicly. The legislators, meeting in the territorial statehouse in Fillmore in December 1855, authorized the election of delegates to attend a convention in late

58. Arrington, 131, 237; *Acts, Resolutions and Memorials*, (1852), 222; (1853–54), 76–77; also Bigler, *Forgotten Kingdom*, 101.

59. "Inconsistent Conduct of the United States towards Her Territories," *Deseret News*, Mar. 8, 1855.

February. For the first time, two of the delegates would be non-LDS, including US Indian Agent Garland Hurt. During the eleven-day convention, the delegates approved a document that, not much different than the 1849 version, declared a "free and independent state" of Deseret. A ratifying vote of the people on April 7 in conjunction with a general Church conference approved the proposed constitution almost unanimously. Apostles John Taylor and George A. Smith were chosen to present the constitution and accompanying memorial to Congress.[60]

After they arrived at Washington, DC, in late June and conferred with Bernhisel and Senator Stephen Douglas, now chair of the committee on territories, they reluctantly concluded that it was not a good time to present a statehood petition. Douglas had become unwilling to be associated with Mormons any longer and advised them to leave the petition with a clerk "and let it follow regular course."[61] The apostles could not find anyone in Congress to sponsor them, the announcement about polygamy having poisoned the well.

In addition to that, the Republican Party had been gathering strength for the past two years in the northern states. At their first national convention, their platform called for the eradication of polygamy and slavery as "twin relics of barbarism." No federal statute prohibited the practice, but that technicality did not soften the repulsion people felt toward it. The timing of the renewed push for statehood could not have been worse.[62] Brigham Young publicly complained about receiving a cold shoulder. Citing again the rule that a territory needed to surpass a given population threshold, he claimed a census that year showed Utah to have 77,000 residents. He expected an additional 20,000 by year's end. Aside from the fact that population was not the main reason the territory's application was being ignored, Young again exaggerated his figures. The estimate three years later by agent Garland Hurt was that there

60. Brooks, ed., *On the Mormon Frontier*, 2:592–95.

61. MacKinnon, *At Sword's Point*, 1:55n7.

62. Foner, *Free Soil*; Young to George A. Smith, July 30, 1856, Smith to Young, Mar. 15, 1857, Brigham Young Office Files; MacKinnon, *At Sword's Point*, 1:136.

were 41,400 people in the territory, and that proved to be a good number. The next year the official 1860 federal census found 40,273 settlers in Utah.[63]

After Governor Young's four-year term ended in 1854, he continued in office despite not being reappointed. US President Franklin Pierce, who was elected in 1852, selected Colonel Edward J. Steptoe as Young's replacement; but Steptoe had been in Utah as a federal road surveyor and investigator of the Gunnison Massacre and knew better than to accept. He recommended that Young be retained. As Pierce was about to leave office in early 1857, and was reviewing the events of his administration with his cabinet, he failed to even mention Utah. The incoming Democratic president, James Buchanan, who was inaugurated on March 4, 1857, was similarly silent. As the oldest chief executive yet at age sixty-five, he began his administration in poor health, unable to easily cope with the press of business. As the nation was fracturing before his eyes, the Mormon question was initially a low priority.

Despite that, within a month of taking office, the president signed orders to Secretary of War John B. Floyd to dispatch 2,500 US Army troops, aided by large supply trains, west to assert their presence in Utah Territory and curb Young's insubordination. In July the orders were amended. The troops would escort Young's successor, Alfred Cumming, to Utah.[64] One of the key catalysts for this was the memorial adopted by the Utah Legislature on January 6, 1857, suggesting that only Latter-day Saints should be considered for federal office in the territory. That compounded the horror stories that had come in at a steady stream from territorial officials.[65]

Utah's lawmakers dispatched a "Memorial and Resolution" on January 16, 1857, ten days after the measure was adopted, in one of the most fateful actions undertaken by the LDS population. In the memorial, federal appointees were characterized as "false hearted

63. Bigler, *Forgotten Kingdom,* 102n49.

64. See Hafen and Hafen, *Utah Expedition*, 27–34, for the initial orders.

65. MacKinnon, *At Sword's Point*, 1: 100–03; Brooks, *On the Mormon Frontier*, 2:616. One distressing report came from Chief Justice John Kinney, another from James Gordon Bennett, publisher of the *New York Herald*, March 20, 1857.

men" and "corrupt demagogues from every section of this widespread republic." The petitioners asserted that "no sensible persons would accept such officers," appointed "contrary to the known and expressed wish of the people." The government men "serve their own selfish purposes totally regardless of the rights of others." The territory would no longer submit to such a "corrupt and base set of officials," the memorial read.[66]

The lawmakers further resolved that while they would observe laws imposed upon them "so far as they may be applicable to our condition in our territorial capacity, we will resist any attempt of government officials to set at naught our territorial laws, or to impose upon us those which are inapplicable and of right force in this territory." It was defiant, promising to "resist any attempt" by federal "officers to bring us into difficulty by misrepresentation or otherwise with either of the departments of government." The legislators provided Bernhisel with a list of selected citizens of the territory, with instructions that the president should use the list in making appointments, or at least choose men with compatible interests in Utah's growth and prospects. It included only one name for governor: Brigham Young. If officials from outside the territory proved to be "political demagogues or bigots," the memorial warned, "we will send them away," and avoid "all social intercourse" with them.[67]

These threats stood in marked contrast to the deferential language the president was accustomed to. The legislators misunderstood how carefully Bernhisel had cultivated good will with the US presidents and senators by exercising diplomacy. They misjudged the depth of wounds inflicted on national leaders by the insults Young had flung at them in his sermons. All their posturing and tough talk did was to confirm to the president that Utah Territory was in a state of rebellion.[68]

---

66. "Memorial and Resolution to the President of the United States, Concerning Certain Officers of the Territory of Utah," Jan. 16, 1857, in Legislative Assembly, Territorial Legislative Records, 2711–18.

67. MacKinnon, *At Sword's Point*, 1:68–73.

68. Cooley, "Utah War," 15–17; Furniss, *Mormon Conflict,* 47–101; Moorman and Sessions, *Camp Floyd*, 3–42.

Complicating matters, Latter-day Saint leaders had been concerned for nearly a decade about their followers' commitment to the Church and to each other. Young saw the unity of the Saints as crucial to building a theocratic kingdom, so he enthusiastically endorsed the Mormon Reformation, a revival-style crusade his counselor Jedediah M. Grant had introduced as a spark beginning in 1855 and then fanned to white-hot heat since then.[69] It absorbed the greater portion of the time and attention of the Church authorities, as more important than forming relationships with outside politicians. The memorial to Congress represented the culmination of this emotion-laden period of literal reformation in all aspects of Latter-day Saint life.

Young believed he understood the true principles of the US Constitution better than anyone in Washington. He considered the Constitution to be a divinely inspired document that had come about, in God's time, to protect the Latter-day Saints at a later time when they would need to have political autonomy. In keeping with that view, he believed the Church already had a right to self-rule. Any interference was considered religious persecution. Of all the missteps that resulted in the alienation of the Latter-day Saints from other Americans, and particularly from elected officials, the developments from mid-1856 into 1857 loom as the most decisive of all, even before the fateful Mountain Meadows Massacre in September 1857.

The way Latter-day Saints saw themselves, they were a chosen people, and outsiders were either potential converts or enemies. This worldview reinforced their perceptions of persecution, creating an almost conspiratorial outlook. No matter how benign an action on the part of the federal government was, it was interpreted as being antagonistic. Young told the Saints, "We are the best people in the world." His counselor Heber C. Kimball spelled out the corollary: "The Gentiles are our enemies; they are damned forever; they are thieves and murderers, and if they don't like what I say they can go to hell, damn them!" To these comments, the listeners shouted "amen."[70]

69. Sessions, *Mormon Thunder*, 203–63; Larson, "Mormon Reformation," 60–63; Peterson, "Mormon Reformation," 23–54, 69–84; Turner, *Brigham Young*, 255–63.

70. Anderson, *Desert Saints*, 420–21. Brigham Young, "Privileges of the Saints," *Journal of Discourses*, Aug. 26, 1860, 8:158; Hardy, *Doing the Works of Abraham*, 129.

The well-mannered territorial delegate, John Bernhisel, got off to a good start with President Buchanan on March 9, five days after his inauguration. They met briefly to discuss the lapsed appointment of Brigham Young. Buchanan thought it best to allow Young to continue in office with an unstated status for the time being. He noted the growing hostility in the country toward Utah over polygamy. He reassured Bernhisel that he was not personally biased and would carefully consider both sides of the issue.[71] Then the memorial arrived from Utah via California and Panama. Already exhausted by illness and the steady throng of office seekers, Buchanan directed Bernhisel to take the document to Secretary of the Interior Jacob Thompson, the cabinet member responsible for territorial affairs.[72] Bernhisel did so and scheduled a follow-up meeting on March 18, 1857, at which Thompson excoriated Bernhisel for "the tone of the memorial," which he said he "did not like" one bit. This put the delegate in a difficult position, probably one of embarrassment more than defensiveness. Thompson thought it was "a declaration of war," "breath[ing] [such] a defiant spirit" that if LDS people found themselves at odds with Washington, they "would have nobody to blame" but themselves. The memorial was "not respectful," he reemphasized. They needed to treat federal officials with respect, regardless of their religious affiliation, he lectured Bernhisel.

For years, students of the Utah War have wondered what it was that triggered President Buchanan's decision to dispatch a large contingent of federal troops to Utah, and whether it was based on misinformation. Was it "Buchanan's blunder," as people later said? Buchanan saw reports from functioning territorial appointees to lay the groundwork for his decision. The final blow, as evidenced by Secretary Thompson's reaction, was the statement of disloyalty from the territorial legislature. It became the foremost reason federal authority needed to be reasserted where the government's rule had been openly flouted from the beginning.[73] It had such an effect on Bernhisel, as

71. MacKinnon, *At Sword's Point,* 1:103–04.
72. Nevins, *Emergence of Lincoln*, 2:72–77, for more on Thompson.
73. MacKinnon, *At Sword's Point*, 1:230–43.

well, that he waited half a month to prepare a report for Governor Young, having clearly lost his nerve, and in anticipation of Young's explosive response. Historian William MacKinnon noticed that "instead of swinging into action" when something was needed "to moderate the administration's negative reaction, Bernhisel grew lethargic, if not fatalistic. He withdrew from the fray" and retreated to his childhood home in Pennsylvania, penning his letter to Young on his return to Washington. This left Young in the dark for over two months after Bernhisel had met with Thompson. The letter was written on May 2 and reached Utah on May 29. By then the US Army was well into its preparations to relocate to Salt Lake City.[74]

Thomas Kane told the US Attorney General, Jeremiah Black, he hoped no harm would come to the territory as a result of Bernhisel's abandonment of his post in Washington, DC. After sending a letter to Buchanan and receiving no reply, Kane himself also became temporarily less committed to the Mormon cause. In a letter to Brigham Young in May, he announced his departure from politics for the moment, having failed in his efforts on behalf of the territory.[75] When Young received these communications, he had already traveled to Fort Limhi, Idaho, on a reconnaissance expedition to see if anyone was aware of government agents or soldiers on the trail. Bernhisel disclosed "a disposition in both houses of Congress and throughout the length and breadth of the land, never to admit Utah into the Union with her 'peculiar institution' [of polygamy]. I regret to say," he continued, "that within the last few months prejudice against us as a people has greatly increased, not only at the seat of central government, but throughout the extended republic."[76] With more candor, Bernhisel might have explained that this "prejudice" was in reaction to the legislature's memorial and President Young's brag that he could not be removed from office.

When the army was dispatched, eastern newspapers publicized the resignation letter of Associate Judge of the Utah Supreme Court

74. MacKinnon, 1:103–07, 112, 120–21, 135.

75. Grow, *Liberty*, 159–70.

76. Bernhisel to Young, Apr. 2, 1857, Young Office Files; Bigler, *Forgotten Kingdom*, 144–46.

William W. Drummond. That only belatedly added fuel to the fire of animosity toward Utah.[77] There were no diarists within Buchanan's inner circle, so there is no direct confirmation of how important that letter was. It arrived toward the end of May when preparations were already being made for war.[78] There had been an earlier complaint from Drummond that was received at the capital by March 19 that may have colored Secretary Thompson's reaction, and it certainly influenced James Gordon Bennett in his editorial for the *New York Herald*. Bennett supported the need for Buchanan to address two questions immediately: the threat of more violence in Kansas and sedition in Utah. The *Herald* was widely read, so its conclusion that "the leading men of the [LDS] church" were "traitorous" carried weight. But as MacKinnon has suggested, the "real catalyst for the change" in the Buchanan administration was the memorial from the Utah legislature.[79]

United States Attorney General Jeremiah S. Black received a letter on March 20 from Utah's chief justice John F. Kinney requesting an extended leave of absence during the existing state of uncertainty. Actually, Kinney had already left. He was unable to carry out the functions of his office due to Young's constant interference, he contended. By the time the letter arrived, Kinney had arrived in Washington and met personally with Black to recount numerous additional examples of "what he believed to be Brigham Young's perversions of Utah's judicial system." The view of the Justice Department was that the governor should be removed from office and federal troops stationed in the territory for the protection of the attorneys and judges. He urged Black to share this information with other cabinet members.[80]

Another document delivered to Black at the same time came from the Utah surveyor general, David H. Burr, who heaped additional criticism on Young. Earlier in the year, in February 1857,

77. Bancroft, *History of Utah*, 504; Creer, *Utah and the Nation*, 125; Cooley, "Utah War," 15–17; also Hafen and Hafen, eds., *Utah Expedition*, 363–66.

78. Furniss, *Mormon Conflict*, 67–68; Moorman and Sessions, *Camp Floyd*, 10–15.

79. MacKinnon, *At Sword's Point*, 1:100–03.

80. MacKinnon, "And the War Came," 22–37.

Burr had proposed adjustments to land policies in a speech before the territorial legislature. Afterward Hosea Stout recorded in his diary that "feelings were very high." It constituted, in Stout's mind, "a contest for the supremacy of our laws in our own courts over the unlawful usurpation and rulings of the district courts."[81] This was typical of the extreme rhetoric and defensiveness of local legislators. The fact was that Utah enjoyed the greatest control of its court system of any US territory.[82] That would not be the case much longer. The federal government was unhappy with how land ownership had been handled in Utah, without complying to federal law. Settlers claimed ownership without purchasing or registering their property, and thus claimants had to be told that their property holdings were tenuous. Thousands of people, many from Europe, who had converted to Mormonism and made the arduous journey across the ocean and prairies, built cabins, farmed, and raised cattle, were now learning they had done so on land that was not the Church's to give away and could potentially be seized, so it was a sensitive topic.[83]

Burr was respected in Washington as a cartographer who had frequently been employed by the federal government and the states. The Latter-day Saints adopted the tactic of looking into his background and attacking his character and competence. Whatever truth there was to it, he was a credible witness to members of Buchanan's cabinet. In Burr's letter he warned that any new governor would probably risk assassination. Mirroring Kinney's recommendation, he advised a military escort, though downplaying the need for a large force over an extended period. A report from Indian agent Garland Hurt contained even more of the same warnings about how precarious the situation was. With so many disturbing dispatches arriving simultaneously, it is no wonder Buchanan came to a determination

81. Brooks, *On the Mormon Frontier*, 2:622; also MacKinnon, *At Sword's Point*, 1:60n21.

82. Alexander, "Utah Federal Courts," 25–74; Allen, "Unusual Jurisdiction," 133–40.

83. Larson, "Land Contest in Early Utah," 309–25; Linford, "Establishing and Maintaining Land Ownership," 126–43.

to do something decisive.[84] He was shocked by the sensational nature of the charges. Even if he dismissed the account of Judge Drummond, who was being discredited because of his own bad behavior, Buchanan could not ignore the corroborating testimony of the others.

As the first decade of Mormonism in what was initially called Deseret came to a close, the settlers of the Great Basin were disappointed to realize they had not yet gained a measure of autonomy through statehood. The position promoted by Church leaders was that this was due to prejudice, evil, oppression, and persecution, which was at best self-defeating. It overlooked the fact that the nation had had abundant opportunity to appraise the theocratic bent, ambition, and defiance of the settlers. As the divergent positions hardened on both sides of the question of whether to grant self-determination for a part of the country that was ambivalent about its loyalty to the United States, it meant that for years to come no other territory stood less of a chance of being admitted as a state than Utah.

84. Alexander, "Conflict and Fraud," 119–25; MacKinnon, *At Sword's Point*, 1:108–09; Stampp, *America in 1857*, 201.

2

THE ARMY MARCHES TO UTAH

1857–72

The next fifteen years were fraught with tension and the possibility of violent conflict between Latter-day Saints and the federal government. At least ten anti-Mormon or anti-polygamy bills were introduced in Congress. Not dissuaded, Latter-day Saints submitted two more separate petitions to be admitted as a state, one in 1862 and the other in 1871, the first quickly rebuffed, the second for a time holding some hope of progress. The most devastating development after the so-called Mormon War, from the LDS perspective, was the appointment of Judge James B. McKean, who arrived in the territory poised to stamp out polygamy. He was thwarted within two years, but if he had succeeded he would have inflicted great political and social devastation, and temporarily he did so, to a degree. More than a few outsiders predicted that his zeal would meet with resistance and potentially lead to another armed conflict. As determined as President Buchanan was to resolve the Utah problem militarily, his successor Ulysses S. Grant, elected in 1868, would prove to be even harsher in his policies against Mormons. In fact, he was probably, in association with his appointee Judge McKean, the most bitter antagonist of the Latter-day Saints since Missouri Governor Lilburn Boggs. It is difficult to imagine how a presidential administration could have behaved more sternly toward the Church and its members, without major violence.

Responding to the territory's insulting memorial to President Buchanan (discussed in chapter 1) and negative reports from federal officials, in mid-1857 the decision was made to order a large proportion of the entire United States Army to march on Utah. William S. Harney was the best-known general at the time, and when he was recalled from a campaign against the Seminole Indians in Florida some observers already assumed he was the one who would be given command of the expeditionary march to Utah. He would have been happy to oblige, but was assigned to "Bleeding Kansas." Colonel Albert Sidney Johnston of Texas was the one who received the appointment to assemble troops to invade Utah in August 1857.[1]

Although Brigham Young had heard rumors of the Utah Expedition as early as June,[2] it was not until midday on July 24, 1857, during the tenth anniversary celebration of the original pioneers' entry into the Salt Lake Valley, that the news was confirmed. At a mass gathering of people who had traveled to a mountain resort to celebrate the day, three riders in dust-caked clothing arrived with information for Young about the army being underway. He received it calmly and without public comment until later in the day. First he discussed its import with some of the other leading Church authorities who were present. When the assembled crowd of over 2,500 prepared for evening prayers, Daniel H. Wells, general of the still-active Nauvoo Legion, matter-of-factly informed them of the news and told them to return to the valley the next morning and begin considering what defensive measures might be necessary.

The first perceptible steps toward military preparation came on August 1 when General Wells told subordinate militia officers that the advance of troops was "tolerably well authenticated," and that the army's intent was to "invade Utah territory." He informed the officers that mobilization orders would be issued. Later in the month there was evidence that Young might announce an intent to resist the armed forces "from coming into this territory under any pretense whatever." He noted in his diary that he had become "fixed in my determination not to let any troops enter this territory … and make every preparation to give the U.S. a sound drubbing. I do not

1. MacKinnon, *At Sword's Point*, 1:126–27, 130–33, 184, 282.

2. Brigham Young, "True Happiness," *Journal of Discourses*, July 5, 1857, 5:1–5.

feel to be imposed upon any more." This kind of defiance was uttered publicly as well, not only by Young but by counselor Heber C. Kimball and apostle John Taylor.[3] Young waited until September 15, 1857, then declared martial law and ordered all military forces under his command to hold themselves ready.[4] Incredible as it seems for a sworn territorial governor to declare war on the United States, Young must have had but little idea of the potential military power he was standing up to. It seems he believed the crisis would be averted, perhaps by God's intervention, and that it was his task to discern and carry out God's will and nothing more.

He believed the real intent of the army was to seize him and take control of the government. Rather than allow that, he came to the determination that he would burn the urban core of Salt Lake City and direct its inhabitants to flee into the hinterlands. Although Captain Stewart Van Vliet, the quartermaster of the invading army, held a reasonably cordial discussion with Young, and Van Vliet warned that "if the Territory should resist the orders of the [war] department [they] should be committ[in]g an overt act [of treason]," Young refused to be intimidated. He proclaimed that he would "have neither their soldiers [n]or officers any more here at all." The report Van Vliet made to Washington helped President Buchanan confirm that "the Mormons were now in armed rebellion against the government." Historian John Turner concluded that Young's proclamation not to allow military into the city "was a distinctly unwise and dangerous step," especially considering Young's intent to stall the army's advance. However, he did accomplish that for a time. The primary result of his bluster, however, rather than gaining the sympathy of the nation, was to provide a solid case for treason indictments against him and his colleagues.[5]

As the stage was set for a calamitous conflict, Utah militiamen

---

3. Roberts, *Comprehensive History*, 4:239; Brigham Young diary, Aug. 11, 1857, Young Papers; Brooks, *Mountain Meadows Massacre*, 19n2. See Kimball's 1857 sermons in the *Journal of Discourses*, 5:164, 253–54, 274–75, 334–35, and Taylor's, 5:112–23, 150–58, 186–90.

4. Arrington, *American Moses*, 254–55; MacKinnon, *At Sword's Point*, 1:234–35, 285–90.

5. Stott, *Search for Sanctuary*, 106–07; Turner, *Brigham Young*, 269, 271–74, 282–84.

sought to thwart the invasion by burning supply trains, rustling cattle, and slowing the advance, which they impressively accomplished for a time, halting the invading army at the onset of winter in Wyoming. Thereafter, calmer diplomatic negotiators, starting with Thomas Kane and then the official peace commissioners Lazarus Powell and Ben McCulloch, were able to diffuse the threat and, amazingly, bring about an acceptable accommodation and eventually amnesty.[6] For the moment, Young added fuel to the controversy by publishing an intemperate protest against Buchanan in a mid-August editorial in the *Deseret News*. It was likely intended to rally citizens of the territory, and Buchanan probably never received the message himself, but outsiders took notice of it. "If you intend to continue the appointment of certain officers, we respectfully suggest that you appoint actually intelligent and honorable men, who will wisely attend to their own duties, and send them unaccompanied by troops, which you yourself know are of no lawful use here." If the people of the territory were provoked, he wrote, they would exploit their prerogative of "using that class of officials strictly in accordance with their deserts," coming very close to the nineteenth-century idiom "use up," meaning to murder.

The editorial was unsigned, but could not have been printed without Young's oversight. Its confrontational tone bears his fingerprints, his style of diplomacy being aggressive and blunt, and he said much the same thing in his public discourse of August 16, 1857, only a portion of which was published. Claiming to know precisely what orders the coming troops had been given, he said they had been told "to use up [kill] the [Church] leaders, break up their organization, disperse the people, and call in our Gentile brethren and break up this kingdom called Latter-day Saints." He vowed again that US troops would not set foot in his domain. His assertion was, "I will fight them and I will fight all hell [rather than] lamely submit to such outrages and wrong oppression." In the same speech, he threatened that if the Utah

6. Moorman and Sessions, *Camp Floyd*, 21–24, 42–43; MacKinnon, *At Sword's Point*, 1:329–43; Bigler, *Forgotten Kingdom*, 152–54; also Journal History, June 12–13, 16, 24–25, 30, 1858.

Expedition continued west, he would no longer restrain the region's Native Americans from attacking emigrants on the Oregon Trail. It is a point of debate whether this influenced the Church members who three weeks later participated in the Mountain Meadows Massacre, but the circumstantial evidence is persuasive.[7] At least, the fiery speeches by Young and his associates during the tense summer of 1857 constituted what historians have seen as Young's declaration of secession from the union and threat of violence.

There were equally inflammatory pronouncements from other Church leaders, published in the Church-run *Deseret News* and reprinted in other newspapers around the country, creating alarm among outside readers. While the *Deseret News* omitted the most strident statements, non-LDS travelers heard them and passed them on to reporters when they reached their destinations. Outsiders were shocked at the intemperance of these statements issued from the pulpit of the Tabernacle. The foremost historian of the conflict, William MacKinnon, found that even "members of [Young's] own Church]" understood his "volcanic rhetoric" to convey a message of secession from the country.[8]

Fortunately Thomas L. Kane, the first of several impressive non-LDS lobbyists, sought to calm the waters.[9] The Buchanan administration should be credited for allowing him to seek a peaceful solution in an unofficial trip. He and the peace commissioners, Powell and McCulloch, eventually found a successful resolution to the conflict.[10] There had not been a time in the country's history when a territory exhibited more bitterness and alienation in its campaign to become a state, often going out of its way to antagonize those it hoped to receive favors from rather than looking for a path to reconciliation.

---

7. Bagley, *Blood of the Prophets*, 81–102; Walker et al., *Massacre at Mountain Meadows*, 96–98, 145–47; Lyman, *Overland Journey*, 125, 128–29. This is certainly true regarding the earlier Mormon Reformation, which inclined the settlers of southern Utah to interact with hostility, if not fanaticism toward most outsiders.

8. MacKinnon, *At Sword's Point*, 1:229–43.

9. Furniss, *Mormon Conflict*, 62–69; Hafen and Hafen, *Utah Expedition*, 267–86; Grow, *Liberty*, 159–70; Turner, *Brigham Young*, 290–96.

10. Unlike Kane, Powell and McCulloch were firm with Young, as they were also with Col. Johnston.

When the *Washington Union* offered what might be termed the party-line report on February 16, 1858, in the nation's capital, it claimed the troops had been mobilized to protect settlers from an Indian menace. It took note of "the flagrant insubordination of the Mormons" only to defend the necessity of sending troops "as a posse to sustain the authority of the executive and judicial officers of the federal government." This was done "strictly with reference to these two considerations and not in the character of an invading force against a hostile country," the editorial explained. It was not done to wage war or as an exercise in religious persecution, but because of "the duty which rested upon the president to see the laws of congress faithfully executed in our own territory."

In a sense, the editorial gave an accurate summary of the Buchanan administration's view that there was a rebellion that needed to be put down, whether it was to be done by police action or military conquest. As alarming as it appeared, it would soon fade in people's minds as the Civil War approached, the Deep South beginning its secession four years later. In December 1860 William H. Hooper, the new Utah territorial delegate to Congress, expressed his confidence to apostle George Q. Cannon that three-fourths of the Republicans in the House of Representatives would vote to admit Utah as a state in order to put that controversy to rest, in light of the larger problems they faced. "Many say they would gladly 'swap' the gulf [of Mexico] states for Utah." The territory received praise for not joining with the southern states, something the southern congressmen suggested Utah should do.[11] Hooper told Cannon he saw an opportunity to "show our loyalty by trying to get in, while others are trying to get out, notwithstanding our grievances, which are far greater than those of any of the seceding states." His optimism at a time when the country was distracted by war helped stimulate another ill-fated petition for statehood.

In December 1861 George A. Smith, a member of the territorial House of Representatives, showed President Young a draft of a bill

11. Roberts, *Comprehensive History*, 5:1–3. The Buchanan administration spokesman, the *Washington* [D.C.] *Union*, suggestion of any type of related "Indian menace" proved to be a total fabrication.

calling for a convention to write a state constitution. Young approved of it. "If they don't" accept it, he said to the legislator, "tell them that we will organize a state government [ourselves] and control [it]." He added that "we must soon organize a government for ourselves, and take care of ourselves," illustrating how little he had learned about Washington's response to ultimatums. His threats would continue to kill any hope of success in moving toward self-rule.[12]

After Governor Alfred Cumming's term ended, the third individual appointed to be Utah governor was forty-one-year-old John W. Dawson, former editor of the *Times* in Fort Wayne, Indiana. After his appointment by President Abraham Lincoln in October 1861, he hurried to Utah before the US Senate had even confirmed his appointment. Three days after his December 7 arrival, he delivered a message to the legislature and appealed for them to remain loyal, implying that there was some question about whether they would. In fact, only a fraction of the Latter-day Saints was from the American South, so his audience had no quarrel with his appeal to back the Union. Then the governor requested an annual tax of about $27,000 to help underwrite the war and recommended several changes in the territory: public schools to replace the congregationally based schools, a new land survey, and sale of public land to immigrants to raise funds. This implied to his audience that he wanted to encourage non-LDS immigrants to settle in the territory—people who could afford to purchase land. It implied a decertification of the existing land titles LDS people had claimed without asking for the federal government's approval.[13]

Brigham Young instructed lawmakers to ignore the governor's speech. He had said the same about Governor Cumming's final message in 1860, and he would say so again regarding Governor Stephen Harding's address in December 1862. In line with Young's instructions, Governor Dawson's address was left out of the official record. If they paid the war tax, Young said, or what he called the

12. Kenney, *Wilford Woodruff's Journal*, 5:605; also Church Historian's Office Journal, Dec. 15, 1862.

13. "Governor's Message," *Deseret News*, Dec. 18, 1861; also Lamar, *Far Southwest*, 356–57, 387–88; Roberts, *Comprehensive History*, 5:13–14.

"loyalty tax," next they would be required "to send 1,000 men to the [civil] war." He would "see them in hell before I will raise an army for them," he insisted.[14] Instead of pursuing Dawson's recommendations, the legislators enacted a bill for another constitutional convention intended to free themselves of appointed governors. Dawson vetoed the bill, claiming they had not allowed Congress sufficient time to consider Utah's previous request in 1856. To President Lincoln a month later on January 13, 1862, Dawson reported more candidly that the legislature was intent on setting up their own state government, something they expected to have operational soon, whether or not Utah was admitted into the union.[15]

His suspicion was confirmed a week later when, on January 20, when the convention delegates met and elected Daniel H. Wells as president and William Clayton as secretary. Wells was Young's second counselor and Clayton, who had been a clerk for Joseph Smith, worked closely with Young on Church projects. The committee for drafting the constitution included apostles George A. Smith and John Taylor, along with future apostle Albert Carrington and LDS territorial judges Elias Smith and Zerubbabel Snow. A five-man committee was assigned to draft a memorial to Congress.[16] The constitution the convention was intended to draft had already been written and was adopted the next day, with a general election scheduled for the first Monday in March to vote on the constitution and elect US senators and a governor in case the constitution passed. The name of the state would again be Deseret. Young was the gubernatorial candidate. Although the vote was never completely reported, it was said to be virtually unanimous with no dissenting votes out of almost 10,000 ballots cast.

Governor Dawson did not stay until the election. A young widow, Albina Merrill Williams, who was doing some sewing for

14. Church Historian's Office, Journal, Dec. 11, 1860. A number of LDS volunteers joined their home-state military units, representing almost every part of the country, including nine southern states, and served on either side of the war (Alford, ed., *Civil War Saints*, appendix).

15. John W. Dawson to Abraham Lincoln, Jan. 13, 1862, Robert Todd Lincoln Collection; Bigler, *Forgotten Kingdom*, 201–02; Whitney, *History of Utah*, 2:37.

16. *Deseret News*, Jan. 22, 1862.

him, said he made a pass at her. Out of fear of retaliation, he decided to retreat to Indiana on an afternoon stagecoach, protected by a group of young men who were recommended to him as bodyguards as he crossed through the adjacent eastern mountains. The first night out, the driver revealed himself to be a relative of Mrs. Williams. He and the guards beat Dawson. When the governor arrived in Indiana and wrote to Lincoln on January 13, he reported that he had not yet fully recovered.[17]

The territorial secretary, Frank Fuller, a non-LDS appointee, became acting governor and diplomatically endorsed the on-going effort to achieve statehood, as did the reappointed territorial chief justice, John F. Kinney.[18] As Dawson had predicted, Young called the "state legislature" into session on April 14 and delivered a "gubernatorial message," published in the *Deseret News*. Thomas Kane's fears had come true. The LDS-backed government now existed openly, separately, alongside the secular one. It was a dangerous game the Church was playing, but its members fell in line by granting their allegiance to it and ignoring the federal government.

According to Wilford Woodruff, Young argued privately that "we have got to frame our own government and govern ourselves[,] [for] we shall not be governed ownly by the devel [devil] & wicked men and go to hell together." He again ridiculed the population threshold of 60,000, even though it rarely had been mentioned in Washington. He cited Secretary of State William H. Seward's statement that the only qualifications for a new state were "a substantial civil community and a republican [representative] government."[19]

The Church president rejected the idea that the settlers needed to prove their loyalty before they could be accepted as a state. They were not aliens, he insisted, but "tried and firm supporters of the Constitution." He said so without apparently seeing the irony in

17. Dawson to Lincoln, Jan. 13, 1862; also Whitney, *History of Utah*, 2:38; Stenhouse, *Rocky Mountain Saints*, 592.

18. "Proceedings of the Convention," "Speech of Hon. John F. Kinney," Deseret News, Jan. 29, Feb. 5, 1862. Brigham Young probably never knew about Kinney's negative reports to the Buchanan administration (chap. 1).

19. *Deseret News*, Apr. 16, 1862. Kenney, *Wilford Woodruff's Journal*, 6:40; Roberts, *Comprehensive History*, 5:5n12.

the fact that they were now running their own unauthorized government. "What are they going to do about it?" he asked his inner circle.[20] Lincoln ignored the brashness of Young's rhetoric, partly because of the demands of presiding over the war. A few days before Young's address to the faux legislature, nearly 20,000 soldiers were killed or wounded in the Battle of Shiloh in Tennessee.[21]

Brigham Young has often been characterized as an astute politician, an able leader, but it is difficult to see how his dealings with Washington merit that assessment. He played to the gallery by being discourteous to federal officials, which was unwise at best and dangerous at worst. He personally did as much as anyone to thwart Utah's admission to the union, not only in the earlier attempts, but even after his death in 1877 as reports of hostile comments he had made continued to generate deep-seated resentment throughout the country. This penumbra would not subside in places of national power until a significant portion of Young's generation, especially contemporaries in Congress, had passed from the scene.

He specifically argued on January 23, 1862, that since the US Constitution did not expressly grant Congress the power to create territories, it lacked authority to do so. Only the people of the territory themselves had that right, Young reasoned. He considered this legal argument to be sufficient justification for reestablishing a fully operational State of Deseret, the same government he and his inner circle had tried to create in 1849.[22] Political theorists think the acceptance of a political entity within a national government is an inherent power for any country, although some Democrats in Young's time would have applauded his resistance of federal authority under the doctrine of states' rights.

In the territorial election in Utah, there was, as usual, only one candidate per office—individuals the Church had endorsed. People obligingly voted for the proposed senators, George Q. Cannon and

20. Roberts, 5:4; Kenney, 6:10–11.

21. Among the fatalities was General Albert S. Johnston, who had led the Utah Expedition in 1857.

22. Bigler, *Forgotten Kingdom*, 205.

William H. Hooper. Cannon was born in Liverpool and had only been a US citizen a few years (or arguably not even yet) and was at the time a counselor in the British Mission. Even so, he hurried to Washington and joined Hooper in mid-June 1862 in presenting the statehood petition to Congress. The vice president, Hannibal Hamlin, introduced their petition to the Senate. Senator Milton Latham of California requested that Cannon and Hooper be admitted as elected officials, which was denied. The consideration they were given was because even though the territory was in rebellion, it had not joined the Confederacy. Even so, the petition was tabled and nothing more came of it.[23]

Church members were quick to see Washington's rejection as a form of religious persecution. Future apostle Orson F. Whitney captured the mood in Utah when he wrote that "the wall of prejudice was too thick to be penetrated." Some people assumed that since the State of Deseret was a poorly kept secret, the memorial gave Congress a chance to either bless the reality of it or allow it to continue by looking the other way. The nation's lawmakers disagreed. An ad hoc government was treacherous, and if it were not for the Civil War, their passive aggression might turn into overt military action. In the background was a persistent irritation over the territory's marriage arrangements. When Orson Whitney composed his history of Utah, the first volume published in 1892, he was a young polygamist and Salt Lake City bishop. As the grandson of Heber C. Kimball and stepson of Joseph Smith by a polygamous wife, he moved in the Church's inner circles and doubtless had reasons and sources behind his conclusion that "had the Mormons been willing to abandon polygamy in 1862, thus meeting the Republican party half way, it was not improbable that Utah, in view of her loyal attitude [by not joining the Confederacy], might have been admitted into the union." He may have been right, but polygamy was not the only obstruction. Even if it was, Young and others in the hierarchy had not yet given a moment's consideration to abandoning

23. Whitney, *History of Utah*, 2:58–59; *Deseret News*, July 2, 1862.

polygamy in the 1860s.[24] Their hostility to Washington was first and foremost the reason they were not given consideration in the nation's capital when they requested statehood.

Congress was more attentive when it came to a bill that Vermont Congressman Justin R. Morrill had been nurturing for at least five years. In April 1862 Morrill introduced a measure "to punish and prevent the practice of polygamy in the territories of the United States."[25] It included a revocation of the territory's charter incorporating the Church of Jesus Christ of Latter-day Saints. Church property worth more than $50,000 was to be placed in the hands of a chancery court receiver. John Bernhisel, reelected as territorial delegate, knew better than to expend energy trying to check the bill's progress. It was the first action the Republican Party had taken to fulfill a platform promise in the absence of the southern states-rights proponents who were no longer present to oppose the expansion of federal authority to marriage.

Even as Deseret's representatives argued their case for statehood, Congress was thus considering the law aimed at them, intended to punish the Church and impose a fine on individuals of up to $500 and five years in prison if guilty of bigamy. It was the first in a long line of legislative actions intended to bring the Latter-day Saints to heel. The bill removed the authority of LDS priesthood holders to perform marriages. It cancelled all other laws related to what was "evasively called spiritual marriage, however disguised by legal or religious forms." Lincoln signed the bill on July 1, 1862, but in keeping with his general policy regarding the Mormons, made little effort to enforce it. Since the Latter-day Saints regarded the measure as unconstitutional, they too ignored it. David Bigler observed that "the spirit of Deseret lived on as if nothing had happened."[26]

As the year ended, Brigham Young and the legislators again found a way to alienate themselves from Congress, for the first time directly offending the Lincoln administration. The Utah legislative

24. Amasa M. Lyman, "Marriage: Its Benefits," Apr. 5, 1866, *Journal of Discourses*, 11:198–208.

25. Firmage and Mangrum, *Zion in the Courts*, 252–53.

26. Bigler, *Forgotten Kingdom*, 217–18.

session of 1862 opened on December 10 in the old Council House in Salt Lake City, presumptuously renamed the State House. The new governor, Stephen S. Harding, was invited to address them. He arrived at the hall accompanied by commanding officers of the US Army stationed at nearby Fort Douglas. The intent of his message was to warn "against such dangerous and disloyal" voices as those who recommended disregarding laws passed by the US Congress, an oblique reference to the Morrill Act and to Brigham Young.

The Church president took umbrage and said he thought the speech "should not be printed."[27] Accordingly, the governor's speech was left out of the published proceedings that were released in March 1863. In its place were denunciations of the US government by Brigham Young, John Taylor, and Orson Pratt, although edited to appear less extreme than what they had actually said.[28] The published version left out Young's comment that "we are called the state legislature but when the time comes we shall be called the Kingdom of God." Left intact, however, was his prediction that one day "this body of men will give laws to the nations of the earth." Young extrapolated in private that with the Civil War in progress, the time would soon be upon them when they would acquire jurisdiction over the nation. "Our government is going to p[ie]ces and it will be like water that is spilt upon the ground that cannot be gathered," he said. Very soon the brethren would "prevail over all our enemies." Almost every member of the legislature was in the Council of Fifty, once the "ghost government of Deseret," but no longer, because now they were openly taunting the federal government, meeting after each legislative session and repassing the same bills as if they had the real authority, not the secular institution.[29]

Despite the legislature's snub of Governor Harding, the *San Francisco Evening Bulletin* published his speech verbatim on January 1,

27. Church Historian's Office Journal, Dec. 11, 14, 1862; Roberts, *Comprehensive History*, 5:20, 22.

28. Tullidge, *History of Salt Lake City*, xxxiii, 291–305, for Harding's speech in full; Campbell, *Establishing Zion*, 294–95.

29. Kenney, *Wilford Woodruff's Journal*, 6:71, 92–93; Hansen, *Quest for Empire*, 142–46. This eventually became a rather meaningless practice and was recognized as such.

1863. Three weeks later Harding informed vice president Hamlin that his message had been "suppressed through the influence of prominent citizens of the territory," by which he meant Brigham Young. A month after that, the US Senate printed a thousand copies of the address and distributed it throughout Utah Territory. Pointedly mentioning Young's intent to preside over a "theocracy," the senators added an avowal that it would not happen.[30] It was once again defiance of Washington, and not religious prejudice, that sparked the most resistance to statehood. Not even polygamy, at least for the time being, had been the primary infraction.

That same January, Young, who continued to use the title of governor, told the legislators that Congress had not had time to consider Utah's statehood request, due to its heavy work load "pertaining to the conduct of the war" and "restoration of the union." The truth was that Congress had composed enabling acts for four western territories: Colorado, Nebraska, Nevada, and Utah, and only Utah's had failed to emerge in a bill from the House Committee on Territories, the official reason being that the territory still had just 40,000 residents according to the 1860 census. If that were the legitimate reason, Colorado and Nevada would not have qualified either, and Nevada would be admitted in 1864 with significantly fewer residents than Utah.[31] Unlike the other territories, this was Utah's third full-fledged attempt to be considered. The war was an issue, and Washington had opted to postpone dealing with the insurgency in Utah, but no one should have assumed that Washington had accepted the mythical Deseret as a fait accompli.

In May 1863 the editor of the *Deseret News*, Albert Carrington, lamely attempted to explain the failure to publish Harding's message. It was optional, he wrote, when in fact it was a statutory obligation. The delay was prompted by the "hope that his excellency might thereby consider his folly, mend his ways and pursue the course which he promised in the latter part of his initial message,"

30. *San Francisco Evening Bulletin*, Feb. 13, 1863; Harding to Hamlin, Jan. 22, 1863, cited in Whitney, *History of Utah*, 2:89–90; Bigler, *Forgotten Kingdom*, 214–15; Stenhouse, *Rocky Mountain Saints*, 678–73.

31. Journal History, Jan. 19, 1863; Elliott, *History of Nevada*, 77–89.

the editorial read. With each fresh insult, such as this one, thrown in the face of federal officers, the Saints lost allies. One former friend was US senator Orville H. Browning of Illinois, who introduced a bill in December 1863 to limit the jurisdiction of Utah's probate courts and give exclusive authority to the governor to muster militias, thereby altering the structure of the Nauvoo Legion, and to the US marshal for summoning jurors. This appeared to LDS leaders to be punitive, but it actually would have brought the territory in line with most other territorial jurisdictions. The House Committee on the Judiciary tabled the bill, Hooper reassuringly reported, but soon enough measures like these would be passed.[32]

President Lincoln continued to demonstrate his disinclination to perpetuate strife in Utah when the Civil War was drawing toward its close. He replaced the stern and unpopular Harding with the more conciliatory James Duane Doty as governor. Doty had previously been the Utah Superintendent of Indian Affairs. Lincoln balanced that concession by replacing Chief Justice John F. Kinney, who was thought by the non-LDS population to have become too friendly with Church leaders, with John Titus of Pennsylvania. In response, Church authorities helped elect Kinney as the territorial delegate to Congress, the first and only non-Church delegate who would serve in that post. In Washington he defended his constituents' religious practices, and on March 7, 1864, introducing a bill for statehood, he delivered a two-hour address before the House of Representatives in which he compared other recent states as "infants in age and population compared to Utah."[33] This proved no more successful than previous attempts to interest Congress in Utah statehood.

The population in the territory became a convenient excuse for rejecting Utah's petitions. If it was a genuine consideration, it was a minor concern. Nevada was admitted in 1864 with about 20,000 residents. The difference was that Lincoln knew Nevada would vote Republican, while Utah would vote solidly for the Democrats, if

32. Roberts, *Comprehensive History*, 5:331–40; *Congressional Globe*, Jan. 16, Feb. 13, 1863.

33. *Congressional Globe*, Mar. 19, 1864.

allowed, and Lincoln needed states to vote for the Thirteenth and Fourteenth Amendments and in the electoral college for the approaching presidential contest.[34]

Between 1863 and 1868, there was, mercifully, something of a respite in the conflicts involving Utah Territory. The new governor shied away from controversy up to his untimely death in 1865, two months after President Lincoln's assassination. Lincoln's successor, Andrew Johnson (1865–69) showed as little interest in the mountains and deserts of Utah as his predecessor had, although the hiatus proved to be a calm before the storm. An early hint of what was to come occurred on June 11, 1865, when Schuyler Colfax, Speaker of the US House of Representatives, and Samuel Bowles, editor of the *Springfield* (Mass.) *Republican*, met twice with Brigham Young in Salt Lake City. While visiting the city, Colfax addressed a gathering of onlookers from his hotel veranda, enumerated what could be expected from the government and what the government should expect of the territory's citizens, namely "allegiance to the Constitution, obedience to the laws and devotion to the union."[35] In a meeting with Young, the LDS leader asked what Congress intended to do about polygamy now that the slavery question had been resolved. Colfax answered that he "thought it about time that another revelation was had abolishing it."

Young wanted to keep the interchange cordial and let the comment pass, leading Colfax and Bowles to think it was possible to see plural marriage as a bargaining piece. Their misapprehension indicated how far apart the two sides were. Two weeks later, in late June, the chair of the House Committee on Territories, James M. Ashley of Ohio, visited Salt Lake and met with apostles George A. Smith and John Taylor, and then with leaders of the territorial legislature. Ashley spoke pessimistically of Utah's prospect for statehood because of the mounting opposition to polygamy he was seeing throughout the nation. He met with Young and told him that additional imminent legislation would enforce the Morrill

34. Bullard, "Abraham Lincoln," 210, 313.

35. Neff, *History of Utah*, 653–55; Roberts, *Comprehensive History*, 5:172–76.

Act. Young replied that in the past when pressure was applied by stationing troops in Utah, for instance, the Church's beliefs and practices had not changed, nor would they in the future.[36] Ashley carried this to Washington. He was the one person in the country who could give Utah what it was seeking, and Young had treated him with indifference that fell short of diplomacy.

It is no coincidence that, except for the toothless 1862 Morrill Act, the steady stream of bills to restrict Utah self-government commenced after the crusade to eradicate slavery had been completed. In June 1866 Senator Benjamin Wade of Ohio suggested taxing Church property, requiring that the Church publicly disclose its finances, placing the appointment of territorial military officers under the governor's jurisdiction, and other measures to rein in the Church and broaden the government's authority.[37] The bill was reported out of committee on July 12, 1866, but died on the calendar. In early 1867 Senator Jacob Howard of Michigan suggested sending troops out west for the "protection of Gentiles in Utah." The *New York World* objected to another "Mormon war ... under present circumstances ... [that] would be a prodigal squandering of the national resources."[38] Americans had come to conclude that the Utah Expedition was a financial disaster with nothing to show for it.

Latter-day Saints, in their newspaper editorials, suggested that statehood would "take the trouble off the hands of those who are concerned about our peace and prosperity." The territorial delegate, William Hooper, regrettably informed George A. Smith in January 1867 that he had bad news and good, that even if it were possible to get an enabling act passed, President Johnson would "never sign it." That was the bad news. On the bright side, he predicted that the Wade–Howard measure to send troops to the Great Basin was going to fail.[39] In both cases he was correct.

36. "Hon. Schuyler Colfax's Journey," 233–251; Bowles, *From across the Continent*, 83–84, 113; Manuscript History of the Church, 1865, 419–21; Stenhouse, *Rocky Mountain Saints*, 614–15.

37. *Congressional Record*, July 12, 1866; also Poll, "Twin Relic," 133.

38. *New York Times*, Jan. 7, 1867; *New York World*, Jan. 8, 1867; Whitney, *History of Utah*, 2:175.

39. Whitney, 2:177; Hooper to Smith, Jan. 12, 1867, Smith Papers.

Back in Utah the legislature drafted another memorial to Congress, this time asking for the repeal of the Morrill Act. Indicating a serious lack of appreciation for what their delegate in Washington was facing, they lectured Congress about the virtue of polygamy as a "divine doctrine" and argued that polygamy had to be accepted, since it had been in practice in the territory for many years. Further, it was their Constitutional right to marry as they pleased. These argument were mainstays of the LDS defense of polygamy for years. Senator Aaron H. Cragin of New Hampshire responded on December 13 with a bill proposing the abolishment of jury trials for polygamy cases and of the need for indictments. The next month, January 1868, Hooper wrote that he would meet with Cragin to try to dissuade him.[40] Whether or not his discussion with the senator made any difference, the Senate allowed the bill to die. However, it was re-introduced, with amendments, the next year.

In mid-1868 the non-LDS citizens of Utah Territory ran their first candidate for congressional delegate against Hooper, a local merchant originally from California, William McGrorty, who received 105 votes to Hooper's 15,179. Hooper's fitness was challenged by attorney C. B. Waite, who had been an associate justice of the Utah Supreme Court. He argued that Hooper's connection to the LDS Church and State of Deseret showed him to be a traitor to the country, especially for having allegedly sworn an oath against the United States in the LDS temple. In the US House Committee on Elections, the committeemen found these accusations to be "absurd."[41] That did not mean they were necessarily supporters of Utah, however. Early in 1869 the House committee chair, James Ashley of the Committee on Territories, recommended shaving off large segments of Utah's landmass to be added to Colorado, Nevada, and Wyoming, with just a narrow strip in central Utah left to the Mormons. He openly admitted

40. *Deseret News*, January 8, 1868; Hooper to Smith, Jan. 8, 1868; Roberts, *Comprehensive History*, 5:229.

41. Roberts, 5:366, 375, 378; also Baskin, *Reminiscences*, 23–29.

that his goal was to make Utah statehood impossible.[42] The respected Massachusetts newspaperman Samuel Bowles mocked this measure as outrageous. Nevertheless, the proposal should have given the Utah legislature an important insight into the thinking of the committee.

Ashley's bill was followed by one suggested by Congressman George W. Julian of Indiana to "discourage polygamy in Utah by granting the right of suffrage to the women of the territory."[43] To his surprise, the territorial delegate spoke in favor of this. Julian asked Hooper if the "leading men" in the LDS hierarchy would agree, and Hooper assured him that there was no reason for them not to. The bill stalled in committee, but in February the next year lawmakers in Utah were convinced that it was such a good idea, they passed their own statute granting women of twenty-one years of age and older the right to vote in all elections. Territorial Secretary Stephen A. Mann signed the bill on February 12, 1870, although the newly appointed governor, J. Wilson Shaffer, challenged Mann's authority to do so when he reached Utah. Nevertheless, the law remained in effect and Utah joined Wyoming Territory, which had recently passed a similar law, as the only areas in the United States that granted women suffrage. By chance Salt Lake City held a municipal election before Wyoming, so that Brigham Young's niece, Seraph Young, was apparently the first woman in the nation to vote.[44]

Schuyler Colfax joined Ulysses S. Grant on the Republican ticket in 1868 and became vice president in March the next year. Orson F. Whitney thought it was Colfax's influence that turned the hero of the Civil War against the Latter-day Saints. One might have more reasonably suspected the reverend John P. Newman, the Senate's chaplain, but for whatever reason, Grant's hostility

---

42. *Congressional Globe,* Jan. 14, 1869, 363–64; also Lyman, *Overland Journey*, 209, 213, 263n31; MacKinnon, "Like Splitting a Man Up His Backbone," 116–17.

43. *New York Times,* Jan. 25, 1869; Bowles, *Our New West*, 264; *Congressional Globe*, Mar. 15, 1869.

44. Bigler, *Forgotten Kingdom*, 283; Arrington, *American Moses*, 365; Van Wagenen, *Sister-Wives*, 6–8; Van Wagenen, "In Their Own Behalf," 31–43; Madsen, *Battle for the Ballot,* 60–74; Wells, "History of Woman Suffrage," 33–52.

remained fervent and consistent. During the summer of 1869, Colfax made a second trip to Utah without calling on Church leaders, Brigham Young being rumored to have recently called Grant and Colfax drunkards and gamblers. Opinions heard at a banquet hosted by the non-LDS dignitaries of the city was credited by Whitney for being the genesis for the Cullom Bill, which was proposed in early 1870 and is discussed below.[45]

In the fall of 1869, only months after the transcontinental railroad was completed at Promontory Summit, Utah citizens staged a "mammoth mass meeting" to petition Congress once more for recognition as a state. When the petition arrived back east, it was ignored. Other senators and congressmen visited Utah when it became easier to do, after the transcontinental railroad was completed, along with large numbers of other visitors of diverse backgrounds. US senator Lyman Trumbull of Illinois called on Young on July 10 for a pleasant meeting that led to the senator's later support of the territory. Other senators from Missouri, New Hampshire, and Ohio, and a few congressmen conferred at different times with Young and attended Church services at the Tabernacle.

The most comprehensive legislation inimical to Church interests was sponsored by a former member of Lincoln's Illinois law office, Congressman Shelby M. Cullom. His intent was to eliminate the judicial privileges the territory enjoyed, based on suggestions by Robert N. Baskin, the attorney, formerly of Philadelphia, who opened a law office in Salt Lake City in 1865. Baskin told the House Committee on Territories that they needed to take "draconian measures" to blunt the broad jurisdiction of the probate courts in Utah. The Cullom Bill authorized the governor to appoint and remove probate and other judges. It gave federal officials the ability to requisition army troops to enforce the law. It prescribed a sentence of up to five years in jail and $5,000 for "unlawful cohabitation," a new term that avoided the need to document that a plural marriage ceremony had taken place. There would also be secret ballots for the

45. Whitney, *History of Utah*, 2:320–21, 325; Roberts, *Comprehensive History*, 5:283–85.

first time, and all laws not consistent with federal statutes would be repealed, specifically the territorial land law.[46]

The bill aroused such concern among the Church leadership that apostle George Q. Cannon was sent to Washington, DC, to help Hooper oppose it. The apostle's opinion was that the law was more suitable for what he called the subjugation of African slaves than for the direction of civilized people. Hooper admitted to George A. Smith in January 1870 that "there is nothing we can do which will stop the cry or satisfy the determined opposition which is apparent in every direction." He recommended that they hold their anchorage "and ride out the storm which the devil has raised and is now spending its fury." There was nothing their enemies "will leave undone," he predicted. "The prejudice here is far heavier than I have ever felt it before." He was only convinced by his faith that their opponents would ultimately fail, that the Church would "come off as heretofore triumphant." For his part, however, Ulysses Grant stood clearly "in favor of blood letting," according to Hooper. After resigning himself to the fact that there was no hope for the immediate future, Hooper still devoted himself full-time, through February and most of March, to lobbying Congress.[47]

Women in Utah reacted with a huge rally against the Cullom and associated bills at the old Tabernacle on January 13. Five or six thousand members of the female Relief Societies braved bad weather to overflow the building. They had no complaints about their polygamous husbands, they said, and denounced the legislation for infringing upon their religious liberty. With defiance equal to that of their male co-religionists, they declared that they would "ignore any act they deemed unconstitutional." News of this gathering was carried nationwide, surprising people with the solidarity on the part of those whom they thought needed to be rescued from polygamy.

The protest was supported by a group of ex-Mormon merchants known as the Godbeites (GOD-bee-ites), after one of their founders.

46. Baskin, *Reminiscences*, 30–31, 73–82, 164–172; Maxwell, *Robert Newton Baskin*, 109–10; "Execution of the Law in Utah," *House Reports*, 1870, Serial 1436, 11–19.

47. Whitney, *History of Utah*, 2:393–94; Hooper to Smith, Jan. 11, Feb. 1, 17, 25, Mar. 28, 1870, Smith Papers.

They held their own meeting in March to protest the recent congressional bills. The first speaker, Eli B. Kelsey, a polygamist no longer affiliated with the LDS Church, wanted to uphold the nation's laws but "could not ask people to break up their families and bastardize their children." Elias L. T. Harrison, one of the key intellectual formulators of the new movement that opposed Brigham Young's economic and political policies, expressed a similar hope that there would be no ex post facto injustice to current polygamists. Another speaker, William H. Shearman, advocated a respectful appeal to senators to reconsider this policy, feeling that earlier demonstrations had only "aroused the antagonism of the nation."[48]

Back in Washington, Hooper engaged thirty-two-year-old Thomas Fitch, then a Nevada congressman, to speak against the Cullom Bill on February 23, 1870. Whitney considered his speech a masterpiece of "lucid logic and brilliant eloquence," and Hooper too reported that it was "one of the best [speeches] delivered in the house for years." Congressman Samuel B. Axtell of California, a future governor of Utah Territory and someone who was friendly to the Mormons, also spoke against the bill. Hooper too stood before the congressmen and accused the bill's sponsors of confusing polygamy with adultery. There were biblical precedents for the former, he argued. As eloquent as the speakers were, their persuasive efforts were lost on Congress. Cullom, according to Hooper, succeeded by appealing to prejudice. The bill passed the House, 94 to 32, the same day as the speeches.[49] Getting the bill passed by the Senate was another matter. Senator Cragin's bill addressing the same topic was preferred over the Cullom bill, and Hooper learned from Senator Jacob Howard of Michigan, "confidentially, but reliably," that the Senate would not pass the Cullom measure, adding enthusiastically that even the newspapers were "down on the bill."[50]

On his first visit to Utah, vice president Colfax had encouraged

---

48. Whitney, *History of Utah*, 2:395–401, 408–14, 435–37.

49. Moody, *Extraordinary Memoirs*, 231; Baskin, *Reminiscences,* 50; Cullom Bill, *House Reports*, no. 21, 41 Congress, 2nd session, Part 1, appendix, 173–77, Part 3, appendix, 1518; Hooper to Smith, Feb. 25, 1870; Roberts, *Comprehensive History*, 5:235–36.

50. Hooper to Smith, Feb. 1, 25, Mar. 28, 1870.

William S. Godbe and others who considered Young's political and economic policies to be anti-American.[51] In March 1870 Godbe himself journeyed to Washington, where Colfax introduced him to President Grant. In a "cozy" discussion, the president listened attentively to the plea to not increase the federal troop level in the territory. Grant pledged to only send as many as were needed to serve as a token presence and "moral force."

Godbe also met with Cullom to review his bill's provisions and make recommendations. The congressman complained that Godbe wanted so many alterations, they would nullify the bill's intent. He nevertheless agreed to delay it, persuaded by the plea for time to allow LDS people to absorb the "new education" they were receiving through contact with outside people passing through the territory on the railroad. Godbe's negotiations proved to be of momentous significance, and the bill progressed no further in the US Senate.[52]

Another opponent of the bill was Senator Aaron A. Sargent of California, who had close ties to the railroads and later played a major role in modifying some of the harshness of later bills. The Central Pacific Railroad had an interest in keeping Latter-day Saints satisfied and wanted to tone down or quash legislation that was detrimental to the region. As for the Cragin Bill, George A. Smith received a note from a senator who was a Reconstruction Republican from Louisiana, John S. Harris, predicting that "there will be no further action on Senator Cragin's Bill." That proved true. Only six senators were present when Cragin spoke on the Senate floor to urge support.[53]

The Godbeites joined with other non-LDS people in opposing "despotism and tyranny in Utah" on July 16, 1870, at a convention to organize the Liberal Party in the town of Corrine at the northern end of the Great Salt Lake. It nominated General George R. Maxwell as its candidate for Congress. In the ensuing fall election, Maxwell garnered 1,500 votes, to the disappointment of the

51. Tullidge, *History of Salt Lake City*, 467–69; also Walker, *Wayward Saints*, 220–21.

52. Whitney, *History of Utah*, 2:438–39; Lyman, ed., *Candid Insights*, Apr. 19, 1892, 329; Tullidge, *History of Salt Lake City*, 399–402.

53. John S. Harris to George A. Smith, June 5, 1870, Smith Papers; also Hooper to Smith, May 21, 1870. Harris and Smith had been boyhood friends.

LDS-led People's Party, which suspected vote tampering. Much like William McGrorty before him, Maxwell protested Hooper's candidacy by pointing out that he had served in the Nauvoo Legion in the 1857 fight against the US Army. Once again, however, the imbalance of Maxwell's 1,500 votes to Hooper's nearly 22,000 proved persuasive to the House Committee on Elections.[54]

In June 1870 President Grant appointed forty-nine-year-old James B. McKean as chief justice of the Utah Supreme Court. McKean was a son of a Methodist minister—no friend of the Latter-day Saints. Apparently John P. Newman, the Senate chaplain and pastor of the important Metropolitan Methodist Church in Washington, D.C., had suggested him.[55] McKean came to be called the "missionary jurist," his intent being "grinding to powder" the "disloyal high priesthood" of the LDS Church. In a most questionable move, he transferred the supreme court from territorial jurisdiction to the federal court system so he could empanel juries comprised exclusively of non-Mormons—until the Englebrecht decision of the US Supreme Court disallowed it in 1872. He also blatantly described the January 1872 case of *People v. Brigham Young* as "federal authority versus polygamic theocracy."[56]

He was on his way to becoming among the most oppressive outsiders in LDS history in the way he enforced arbitrary rules, insisting that wives testify against their husbands, contrary to the legal norms elsewhere. Church leaders engaged the former congressman Fitch of Nevada, after he lost his reelection in 1870 and was practicing "mining litigation" in Utah, to construct a defense against the territorial officials. The attorney asserted that McKean, "by his rulings," had enforced the Cullom Bill "in advance of its passage by Congress" (including aspects never enacted into law). It was only because of the court's bias, Fitch maintained, that prosecutor Robert Baskin won easy victories against Latter-day Saints.[57]

54. Roberts, *Comprehensive History*, 5:367.

55. Alexander, "Federal Authority," 85–100; McFeely, *Grant*, 503. The reverend Newman was close enough to Grant to attend to his death fifteen years later.

56. Whitney, 2:541–43, 555, 558–600; Tullidge, *History of Salt Lake City*, 587–88.

57. Roberts, *Comprehensive History*, 5:645–47; Whitney, *History of Utah*, 2:647.

On January 10, 1871, federal officials took another bold step in bending the system to their favor by seizing the territorial prison so they could fill it with polygamists. McKean prosecuted Latter-day Saints under the Utah statute on adultery rather than the federal anti-polygamy law because the former was harsher. Given that he ignored other territorial laws in favor of federal statutes and procedures, it indicated the selectivity of his enforcement. He boasted that a Latter-day Saint accused of adultery would automatically be convicted and receive a severe sentence.[58] This attracted the attention of the editor of the *Omaha Herald*, George L. Miller, who pointed to it as an example of corruption in the judicial system. The moral outcry over polygamy had sometimes been contrived by politicians "for their own aggrandizement," he concluded.[59] Even the fervid anti-Mormon politician Fred T. Dubois of Idaho would later concede that many politicians opposed polygamy for their own political benefit.[60]

McKean had been a colonel in the Union Army. He approached the law, during his time in New York, the same way he organized a military campaign. A critic wrote in the *Albany Law Journal* that McKean had forgotten about "justice" and the need to be "impartial." Fitch wrote facetiously that at least McKean had not persuaded the military at Fort Douglas, in the hills above Salt Lake City, to employ its guns in the contest over governance. Baskin said, without irony, that personally he would have called up the troops.[61]

A glimmer of support for Utah Territory came when William C. Staines, one of the Church's emigration agents in New York City, informed Brigham Young in mid-1871 that Senator William M. Stewart of Nevada had put in a good word for them. Speaking to emigration commissioner Bernard Casserly, Stewart had described Mormons as "good people" and many of the federal officers as "scoundrels." Like Fitch and Sargent, Stewart was allied with the Central and Southern Pacific Railroads. Apparently, the way around

58. Linford, "Mormons and the Law, 331.
59. George Miller, in Whitney, *History of Utah*, 2:408, 617–19.
60. Clements, *Fred T. Dubois*, 38n42, 48.
61. Fitch and Baskin, in Whitney, *History of Utah*, 2:580–81, 621–22.

the political impasse on statehood hinged on economics. A Church agent/board member with the Boston-based Union Pacific Railroad Corporation, Bishop John Sharp, reported that the territory had friends at UPRR. When the railroad completed its line between Omaha and Utah and met the Central Pacific Railroad from California, that Union Pacific used its influence to dampen legislative threats, and would continue to do so, Sharp promised.[62] It might be said that the railroad lobby was the decisive factor even regarding statehood, if sufficient documentation could render a definitive assessment. Leland Stanford and other railroad magnates were similarly consistent in their support of LDS civic autonomy.[63]

McKean felt otherwise, and considered it more important to pursue and arrest the Church's leaders, not just the rank-and-file. On October 28, 1871, he arrested Daniel H. Wells, a counselor in the First Presidency and mayor of Salt Lake City, for polygamy and for ordering Bill Hickman to murder Richard Yates in November 1857 during the Utah War. Young was indicted on the same charges. Young appeared in court on October 16 to plead not guilty and then leave town to spend the winter in St. George, led to believe his case would not come to trial until the spring. In fact, Baskin and McKean set a court date of November 20. [64] It would not be possible to travel back on three hundred miles of snowbound and muddy roads in time for court. Young's attorneys were denied a request that McKean change the date.

Visiting the city and present in the courtroom that day were Senator Oliver P. Morton of Indiana and William P. Fishback, editor of the *Indianapolis Journal*. Fishback published a critique of how McKean and Baskin were trying to "precipitate a collision between the federal authorities and the Mormons in a contest in which the government occupies a false and untenable position." Fishback wrote that both he and the senator considered it "folly" and "utter recklessness" and

62. William C. Staines to Brigham Young, Aug. 22, 1871; Leland Stanford to Young, May 18, 1871; John Sharp to Young, Oct. 22, 1871, Young Office Files.

63. Lyman, *Political Deliverance*, 69–95.

64. For more, see Whitney, *History of Utah,* 2:629–38; MacKinnon, *At Sword's Point*, 1:298–301; Turner, *Brigham Young,* 285–86.

regretted "the grave results that must necessarily ensue," which were civil war. That is, unless the president "interferes with the schemes of the petty lords of misrule, who are doing their utmost to bring it to fruition."[65] In the face of such ridicule, McKean succumbed to the demand to reschedule the court date to December. Young did his best to return by then but did not quite make it.[66]

US Attorney Charles H. Hempstead had earlier been with the California volunteers stationed at Fort Douglas and was an acquaintance of President Grant. In September 1871 he resigned from office after three years, saying he had become tired of McKean's methods. He would not "further prosecute rulings of the McKean court," he said. Essentially switching sides, he remained in the city another year to serve with Fitch in representing Latter-day Saints. His replacement as US Attorney was George C. Bates, a former Whig Party enthusiast who had practiced law in Chicago, whose appointment elicited praise from Brigham Young's son-in-law Hiram B. Clawson. As nearly as Clawson could tell, Bates "intended to discharge his duties without prejudice." That would represent a turn from the "reformist agenda" of the existing federal officials. Some "conservative members of congress," Clawson wrote, specifically Senator Lyman Trumbull of Illinois, were "anxious to have the present persecutions stopped." Bates had "on several occasions expressed himself decidedly against the course pursued by [the federal] ring," the term employed to describe the men sent to Utah from Washington and sympathetic non-LDS community connected to the *Salt Lake Tribune*, the rival of the Church-supported newspaper.[67]

A former acting governor of Utah Territory, the non-LDS attorney Frank Fuller, let Clawson know in December that Bates wanted to confer with Young. Everyone assumed that Young would flee the territory rather than remain to stand trial. Fuller and Fitch advised him to stay and "fight [the federal judges] in their own court

65. Roberts, *Comprehensive History*, 5:390–401.
66. Whitney, *History of Utah*, 2:658–666.
67. Hiram B. Clawson to Brigham Young, Oct. 31, 1871; Clawson to Young, Dec. 11, 1871, Young Office Files; also Whitney, 2:649.

room," something the latter repeated in a letter of December 12.[68] Young took the advice and surprised opponents by appearing before Judge McKean on January 2, 1872, after a difficult journey from St. George. His attorney requested that he be allowed to go free on bail.

When high-ranking LDS leaders were arrested, they were often treated well. When Mayor Daniel H. Wells was arrested for murder, he was placed in the custody of General Henry A. Morrow at Fort Douglas and "extended every courtesy." Morrow assigned Wells to officers' quarters. He invited him to Sunday dinner with his family and even called on Wells to offer a blessing on the food.[69] The attorneys Fitch and Hempstead convinced McKean to grant Wells bail, to the disappointment of prosecutor Robert Baskin and US Marshal George Maxwell.[70]

Since McKean had declared the territorial courts to be federal, the territorial legislature refused to allocate funds to maintain their operations. Bates was forced to travel to Washington in December 1871 to ask for funds. Attorney General A. T. Akerman told him the Treasury Department did not feel at liberty to allocate money for a purpose not clearly outlined in the existing statutes. The chair of the Senate Judiciary Committee, Lyman Trumbull, and US Solicitor General, Benjamin H. Bristow, assured Bates that funds would be appropriated. Until then, judicial matters were brought to a standstill in Utah, all court proceedings postponed until the spring of 1872, including Brigham Young's case. By the time the budget problems were resolved in March, virtually all cases which McKean had commenced had been nullified by the momentous *Clinton et al. v. Englebrecht* US Supreme Court decision that freed Young and everyone else who had cases pending. In the meantime Senator Cragin found the situation dire enough to resubmit his amended bill.[71] That meant the legislative onslaught would continue.

68. Thomas Fitch to Brigham Young, Sept. 23 and Dec. 12, 1871, Young Office Files.
69. Whitney, *History of Utah*, 2:638–40.
70. Hiram B. Clawson to Brigham Young, Oct. 31, 1871, Young Office Files.
71. Whitney, *History of Utah*, 2:653–56; *New York Times*, Dec. 11, 1871.

At this juncture, former congressman Fitch added fuel to his side of the fire by writing to the *New York Times* accusing the Grant administration of being inspired by something other than justice, but that most Republicans in Congress had "neither the disposition nor the courage to oppose Grant's Utah policy." Fitch predicted that if McKean's efforts to suppress polygamy failed, Congress could be expected to enact something "outrageous" along the lines of martial law. That was actually among the options Grant considered. Thus Fitch encouraged Church leaders "to accede to the suggestion that polygamy be given up for the future, on condition of her [Utah Territory] being admitted to the union as a state." In the same letter, he tantalized Young with the reminder that "a state government means self government at home, exemption from persecutions and plunder, political power at Washington, the power to enforce justice, peace, prosperity, and progress."[72]

A week earlier, on December 5, 1871, former acting governor Frank Fuller had sent President Young a similar proposal that they engage in a simple swap: "Under the circumstances, if Utah should propose to accede to the suggestion that polygamy be given up for the future, on condition of her being admitted to the union, it is probable that such a proposition would be accepted." There were conditions. Utah would need to be admitted as a Republican state and "the Gentiles" would need to be allowed to "run the new state for a year or two: and congress will force a constitutional prohibition of polygamy so far as future marriages are concerned." As history would eventually show three decades later, these were the type of concessions that finally proved to be the only practicable way forward.[73]

Since Young did not offer a response, on December 11 Fuller made a more detailed proposal to George A. Smith, explaining his disappointment that he had not received a reply from President Young. He reminded Smith that anti-polygamy pressures were mounting to an unprecedented peak, with the suggestion that

72. Thomas Fitch to Brigham Young, Dec. 12, 1871, Young Office Files.

73. Frank Fuller to Brigham Young, Dec. 5, 1871, Young Office Files; Lyman, *Political Deliverance*, 130–31, 155, 168–69.

Congress would take away all vestiges of self-government from members of the Church. Fuller proposed that Latter-day Saint leaders allow their non-Church friends in Congress to take the lead in a prompt and concerted effort. He pointed out that an enabling act sponsored by friends rather than hostile enemies would make all the difference to their future peace and prosperity. He also pointed out that a Colorado statehood bill was vetoed by Grant's predecessor, Andrew Johnson, because the electorate had not demonstrated itself to be sufficiently compatible with the Republican Party.[74]

The first state officials should therefore be non-Mormons who had proven themselves to be cooperative with Church leaders, Fuller argued. He mentioned that George Q. Cannon, known to be popular with his peers in Congress, should remain there as Utah's first voting member of the House of Representatives. The constitutional convention, by contrast, should have few, if any, polygamists as delegates. The majority should be "friendly Gentiles," and the mostly LDS legislature should stay in the background. "The war [against polygamy] has scarcely begun," he warned. If Utah committed itself to the Republicans, the Democrats in Congress would understand that the commitment was only "skin deep" and could be reversed.[75]

The Church leadership decided to neither heed Fuller's advice nor to openly oppose any of his suggestions. In January 1872 the territorial legislature enacted one more bill appropriating funds for a constitutional convention—the fourth one to that point in time. Utah's governor since 1871, George Woods, vetoed the bill. A former Missourian and recent Oregon resident, he argued that it was Congress's prerogative to initiate the process. Statehood was not a right, he lectured, "but a privilege." Virtually every Utahn disagreed with him. "Utah should place herself in harmonious relations with the general government," the governor continued.[76] The legislature ignored his veto and announced a convention to be held February 19, 1872. The momentum for this civil disobedience was aided

74. George A. Smith may have unofficially condoned continuance of these steps, but would not have committed the Church to approve the entire process.

75. Frank Fuller to George A. Smith, Dec. 11, 1871, Smith Papers.

76. Journal History, Jan. 27, Feb. 15, 1872.

by non-Mormons led by Thomas Fitch and friendly US Congressmen. Half the convention delegates representing Salt Lake County were non-LDS (ten Mormon, nine non-Mormon), which was of itself something of a breakthrough.[77]

Fitch had been a key delegate in the successful Nevada constitutional convention in 1864, making him a natural strategist for Utah's attempt to beat the odds. When he suggested that they follow whatever advice Congress deemed necessary regarding plural marriage, there were mixed feelings among the Utah polygamists, but as historian and local Church leader Orson Whitney wrote, some of them were all the more "earnest in their efforts to throw off the shackles of territorial serfdom." On the second day of the convention, Fitch delivered an eloquent address. He had quite clearly formulated a strategy with congressional friends and now stated: "I am not here to attack polygamy from a theological, moral, or a physical, but from a political standpoint," he said. It had been allowed to exist "by the sufferance of a people who now declare that it shall exist no longer." The trenchant question was whether "this people [can] hope to retain polygamy against such influences and such antagonisms as faced in the nation at large?" His warning to supporters of polygamy was ominous: "If you do not by this concession successfully organize a state government for yourselves now, the day is not far distant when your foes will organize one over your heads and organize it upon such terms as will ostracize your most honored citizens from public places, if it do[es] not disfranchise the [entire] body of your voters." His appraisal was blunt and accurate, but two decades ahead of its time.[78]

Those leading the convention wanted to inquire of Congress what conditions involving plural marriage would satisfy the nation. The delegates "pledge[d] to abide" Washington's advise "if the majority of the voters in the territory" agreed to it. The proposed

77. Whitney, *History of Utah*, 2:691–92; Roberts, *Comprehensive History*, 5:460. There had been no expressed approval of these steps by Young or Cannon, who clearly intended to halt matters if they came close to prohibiting plural marriage.

78. For Fitch's entire speech, see Tullidge, *History of Salt Lake City*, 563–579.

constitution, similar to the 1862 version, was ratified by hopeful citizens by a vote of 25,160 to 365.[79] The convention chose two senators, Fitch and Hooper, and Fuller as a congressman. Giving two out of three seats to non-Mormons was a significant concession.

Immediately after the close of the convention, Fuller, Fitch, and several prominent LDS men called for a political meeting in Salt Lake City two months hence, at which they intended to organize a territorial Republican Party. It would be the first known effort to link territorial organizations with national parties. They sent delegates to a Republican national convention but were refused seats, in favor of the representatives of Utah's Liberal Party. One week after the territorial Republican meeting, Democrats held their own convention that was attended by Utahn Hadley D. Johnson, a former party congressman from Iowa. However, the local groups had not sufficiently consulted the national parties, which were clearly not on board with these efforts. It would still be twenty years before the territory would have Democrats and Republicans.

When the conventions were being held in Utah, an unsolicited admission bill was introduced to Congress by Representative James G. Blair of Missouri. Speaking in support of it on February 17, 1872, he proposed that since LDS marriages had been performed when the region was still part of Mexico, the country should recognize the wives and children from that period to the present as legitimate. Originally the settlers had not been constrained by US laws, he pointed out, and they could be grandfathered in.[80] Congress took a dim view of the suggestion, nor was Utah ready to give up future marriages in exchange for recognizing exiting ones. As far as the LDS citizens were concerned, they were being threatened, as surely as if it were the former military invasion, this time through legal maneuvers. They had allies in Congress who had thus far successfully de-fanged the most dangerous bills, but that trend would not last forever.

---

79. "Admission of Utah into the Union," legislative resolution, *House Miscellaneous Documents* 165 (42–2), 1872, Serial 1526.

80. Roberts, *Comprehensive History*, 5:438.

The bitterness of the McKean crusade, contrasted with the effective opposing arguments of former Nevada congressman Thomas Fitch, placed Utahns in a complex situation. Many citizens appeared to be leaning in favor of statehood, even with the distressing terms they were being offered in regard to plural marriage, but this was likely not yet anything close to a majority of the territory's citizens. The early months of the ensuring year and the future treatment of the just-submitted fourth attempt at statehood were then awaited with considerable apprehension.

3

LOBBYISTS, THE POLAND ACT, AND A SERIOUS STATEHOOD EFFORT

1872–80

The year 1872 began with a determined fourth attempt to achieve the impossible. In late 1871 and into 1872, amid a continued onslaught of anti-polygamy legislation in Congress, the effort toward statehood appeared to have some realistic prospects for success, although still contingent on Latter-day Saints giving up plural marriage. As Church leaders and judges butted heads, interested people ultimately witnessed an unexpected turn-around in the downfall of Judge James B. McKean and the emergence of apostle George Q. Cannon as a major figure in LDS politics.

After the constitution was drafted in February 1872, an election to ratify it was scheduled for late March. Without waiting to see the results, the three men who were to accompany it to Congress, George Q. Cannon, Frank Fuller, and Thomas Fitch, knowing what the vote would be, embarked by train for the nation's capital and arrived there on March 16. They joined the territorial delegate to Congress, William Hooper, who by then had been in Washington for over six successive years, plus a separate earlier term. When Cannon conferred with him, he was startled to learn that Hooper, acting on advice from friends and contacts, had concluded to postpone the push for statehood. Exhibiting a more aggressive temperament, and perhaps naivete about the situation in Congress, Cannon resolved to keep the memorial and constitution on track.

Working with experienced lobbyists Fitch and Fuller, Cannon conferred with senators and congressmen from New England, especially. It was a bad time. Most officials were preoccupied with the upcoming fall elections. Some of them confided that they would feel more comfortable supporting such controversial legislation after the election. Cannon took that to heart and resolved to put the art of lobbying to practice, to find out, by putting a considerable number of elected men through what he called "a thorough test," what their true principles might be. He confided to Brigham Young that "the secret strength of our enemies and chief difficulty that we have to contend with" was fear of a public backlash for sympathizing with an unpopular Church, an issue slightly separate from statehood but an impediment nonetheless. Until he had observed it up close, he wrote, he would not have believed that "men could be so cowardly" in defending basic rights.[1] He was learning through his interactions, with some direction from Fitch, what kind of strategy would ultimately prove successful.

After well over a month, Cannon and Hooper scheduled an interview with President Ulysses S. Grant as he was beginning his fourth year in office. Two days before that meeting, Cannon philosophically reflected to Brigham Young on March 31, 1872, about how spectacularly the previous attempts at statehood had failed. The 1856–57 effort resulted in troops being dispatched to the territory. The 1862 attempt triggered the Morrill Act that made polygamy illegal. Cannon now wondered what the current campaign would produce, but expressed belief that if they asked for bread and were given a stone, using the biblical analogy, Congress would pay for it by some act of cosmic justice.

When Cannon and Hooper met with Grant, the apostle was pleased to find the president in a pleasant mood and friendly, though not inclined to commit himself in any way on Utah. The day afterward, when the Utah memorial was introduced to the House and

1. George Q. Cannon to Brigham Young, Mar. 16, 31, Apr. 1, 3, 1872, Young Office Files. Cannon said the two non-LDS agents were frequently asked how many wives they had.

Senate territorial committees, instead of dying there, the documents were ordered printed. Significantly for the first time, hearings were scheduled. There had been no previous attempt that had progressed that far. Simultaneously on April 1, Daniel Voorhees of Indiana, a Democrat, introduced an anti-Mormon bill intended to add teeth to law enforcement in Utah. Voorhees had recently been with Judge McKean and doubtless obtained the component material from Robert Baskin, who would draft a lot of the legislation over the next few years that was inimical to the Latter-day Saints throughout.[2]

In Cannon's April 3 letter to Young, he pointed out that the Voorhees Bill anticipated a pro-McKean decision in the pending Englebrecht case. The high court received briefings on March 23. Cannon predicted that if the Supreme Court struck down McKean's judicial rulings, the Voorhees Bill "would be a nullity." Somewhat surprisingly, Nevada Senator William Stewart, who was a knowledgeable insider with connections to the railroad lobby, informed Cannon that he expected a decision favorable to the Church. If that were the case, he suggested that the new US Attorney General, George H. Williams, should be consulted on how to draft legislation that would be fair to Utah but that would shield congressmen from "accusations" of "favoring the Latter-day Saints."[3]

The apostle learned that sentiments of support were sometimes mixed with an equal dose of duplicity. He suspected Senator Stewart's ambition behind his hope that Utah achieved statehood, and instead intended that Utah would actually be combined with Nevada for a larger state with a greater population, all to Stewart's benefit. It would alleviate the allegation that Nevada should not have been made a state in the first place. "Utah and Nevada might be 'married,'" Cannon wrote, "and Stewart be profited by [the] wedding." That possibility never appeared in public discussion, but it was a scenario Cannon probably labored behind the scenes to thwart because of how it would impinge on Utah independence and the ability of the Church to control its political future.

2. Cannon to Young, Apr. 1, 1872; also Baskin, *Reminiscences,* 25–26, 28, 206.
3. Cannon to Young, Apr. 3, 1872; also Elliott, *Servant of Power*, x.

Meanwhile, another legislative dart was introduced by New York congressman and future US vice president William Wheeler to limit Latter-day Saint participation in Utah elections. Cannon called it a plan "to promote purity" among Latter-day Saints, a morality test to exclude polygamists, no doubt authored "by Satan." When Hooper asked Wheeler about it, the congressman confessed that he knew little beyond the fact that "it was handed to him to present" to the committee, probably by McKean or Baskin. Wheeler assured Hooper that he had no personal interest in legislating against the Latter-day Saints. He expressed surprise to learn that a clique of only about two hundred men in Utah Territory wanted to gain political control by preventing Mormons from voting. This group, led by men, some of whom were aiming to protect their fortunes in mining through legislation, came to be called the *Tribune* ring.[4]

Perhaps because of the uncertainly over the outcome of the Englebrecht case, Baskin and McKean stepped up their efforts to push the Voorhees Bill through as quickly as possible. John A. Bingham, an Ohio Republican and chair of the House Judiciary Committee, requested two days of floor exchange to consider the bill. This made Cannon particularly anxious about the "sea of travails" the bill's passage would create. On April 12, 1872, Fitch, Cannon, and Hooper appeared before the Senate Committee on Territories. Fitch spoke for twenty minutes, emphasizing the urgent desire of Utahns for statehood, suggesting that they were to the point they would probably give up polygamy to receive that privilege. Fitch "very neatly and satisfactorily [adhered] to our views as we conversed upon them before we left home" except on that one point, Cannon wrote to Young. A throw-away comment that might have been forgotten, he thought, had Fitch not elaborated in the informal question-and-answer period. In "a conversational" way, the spokesman "came to this gradually," finally "dwelling at some length upon the ways we [the Latter-day Saints] had endured" hostile treatment and would do what was necessary to find relief. Fitch "conveyed the idea that, in

4. Cannon to Young, Apr. 4, 1872; Tullidge, *History of Salt Lake City*, 467.

his view, polygamy was a dying institution." He cited the example of two favored older Latter-day Saints, William Jennings and Edwin D. Woolley, who had lost wives to death and separation, reducing their number of wives to the legal limit, and had decided to leave the matter that way rather than seek more wives. Cannon explained that their lobbyist was oblivious to the blow he had leveled or how "repugnant to our feelings" his suggestion was, particularly to suggest the erosion of loyalty to the practice of plural marriage among the presumed faithful.[5]

The truth was, Cannon himself was going through some soul-searching, seeking assurance that he was yet firmly on the proper course. He recalled that the Latter-day Saints had moved far from the settled United States for the express purpose of practicing their religion without interference. Now they were asking to be brought into the national fold through compromise. He felt that some agreement could be reached that the Church could "honorably accept," but it would certainly need to include the continuation of plural marriage, since "God had revealed it" to his prophets. Cannon was summoned to the committee on April 13 to answer questions that still troubled the senators. One of the most persistent was whether Gentiles could "receive equal justice to a Mormon" in Utah Territory. Cannon affirmed that they would. Another question was whether plural marriage was compulsory; stated another way, how did leaders regard those in the Church who did not comply with the principle? Cannon assured them that it was left to each person's individual conscience to decide whether or not they felt called to participate in the practice. When queried about whether polygamy might be phased out in order to achieve the political franchise, Cannon hedged. He said that the citizens of the territory had met every requirement that had been asked of them in applying for recognition as a state. "Our religion ought not to be questioned," he stated, only whether they were "republican," or what we might today opt to characterize as democratic.[6] He also made an appearance before

5. Cannon to Young, Apr. 12, 13, 16, 1872.
6. Cannon to Young, Apr. 12, 13, 1872.

the House Committee on Territories to give substantially the same testimony, albeit a bit more candidly.

A less-capable representative may not have successfully juggled multiple objectives: shepherding the statehood petition through the committees in both houses of Congress; protecting polygamy as a divine institution; and interacting with President Grant, while simultaneously opposing Grant's reelection as the most unsympathetic person, from the perspective of Latter-day Saints, ever to have occupied the White House. Cannon also had to neutralize the havoc wreaked by Judge James McKean and other hostile activists at home and in Washington. The pivotal Englebrecht case remained under consideration. If it proved to be unfavorable to the Church, it would validate the judicial improvisation of McKean's court. Almost as soon as Cannon reached Washington, a letter from Brigham Young urged him to go to the new US Attorney General, George H. Williams, and recommend that John F. Kinney, Utah's former chief justice, be appointed to replace McKean.[7]

Suspense ran high when the Supreme Court deliberated the Englebrecht case. Almost two years earlier in the summer of 1870, non-LDS liquor dealer Paul Englebrecht had gone to court to challenge the validity of Salt Lake City ordinances limiting his business. He possessed several liquor licenses but had been arrested a half dozen times on various charges. On August 27 LDS alderman Jeter Clinton issued a warrant for the destruction of his inventory, which was carried out by city officials and policemen in the presence of witnesses. Two days later a US marshal arrested the officials who had carried out the order, based on a warrant from the territorial district court. Englebrecht filed a civil suit for treble damages. The jury selected by the marshal consisted entirely of non-LDS citizens, so it was not entirely surprising that the defending city officials, all Church members, were convicted.

An appeal from the city attorney asked to have the decision set aside because the jury had not been selected according to Utah

7. Brigham Young to George Q. Cannon, Mar. 16, 1872; also George A. Smith to George H. Williams, Mar. 16, 1872, Young Office Files.

law.[8] Judge McKean heard the appeal. His entire career had been noted for a disregard of territorial statutes. He was the one who had given the US marshal, rather than the Utah marshal, the authority to summon the jury. His ruling in support of the lower court was not a surprise. The city officials appealed the case to the US Supreme Court. After the court heard arguments in early 1872, the anticipation mounted as each day passed, approaching an announcement of the decision. At one point Cannon was pleased to inform Brigham Young that, while he was walking on Pennsylvania Avenue on April 12, Supreme Court Justice Stephen J. Field hailed him and confided that the delay had nothing to do with indecision. It was simply because the justice assigned to write the majority opinion had not yet completed his task. He thought that it would be announced early in the ensuing week. The exchange on the street indicated that Cannon had won the respect of some government figures. What the apostle feared was that President Grant had pressured the Supreme Court to rule against the Church. He was not yet sure what to think, because the Church had never yet received a positive decision from the high court. Adding to the suspense was the speculation that if the court upheld McKean's crusade, Brigham Young would go to jail. On the other hand, a defeat for President Grant could generate a stimulus for new anti-polygamy legislation.[9]

Utah prosecutor George Bates and Judge McKean traveled to Washington to lobby officials and hear the outcome of the Supreme Court case. McKean had the ear of President Grant, and Bates was on friendly terms with Attorney General George Williams and Solicitor General Benjamin Bristow. Bates and Baskin also each appeared before the House Judiciary Committee in early March, the latter to deliver a petition signed by 300 Utahns, intended to counter a petition by the former that was signed by 1,500 Utahns. The original petition asked to remove McKean from office. On April 15, 1872,

8. Whitney, *History of Utah*, 2:560–62.

9. Cannon to Young, Apr. 12, 1872; Fitch to Young, Mar. 17, 1872, Young Office Files. Justice Field would later side with the Church in writing a dissent in the momentous *Reynolds* case of 1879. He would also rule against the Church, prominently in *Davis v. Beason* in 1890.

all the parties were in place for the Supreme Court's announcement of its decision in the most important ruling to date regarding the government of Utah, specifically the question of jury selection. Surprisingly, it was a unanimous decision, and it went against the federal officials. McKean's court lacked authority to empanel juries chosen by the US marshal, the Supreme Court ruled. In addition, the earlier decisions reached in any case involving such juries were invalid. Virtually all decisions McKean had rendered in the previous twenty months were at that moment nullified.[10]

Seated directly in front of Chief Justice Salmon P. Chase, Fitch demonstrated his elation by waving his arms. McKean sat stone-faced, "almost in despair," as he tried to grasp the extent of the death knell to everything he had done. After Baskin recovered from utter disbelief, he lost his temper and denounced the verdict in a voice that was loud enough for everyone to hear. A congressman jokingly wondered if Cannon had enough women to offer the justices prizes. Cannon's response was to joke that the Church might accommodate the justices, but not members of Congress. To Young, Cannon subsequently expressed heartfelt gratitude for the outcome, assuring the Church president that he could rest easy. Young was now free of judicial entrapment.[11]

Bates, who had been asked for his resignation as US Attorney for Utah but had not tendered it, pilloried McKean by writing a caustic review of the judge's actions and gloating about the outcome. This confirmed that the judge had "disgraced" himself and "abused" the judicial system, he contended. "A careful search of the records" would reveal "packed grand and petit juries, a corrupt judge, a pretended United States district attorney [Baskin] appointed by that judge," and immunity for "an atrocious murderer" in exchange for William Hickman's "perjury."[12] Bates remained in office long

10. Whitney, *History of Utah*, 2:676–81; *Clinton v. Englebrecht*, 80 U.S. 434 (1871); Firmage and Mangrum, *Zion in the Courts*, 141–47, 242n130.

11. Whitney, *History of Utah*, 2:681–90; Cannon to Young, Apr. 15, 1872.

12. Tullidge, *History of Salt Lake City*, 512–13; also Baskin, *Reminiscences*, 13–16, 36–37, 513–22. Bates had been informed of his supposed dismissal by the Rev. Newman, who was not an appropriate source for such a notice.

enough to facilitate the release of McKean's prisoners, which took him nearly to the end of 1872. It was assumed that McKean would resign, but he stubbornly stayed put.

Cannon finally met with Attorney General George Williams on April 17 and urged the reappointment of Kinney to replace McKean. Not wanting to monopolize the attorney general's time, Cannon courteously arose to take his leave, and two times Williams asked him to remain and expressed sympathy for Latter-day Saints. Cannon knew this did not change the reality that Grant was still supporting McKean, and Williams himself would be temporarily replaced a few weeks later by Solicitor General Benjamin Bristow and then three years later forced to resign in a cloud of corruption. In any case, Cannon sought direction from Williams on how to get the old verdicts overturned and prisoners released in Utah. Four days later he was told he should include all relevant names on one *habeas corpus* petition and submit it to Cyrus M. Hawley, Utah territorial district judge. Hawley proved to be of little assistance. Other Utah judges were more attentive, to the extent that all the affected defendants were freed within a period of a week. Cannon again assured President Young that he would not be re-arrested.[13]

As Brigham reported to his brother Edward in Wisconsin, the non-LDS prisoners were celebrating in the streets, while "our people conducted themselves as usual, seemingly, as if nothing had happened."[14] Other accounts reported more merriment than Young's muted report suggests. He was disappointed that McKean was staying in office despite having overstepped his bounds. "The grip they hold on us they are not willing to loose," he wrote.[15] There was muted celebration among the Utah delegation in Washington over the Supreme Court ruling, tempered by a worry regarding retaliatory legislation to follow. Instead, as Cannon learned from a trusted source, the Voorhees Bill, for instance, was fated to "sleep in the hands of the committee" until next session. The Utah lobbyists

13. Cannon to Young, Apr. 17, 25, 1872; also Nevins, *Hamilton Fish*, 662, 769–72, 818.

14. Brigham Young to Edward Young, Apr. 24, 1872, Young Office Files.

15. Young to William H. Hooper and George Q. Cannon, Apr. 20, 1872, Young Office Files.

were informed that Chairman Bingham had clashed with Voorhees. As a result, Bingham introduced his own bill with similar provisions but better prospects for success among the majority Republicans than from Democrat Voorhees's legislation. Cannon wrote almost jovially that so many anti-Utah bills had been proposed, they were "likely to strangle one another."[16]

Senator Aaron Cragin, whose bills in 1867 and 1869 had posed such a threat, now confided to Cannon and Hooper that McKean and Baskin were disappointed that Cannon was so active in Washington, a backhanded compliment to his effectiveness. While formerly no friend of the Mormons, Cragin admitted he was "disgusted with Baskin's appearance and talk." He divulged that there was a "strong feeling against McKean in many quarters." His extreme position and methods were "looked upon as shameful to many members" of Congress. Cannon was trying to exploit these views ("strengthen feelings") for the Church's benefit, he reported to Young.[17]

Fitch too noticed a dramatic change in attitude about Utah in the wake of the Supreme Court decision. Congressman Austin Blair of Michigan, who had earlier supported passage of the Cullom Bill, now expressed himself in favor of Utah statehood. On April 1 and 3, Fitch wrote to Young that McKean was lobbying assiduously to get the Voorhees bill passed, but it was seen as "a rehash of the Cullom Bill" and had little prospect for passage in the Senate that spring. Before Fitch testified on April 12 and 18 to the committees on territories, he realistically agreed with Hooper that there was not much chance for Utah's admission as a state that session. Everyone conceded that it would be best to continue their efforts next year without haste and accept that for the moment they would retain their territorial status.[18]

Cannon wrote a mysterious letter in mid-April to Young's counselor Daniel H. Wells. Parts of it were in Hawaiian to conceal

16. Cannon to Young, Apr. 27, May 8, 9, 1872.

17. Cannon to Young, May 9, 10, 17, 1872, Young Office Files.

18. Thomas Fitch to Brigham Young, Mar. 17, Apr. 3, 1872; Cannon to Young, May 8, 1872, Young Office Files.

the message if it were intercepted. Cannon reminded Wells that Joseph F. Smith, who like Cannon had been in Hawaii as a missionary, could translate those portions of the letter. The concealed portion asked for authorization to invest "a few thousand dollars" in bribes to block threatening legislation. He promised that only he and Fuller would undertake the business and would "go slow," meaning they would be careful.[19] Wells's answer has not survived. It may have been concluded that it was unnecessary to resort to such political gamesmanship in the wake of the Englebrecht decision. On the other side, a prominent Utah mine owner and banker, Joseph R. Walker, was in Washington and boasted, on a night when under the effects of alcohol, that he was spending $200,000 to block the attempt to gain statehood. Cannon heard that several officials had received large sums from Walker.[20] It was the Gilded Age, and such methods were not altogether unexpected.

When Cannon, Fitch, and Fuller met with the House Committee on Territories on April 18, it was the first time this committee heard actual testimony about advancing Utah from territorial status to statehood. Fitch made a presentation like the one he had offered to the Senate Committee on Territories but with fewer comments about plural marriage, only to suggest that something might be inserted into the constitution offering leniency for existing marriages. Congressman George C. McKee of Mississippi commented that a similar concession had been offered earlier at a crucial juncture in Reconstruction, allowing representatives of southern states to be readmitted without requiring them to engage in a breach of principle, from their perspective. The congressman recommended a similarly lenient approach regarding the Later-day Saints.

Cannon privately confessed to Young to being alarmed at the requirement, saying "this they all thought would answer. I was much chagrined at the supposition." Doubtlessly correct, Fitch assumed the citizens of Utah would not achieve statehood without concessions on

19. Cannon to Daniel H. Wells, Apr. 16, 1872, Young Office Files.

20. George Q. Cannon to Daniel H. Wells, Apr. 16, 1872, Young Office Files; Cannon to Young, Apr. 22, 1872.

plural marriage. Cannon still persisted in the Latter-day Saint position that polygamy was protected by the First Amendment. He had earlier disclosed to his religious leader the assumption that Congress intended to "exact from us the relinquishment of celestial marriage," that "some [of them] talk as though we owed it to them or the country to sell our eternal salvation and exaltation" for statehood.[21]

Cannon hoped to have the chance to promote "further understanding and airing of the situation" before any such concessions were demanded. If allowed to, he would clarify his sentiments before the House Committee on Territories. In either case, he would do his best to allow "no bill to leave the committee room that is not what we want," explaining that it would be advisable for the Utah delegation to clearly declare what was desired and what conditions were off the table.[22] A week later, on April 25, according to his request, apostle Cannon testified alone before the House committee. After determining that an anti-polygamy provision was in fact demanded, he declared that "we did not want a constitution containing a clause prohibiting polygamy." He assumed the Mormon people would vote against it, as he also certainly would, he told the surprised committee members. After overcoming the impact of hearing this, the committee expressed appreciation for his frankness, stating that they were glad he had not concealed his and his associates' true feelings under the pretext of some diversion.[23]

That being said, his candor doomed Utah's fourth attempt at statehood and cast a shadow over such prospects for the next decade. Cannon knew how Brigham Young felt about it, that polygamy was not negotiable. Congress at least seemed to be moving in the direction of less antagonism toward the LDS faith, so that in the near

---

21. Benedict, *Compromise of Principle*; Cannon to Young, Mar. 31, 1872. The highest priority was thus neither statehood nor protecting Latter-day Saints from anti-Mormon onslaughts, but rather retaining the "peculiar" practice of plural marriage at all costs.

22. Cannon to Young, Apr. 18, 1872. What Cannon desired was to admit Utah without restrictive constitutional provisions "and leave us and our institutions to the [possible] attrition and influences to which their people will be exposed and if we cannot survive this contact, the matter [would be] solved." On the other hand, if Mormonism's distinctive form of matrimony could survive, it should be so allowed.

23. Cannon to Young, Apr. 25, 1872.

future things might be more bearable. This was the last attempt to win a star on the flag during Brigham Young's lifetime. Young died five years later in August 1877. His successor, George Q. Cannon's uncle, was John Taylor, a man who was equally determined not to abandon plural marriage. In hindsight, it was only a matter of time before that would have to be done. When Fitch learned of Cannon's intransigence, likely when on his way back to Utah, he would have been displeased. He had tethered himself to Utah on the assumption that he could win a Senate seat after statehood. According to Fitch's biographer, he was upset enough that before long he left Utah permanently. When he composed his memoirs in 1903, he barely mentioned Utah. He considered the LDS leaders unreasonable, and that he had pursued the only way forward.[24]

Fitch's wife was an accomplished actress and poet who participated in the Washington social scene. Anna Shultz Fitch learned in her own arranged conversation with President Ulysses Grant of the president's intent was to wait until the non-LDS population in Utah Territory overwhelmed the LDS portion, because in his view Mormons could not be trusted. He would veto any Utah statehood bill that came to him, he said. Frank Fuller soon heard much the same thing from Grant himself. The president said bluntly that he would not grant statehood "to any body of people until they were fitted for it," so that neither New Mexico nor Utah would be accepted into the alliance of states. In both instances, he said, their people had "set at defiance the laws of the country."[25] Cannon knew that his fellow lobbyists saw things differently than he did. He noticed how restive Fitch grew, especially when his current retainer fee expired and he became anxious to get back to Utah to his law practice. As far as Cannon was concerned, they could do without him for now, but he felt they would need him again during the ensuing winter session.[26]

24. Moody, ed., *Extraordinary Memoirs*, viii–ix, 88.

25. Fitch to Young, Apr. 25, 1872; Fuller to Young, May 16, 1872, Young Office Files; Fuller to George A. Smith, Dec. 11, 1871, George A. Smith Papers; Cannon to Young, May 17, 1872.

26. Cannon to Young, Apr. 24, 27, 1872. The parallels between Fitch's efforts and those later of Isaac Trumbo are in contrast to the integrity and transparency that Cannon demonstrated toward almost everyone else.

On May 21 Representative John Bingham tried to get his anti-polygamy bill reported favorably out of committee. Sources favorable to Cannon assured him they would vote for it only after it had been "stripped of its most objectionable features." Ultimately it was stalled until the end of the session, and all told, there had been "no less than seven separate anti-Mormon bills introduced into Congress that session, the direct object of which has been to cripple or destroy us," Cannon told Young. With a caustic bite, he concluded that this indicated "the estimation in which the work and people of God are now held." What preoccupied the lobbyist at the time was the upcoming presidential election and how it had brought partisan politics to a boil.

Cannon saw in it an opportunity to wound Grant; at least, he decided to add his influence to the mix by first consulting with Thomas Kane of Pennsylvania, still a friend to the Mormons. Kane was acquainted with New York newspaper editor Horace Greeley and said he would deliberate with him about how to help wrest the presidency from Grant.[27] Greeley had formed his own opinion about Latter-day Saints and was inclined to take a stand for their fair treatment. He conceded that the territory had too few people to make a state, but in his correspondence with Kane he expressed dissatisfaction with Judge McKean's bullying. At the end of April 1872, Kane advised Cannon against sending a Utah delegation to the Republican national convention in June. Since Grant controlled the regular Republican Party, the president's opponents had organized a rival Liberal Republican Party to appeal to disaffected Democrats as well as Republicans. Kane urged Cannon to quietly attend the Liberal convention in Cincinnati in May. The new party would stress Lincoln's goal of "malice toward none," which meant, among other things, amnesty for ex-rebels from southern states. Another uniting principle was objection to Grant's use of the spoils system, or appointing unqualified party members to office. In the view of the dissenters, this constituted corruption. What Kane did not soon

27. Cannon to Young, May 21, 23, 24, 25, 26, 1872; Grow, *Liberty*, 249–53; Fales and Flake, *Mormons and Mormonism*, 366, 374, 376, 379, 380.

disclose to Cannon was that the Liberal Republicans wanted to nominate Greeley as their presidential candidate if he would abandon his support of protective tariffs so that he could appeal to Democrats.

Cannon had assumed that Kane was too ill to attend the convention. Yet upon arrival, he discovered Kane to be hard at work trying to remove an anti-Mormon plank from the proposed party platform. The non-LDS ally argued that support for Utah constituted opposition to Grant, and their support would furthermore encourage the administration to take less harsh positions against the people of Utah. Greeley received the nomination, and an exhausted Kane, who succeeded in helping draft an acceptable platform, requested Cannon to accompany him back to Pennsylvania on the train, which Cannon did. Kane slept all the way home. When the Democrats held their convention in Baltimore in July, they also nominated Greeley as their presidential candidate, the only time this has happened. Unfortunately, Greeley performed badly at the polls. The only states he won usually went Democratic. His campaign was not without its impact, however. It publicized reforms that were incorporated into the next decade of federal legislation.[28] The opponent won a larger majority than anyone had received in recent memory, the key to Grant's success being his record as commanding general of the Union Army during the Civil War.[29] This was the last of Thomas L. Kane's many heroic services to the Church of Jesus Christ of Latter-day Saints.

In the waning days of the congressional session in the spring of 1872, Cannon had commented that "the devil is busy and full of tricks," and he, Hooper, and Fuller had their hands full monitoring the last-minute rush of legislative business. As always happened at the end of a session, the rules were slackened and proposed laws managed to slip in without time for the opposition to mount a defense. For instance, Senator Aaron Cragin introduced another (unsuccessful) Utah bill. For this and other legislation, Cannon acquired

28. Hale, *Horace Greeley*, 330–53; Van Deusen, *Horace Greeley*, 400–24. Both Greeley and his wife died of natural causes within a month of the campaign, even before the electoral votes were tallied.

29. McFeely, *Grant*, 383–84.

an undetermined, but considerable, number of congressional allies who promised to block it. The session proved to be important in Cannon's development as a seasoned lobbyist. One of his allies was Congressman Benjamin Butler of Massachusetts, a Republican and former Civil War general who Cannon said "stood manfully for the people of Utah against inimical legislative measures." Cannon also mentioned the support of Republican reformers Charles Sumner of Massachusetts and Carl Schurz of Missouri, the two of them "blast[ing] Grant" with criticism for his administrative policies.[30]

Back in Utah the previously mentioned Godbeites, critical former Mormons who sometimes pulled in other directions from the *Tribune* ring, now united with the anti-Mormons in opposing statehood. They helped circulate petitions to show Washington there were more people in the territory than Mormons—people who were unhappy with the plenipotentiary power of Brigham Young. In their view, most of the territory's citizens were still incapable of personal independence from the Church, which would be necessary for "maintaining a republican government." The Godbeites submitted to Congress a petition in the fall of 1872 with 2,700 signatures to maintain the territorial status quo.[31] Attempting to weaken this, LDS bishops in Utah had threatened Church members with excommunication for signing the petition. Among those who signed were former LDS apostle and Godbeite activist Amasa M. Lyman, his plural wife Priscilla Turley, and their adult son Theodore. For doing so in defiance of their bishop, the latter two were excommunicated in December 1872.[32] There were isolated instances in other territories of people opposing statehood, but never on this scale until the modern example of Puerto Rico.

After Cannon had proven himself as a political operative, in August 1872 he was elected territorial delegate. The Liberal Party

30. Cannon to Young, Apr. 29, May 1, 6, 8, 21, 23, 1872; Fitch to Young, May 1, 1872.

31. Bigler, *Forgotten Kingdom*, 293–94; also "Memorial of the Legislature of Utah," Apr. 1, 1872, "Memorial of Citizens of Utah against Admission," May 6, 1872, Misc. Docs. 155, 208, 42d Congress, 2d Session, House of Representatives.

32. Edward Partridge Jr. journal, Nov. 9, 16, Dec. 7, 1872; also Lyman, *Amasa Mason Lyman*, 464.

candidate, George Maxwell, lost by a vote of 20,969 to 1,942. The historian Edward W. Tullidge described raucous Liberal Party rallies where firearms were brandished and violence threatened. To their credit, city officials and law enforcement officers exhibited enough restraint to prevent the demonstrations from turning into riots.[33] Maxwell protested the election because of Cannon having sworn a vow in the LDS temple that Maxwell said would make it impossible for him to be loyal to the United States. The Utah governor and territorial secretary dismissed the claim and certified Cannon's election. A peculiarity of the era was the extensive period of time between an election and when a winning candidate was sworn into office, in this case where the election was in August 1872, Cannon's term would not begin until December 1873. Hooper remained the lame-duck delegate for another session, the reasoning behind this being that the incoming representative would have time to prepare and learn the ropes. However, the existing delegate was discouraged and ill, so when Cannon arrived at the capitol in the fall of 1872, he unofficially took over much of the longtime delegate's work. A Cannon biographer explained that "officially, his delegate tenure lasted the eight years from 1874 to 1882. But he had certainly made his presence known in Washington" before that.[34]

Maxwell was still not prepared to admit defeat. He too traveled to Washington, where he gained the ear of Representative Clinton L. Merriam of New York. Merriam had the House Committee on Elections investigate Maxwell's claim. Its finding that Maxwell had no right to the seat did not stop Representative Gerry W. Hazelton, a Wisconsin Republican, from pushing through a resolution that was adopted on January 11, 1875, excluding Cannon from the House until a new investigation could be conducted. By that time the session was so near its end that the action was never carried out.[35]

Cannon's diary, supplemented by his detailed letters to Brigham Young, allows for a remarkable insider's view of events as they

33. Tullidge, *History of Salt Lake City*, 592–93.
34. Whitney, *History of Utah*, 2:730; Bitton, *George Q. Cannon*, 174–81.
35. Roberts, *Comprehensive History*, 5:369–71.

transpired in 1873 during the congressional fight over Utah's future. Unfortunately, no known sources exist for the opponents' side of the struggle. In those days a new session began in December with some preliminary business before the normal Christmas recess arrived. When everyone was back in town, a primary agenda item was resolving the territorial questions. During discussion about Colorado, William Hooper proposed an amendment to grant the same status to Utah at the same time. Friendly California senator, Aaron A. Sargent, sweetened the package by adding moderate restrictions regarding polygamy.[36] This generated such animated debate that in a charged discussion on January 28 Hooper and Sargent attempted to withdraw their amendments, based on the crushing criticisms their proposals received. William H. Clagett, Republican delegate from Montana Territory, also launched a "fierce and brutal" attack on Utah's citizenry, much of what he said being untrue. No one stepped forth to correct his misrepresentations. The Idaho Democratic delegate who resided part-time in Salt Lake City, Samuel Merritt, was "evidently pleased with the performance," even though he admitted that some of Clagett's statements were false. Hooper stood to reply, but he was a poor speaker and garnered little sympathy compared to the rapt attention Clagett had received. The delegate prepared a written response to set the record straight, but it too received little attention.[37]

On Monday, February 3, Clagett and Merritt were asked to confirm to President Grant the "terrible condition of affairs in Utah," as they had been conveyed to him by the reverend Newman. They said it was true that the Utah legislature passed statutes that "discriminate with great severity against those who do not belong to Brigham Young's Church, so that it amounts to virtual exclusion." The president decided that "the final issue with Utah cannot be avoided." That same day, he did something rare for a chief executive in the nineteenth century. He

36. William Hooper, "Colorado Territory," *Congressional Globe*, Jan. 29, 1873; George Q. Cannon journal, Jan. 28–29, 1873. This journal, published in Tullidge, *History of Salt Lake City*, appears to be an almost complete version for the period, also now thankfully available online with few redactions.

37. Cannon journal, Feb. 2–5, 1873; Hooper, *Vindication.*

personally went to the capitol building and, explaining that "Utah affairs had called him there," conferred with members of the judiciary committees of the House and Senate. He urged them to do what they could to curb the excesses of the LDS legislature. He said that if the congressional session ended on March 4 "without legislation, he would put his troops into Utah and nail the thing by that means."[38]

On February 5 Merritt reintroduced aspects of the Voorhees Bill for more federal control and to suppress the Church's influence. Cannon predicted that this would result in more carpetbagging and "open wide the doors for every species of corruption to flow in unchecked." Rather than bringing the two sides together to work out a compromise, the gap was widened, the issues wildly misrepresented, and an avalanche of bills kept coming. On Friday, February 7, Republican senator Frederick T. Frelinghuysen of New Jersey introduced legislation similar to Merritt's that would quickly gain traction in both houses.[39]

In an interview conducted by a *New York Herald* reporter, Grant said he wanted to see laws that "would at once quiet the disturbance" in the Great Basin "by making the federal authority supreme." Despite the Supreme Court's ruling, he wanted to revisit the selection of jurors and take it out of the hands of LDS authorities. It was the only way polygamy could be suppressed, he said. What an irritation to see "the impudent encroachments of Mormonism," he said. They were "a reproach to the nation." "We have temporized enough," he insisted. One way or another, he would "compel Mormon leaders to act as loyal citizens of the republic."[40] This approach, as reported in the *Herald*, did not reflect a consensus of public opinion, even among political leaders.

Cannon reported that the shrill comments of the president in the New York article "fell like a wet blanket upon the members" of

38. Whitney, *History of Utah*, 2:720–35.

39. Cannon journal, Feb. 5, 7, 1873; Roberts, *Comprehensive History,* 5:436–37. A primary aim of Grant and the largely mining-backed Tribune ring was taking government power away from elected territorial officials and placing it in the hands of federally appointed officials.

40. *New York Herald,* Feb. 14, 1873; Cannon journal, Feb. 13, 1873.

Congress when the Washington papers picked it up. The legislature was not in a mood to allow the president to usurp their authority. Between the positions of the states' rights Democrats and the rival Republican faction that called themselves Half-breeds, there were plenty of opponents to the president's goal of intervening in Utah. Moreover, when Grant sent a formal message to Congress urging a bill, probably suggested by Baskin,[41] it backfired spectacularly, according to Cannon. "I never saw a document read which appeared to attract less attention than did this," he wrote to Young. Cannon was quick to move among the legislators, "conversing as I had opportunity," encouraging resentment of the president's tendency to lecture Congress. Cannon noted that "a better feeling prevails" toward Utah "than I could expect under the circumstances." The slump in Grant's popularity in Congress, in contrast to his popularity with the voters, was working to Cannon's and Hooper's advantage in an uneven contest against the anti-Mormon ring.

On the other hand, there were Stalwart Republicans in the Senate who agreed that anti-Mormon legislation was second in importance "only to appropriations." One of them, the chair of the House Judiciary Committee, grudgingly allowed Fitch opportunity for written arguments plus ten minutes to verbally counter assertions against the anti-Mormon Frelinghuysen bill. A standoff ensued when Utah antagonist Clagett tried to speak and was blocked by temporary Speaker of the House James A. Garfield, who had visited Utah the previous year and generally liked what he saw. Later Speaker James G. Blaine, another dignitary who had recently visited Utah, refused to allow time from the bill's proponents. Garfield and Blaine were increasingly powerful Half-breeds who were on good terms with Cannon and interested in Utah affairs. They were consistently effective intra-party opponents of the president.[42]

Merritt told Cannon his punitive bill would easily pass because all the machinery was in place to prevail in the House, after which

41. Roberts, *Comprehensive History*, 5:433; "Message from the President," Senate Executive Document 44, *Congressional Record*, Feb. 14, 1873.

42. Cannon journal, Feb. 5–14, 1873; Morgan, *Hayes to McKinley*, 58–75, 84–96.

its Senate companion would also quickly be approved. Cannon's reaction, according to his journal, was to pray for intervention and get busy behind the scenes talking to newspaper editors, congressional staff, and religious leaders, employing methods he sometimes referred to in his diary and elsewhere as "clandestine." He found something of an ally in General William T. Sherman, whom Grant had dispatched to Utah in late 1870 to investigate the situation. The general was well known for his hardline approach during his prosecution of the Civil War, but he felt that Grant's approach to Utah was too harsh.[43] Even at a dinner party he was attending with Grant, he said the policy was "all wrong." That elicited laughs from guests who said he must have become converted to polygamy. In the Senate, where Hooper was concentrating his effort, the Utah delegate convinced Republican Senator John Pool of North Carolina to amend the Frelinghuysen bill to temper it. Pool agreed, but the committee rejected the amendments before reporting the bill to the entire Senate for floor debate.[44]

Cannon vividly described the back-and-forth repartee as the bill was discussed. Church opponents fought "inch by inch," he wrote, standing to deliver screeds against Utah: John A. Logan of Illinois, William Windom of Minnesota (both Republicans), Allen G. Thurman of Ohio (a Democrat), and others who were responded to by LDS-friendly senators Lyman Trumbull of Illinois, William M. Stewart of Nevada (Republicans), Thomas F. Bayard of Delaware (Democrat), and several others who were equally enlivened by the controversy. The defenders of Utah were appalled by the suggestion that deputy marshals should be given authority to call on the military, or what they characterized as an "appeal to the bayonet to enforce civil process." It did not matter. The measure passed 29–10. Thirty-nine senators made it a point of being absent or abstaining rather than go on record opposing Grant. The companion bill in the House of Representatives came up for debate on Saturday, March 1, 1873, four days before adjournment. As the debate extended into the evening

43. Cannon journal, Feb. 22, 1873; Roberts, *Comprehensive History*, 5:348.
44. Cannon journal, Feb. 11, 14, 1873.

on Sunday, a nearby committee room was prepared for a celebration. Some of the congressmen, including committee chairman Bingham, began sampling the spiked punch prior to getting the bill properly brought to the floor that night, slowing down the process.[45]

Monday was characterized by the normal end-of-session rush, along with the impeachment of two midwestern judges, which unexpectedly monopolized the floor time. The proceedings continued on past midnight, then adjourned before the Utah bill was voted on. That naturally drew a sigh of relief from Cannon. However, the House reconvened at 9:30 a.m. the next morning, ready to pass the bill. Senator Aaron Sargent, a friend of Utah, pointed out that a quorum was not present, so that the vote had to be postponed until shortly before noon. When enough senators were present, they voted to transact no further legislative business, thus allowing the Frelinghuysen bill to die. Furious, Clagett alleged that Mormons had spent hundreds of thousands of dollars to bribe members of the House Judiciary Committee. This time, at least, it was probably simple mismanagement. Cannon ascribed the success to God, "who was … mightier than they all."[46] Many Congress watchers were shocked.

After half a year's respite from legislative infighting, President Grant called on Congress in his annual message on December 1, 1873, to once-and-for-all solve the "Mormon problem." In his view "affairs in Utah require your early and special attention."[47] A month later, on January 5, 1874, Vermont's Luke P. Poland, a one-term congressional Republican, introduced a bill in the House "relative to courts and judicial offices in the territory of Utah," with the intent of satisfying Grant and the public sentiment he stirred up.[48] If passed, it would weaken the probate court system and entirely eliminate the territorial marshal and territorial attorney, allowing federal officials to oversee the courts. As Orson F. Whitney saw it, the bill's "provisions discriminated against the majority of the citizens of

45. Cannon journal, Feb. 25, Mar. 1, 1873.

46. Cannon journal, Mar. 3, 4, 1873; Tullidge, *History of Salt Lake City*, 605–07.

47. Richardson, *Messages and Papers of the Presidents*, 9:4162–64 (Feb. 14, 1873); 4189–4209 (Dec. 1, 1873).

48. For the complete bill, see the *Congressional Record*, 1874, 253–56.

the territory." President Grant sent another message to lawmakers on February 14 urging passage of this or whatever other laws they thought would see to the "needs" of Utah. Some 2,000 miles away, the Utah Territorial Legislature responded with a memorial to Congress suggesting that the federal government create an investigative commission to determine actual conditions in Utah. The governor, George L. Woods, vetoed the bill, calling it "improper." It was sent to Congress nevertheless, but without response. Members of the House and Senate judiciary committees were confident of their own assessments, backed by Governor Woods, that politics in Utah were controlled by Mormons and governance needed to be wrested away from them.[49]

On January 9, 1874, Cannon secured another interview with President Grant. He encouraged Grant to consider the idea of an investigating committee. The president was noncommittal, but agreed in principle. Ten days later Cannon returned with a copy of the memorial from the Utah legislature. Grant commented that the investigating should have been done much earlier, but did not say whether it should still be undertaken. With the weight of public opinion on his side, he was finding more support in Congress for closing down the long-criticized probate court system of Utah. The calls to do something about the territory were becoming more strident.[50]

When Cannon testified before the Senate Judiciary Committee on February 16, the chairman refused to grant him enough time to deliver a prepared statement. There would not be an investigative delegation, members of the committee told him. Discouraged, his spirits were nevertheless lifted when he later passed the Idaho delegate, Samuel Merritt, in the hallway and got a glimpse of how things looked from the other side. "You told me in Salt Lake City that the Lord was on your side," the Idahoan said, "and I am damned if I don't begin to believe it." Cannon's reply was, "You will find it out." Merritt quipped, "Bully for the Lord," an idiom that meant good for you/him.[51]

49. Whitney, *History of Utah*, 2:738; Roberts, *Comprehensive History*, 5:431.

50. Cannon to Young, Jan. 10, 1874; "Memorial of the Legislative Assembly of Utah," *Congressional Record*, House Misc. Doc. 139; Cannon journal, Jan. 23, 1874.

51. Bitton, *George Q. Cannon*, 188–89.

On March 2 Cannon again introduced an enabling act, accompanied by the constitution of 1872. This action makes little realistic sense unless simply to keep statehood hopes alive among Utah citizens. Most officials of the United States government and majority of informed citizens recalled Cannon's recent frank declaration that he and his people would refuse to make concessions regarding plural marriage. But the delegate even stopped by the White House to let President Grant know what he was doing and again was "treated courteously," he reported.[52]

On the legislative front, the Baskin–McKean and *Tribune* faction remained far from defeated, even by the Englebrecht decision. Instead of retreating, they returned to their often-successful legislative approach and threw their full support behind Representative Luke Poland's bill. Even the sponsor himself recognized that the bill had insurmountable problems.[53] Encouraged to do so, he dramatically toned down some of the more draconian provisions, admitting on June 2 when he introduced the revised version that he had overreached. Commenting on it later, after considerable amending, he termed it "remarkable for its moderation when compared with previous bills that have been before the house upon this vexed subject of the territory of Utah."[54]

Realizing that the bill was not the sole result of Poland's doing, Cannon complained to Kane that his opponents enjoyed a network that reached "horizontally" into many, if not most, places of national government. Yet he said his own cause enjoyed a less broadly based, but also effective, "invisible vertical influence, which was also at work." This probably referred to several quiet centers of legislative power, including lobby interests.[55]

---

52. Cannon journal, Mar. 2, 1874.

53. Whitney, *History of Utah*, 2:739–40, indicated that "Poland withdrew his [original bill] and presented one considerably modified," meaning less oppressive to the Utah majority. This portion of Whitney's history was ghostwritten by the delegate's oldest son, John Q. Cannon. See Lyman, *Candid Insights*, 329.

54. See Roberts, *Comprehensive History*, 5:434–36; Cannon, George Q. Cannon Journal, May–June 1874.

55. Bitton, *George Q. Cannon*, 189–90. Cannon's biographer probably incorrectly assumed the reference was to divine assistance.

In the congressional debate that began June 2, Cannon defended the beleaguered probate courts. He explained that the federal courts heard cases only in Beaver, Provo, and Salt Lake City, while the probate courts (courts of original jurisdiction since 1852, not simply arbiters of inheritance) were everywhere. He cited Beaver as an example of the inconvenience of the three federal courts. Beaver was a hundred miles from St. George. The probate judges were mainly local bishops, part of the lay ministry the Church relied upon. "There is probably no officer in Utah territory, if he belongs to the Mormon people, who does not hold some position in the church." It was "the privilege of every worthy man of their organization to be an elder, and when called upon, to make himself useful in preaching." This hardly constituted a serious mixing of church and state affairs, Cannon reasoned to deaf ears. The House passed the Poland bill by a vote of 159 to 55, with 75 abstentions.[56]

The counterpart in the Senate was to be debated three weeks later on June 23. By that time it had been so extensively pruned and amended, some of its original backers no longer considered it a remedy for the problem it was intended to address. The sponsor maintained a conciliatory tone and continued to invite whatever suggestions could improve it. Responding to the call, Utah backers quickly relieved it of section 7 disallowing common-law marriage and added an amendment allowing cases in territorial courts to be appealed to the US Supreme Court. When LDS-friendly Senator Aaron Sargent proposed adding several complex final proposals, he was allowed to do so "without opposition" because the session was nearing adjournment. The opposition responded with their own amendment allowing Gentiles who had abandoned Utah Territory during times of unrest to sue for restitution of property without regard for a statue of limitation.[57]

---

56. "Legislative Debate on the Poland Act in the House," *Congressional Record*, June 2, 1874.

57. "Legislative Debate," June 23, 1874. Cannon's grandson, Mark W. Cannon, with access to family notes and correspondence, wrote in his Harvard dissertation, "Mormon Issue in Congress," 57–60, 288, that Sargent enlisted the help of Republican congressional leaders and alluded to his willingness to filibuster if necessary.

Sargent appeared to be fair-minded. That he was not exactly partisan was evident in his statement that care needed to be taken because of the "high condition of fanaticism" in the territory, so that their actions did not provoke "a civil war there." That result, because the citizens were no match for the US Army, would be "desolation." He believed that with "the progress of time [and] the influx of Gentiles," prejudices would melt "like an iceberg in warmer water." If the nation was patient, the Mormons would come around to respect the rule of law and honor the norms of American society. Having said that, he struck the requirement that alimony would be a required element of divorce proceedings. He added an allowance for weddings to be solemnized without formal documentation. He cut a proposed disqualification of jurors who subscribed to polygamy but did not practice it. Another modification allowed attorneys in polygamy cases to use pre-emptory challenges in jury selections. At that, the bill passed the Senate and was quickly approved in the House. President Grant signed it into law the same day, June 24, 1874. It was the only partial legislative victory against the Latter-day Saints since the Morrill anti-Bigamy Act of 1862.

Even in its attenuated form, the Poland Act weakened the local courts. It removed chancery, civil, and criminal jurisdiction, so that the probate courts were left with estate matters, divorces, and issues involving guardianship. The selection of juries was to be done in cooperation with clerks of the federal district courts. At the same time, justices of the peace were given more responsibilities. Citizens were given the right to appeal bigamy and capital cases to the US Supreme Court. The new law also eliminated elected territorial attorneys and marshals in favor of appointed US attorneys and marshals.

This became the tool by which polygamists were pursued for the next eight years until the Edmunds Act, and later Edmunds–Tucker Act, would enhance the possibilities for prosecution. It was less radical than feared, but still difficult to defend against.[58] Latter-day Saints were not immediately able to recognize that the wall surrounding polygamy had been breached and that it would tumble

58. Whitney, *History of Utah*, 2:740; Roberts, *Comprehensive History*, 5:442.

in less than a decade and a half. In the short term, Cannon had scored a success by limiting the damage and satisfying detractors to the point that they did not then see the need for other laws to rein in the Latter-day Saints. The Poland Act stands as the only such law passed during Cannon's entire years of service until the Edmunds Act intentionally removed him in 1882.[59]

It is unclear exactly why Senator Sargent felt such sympathy for the Latter-day Saints. But his support was probably derived from his association with railroad interests. It was the aim of a broad alliance of railroad companies to maintain peace and harmony in areas they serviced, and they became the most powerful allies of Latter-day Saint interests through an extensive lobbying network. The LDS Church came under their influence and soon conscientiously followed their instructions in political matters, with the aim being statehood, scrupulously avoiding any of the missteps that had posed problems earlier.[60]

When Cannon stood for reelection in the summer of 1874, his challenger was none other than Robert N. Baskin. Cannon won, 22,260 to 4,513. The Liberal Party was doing slightly better, but not yet a serious threat. It once more challenged Cannon's claim to have been naturalized in 1854, since at the time he was serving a mission to the Sandwich Islands. As a member of the LDS Church, his highest loyalty was to the Church rather than to the country, they also stressed. Cannon's attorneys included longtime New York Congressman Charles A. Eldridge. They answered that Cannon's service as a delegate to Congress was evidence of his loyalty to the country, and that his time in Hawaii ended in 1854. After a brief hiatus in Utah, he oversaw publication of the LDS newspaper, the *Western Standard*, and the Book of Mormon in Hawaiian, from a print shop in San Francisco through 1855. With that clarification the House felt it could do nothing other than

59. Cannon was removed for being a polygamist, but Liberals were more happy to see him go because of his effectiveness as a legislative opponent.

60. Lavender, *Great Persuader*, 287, 346; Lyman, *Political Deliverance*, 73–92; Lamar, *Far Southwest*, 370. This law, later upheld by the US Supreme Court, breached some of the walls of the defense of polygamy and self-rule.

begin to accept him as a delegate, beyond ordering an investigation into his background, which Congress did.[61]

Near the end of the Republican dominance of the House of Representatives, Washington was adjusting its attitude about the appointment of territorial officials. Grant assigned Samuel B. Axtell to replace Governor Woods. Axtell arrived on February 2, 1875. He had been a miner and county attorney in California, and during two terms in the US House of Representatives he had formed a close friendship with William Hooper. He had a working knowledge of and interest in Utah. He was one of two Republicans who had spoken against the Cullom Bill in 1870. His appointment came partly through the influence of Senator Sargent of California.[62] His downfall was his overly cordial association with the Latter-day Saints. The anti-Mormon Liberal Party in Utah was instantly offended by this and registered its complaint with Grant, who only four months later ordered Axtell transferred to New Mexico, to be the territorial governor. On June 8 Grant appointed his friend George W. Emery to fill the vacant office in Utah. The new governor was a New Englander who was living in Tennessee at the time. His term would be noteworthy for lasting five years, a lengthy term of office for a Utah appointee. He also stood out because he chose to remain neutral on Utah affairs. Grant surprisingly approved of this approach, and even encouraged it. He told Emery to "deal justly between man and man, avoiding all extremes," and to especially resist pressure from the anti-Mormons. Grant and his wife, Julia Dent Grant, decided to visit their friend in Utah Territory in the fall of 1875 to observe conditions for themselves. It was a significant achievement for Governor Emery. LDS leaders went out of their way to be gracious hosts, meeting the Grants at the main railroad junction in Ogden and accompanying them by private train to Salt Lake City. There they were picked up by carriage and driven through welcoming throngs lining South Temple Street. Seeing smiling children backed

61. Cannon, "Mormon Issue in Congress," 53–56, 60–62; also Bitton, *George Q. Cannon*, 172–74, 186–87, 191–95; *Congressional Record*, Dec. 6, 1881, 42.

62. Roberts, *Comprehensive History*, 5:595–601.

by parents, Grant asked Emery whose children they were. They were Latter-day Saints, the governor replied. Grant "thoughtfully gazed for a few moments upon the lovely scene before him, and then murmured in a meditative tone, 'I have been deceived.'"[63]

The next day while Grant toured the broader valley and mountain areas, his wife was brought to tears attending a Tabernacle organ concert by Joseph J. Daynes. She afterward made a comment about "these good Mormon people."[64] When the Grants returned to Washington, the president was notably silent about Utah. Except for a repeated commitment in December 1875 in his annual message regarding the need to see polygamy abolished, he kept quiet about the Mormons his last two years in office. Others too had mellowed in their views. Senator Isaac P. Christiancy of Michigan introduced a bill in 1876 to exclude advocates of polygamy from juries, and when Cannon met with him to suggest that he had "gone too far," Christiancy agreed and said he would not press his bill. He had probably been induced to introduce it at the request of the Baskin clique. Other silent interests worked to promote the bill as it journeyed through the process without further impetus from Christiancy. There was a telling connection between the senator and Utah prosecutor George Maxwell. Christiancy's son James had been an officer in a Michigan cavalry unit with Maxwell during the Civil War. That may have been the way the father was introduced to Utah issues, through his son.[65]

Baskin testified before the Senate Committee on Territories in favor of another bill addressing polygamy. Cannon felt obliged to speak against it. He did so, and that was the last he heard of the bill. With Democrats thereafter gaining a majority in the House, Latter-day Saints would enjoy a respite of six years. This is why Cannon, who had four wives, was spared hearings on his status. Baskin ran

63. Whitney, *History of Utah*, 3:116, 118; Roberts, *Comprehensive History*, 2:778–79, 3:118, 5:505. It is doubtful Newman was influential thereafter.

64. Whitney, 2:777–79.

65. Richardson, *Compilation of Messages*, 9:4286–4310; Maxwell, *George R. Maxwell*, 43–44; Baskin, *Reminiscences*, 73. This cavalry unit was commanded by George Armstrong Custer.

against Cannon again in 1876 and lost again, and in the next election two year later the Liberals neglected to sponsor a candidate at all, leaving Cannon unopposed. The next time Congress passed another anti-Mormon law would be in 1882 when the infamous Edmunds Act surfaced. In the meantime, everyone was taking a wait-and-see attitude about what effect the Poland Act would have. Following the trouble the Poland bill had in committee, no one was eager to repeat that experience. Many bills that were suggested died in committee or on the calendar.[66] The Democrats, in their support of fair treatment, wanted the allegiance of Utah voters. Of course there were other issues that demanded the lawmakers' attention: a controversial presidential election in 1876, currency questions, civil service reform, the end of Reconstruction, and the ever-complex business of appropriations, immigration, and tariffs.[67]

It had been a turbulent decade for the LDS Church. Never before had there been such an onslaught of bills scrutinizing Mormon governance, beliefs, and practices. President Grant addressed these with varying degrees of urgency, almost until the end of his term in 1877, the year Brigham Young died. It was the end of an era on both counts, characterized in Congress and in Utah by a deadlock between the federal government and a desire for home rule. Congress had made its position clear that polygamy had to go, as a non-negotiable prerequisite for statehood. On the other side of the question, there was no compromising the LDS commitment to plural marriage. The next LDS president, John Taylor, would go into hiding rather than forfeit his marriages and die in exile in 1887. As the 1880s approached, George Q. Cannon was optimistic. Little did he know that it would be a decade of anything but calm. His time thus far in Washington had provided him with invaluable experience in observing alliances, manipulations, and corruption constituting a part of the process in the Washington environment. He had learned how the sausage is made, so to speak. Among his other

66. Bitton, *George Q. Cannon,* 198–199; Cannon, "Mormon Issue in Congress," 60–62, 64.

67. Morgan, *From Hayes to McKinley,* 12–15, 73–78, 120–22.

lessons were the value of person-to-person interactions, frankness, and reciprocity. He knew the results of poor leadership, loose lips, and unreasonableness. On the other hand, everyone drew a line in the sand at some point, on principle or for constituencies, and that was allowed as long as a politician respected opposing views and engaged in the give-and-take of theories and solutions—the stuff of statesmanship. That kind of negotiating ability would be in high demand over the next ten years.

4

PRESSED TO THE WALL

1880-85

Latter-day Saints would soon directly challenge anti-polygamy laws with a test case they were certain would guarantee them their constitutional rights. They were disappointed. As the wheels of justice turned, the Church advised high-profile polygamists to either leave the country or go into hiding. There was some hope the situation would improve when the first Democratic president since James Buchanan was elected. However, Grover Cleveland proved no more lenient at first in administering the law than his predecessors. With the LDS leadership in hiding and unavailable to counsel the membership, the rank-and-file were more or less on their own, just when they were most in need of guidance the outlook appeared bleak.

The message the Church members heard when the leaders communicated by letter was one of resistance. The federal intervention in the territory was equated with Satan's attempt to lead humankind astray. During this time LDS people remained generally loyal to the hierarchy and to "the principle" of polygamy despite suffocating efforts by deputy marshals, prosecutors, and judges to find and arrest those who had more than one wife. This was one of the most extensive episodes of civil disobedience in the history of the country.

In the drawn-out court case involving the divorce of Ann Eliza Webb, the woman who called herself Brigham Young's "nineteenth wife," although she was actually fifty-third, Judge James McKean was clearly aligned with the prosecution. The case was filed in July 1873.

After the final judicial decision was rendered nearly two years later in February 1875, McKean assessed Brigham a fine of $3,000 for court expenses and alimony of $500 per month, an amount so high for the day that newspapers across the country scoffed at it.[1] Journalists also wondered why McKean had not excused the frail seventy-four-year-old defendant from having to attend trial each day. President Ulysses S. Grant finally agreed with the newspapers that McKean was once again overstepping his bounds, and within a week of McKean's decision, even in light of Grant's visceral disapproval of polygamy, the judge was asked to step down. David B. Lowe, a Republican from Kansas, was appointed to replace McKean. He arrived in Utah in April 1875 and briefly oversaw the Young–Webb divorce case before resigning. His replacement, Alexander White, was never confirmed by the US Senate and therefore dismissed.[2] The revolving door of federal territorial officials continued to spin.

Ever since passage of the Morrill Act of 1862, Latter-day Saints were convinced that if it were reviewed by the US Supreme Court, the justices would find it to be an unconstitutional infringement of basic rights. After the Englebrecht decision struck down Judge McKean's activism, a sentiment developed, even in the Church, that a definitive judgement was needed. Utah territorial attorney George C. Bates said so when visiting the nation's capital in 1872. He said he was going to indict leading Latter-day Saints, with their consent, and try them for violating the Morrill Act. Grant replaced Bates with William Carey. It turned out that Carey also approved of the idea of a test case. When George Q. Cannon was arrested on October 21, 1874, Carey thought he would be the right person to undergo the strain of a drawn-out appeal. Cannon, by then one of Young's counselors in the First Presidency and territorial delegate to Congress, thought otherwise. In quiet negotiations with the new US District Attorney, it was agreed that the Church would provide someone else for a representative case and that the essential evidence would be turned over to the prosecutor in return for dropping the charges

1. B. H. Roberts, *Comprehensive History*, 5:454.
2. Alexander, "James B. McKean," 85–100.

against Cannon and others whose cases were then pending. Cannon asked friend and protégé George Reynolds, a Church secretary, if he would supply his marriage records to the district attorney for the benefit of the Church. Reynolds willingly agreed.

On October 23, 1874, Reynolds, then thirty-two and working in Brigham Young's office, was indicted before the fair-minded Judge Phillip H. Emerson. On April 1, 1875, the Church secretary appeared in court, represented by none other than McKean's longtime critic George Bates, along with his new law partners Zerubbabel Snow and Jabez Sutherland. The jury had seven LDS and five non-LDS men on it. According to a previous agreement, friendly witnesses gave evidence of Reynolds's second marriage to Amelia Jane Schofield. There were a number of procedural errors, the defendant not being asked for a plea until after he was found guilty, for instance, at which time he declared himself the opposite. It was also significant that the judge advised the jury to disregard religious beliefs, which "can have nothing to do with this case," he said. It took a half hour for the twelve men to find Reynolds guilty. Emerson then declined to impose punishment, thinking the law did not require it. It was only after prosecutors Carey and Baskin insisted, that Emerson brought Reynolds back to court on Saturday, April 10, and sentenced him to a year in prison and a fine of $300. When the defendant's attorneys appealed to the territorial supreme court, Emerson accepted Reynolds's bond and allowed him to go free.[3]

On June 7 the three-judge territorial supreme court heard the defense's appeal. Twelve days later the court set aside the original indictment on grounds that federal law had been followed, instead of territorial law, in determining the size of the grand jury. A second indictment was therefore obtained, and Reynolds was arrested again on November 1. He pled not guilty. Judge Alexander White presided, beginning December 9. This time Reynolds was represented by non-LDS attorney Parley L. Williams. When the prosecution asked that the evidence obtained during the first trial to be allowed, Williams objected. The defendant was no longer cooperating, and

3. Van Orden, *Prisoner for Conscience' Sake*, 61–62, 66–72, 84–85.

the crucial testimony of the second wife was then no longer available. White accepted the previous evidence and informed the jury that the issue before them was only whether Reynolds was already married when he took a second wife. There "must be some limits to the high constitutional privilege" of freedom of religion, he added. Carey, serving as the prosecutor, was unskilled, Reynolds found—so much so that Judge White had to assist him throughout the proceedings. This time it took the jury two hours to find Reynolds guilty. On December 21 White sentenced Reynolds to two years' hard labor and a fine of $500. The territorial supreme court upheld the decision on June 13, 1876.

An appeal was immediately filed with the US Supreme Court. After a wait of eighteen months, news came that the court would accept the case and hear arguments three months later in March 1878. The expedited schedule had to do with the court's decision, after accepting the case, to reclassify it as a criminal matter and move it up on the calendar. This caught the Church off guard, without representation. Cannon asked Chief Justice Morrison R. Waite if the defendant could have time to assemble a legal team, but Waite was unsympathetic to the request. Thomas Kane suggested to Cannon that he approach George W. Biddle, a renowned Philadelphia attorney. Biddle said he was willing but that his schedule was full during the March slot. Cannon met several times with solicitor general Samuel F. Phillips and US Attorney Charles Devens before he obtained a postponement to November, probably because of Biddle's prominence.[4] In the meantime, Reynolds was in prison, his request to post bail having been denied.

Biddle was less interested in participating in a test case than in getting his client freed over procedural errors. The court, on the other hand, was not disinclined to pursue weightier issues. Biddle also argued that the Morrill Act infringed on states' rights. No, said the court. In their brief, Biddle and his team had mentioned the size of the grand jury and the fact that the jury received prejudicial instructions to overlook the First Amendment's protection of religion.

4. Bitton, *George Q. Cannon*, 218–20.

The reason the case produced what became known as a landmark decision was because Chief Justice Waite perceived in that remark an issue of "whether the First Amendment's guarantee of the freedom of religious exercise would excuse otherwise criminal conduct." The constitution prohibited Congress from passing laws regarding the "establishment of religion, or prohibiting the free exercise thereof," he wrote, but this was different. This dealt with more than "mere opinion," but with "actions which were in violation of social duties or subversive of good order." He wrote that "polygamy has always been odious among the northern and western nations of Europe," from which the American traditions and institutions sprang.[5]

The court determined that it was "within the legitimate scope of the power of every civil government to determine whether polygamy or monogamy shall be the law of social life under its domain"; whereas lawmakers "cannot interfere with mere religious belief and opinions, they may with practices." In other words, people can believe what they want, but they cannot engage in whatever behavior they please. The rulings of the lower courts would stand, the January 6, 1879, decision read. Reynolds would serve out his sentence in prison. More than 32,000 Utah citizens requested that he be pardoned, and Cannon presented the signatures to President Rutherford B. Hayes himself, who said the petition deserved attention but took no action. Cannon had the "hard labor" portion of the sentence mitigated so that Reynolds could spend most of his term as an office clerk and school teacher for other prisoners. Because of his good behavior, his two-year sentence was shortened by 144 days, almost five months, and he was released toward the end of January 1881.[6]

Many national leaders considered the *Reynolds* decision to be the ultimate solution to a long-standing question. That being the case, people were willing to see all Latter-day Saints pardoned for violating the Morrill Act prior to the Reynolds verdict, on condition that they would thereafter obey the law. Among those holding

5. Firmage and Mangrum, *Zion in the Courts*, 153–59.

6. Whitney, *History of Utah*, 2:70, 88–90, 3:49–57; Roberts, *Comprehensive History*, 5:471–74.

this view were US vice president William A. Wheeler and Supreme Court Justice Stephen J. Field. There was no perceptible response from LDS leaders suggesting they would even consider such conditions. Outside of Utah, the verdict was viewed as having struck a "death blow to polygamy." Many observers anticipated wholesale prosecutions in the immediate aftermath of the ruling. The *Salt Lake Herald* observed that a considerable number of anti-Mormon petitions were presented to Congress immediately after the Reynolds verdict to exploit "whatever feeling of prejudice against the Mormons" might have been generated by the decision.[7] Cannon commented dryly that "petitions continue to pour in from all parts of the country primarily from the women of religious sects asking for additional legislation to make more effective the anti-polygamy law of 1862." This, he observed, "evoked a power which politicians do not like to displease."[8]

Prior to *Reynolds v United States*, the harshest punishments for polygamy had been legislatively and procedurally forestalled by the Englebrecht case. The court decision now provided an impetus for more proscriptive enforcement, the first step in a return to the approach of the early 1870s and a law-enforcement crusade to overshadow anything Judge McKean had tried. The LDS historian Richard D. Poll commented that *Reynolds* required the Saints to assume a "new position ... The law must be obeyed or a new basis for continuing to ignore it must be found." But apparently not realizing how dramatically the court decision had changed the legal landscape, LDS leaders continued to speak with high-minded rhetoric about constitutional rights, liberty, and freedom. While some put on a brave face as they talked about the divine protection God would surely grant them, their legal defenses had been virtually swept away. They faced increasingly harsh judicial blows and the rising onslaught of investigations by federal marshals. This engendered a top-to-bottom disruption of the community—its economic stability, religious

7. *Salt Lake Herald*, Jan. 8, 11, 19, 1879.

8. Cannon journal, Jan. 15, 1879. For petitions to Congress to curb polygamy, see *Congressional Record*, Apr. 15, 24, 29, 1886.

practice, and family life.[9] Nevertheless, Church authorities simply encouraged continued resistance.

The fierce anti-Mormon sentiment was enhanced by the return of a Republican majority in the US House of Representatives in the election of 1880, soon followed by a plethora of anti-polygamy bills. Rutherford B. Hayes observed in his third annual message to Congress on December 1, 1879, that the Morrill Act, passed seventeen years earlier, had not succeeded in halting polygamy. He opined that "stringent" new legislation was required.[10] The floodgates opened.

Only twenty-four hours after Hayes's message, Congressman Thomas L. Young, an Ohio Republican, introduced a bill that would assign successive prison sentences for each separate period of conjugal relationships, something that became known as the segregation of sentences. If incarcerations were limited to three years for this type of infraction, two counts would allow a sentence of six years. Edwin Willits, one of many Republicans from Michigan who became involved in sponsoring anti-polygamy legislation, introduced three bills less than two weeks later. The first would ban those who either practiced or simply believed in polygamy from serving on juries. The second would allow prosecution for "unlawful cohabitation" rather than bigamy, eliminating the necessity of proving a wedding had taken place. The third bill would expand the first by prohibiting any proponent of polygamy from voting or holding elective office.[11]

The avalanche of bills continued on December 10 when Republican Congressman Julius C. Burrows, also from Michigan, proposed an anti-polygamy amendment to the US Constitution. This was referred to the House Judiciary Committee, while Willets introduced another bill, this one intended to close a loophole in his first proposed legislation by requiring voters to swear an anti-polygamy oath. The Willets bills failed, but these concepts would surface again to be incorporated into subsequent successful legislation,

9. Larson, *Americanization of Utah*, 91–138.

10. Morgan, *From Hayes to McKinley*, 119–20; Richardson, *Compilation of Messages*, 10:4509–33.

11. "A Bill Relating to Bigamy," "Polygamy," *Congressional Record*, Dec. 2, 10, 1879, Dec. 16, 20, 1881.

particularly the Edmunds Act of 1882. In February 1880, Arkansas Democratic senator Augustus H. Garland introduced a bill with features of the earlier House proposals, with the humanitarian allowance for children of plural marriages born before November 1, 1879, to be considered legitimate. This ethical gesture was intended to protect the inheritance rights of children. It was hoped it would encourage polygamists to cooperate with law enforcement.[12] The bill was nevertheless set aside without being acted on.

It was a turbulent time for Utah's delegate, George Q. Cannon. He was mostly treated with respect despite the hostility his colleagues demonstrated toward polygamy. He even received an appointment to the all-important House Committee on Territories from Speaker Samuel J. Randall prior to the Republicans takeover of the House at the end of 1880. Some legislators looked at the question of statehood independent of the polygamy question. Congressman Fernando Wood, a former New York City mayor and a current Democratic Party leader, went on record saying he did not care about religious issues at all. He and other Democrats were more concerned about assurances Utah would vote Democratic. Cannon replied that Utah could be counted on to be as true to the party as Texas, which was known for having few Republicans, if the party supported issues of importance to Utah.[13]

On March 1, 1880, Eli H. Murray replaced Governor George W. Emery. The new governor had been a Union officer with General Sherman on his march through Georgia during the Civil War. A tall handsome Kentuckian, he was known for his amiability and courtesy, and he made friends easily, sometimes among the Latter-day Saints, as well as among the Gentiles. He disliked the LDS Church itself, as an institution, and what it stood for in his mind, and allied himself with those who opposed the ecclesiastical hierarchy. When Salt Lake City officials learned in 1880 that President Rutherford B. Hayes was going to visit Utah in September, these predominantly LDS office holders telegraphed the White House offering to host

12. Roberts, *Comprehensive History*, 5:11, 610.
13. Bitton, *George Q. Cannon*, 225; also Alexander, *Utah*, for the political shifts.

him. After a long delay, the White House responded that Governor Murray would oversee the president's itinerary, which meant in essence that the Church leaders would be shunted aside. The First Presidency chose to ignore that information and do as they had five years earlier when President Grant visited and take their own train forty miles north to the transcontinental railroad connection in Ogden. There they had the presidential cars connected to a locomotive of their own from the Utah Central branch line, and as the passenger cars were being hitched George Q. Cannon greeted Hayes. An invitation extended to join the LDS President John Taylor in his car was accepted. Throngs of Latter-day Saints, young and old, crowded along the tracks southward through Davis County and into Salt Lake City. The following day the presidential party visited the Tabernacle, the unfinished temple, and other points of interest, escorted by non-LDS committeemen as well as by LDS guides. Despite this cordial interaction, Hayes continued to see Mormons as subversives who needed to be brought into line.[14]

Several months later in December 1880, in President Hayes's final State of the Union message, he called anew for legislation involving Utah. This time he recommended dissolving the territorial legislature and replacing it with an appointed commission. As outrageous as it appeared to be, the suggestion became the standard of the Utah Liberal Party through the decade. Then the new Republican president, James A. Garfield, mentioned polygamy explicitly for the first time in an inaugural address. Others had mentioned it in their annual reports to Congress.[15] Four months after his inauguration, he was fatally wounded by an assassin, dying on July 2, 1881, succeeded by vice president Chester A. Arthur. In President Arthur's first annual message, delivered December 6, he too stressed the need for anti-polygamy legislation.[16] Thus, within one year, three different US presidents had spoken against polygamy in the country's

14. Whitney, *History of Utah*, 3:107, 120–25.

15. Richardson, *Compilation of Messages*, 10:4553–79, 4596–602. Cannon, who considered Garfield a friend of the Latter-day Saints, was hurt by his remarks. See Cannon, "Mormon Issue in Congress," 68n3; Cannon journal, Mar. 4, July 4, 1881.

16. Chester A. Arthur, "First Annual Message," in Richardson, 10:4624–4652.

highest-profile addresses. Part of the Republican Party platform, in the party's return to the majority in both the House and Senate in the fall 1880, argued that slavery had been conquered, so it was time for "its twin barbarity, polygamy, [to] die in the territories." Many Republicans began to work feverishly toward that end. Richard D. Poll tracked the bills: "The first session of the forty-seventh Congress, that which met from December 5, 1881, to August 8, 1882, saw no less than twenty-three bills and amendments on polygamy matters introduced, of which only one [Edmunds Act] came to a vote in either chamber."[17]

The same elections of November 1880 also saw a concerted effort from Utah's Liberal Party to displace Cannon as the congressional delegate. Allen "Green" Campbell, who owned some high-yield mines in Beaver County, was the party's contender. He and other Liberals included in their campaign an effort to discredit women's suffrage, a tactical error when it was picked up by anti-polygamy Republicans in Washington. The results of the election proved similar to previous contests: Cannon received 18,568 votes and Campbell 1,357. Despite the disparity, the governor granted Campbell the certificate of election and filed it with the territorial secretary. The pretext for doing so was an unsubstantiated charge that some ballots had been cast illegally. In Washington the outgoing clerk of the US House of Representatives, George M. Adams, placed Cannon's name on the House roll for having received vastly more votes.[18]

During the next six months, the "Utah question" faded until the opening of the new congressional session on December 6 erupted over the clerk's decision to seat Cannon. The Republicans thought the seat should go to Campbell. Neither man was immediately given the spot because the Edmunds Bill was under consideration, and if it passed, its provision that polygamists, and believers in polygamy as a religious doctrine, could not vote, serve on juries, or hold office would disqualify Cannon. Bill 353, as it was designated, was Senator

17. Roberts, *Comprehensive History,* 3:606; Poll, "Twin Relic," 166, 187; McKee, *National Convention and Platforms*, 172.

18. Whitney, *History of Utah*, 3:136, 140, 156–57, 168–69; Bitton, *George Q. Cannon*, 239–42, 248–50.

George F. Edmunds's expansion of the Morrill Act, submitted on December 12. Its key provision made unlawful cohabitation, or residence with a woman other than one's legal first wife, punishable by six months' imprisonment and a fine of up to $300. Children born prior to January 1, 1882, would be eligible for inheritance, but not those born afterward, who would furthermore be considered legal evidence of cohabitation. There would be no more elections for territorial officers, their seats vacated. The US president would appoint a five-member commission to oversee all future elections in the territory. Cannon's defense for being seated in Congress was that to apply the law to him would be an ex-post-facto application of it.[19]

Sympathetic observers soon realized that if the bill passed, Utah might be governed by a small minority of non-Mormons, on the assumption that even monogamist Latter-day Saints would refuse to take the test oath. In fact, there had never been truly democratic elections in Utah, and to some Americans a fair set of voter rules in the territory was long overdue. In discussing whether to seat Cannon, the opposition led by Dudley Haskell, a Kansas Republican, advanced the legalistic argument that the election had been certified to go to Campbell. Among those who argued against him were S. S. "Sunset" Cox, a Democrat from New York who concluded his speech by saying, "It is not a question of how many wives, but how many votes" a man had. A report from the House Committee on Elections a month later suggested that Campbell's meager share of the votes did not justify his installation, even if Cannon were denied the seat. In light of Congress's ability to set its own rules, the committee suggested that it reject both candidates, Cannon because he was living in polygamy, and allow a new election to be held.[20]

The Senate Judiciary Committee advanced the Edmunds Bill to the floor with its endorsement on January 23, 1882. Edmunds had worked feverishly to get the bill advanced on the calendar to February 15, even writing an article for *Harper's Monthly* under the

19. Goodwin, "Political Attitude of the Mormons," 276–86; Cannon, "Utah and Its People," 451–466; *Congressional Record*, Mar. 8, 1882.

20. Firmage and Mangrum, *Zion in the Courts*, 10, 161–67; Whitney, *History of Utah*, 3:171–73, 175–76, 184–85.

headline, "Political Aspects of Mormonism," to pique the nation's interest. The floor debate lasted two days. Edmunds said the purpose of the act was "to redeem this territory of Utah from the absolute domination of 2,000 polygamists." In a veiled threat, he reminded his fellow senators of the mood of the nation, saying that "there is no constitution but the will of the people," and at the moment it was "an angry mob."[21]

Most of Edmunds's opponents were states-rights Democrats from the South. For several years Latter-day Saints could count on up to a dozen prominent southern senators to speak out against infringements on religious practices. For instance, Senator Wilkinson Call (D–Florida), a longtime friend of the Church cause, challenged the creation of the Utah Commission, which he said "virtually declares that the president may give the whole political power of elections in the territory of Utah to five persons, nominated by himself and confirmed by the senate." While he personally abhorred polygamy, he was "not willing to persecute a Mormon at the expense of the Constitution of the United States." Other southern Democrats offered variations on the theme, all saying they despised polygamy but fearing the result of federal overreach.[22] The Edmunds bill still passed the Senate on February 18, 1882, without difficulty.

It was then railroaded through the House the next month on March 13–14 after four hours of tumultuous debate. Representative Aylett H. Buckner (D–Missouri) charged that the point of the bill was to deny Cannon his election simply by declaring his lifestyle illegal. New York manufacturer Abraham Hewitt (D–New York) offered more philosophically that if the point was to "stamp out polygamy," it could be done "without resorting to a remedy which, if generally applied, would violate our whole political system and convert our elections into a mockery of justice." Despite their pleadings, the Edmunds Act passed without alteration on March 14, 1882, in

21. Poll, "Twin Relic," 187–89; Edmunds, "Political Aspects of Mormonism," 285–88.

22. Buice, "Stench in the Nostrils," 100–12. The unique Utah Commission turned out to be one of the most positive governmental innovations of the entire era.

a lopsided vote of 199 to 42. It was signed into law by President Arthur on March 22.[23]

It would take considerable time for most Latter-day Saints to learn the details of the law. What they would discover was that it allowed them to vote if they affirmed, by means of a "test oath," that they would not aid or abet anyone else in the practice of plural marriage. Utah commissioner John A. McClernand later observed that many monogamous Mormons soon proved "willing" to take the oath and, remarkably, even "cast ballots in favor of restricting plural marriage." To the extent that this was true, it indicated a lessening of the grip on political dominance that was long enjoyed by Church leaders who were now absent and on the run.[24] It took a decade to develop, but Latter-day Saints gradually grew into the kind of voters federal legislators wanted them to be, less beholden to the political decisions of the Church.

Overlapping passage of the Edmunds Act was the culmination of the question of whether Campbell or Cannon would be recognized as territorial representative. Cannon was permitted the rare privilege on April 19 of addressing the House prior to its vote on whether he would be seated. He said he was "one of those people who are everywhere spoken against," and his opponent was of the type who was willing to "strike down a people against whom popular sentiment is strong." He was applauded and warmly congratulated for his candor, but the vote was only 79 in his favor and 123 against him. This did not mean Campbell would be given the post, however. It was stipulated that a replacement delegate would be elected later in the year. Cannon remained in Washington at President John Taylor's request, to be a "watchman at the gates of the enemy." He followed Thomas Kane's suggestion that he engage Jeremiah S. Black, who had served in James Buchanan's cabinet as US Attorney General, as a lobbyist, to help stem the tide of actions inimical to the Church and its members.[25]

23. Whitney, *History of Utah* 3:176–83.
24. Shelby M. Cullom to John A. McClernand, July 29, 1887, McClernand Papers.
25. Whitney, *History of Utah* 3:191–94; Bitton, *George Q. Cannon*, 258–59.

Even while the Edmunds Bill was roaring through Congress and Cannon's seat was slipping out of his grasp, Utah's territorial legislature launched another attempt in February 1882 to seek the elusive goal of statehood. This time the movement was led by apostle Daniel H. Wells in the upper house of the legislature, affirming Utah's right to its own representation, to a "republican form of government," for their posterity to "enjoy the blessings and liberties that the founding fathers had fought to secure for citizens of the United States." A constitutional convention was scheduled for April 10. Resolutions were adopted authorizing communities to hold gatherings to select county delegates.[26]

It was another futile gesture, but two days before the Edmunds Act passed, the Utah Territorial Legislature approved a memorial objecting to being ruled by an appointive commission. The legislature asked why Congress would want to "disarrange the political machinery" of the entire territory in order to punish a few offenders of the law. Their case was reasonably well argued, but was too little too late. It did not stand a chance of success in the nation's capital. Nevertheless, in the second week of April the territorial convention gathered in Salt Lake City. This would be the fifth attempt to draft a constitution, and this time the delegates were almost solely of Latter-day Saints, outside of three attorneys who were employed by the Church. As directed by the territorial legislature, the number of delegates was twice the usual thirty-six spots apportioned to legislative districts. The seventy-two men met for two weeks. For the first time yet, they dispensed with the name and concept of Deseret, something that had never been looked on with favor anyway in the halls of Congress. John T. Caine stated the obvious: "We have tried three [four] times to get admission as a state under the name Deseret. And have failed." As an afterthought, he added meaningfully to the epitaph, "I want to try the name of Utah. Deseret may be a sweet name, but it has a sting."[27] At the time,

---

26. Roberts, *Comprehensive History*, 6:71–72; also "Memorial of a Convention to Admit Utah as a State," *Congressional Record*, June 22, 1882.

27. *New York Herald*, Feb. 18, 1882; also "Memorial from Utah," *Congressional Record*, Feb. 18, 1882; *Deseret News*, Mar. 8, 1882. The word *deseret* supposedly referred to a beehive of fellow workers.

the name change passed by unnoticed. It would become a significant element of future proposals, as well as of the state's self-consciousness.

The undistinguished constitution was accepted by the electorate on May 22, 1882, with a vote count of 27,814 to 498. In early June the convention reconvened to approve a memorial that would accompany the constitution to Congress. The monogamous co-founder of the *Salt Lake Herald*, John T. Caine, a Mormon, was appointed to carry the documents east since he was expected to become the territory's congressional delegate. In Washington, D.C., he enlisted the help of Senator Wilkinson Call, a friendly Democrat from Florida, to present the documents in the upper house of Congress on February 23, 1883. The bill received no recognition. At the end of 1883, Caine again offered a similar resolution attached to the same constitution, and that too was ignored.[28]

In June 1882 President Chester A. Arthur acted on one of the provisions of the Edmunds Act to appoint a five-man Utah Commission comprised of Ambrose B. Carlton (D–Ind.), George L. Godfrey (R–Iowa), Algernon Paddock (R–Neb.), James R. Pettigrew (D–Ark.), and Alexander Ramsay (R–Minn.). As specified, the men would serve at the discretion of the president. They met in Chicago on July 17 to discuss their mission and the details of their trip, and the next month found them in Salt Lake City. Their responsibility was to appoint and oversee local people to register voters, supervise the elections, and oversee the counting of the returns. Their first meeting in Utah was unaccountably delayed until August 19, too late to prepare for elections that were traditionally held in August of even-numbered years, so they simply canceled the election. The territorial supreme court justices, John A. Hunter, Phillip H. Emerson, and Stephen P. Twiss, predicted to an interested observer, Senator Elbridge G. Lapman (R–New York), that the cancelation would "cause general disturbance and trouble." In their opinion there needed to be some means of providing "legal successors to all the present incumbents of office," since according to the Edmunds Act the current officials were to be dismissed forthwith.

28. Whitney, *History of Utah*, 3:180–81, 248.

What resulted was Senator George F. Hoar (R–Mass.), chair of the Senate Judiciary Committee, authorizing Governor Murray to appoint whomever he chose for the offices vacated by the Edmunds Act. That approach did not sit well with some of the southern senators, particularly Joseph Brown (D–Georgia), who wanted such appointments to expire within eight months. That stipulation, added to the instructions conveyed to the territorial supreme court by Senator Hoar, was disregarded. In committee debate in the lower house of Congress, Representative George L. Converse (D–Ohio) reasonably suggested that current office holders should stay through the interim if they "had not been guilty of polygamy." That was similarly ignored. Instead, three proclamations from the Utah governor in September and October removed all elected officials from office and replaced them with 174 appointees. Almost all of the new officials were non-LDS, some of them former LDS members. This "office grab" had the support of the local legal profession because attorneys were required to prepare papers for office-holders. There was also the promise of litigation, which attorneys had little interest in interrupting either.[29]

The lobbyist assisting Cannon, Jere Black, pled the Church's cause before the Secretary of Interior Henry M. Teller in late September, arguing that, for instance, it was not right for Utahns to be deprived of a jury of their peers. The new Murray regime was "hardly better than a military commission, 'organized to convict.'" It was also ex post facto, he reasoned, punishing a man for beliefs acquired in the past. It was "an outrage."[30] Mainly outside of Salt Lake City, LDS elected officers resolved to "ignore the governor's appointments, and dispute to the last legal extremity what they considered to be his autocratic use and abuse of 'one man power.'" In rural areas this protest would continue because of popular support and insufficient federal muscle to remove existing office holders in every town. Even in Salt Lake County, when four men sought to file

29. Whitney, 3:208–16; Roberts, *Comprehensive History*, 6:58–59, 62–67; *Deseret News*, Sept. 20, Oct. 4, 25, Nov. 8, 1882.

30. "Black's Bugle Blast," *Ogden Standard*, Oct. 19, 1882.

their bonds and assume their posts as probate judge (U. J. Wenner), sheriff (Arthur Pratt), county clerk (William Nelson), and selectman (Samuel Kahn), they were told to report to LDS judge Elias Smith, who took the matter under advisement and would not allow the new appointees to be installed. Wenner tried to file his bond with the territorial treasurer, James W. Cummings, but was told the territory already held a bond for that particular position and declined to recognize the appointment. Other appointees met with similar opposition and had to contest their appointments in the courts.

One of the most visible cases involved Nephi W. Clayton, a Latter-day Saint whom Murray himself had appointed territorial auditor for a two-year term drawing to a close at the end of November 1880. With the contested portion of his term only one month, the territorial Chief Justice John A. Hunter nevertheless, acting in his capacity as a district judge, denied Clayton his seat for the remaining few days. In another highly visible case, Murray dismissed apostle Franklin D. Richards as probate judge in Weber County and appointed James N. Kimball in his stead. Richards appealed to the territorial supreme court but was unsuccessful there, so he appealed to the US Supreme Court. By means of that obstruction, he was able to hold office a year beyond his dismissal until August 1883.[31]

Another case demonstrated the scarcity of potential non-LDS office holders in some areas. Lorenzo Snow Lyman lived in Parowan during part of his childhood. He left the LDS Church and moved to California, then returned to Parowan for a time in 1882. With no personal contact from Murray, he received indirect notice that the governor had appointed him an Iron County probate judge. In a note addressed to Murray, later published in the *Deseret News*, he stated that he assumed his appointment rested on the fact that he was a rare non-Mormon in the vicinity, and if so, he did not feel right about accepting the position: "I could not have the hearty support of the majority of the community. ... All officers should be elected by the people."[32] The controversy over Murray's appoint-

31. West, *Life of Franklin D. Richards*, 194–95.
32. *Deseret News*, Oct. 4, 1882.

ments ended when the Utah Commission assumed careful oversight of all elections in August 1883.

Another challenge faced by the commission was that the previous autumn, Liberal Party leaders had opposed elections of any kind. The commissioners ignored their boycott and set a November 1882 election date. In the meantime they worked to establish a reasonably good list of county registrars who would purge polygamists from voter registration lists and ask voters to confirm their residency, citizenship, payment of taxes, and affirm the following: "I do further solemnly swear that I am not a bigamist or a polygamist; . . . that I do not live or cohabit with more than one woman in the marriage relation." Despite the present-tense construction of the oath, commissioners excluded men who had formerly lived with more than one wife on the assumption that "once a polygamist, always a polygamist," even if a man had left the LDS Church and become monogamous. Women still usually enjoyed the right to vote, but some were excluded on the basis of their gender and had to go to court to have their right upheld. The *Deseret News* throughout the month of August denounced the oath for asking only about wives and not including mistresses or prostitutes with whom a man may have cohabited. In a published announcement, the First Presidency commented similarly on how the oath seemed to devalue marriage and allow licentiousness. More importantly, the First Presidency encouraged every member who qualified to vote to do so in order to maintain a "free and constitutional form of government in these mountains."

Before the arrival of the commission, the LDS-run People's Party had expressed desire for a special election to select the delegate who would represent the territory through Cannon's unexpired term. Governor Murray ignored the request. The party put forth LDS monogamist John T. Caine as the one to run in November. Caine was a well-known actor, a municipal officer, and a newspaper man. The Utah Commission verified that he was qualified to run, and since he had been designated the Church's candidate, it was assumed he would win. However, for the first time in the history of the territory, things went differently. Instead of taking marching orders directly from Church leaders, people attending the People's Party convention questioned the nomination and considered other applicants, even though Caine ultimately cinched the nomination. It was nevertheless a sign of how territorial politics were evolving.[33]

Many of the early non-LDS settlers in the territory were drawn by potential mining opportunities. The Latter-day Saints had emphasized farming and ranching, and the territorial laws had not encouraged mineral extraction. The Liberal Party invited miners to immigrate and backed the federal government's goal of appointing key territorial officials and minimizing LDS voter roles. As a result, there emerged a cadre of elites who, through mine development and political office, enriched themselves and their friends. Gradually the average non-LDS immigrant came to suspect the motives of these movers and shakers and began to speak in favor of fairer elections. As an example, in late 1879 a mining camp newspaper, the *Silver Reef Miner*, expressed the sentiment that the *Salt Lake Tribune* did not speak for the majority of less well-off non-Mormons laboring in the extreme southern part of the territory, nor did the few activists in the mines who were "rabid vagabonds ... all the time stirring up strife here." They no more represented the larger non-LDS population "than Judas represented the primitive [Christian] church and apostles."[34] The tide was slowly turning nationally as well, leaving behind the harsh statements of Presidents Hayes, Garfield, and Arthur as the high point of negative sentiment against LDS people. Americans did not like polygamy, but they had also grown tired of political exploitation.

After Caine won his party's nomination, he easily emerged as victor in the November 1882 vote. Before the ballot count, attorneys for the Liberal Party submitted formal petitions arguing that Caine was a polygamist in belief and therefore not suitable. The Utah Commission considered this and rejected it. Caine's victory of

33. Whitney, *History of Utah*, 3:226–32; Roberts, *Comprehensive History*, 6:51–52, 60–65.

34. Journal History, Jan. 9, 1880.

23,039 votes to Philip T. Van Zile's 4,884 was certified. It authorized Caine to immediately begin serving through the remainder of Cannon's unexpired term as well. The commission significantly reported to the Secretary of the Interior that the election was conducted free of polygamists. That made it a turning point for non-Mormons in the territory, whose competitive gap was somewhat narrowed. It happened at the same time the exclusivity of the *Tribune* ring was challenged, but also foreshadowed the beginning of an era of exclusive office holding by monogamous Latter-day Saints, previously unexpected by virtually all observers on both sides of the religious divide. After a short delay, Caine was admitted to the US Congress in January 1883.[35]

Meanwhile, Senator Edmunds had grown dissatisfied with the limitations inherent in the bill bearing his name. He introduced another to strengthen the first. Assisted by Senator John A. Logan (R–Illinois), he led the floor debate against Democratic Florida senators Wilkinson Call and Charles Jones. Senator Hoar of Massachusetts spoke against Edmunds's attempt to eliminate women from the polls in Utah. With too many senators expressing reservations about the new provisions, and time running short, the bill died without being voted on. One person keeping a close eye on the proceedings was George Q. Cannon, still in Washington. When Caine arrived, the former delegate initiated him into the intricacies of the position. As the apostle confided to his nephew, George C. Lambert, "it is unpleasant being here in many respects. More so, on some accounts, than when I was a member [of Congress]." At the same time, he found that many of the newly elected congressmen were friendlier than their predecessors.[36]

The Liberal Party in Utah was pleased that polygamists had

35. Commissioner A. B. Carlton said that up to 14,000 polygamists had been disfranchised (Whitney, *History of Utah*, 3:243–47). Adding wives and children to 14,000 fathers, or even children to mothers, quickly tops 100,000 in plural families, but the 1880 US census enumerated only 120,283 Mormons, 14,156 Gentiles, and 6,988 apostates, so the figure is too high ("Report of the Utah Commission, 1882," in *Annual Report of Department of the Interior*, 2:1003–09).

36. Poll, "Twin Relic," 230–33; Journal History, Feb. 5, 1883; also *Congressional Record*, Aug. 2, 1882.

been disfranchised. The Liberals had but few adult females in their group, so they wanted to see women disqualified as well. That would not happen, the chair of the Utah Commission, Alexander Ramsay, asserted. "We don't care how many Mormons vote," he said, "we cannot interfere with their religion, but they must not be polygamists if they want to vote." The commissioners fairly curbed the worst abuses by some former election officials who had allegedly looked the other way while fraud was committed. The governor was disgruntled that President Arthur had not appointed the men he had recommended, resulting in the commissioners acting independently, no longer with prejudice. Historian Orson Whitney thus correctly concluded that "Governor Murray was no longer supreme in the territory." He was more likely on the side of election abuses than helping the commission eliminate them, and therefore not consulted.

Senator George F. Edmunds pressed for additional polygamy legislation, buoyed by the success of his 1882 law. He thought wives should be compelled to testify against their husbands, without limitations. That failed in the face of Jeremiah Black's lobbying among the Democrats, assisted by the prayers of the Saints, Cannon wrote.[37] Unfortunately the lobbyist, Black, died unexpectedly in the autumn of 1883 at age seventy-three.

On April 7, 1882, a snowstorm greeted the first session of the LDS general conference convened in Salt Lake City. President John Taylor drew a parallel between the weather and the approaching judicial storm, counseling his people, with accompanying gestures, to "put up our coat collars and wait till the storm subsides." It was impossible to reason with the opposing side for the moment, but when the "sunshine" returned perhaps "we can talk to them." Two days later in another conference sermon, Taylor specifically warned that "there will be a storm in the United States after a while, and I want our brethren to prepare for it," saying that "the wise will understand." Rather than place themselves in a "state of antagonism" to the country, their duty was to abide by its "unjust, inhuman,

37. Whitney, *History of Utah*, 3:246.

oppressive and unconstitutional law, so much as we can without violating principle." There should be no direct conflict, he urged. At the same time, they should not "sacrifice every principle of human right at the behest of corrupt, unreasoning and unprincipled men."

A friendly correspondent for the *New York World*, Phil Robinson, described the "sobriety" of the congregation. The Church president "commanded respect," and yet it "astonishe[d]" the reporter to observe the way "the great Tabernacle was filled with waves of sound as the amens" to the president's counsel resounded. His position, publicly and privately, was to respect the country's laws in general while offering unyielding defiance to the supposedly unconstitutional laws touching on marriage. In April 1883 he reiterated that "we will contend inch by inch legally and constitutionally for our rights as American citizens."[38]

The storm he predicted would come began in the courts and was gaining momentum. The first cases involved women who were suspected of being plural wives, litigated by US Attorney Philip Van Zile, who had helped Edmunds craft his 1882–83 legislation. First up was Annie Gallifant Connelly, a young woman who was not yet twenty and was pregnant. A grand jury asked her in November 1882 to confirm that her husband was John Connelly, a baker. She refused to do so. Chief Justice John Hunter informed her that if she did not answer, she would be held in contempt of court. When she again refused, he sentenced her to prison. She was assigned a non-LDS physician to provide medical care. He turned out to be someone who had been expelled from the medical association for malpractice. Four days before the child was born, Annie was released from custody, and when her husband was eventually indicted in October 1885 Annie testified that they had been married more than three years, confident that the statute of limitations had expired. It had, which eliminated the possibility that there could be a conviction. It was a loophole that consistently frustrated opponents of polygamy and motivated Edmunds and his associates to try to amend the law.

In another case, this one occurring in the spring of 1883, Belle

38. Larson, *Americanization of Utah*, 103.

Harris of Sevier County was summoned before a neighboring Beaver County grand jury where she was asked if she was married. She had an infant in her arms but claimed "personal privilege" in refusing to answer. She was remanded to the custody of US Marshal Edward A. Ireland, a personal friend of US President Arthur. She reported that she was "kindly treated" at the prison just east of Salt Lake City, situated comfortably in an apartment adjoining the warden's house. After it became clear that the grand jury had overstepped the evidence in her case, Justice Stephen Twiss of the territorial supreme court withdrew the conviction, resulting in Harris's release. When she arrived back home, local officials treated her to a reception at which she was honored for how "nobly" she had "suffered for a principle."[39] This kind of public support for those who were imprisoned became common in the LDS community.

In early 1884 before many men had been fully prosecuted, there was another attempt to compel a wife to testify against her husband. A school teacher in Summit County, Nellie White declined to disclose her marital status. Judge Hunter sentenced her to the penitentiary, and she occupied the same apartment Belle Harris had the previous year. Some of the non-Mormons "took umbrage" at this kind of "leniency." A "more rigorous" investigative method might prove more fruitful, they suggested, according to Whitney. The LDS chronicler noted that Ireland rejected any "unchivalrous" or "cruel" interrogations of women.[40] It went against the grain of social assumptions to treat women, especially white middle-class women, with disrespect.

In contrast to this humane policy toward women, Ireland was less merciful when dealing with the men. His earnestness was nevertheless tempered by the restraint of Judge Emerson, who said he was "averse to making a specialty of any class of cases" and did not want the territory turning to "those extreme policies" recommended by more hostile Liberal Party members. He preferred to "treat polygamy

39. Madsen, "At Their Peril," 441–43; Emmeline B. Wells, "A Few Facts," *Woman's Exponent,* July 15, 1885, 28.

40. Firmage and Mangrum, *Zion in the Courts*, 194–97, 207–09.

as any other crime, but not resort to any extraordinary measure for its extirpation." Emerson was a Republican who resigned when Grover Cleveland, a Democrat, was inaugurated early in 1885. President Cleveland appointed Orlando W. Powers in his place. Powers occupied the position of associate justice for fifteen months without being confirmed by the Senate. Political opponents in his home state of Michigan created enough opposition, joined by Utah Chief Justice John Hunter, who was "not altogether in harmony with the radicals" and "endeavored for that reason to procure [Powers's] removal from office," that Powers was forced to resign.[41] Neither he nor Hunter remained in office very long.

The person who received the higher post had been a law partner of anti-polygamy crusader Shelby Cullom in Illinois. Charles S. Zane was appointed chief justice in Utah in July 1884. During his first four-year term, he acted on the belief that he had been given a mandate to suppress polygamy. His approach was far from that of James McKean, however, in that he respected established legal procedures. As a staunch Republican, he would be reappointed several times to serve until statehood was attained in 1896. Along the way he would become more moderate in his methods, while the pursuit of polygamists by US marshals would intensify. In 1890 he proved to be the first territorial official to accept Church President Wilford Woodruff's assurance that polygamy would be abandoned.[42]

As historian Howard R. Lamar observed, Zane may have been the best representative of a new type of federal appointee, whose formative years were shaped by the trauma of the Civil War. Zane was cut from the same pattern as Judge Jacob S. Boreman of West Virginia, a Union Army veteran who had preceded Twiss as an associate justice of Utah's supreme court. As district judge in the central Utah town of Beaver, he presided over the conviction and execution of John D. Lee in 1877 for participating in the Mountain Meadows Massacre. Boreman had stepped down from the supreme court to

41. Whitney, *History of Utah*, 3:281–83.
42. Alexander, "Charles S. Zane."

practice law privately in 1880 but was reappointed in 1885.[43] Where the Latter-day Saints were concerned, he was a vigorous crusader against polygamy. In fact, like many other judges after 1880, he was neither venal nor vindictive, though determined to enforce the law.

Zane and Boreman remained in office for a good portion of Democratic President Grover Cleveland's first term. Powers remained in Utah after he was removed from office and became a leader in the extreme anti-Mormon clique, and he was joined in temperament by New York transplant Edward Ireland, a Salt Lake City lamp merchant who became the US marshal in 1882. William H. Dickson, a naturalized American from New Brunswick, had also moved to Utah and opened a law practice. In February 1884 President Arthur appointed him US Attorney. He had been the Nevada attorney general and a law partner with former Nevada state senator Charles S. Varian. After his appointment in Utah, Dickson summoned Varian to be his assistant. Both displayed real "zeal and energy," but tempered it with the kind of professionalism Boreman and Zane exhibited, to the extent that even LDS people came to respect them. They were both Republicans and considered themselves united in a legal battle against Mormon polygamy. They did not consider themselves to be battling Mormonism itself, a distinction that was lost on most Church members, who could not see the patriotic side of such men or understand that they considered their involvement a duty rather than a personal grudge. They were very much unlike Salt Lake City attorney Robert Baskin or *Salt Lake Tribune* editor Charles C. Goodwin.

Judge Zane had his mettle tested in July 1884. The Poland Law required that an annual pool of potential jurors be created with equal numbers of LDS and non-LDS people. This functioned adequately for ten years until Zane and his colleagues increased the number of prosecutions, to the point that by August the pool of jurors was exhausted. The law did not allow for another jury pool until the next year. Zane decided he would need to violate that portion of the statute in order to keep the courts open. One of the first cases brought before

43. Lamar, *Far Southwest,* 395–96; Boreman, "Crusade against Theocracy," 11–12.

Zane was that of twenty-seven-year-old future LDS apostle Rudger Clawson, who had been seen in public with Lydia Spencer, a plural wife. Rudger was something of a local hero already because of how he had faced a hostile crowd in July 1879 as a missionary in Georgia. His companion, Joseph Standing, was murdered in that confrontation. On April 24, 1884, Clawson was arrested in Utah and plead not guilty. It turned out that the prosecution did not have enough substantive evidence for conviction. Clawson's wife Lydia had gone into hiding so she would not have to testify. The non-LDS jury was divided. Eight jurors voted for conviction, and four wanted an acquittal. The *Salt Lake Tribune* assailed the four holdouts for not convicting an obvious polygamist, but their fellow jurors said they admired the integrity of those who refused to look beyond the evidence. In early autumn Lydia was located and brought to appear at a new trial in October. She refused to testify. Judge Zane gave her a warning. "You take a fearful responsibility in undertaking to defy the government," he said. She persisted in her defiance, so Zane remanded her to the custody of marshal Ireland, who took her to the penitentiary. The next day, October 25, her husband encouraged her to testify, and she did.

Clawson was thereby convicted, based on his wife's testimony. At the sentencing on November 3, Zane asked him if he had any legal cause why judgement should not be pronounced. The future apostle answered, "I very much regret that the laws of my country should come in contact [conflict] with the laws of God, but whenever they do I shall invariably choose the latter. If I did not so express myself I should feel unworthy of the cause I represent." He invoked the First Amendment's guarantee of freedom of religion. Zane responded, "The Constitution of the United States, as construed by the Supreme Court, and by the authors of that instrument, does not protect any person in the practice of polygamy." The practice of having more than one wife had emerged from barbarism, he said, and LDS people had been misled into thinking it was an acceptable Christian practice. He would have pronounced a smaller fine, Zane offered, "were it not for the fact that you openly declare that you believe it is right to violate the law." He sentenced Clawson to three and a half years in prison and $500 for polygamy, and for cohabitation another six months and $300.

Clawson was taken directly to the penitentiary. When he appealed the verdict, the territorial supreme court upheld the decision and denied his appeal to the US Supreme Court. He became well-publicized because of the length of his sentence. In January 1886 Lorenzo Snow was also sentenced and the two became friends in prison. When Snow became Church president in September 1898, Clawson was called to the apostleship the next month.[44]

At the end of 1883, President Arthur argued that polygamy was so entrenched, it required additional legislation to extricate it. Senator Edmunds revived what he had proposed in 1882. The session ended before his bill was considered. He tried again in 1884. On May 27 the bill came to the floor of the Senate. Joseph E. Brown of Georgia occupied an entire day expounding on his own unique views of divorce in an attempt to stall the legislative progress—a kind of filibuster. When the floor opened again, there followed three days of discussion on whether women should be compelled to testify against their husbands and prohibited from voting, and about the disincorporation of the Church. Senator Hoar wanted women to vote but otherwise supported the bill and lent his name to it while Edmunds was preoccupied with other matters. The bill still failed, 33 to 17. On the House side, discussion was postponed because it was an election year and members were concerned about campaigning. Southern allies had their own reasons to defend the Latter-day Saints and block progress of the Edmunds bill where they could.[45]

In the Utah delegate campaign for 1884, a new first emerged in the parades that were staged with the political trappings of torches, bands, marching units, and campaign rhetoric common elsewhere but new to the territory. Allen Campbell was again offered the nomination of the Liberal Party. When he declined to accept it, the convention's choice fell on US Attorney Phillip Van Zile. The incumbent Caine

44. Details from Whitney, *History of Utah*; Hoopes and Hoopes, *Mormon Apostle*.

45. Richardson, *Compilation of Messages*, 11:4757–75; Buice, "Stench in the Nostrils," 109–12; *Congressional Record*, US Senate, June 5–6, 1882; June 16–18, 1884.

remained the choice of the Peoples' Party. "Never had Utah witnessed such enthusiasm over an event of this character," Whitney wrote.[46] The intent was to imitate national fanfare and downplay ecclesiastical allegiances. In doing so, voters once more showed they were coming of age politically. These things would emerge as important elements in a later, more realistic, bid for statehood.

In June 1884 some Republicans at the national convention attempted to add a plank to the platform endorsing the use of military force to suppress polygamy. That was the year Grover Cleveland became the first Democratic US president since James Buchanan. Citizens in Utah staged a "grand popular" celebration in several cities at Cleveland's win. Delegate John T. Caine sent a telegram to the president-elect on November 8 informing him that "ten thousand citizens of Salt Lake City tonight are enthusiastically celebrating your election. Their joy is as sincere and honest as the jollification is demonstrative." He affirmed that his people looked confidently toward an administration that would be as honest and fair-minded as his tenure as New York's governor had been.[47]

Although non-LDS Democrats in Utah welcomed the new administration, they refrained from taking part in the celebrations. They feared that Cleveland might be more lenient toward polygamists and religious laws would be imposed on them. Sharing this feeling was George Miller, a longtime Democratic national committeeman from Nebraska who used the editorial columns of the *Omaha Herald* to urge fair treatment for Latter-day Saints, even though he could not condone plural marriage. In January 1885, just over a month before Cleveland was inaugurated, Miller sent Cleveland's private secretary and chief advisor, Colonel Daniel S. Lamont, a memorandum on Utah matters for the president-elect's consideration. Explaining that he was speaking for the Mormons as their "recognized friend," he surveyed the background of polygamy and resultant public hostility and warned that the Edmunds Act might disrupt Cleveland's presidency right from the start with a violent conflict.

46. Whitney, *History of Utah*, 3:239–243, 246; Maxwell, *George R. Maxwell*, 44n34.
47. John T. Caine to Grover Cleveland, Nov. 8, 1884, Caine Letters.

Miller urged the president to take a firm position against plural marriage early on to stave off the insurgency. He should also recommend passage of the amendments to the Edmunds Act that would impose "prompt and severe penalties" for Church officials if they performed polygamous marriages in the future, anywhere in the United States. Mormon leaders should not expect leniency from a Democratic administration. Strictness would be the "key that would unlock and solve the Mormon problem by causing the early surrender of the leaders of the church." This could be "the crowning glory" of Cleveland's public service.[48] As sympathetic as Miller was toward the LDS people, he had misgauged their depth of commitment to plural marriage on the part of the hierarchy and the amount of resistance to federal intervention they would still offer.

Cleveland followed Miller's advice in his March 1885 inaugural address. "The conscience of the people," he proclaimed, asks that "polygamy in the territories, destructive of the family and religion and offensive to the moral sense of the civilized world, shall be repressed." This encouraged the anti-Mormons in Utah, including the governor, who on behalf of the "law-abiding citizens" of Utah telegraphed their thanks to Cleveland for his "determination to suppress polygamy." To close observers it soon appeared that Cleveland was in earnest, because he kept unpopular Republican appointees like Murray in office until the end of their regular terms. Cannon wrote to Cleveland shortly after the inaugural address warning him that the Republican appointees would embarrass the new administration through questionable tactics they employed in their raid on Latter-day Saints. They would interpret the speech as approval of their abuses and would know it would be difficult for Cleveland to replace them after having just endorsed them.[49]

While Miller's letter was en route to Washington in January

48. George L. Miller to Daniel S. Lamont, Jan. 26, Feb. 7, 1885; Miller to Grover Cleveland, Feb. 7, Oct. 27, 1885; Miller to W. C. Endicott, Oct. 30, 1885, Cleveland Papers.

49. Richardson, *Compilation of Messages,* 11:4909–50; Nevins, *Grover Cleveland,* 234–65; George Q. Cannon to Grover Cleveland, Mar. 25, 1885, Cleveland Papers. Cleveland fair-mindedly allowed all appointees to compete their appointed terms, in keeping with the spirit of the new Civil Service Act.

1885, Angus M. Cannon, a brother of George Q. and president of the Salt Lake Stake, was apprehended on the street by deputy William Greenman. Before friends could post bail, the deputy had gone to one of Cannon's homes, forced his way in when the maid opened the door, and delivered a subpoena to Amanda M. Cannon in an upstairs bedroom where she was confined with an illness. His boldness surprised her, and it shocked many others.

In Angus Cannon's trial later in the year, Assistant US Attorney Varian argued that "if a man claimed two or more women as his wives and held [them] out to the world as such, he was guilty," even if it could not be proved that he shared a bedroom with any of them. The court agreed. Defense attorney Arthur Brown sided with Judge Zane's previous ruling that unlawful cohabitation entailed "treating more than one woman as a man's wives according to the forms of marriage," not just living in the same house with them. But in his instruction to the jury, Zane agreed with Varian that "it is sufficient to show that [if] a man lives with more than one woman, cohabits with her and holds them out to the world as his wives," he was guilty of unlawful cohabitation. Cannon was sentenced to six months imprisonment and a fine of $300.[50]

Angus's brother, George Q., was one of the most trusted members of the inner circle of Church leaders under Brigham Young and John Taylor. He called Taylor, who was also his uncle, "the best friend I had on earth, for he had been as a father to me in early life." Taylor called him to be his first counselor in 1880. The counselor was fiercely loyal to the president. He always "submitted to his judgement, as my head," he explained.[51] To a similar degree, Cannon displayed unwavering commitment to plural marriage. He saw that it was important enough to Taylor for the president to go into hiding rather than submit to the law. In Taylor's last public sermon at the Tabernacle, delivered ten days after Angus Cannon was convicted, he advised the members to "take care of [your] liberties." He told the Church to "put [its] trust in the living God, to obey every constitutional law,

50. Whitney, *History of Utah*, 3:334–39, 363–72.
51. George Q. Cannon journal, July 25, 1887.

and to adhere to all correct principles." He expressed sorrow that the country was "no longer a land of equal rights." That being so, "we must take care of ourselves as best we may, and avoid being caught in any of their snares." With rhetorical fervor, he asked: "Shall I be recreant to all these noble principles that bind me to my God, to my family, to my wives and to my children ... [N]o never! No Never! NO NEVER! I cannot as an honorable man disobey my God" by submitting to unjust ex-post-facto laws. Then he then went into hiding on the polygamy underground for the next two and a half years until his death.[52]

George Q. Cannon's son, the future apostle Abraham H. Cannon, recorded that the Church leadership was determined "not [to] allow President Taylor to fall into enemy hands," knowing that if he were apprehended he would be imprisoned for the rest of his life. The night after the president's statement of defiance, he, George Q. Cannon, Taylor's secretary L. John Nuttall, and bodyguard Charles Wilcken slipped quietly away. Their plan was to conduct as much Church business as possible from undisclosed locations. Joseph F. Smith, Taylor's other counselor, was able to avoid arrest by returning to the Sandwich Islands where he had served a mission as a teenager. Some Church opponents made much of this supposed abdication of responsibility, but B. H. Roberts defended the presidency by giving biblical examples of leaders who had likewise avoided persecution by disappearing from the public view: Moses, Samuel, David, Obadiah, Elijah, Joseph of Egypt, and Saul of Tarsus. Rewards were offered, which by 1886 reached $300 for Taylor and $500 for Cannon. Historians have pointed to the larger sum for Cannon as an indication of his priority to federal officials.[53]

Going "on the underground" meant taking refuge in hideouts built into homes and buildings and finding retreats in the mountains or in southern Utah's canyon country, taking shelter with Church members for brief periods, and traveling outside Utah as far as Canada to the north and Mexico to the south. There was a

52. *Deseret Weekly News,* Feb. 25, 1885; Roberts, *Comprehensive History*, 6:122–27; Larson, *Americanization of Utah*, 117–18.

53. Abraham H. Cannon journal, Feb. 1, 1885; Bitton, *George Q. Cannon*, 270, 283; also John T. Caine to George Q. Cannon, Jan. 6, 1886, Caine Letters.

communication system to keep them in touch with each other. From the top down, most Church leaders, including even local heads of congregations, were forced to go on the run. They were able to do so with the help of volunteer guards, signal systems, and nighttime transportation arrangements that exasperated the "deps," as deputy marshals were called. The tension, deprivations, and narrow escapes created an abundant LDS lore.[54] The lifestyle was normative for LDS leaders from 1885 to 1890, and to a limited extent during a year or two before and afterward.

An epistle from the First Presidency was read at the April 1885 general conference and then published, claiming that the men "who practice plural marriage are estimated as exceeding but little, if any, over two percent of the entire membership of the Church." The members of the presidency therefore "consider it an act of great injustice to the ninety-eight percent, to be abused and outraged ... because of the 'raid' upon these alleged breakers of the law." The message was meant for foreign consumption. Church members knew, and demographers have since ascertained, that around a quarter of the male members of the Church in Utah were directly involved in polygamy: 30 percent of the heads of households in St. George and 20 percent in Davis County, a lower percentage in urban settings, but a considerable average percentage of the population, especially when the women and children are added to the count.[55]

Similar statements were issued from subsequent general conferences that were held in various locations in northern Utah. Historian B. H. Roberts characterized the epistles as "remarkable for their conservative tone and wisdom; for the total absence of anger or vindictiveness, as also for the scope and variety of the subjects they treated upon." He found them to "compare favorably with the wisest and best state papers ever issued by kings, or presidents, ministers of state or cabinet councils. The flock of Christ

54. Larson, *Americanization of Utah*, 119–23.

55. Roberts, *Comprehensive History*, 6:149, 172; Bennion, "Incidence of Mormon Polygamy"; Daynes, *More Wives than One*, 61, 101, 107, 173–79.

therefore, was supposedly not left without the counsel of heaven or the care of the shepherds."[56]

The first conference after the leaders had gone into hiding in April 1885 was conducted by William Jennings, a former Salt Lake City mayor who had never been in a high Church leadership position. At that conference a committee was assigned to draft a missive to President Cleveland about "the tyrannical conduct of federal officials." It was probably targeted more to the Latter-day Saints, to lift their spirits, than to the US president. For whatever purpose it served, it was presented to President Cleveland in May by John Q. Cannon, George Q.'s oldest son and member of the Presiding Bishopric; apostle John W. Taylor, who was John Taylor's son; and John T. Caine, the recently re-elected territorial delegate. Cleveland listened courteously and stated that he was not behind the new Edmunds–Tucker bill that was making its way through Congress. The people represented by the petition were "entitled to fair consideration and to have the law impartially administered," he affirmed. He promised to appoint officials who knew their duty and would not exceed it. To a considerable extent, he kept that promise when he reached the midpoint of his first term and the tenures of several Republican appointees, including Zane, expired.[57] Even so, the fact that the Church presidency and apostles had gone into hiding probably confirmed to Cleveland that they were not only guilty but fanatically so.

In the short period from the Reynolds Supreme Court case of 1879 to the beginning of the Grover Cleveland presidential administration in 1885, those advocating plural marriage lost considerable hope and perhaps some status even in Utah There had been abundant obedience, commitment, and sacrifice demonstrated. But with hindsight, it becomes clear that the end of the wider practice of the controversial institution loomed far nearer than almost anyone yet realized.

---

56. Roberts, *Life of John Taylor*, 384–85. Actually, as will become clear later herein, the lack of continued advocacy of plural marriage among those not yet committed to it looms as a major cause for the decline of subsequent support for the institution.

57. Whitney, *History of Utah*, 3:378–86; also John W. Young to James Jack, Mar. 4, 1887, Jack Papers.

5

GROVER CLEVELAND AND THE LATTER-DAY SAINTS

1886-87

The election of a Democrat, Grover Cleveland, was celebrated by Utah Latter-day Saints, and then disappointment set in. Cracks started to show in the resolve to defy the Edmunds Act, at least among some of the rank-and-file in the Church. As pressure continued to be applied on the polygamists in the territory, approximately one fifth of them concluded that it would be better to conform to the law rather than to obey ecclesiastical mandates to maintain their resistance. This likely caused more tension within the Church than has previously been recognized, from what little is available in the sources.

The US Supreme Court rendered its decision in *Murphy v. Ramsey* on March 23, 1885, to largely uphold the Edmunds Act of 1882. The plaintiffs had challenged the legality of the test oath the Utah Commission had formulated and the disenfranchisement of Latter-day Saints who would not take the prescribed oath. The newly appointed election deputies and registrars prevented men from registering who had been polygamists, even those who were then living with only one wife. This had been upheld by the lower federal courts. However, the US Supreme Court saw things differently. The court nullified the doctrine of "once a polygamist always a polygamist" and soon gave full legal status to anyone who had given up their previous marital relations to become monogamous.[1] The ruling paved the way for an internal struggle among Latter-day Saints. Some reappraised conditions and concluded that they should do what was necessary to attain their good standing with the courts. This sometimes stupefied the true-blue loyalists among the faithful, who felt that to renounce polygamy was an almost unforgivable offense.[2]

Shortly after the US president's inauguration, George Q. Cannon wrote to President Grover Cleveland to vividly depict the crisis that existed in Utah Territory and neighboring areas. Cannon explained that the Latter-day Saints, numbering what he counted as nearly 200,000 in the Great Basin region, had founded flourishing communities and built productive economic enterprises after their losses to mob violence in Missouri and Illinois. He justified their commitment to a marital system he claimed was only practiced by 2 percent of the Church population.

The delegate went on to complain about judicial officials such as James McKean and his cohorts, who for more than a dozen years had been responsible for harassing Latter-day Saints. Cannon wrote that they were "a class of men whose sole object was political and personal aggrandizement." Republicans were only interested in rule by committee, he ventured, rather than in principles of fairness or good government, especially majority rule. He suggested that Cleveland should replace them with men of his choosing: "You sir have the right to call a halt and to have an investigation made by men who you know and in whom you have entire confidence."[3] The president apparently ignored the delegate's suggestions.

After going into effect in 1883, there appeared to be no hurry to implement the Edmunds Act. The first conviction was in November 1884, and there followed a period in which the prosecutors seemed to be refining their tactics. Late in 1885, after clarification in *Murphy v. Ramsey*, there had been twenty-three convictions and seventeen exonerations for men who promised to refrain from

1. Whitney, *History of Utah*, 3:351, 352–53, 578; also *Murphy v. Ramsey*, 114 U.S. 15 (1885).
2. Allen, "Good Guys," 148–74.
3. George Q. Cannon to Grover Cleveland, Mar. 25, 1885, Cleveland Papers.

cohabiting in the future, comprising over 43 percent of the forty men who were brought to court. There were forty-some-odd other cases still awaiting trial, as well. The deduction of the Utah Commission was that there had been relatively few plural marriages performed in 1885.[4] The conclusion should have been that a major erosion of commitment to plural marriage was underway.

On April 13 of that year, a respected LDS businessman, Orson P. Arnold, was tried for unlawful cohabitation. The true-believer's script was one of defiantly declaring innocence, accepting a sentence, and enjoying a hero's send-off to prison. But Arnold helped turn the tide away from this expectation by pleading guilty and promising to obey the law, for which he was given probation, although he was still fined three hundred dollars. His admission shocked many Latter-day Saints. It was held up by the leadership as an example of weak-willed abandonment of sacred priorities. But by the end of 1885, at least 20 percent of eighty-three Mormons who were indicted for cohabitation chose to follow the same course in a pattern that would grow in occurrence.

In the spring of that year, federal marshals decided to pursue prominent polygamists such as John Sharp, the corporate board member with the Union Pacific Railroad and bishop of the Salt Lake Twelfth Ward, and Septimus W. Sears, assistant superintendent of ZCMI, the Church-owned regional mercantile company. They were set to be tried in September. The delay allowed them to communicate through George Miller of the *Omaha Herald* to President Grover Cleveland that they were prepared to put aside polygamy if they could expect leniency in exchange. Likely at their invitation, Miller visited Utah in July. He was hoping he would be able to meet Brigham Young's successor, John Taylor, and former Utah delegate and counselor in the First Presidency, George Q. Cannon, but the two decided it was too dangerous to come out of hiding to meet him. He probably would have been disappointed anyway because neither man was prepared to budge on the issue of plural marriage.

4. Roberts, *Comprehensive History*, 6:115; also "Report of the Utah Commission, 1885," in *Annual Report of the Department of the Interior*, 2:885–91.

Furthermore, Miller could not have offered any real assurance that Cleveland would ameliorate the track-and-capture crusade even if they agreed to temper their enthusiasm for polygamy.[5]

Sharp was well-known both in the east because of his connection to the Union Pacific and in Utah where he was chairman of the People's Party and a lay bishop. John W. Young, Brigham Young's son who was working as the Church's head lobbyist in Washington and New York, had heard from friendly prominent businessmen that they respected Sharp's decision to give up polygamy. When Sharp reached out to the First Presidency for its approval, however, he was rebuffed. In response he resigned his ecclesiastical and political positions.[6]

It is likely that Miller's visit prompted Cannon to write in August to a Cleveland political confidante, Secretary of the Treasury Daniel Manning. Cannon did not mince words: "If the purpose of the administration is to persecute the Mormons for their religion and to impress them with the idea that [the government's] object is to destroy them because of it, it would be difficult to adopt a better plan." Buried beneath his controlled anger was an olive branch: the apostle assumed Cleveland must not be aware of how serious the situation was. If he did know, then he should be made aware that increased pressure would not compel the Latter-day Saints to surrender. The government's war on polygamy "had only strengthened the resolve of the people to resist," Cannon wrote. To "frighten men into promising to put away their wives and to cease to regard them as objects of their care and protection" was wrong, he concluded.[7]

The next month, non-Mormon merchant C. R. Barratt confided to Miller in Nebraska that there was some potential for violence in Utah. "The situation here ... is strained," he reported, "very possibly

5. Whitney, *History of Utah*, 3:357–59, 420–23; George L. Miller to Col. Daniel S. Lamont, Feb. 7, 1885; Miller to Grover Cleveland, Feb. 7, 1885, Cleveland Papers.

6. J. W. Young to John Taylor, June 2, 1887, John W. Young Papers; also Allen, "Good Guys," 168–71. Young complained that Sharp was a bad example.

7. George Q. Cannon to Daniel Manning, Aug. 7, 1885, Cleveland Papers. Cannon asserted a correct probability that almost any other community in the nation so treated would likely have resorted to "riot and bloodshed," which he suggested was yet possible.

more critical [than] at any time in the past." There had been rumors and threats that the LDS people would finally reach their limit of patience and resort to retribution, but Barratt was unable to give any recent evidence of this. Cannon had raised the same issue a month earlier in an inverse way, citing "no better evidence of the peaceful disposition, of the patience and forbearance and of the loyalty" of the LDS people than its "quiet submission to grievous wrongs inflicted upon them by the present [and past] courts." He charged Republicans with "vindictiveness," and repeated his view that it was counterproductive to try to "compel the Mormons to surrender." With some eloquence, he wrote that "no student of history ought to think that persecution will ever succeed in eliminating from the faith of a people beliefs that are objectionable to those who do not believe as they do." From his own personal experience, he had seen that "when men suffer for a principle it endears it more to them, and they place a higher value upon that than they do upon other principles for which they are not called to make sacrifices." The judicial crusade had "created sympathy for those who suffer" and made defendants appear "truly heroic."[8] Actually, this may have been true in the early part of the decade. He probably did not yet recognize the diminishing resolve on plural marriage among many in the younger generation of Latter-day Saints. It would likely be a few more years before the hierarchy would understand that change.

Cannon reminded Manning that there were thousands of LDS people presently ready to cast their ballots for Democrats. "I take it," he wrote, "that the Democratic party is not so bigoted on this question of religion as, for the sake of appearing as reformers, to destroy its prospects for growth."[9] Given the party's poor showing in the national elections since the Civil War, the argument was apt. He concluded with this: "It seems to me, sir, that it is a great blunder to allow the enemies of the Democratic party to be the means through which its policy upon so important a question ... shall be carried out."

8. C. R. Barratt to George L. Miller, Sept. 27, 1885; Miller to W. C. Endicott, Sept. 30, 1885; Cannon to Manning, Aug. 7, 1885, Cleveland Papers; Larson, *Americanization of Utah,* 80.

9. Cannon to Manning, Aug. 7, 1885.

Manning failed to respond to Cannon, but future changes suggested that Cleveland may well have started to consider Cannon's points.

An alternative scenario was also developing at the same time. With two-thirds of the general Church leadership in hiding, those leading the Church from day to day, including at the local level, were monogamists who could carry on without the threat of arrest. As Wilford Woodruff soon described the situation, "eight of the twelve [apostles], not to mention a great number of prominent [local leaders] throughout the various settlements are unable to appear in public."[10] Some continued to secretly visit their families while in hiding, but they missed being able to speak from the pulpit. No doubt the congregations missed their presence as much as leaders missed them. However, that did not change the fact that while the polygamists were gone, some Church members became more comfortable with leaders who were less radicalized, and the dangers inherent in supporting the existing hostility appeared increasingly senseless.

Cannon's letter to Manning likely asserted more passion regarding plural marriage than most in the rising generation felt about it. There were certainly young polygamists, but far more of the maturing young people were moving toward modernity and moderation over choosing their parents' ordeals with plural marrying. They may have been dubious, and to a degree resentful, of the proclaimed benefits of polygamy. They were, of course, outraged at the indignities their parents had been subjected to by US marshals, in being hunted down and prosecuted, but that too probably worked against the degree of commitment they felt toward personally embracing the institution. During an extended period when polygamists were not in charge and able to encourage the Church through sermons to remain loyal to "celestial marriage," the outlook among many of those in the pews changed. Practitioners of plural marriage were in hiding beginning at least in 1885. Even though John Taylor had drawn a deep line in the sand in his last conference address, he was out of sight, and beyond the sound of his voice people gravitated to safety.

10. Wilford Woodruff and George Q. Cannon to John T. Caine, Feb. 18, 1888; Cannon to Caine, Jan. 6, 1886, Caine Papers.

At least one-fifth of the older polygamous men, who had formerly been among the most dedicated stalwarts, wavered when brought to court, promising to reform rather than be imprisoned. The cracks were widening. An outsider observer, Hadley D. Johnson, a former congressman living in Salt Lake City, asserted in 1886 in a letter to the Utah Commission that plural marriage was becoming "so unpopular that the younger members of the Church will repudiate the system and refuse to engage in its practice."[11]

Even at the height of the Mormon Reformation in the 1850s, more than half the Church membership resisted appeals to embrace polygamy, and they provided long-term examples of how to participate almost fully in the Church without doing so. While Church leaders trumpeted the false "2 percent" estimate of how many men had more than one wife, a figure intended for public consumption, LDS congregants heard the same figures and young people may have wondered why they should go to jail to support something the majority of the membership avoided. It is impossible to measure these momentous changes, except through later events that show the results of this slow change of course.

George L. Miller had not received any assurance of change when his Utah visit was over, but he kept in touch with correspondents in the territory. Sharp and Sears had not come to trial. Barratt, the non-Mormon merchant in Salt Lake City, sent Miller an alarming letter that Miller forwarded to Secretary of War W. C. Endicott, including five *Deseret News* editorials, suggesting that the resistance could soon take on a more threatening complexion. Barratt thought the time had come when LDS rage would boil over, not entirely at non-Mormons, but at ex-polygamists like Arnold, Sharp, and Sears, who were considered turncoats.[12]

On April 28 George Q. Cannon's son Abraham was arrested. He did like Rudger Clawson and expressed devotion to "a higher law than that of man," admitted to having several wives, and proclaimed

11. *Hearing before the Committee on Territories*, 1890

12. Barratt to Miller, Sept. 27, 1885; Miller to Endicott, Sept. 30, 1885; Whitney, *History of Utah*, 3:420–24, 358; *Deseret Weekly News*, July 22, 29, Aug. 5, 12, 19, 1885.

that he was proud to live with them. He was therefore quickly sentenced and became, with Clawson, the face of young Mormons who remained steadfast and had not assimilated to the world's ways. They would remain uncommon exceptions, however. At least a dozen polygamists from outside the city were apprehended about the same time, and a good many of them would recant.[13]

In October Cleveland asked Miller to update him with additional views about the "Utah problem." Miller still thought it imperative that the president emphasize obedience to the law and make sure it was administered fairly. Miller underscored the bitterness the people in Utah felt over the administration not having replaced the Republican officials. Cleveland emphasized that it was important to stay the course, while being careful not to overstep legal bounds. They were both convinced that Latter-day Saints would eventually relent. On that score, if the leaders in hiding were those they had in mind, they were wrong. Miller had not met Taylor and had no real measure of the man. Before Taylor's death, Woodruff spoke of his stubbornness. "No man could alter the opinions of Pres. Taylor," he told other apostles. Taylor spent most of his last three years in hiding, preferring to be a polygamy martyr than enjoy the comforts of his home and office. Cannon supported the same unwavering stance for the remainder of his uncle's life.[14]

Another of Miller's suggestions was more promising. If Cleveland appointed officials who were more sympathetic, it would go a long way toward lowering tensions in Utah. Cleveland should choose men of high character and experience, Miller suggested. They should "establish an atmosphere of appreciation for fairness, justice [and] wisdom that might induce Latter-day Saint leaders," who were "quick and intelligent" men, to "yield respect and … [perhaps] adjustment."[15] Cleveland slowly moved in that direction, replacing the Utah Commission's James Pettigrew in 1886 with

13. Whitney, 3:360–61, 476.
14. Miller to Endicott, Nov. 5, 9, 1885; Grant, *Diaries of Heber J. Grant*, Oct. 5, 1887.
15. Miller to Endicott, Oct. 29, 1885.

Democrat John A. McClernand, a Union general who had participated in the siege of Vicksburg during the Civil War and afterward had been elected to Congress from Illinois. He had the stature and resoluteness to pursue an even course without being intimidated by the three Republicans on the commission. He was joined by an equally firm and fair Democrat, Ambrose B. Carlton of Indiana, who became chairman. The two Democrats markedly altered the image of the federal government in Utah and assured that the Edmunds–Tucker Act, passed in March 1887, would be implemented without bias. These two contributed heretofore largely unrecognized differences in tempering the emotional atmosphere within the territory.

Miller sent Cleveland a hopeful report in late October 1885. Negotiations were underway for a clandestine conference with George Q. Cannon, that had been arranged by John T. Caine. Miller took the westbound Union Pacific train from Omaha to Salt Lake City and arrived on November 6. Caine met him at the train station and drove "by a circuitous route" to the designated meeting place. Miller conferred with Cannon into the night, but without receiving an assurance of acquiescence. Miller informed Endicott that he had been unable to alter any of Cannon's views. He did come away with a critical appraisal of how the Republican deputies and judges had behaved. He called them "Republican bandits who preach the gospel of hate from every federal office in the territory." He urged Cleveland to replace them all.[16]

Ten days after the meeting, on November 19, Cannon wrote Miller to say he had conferred with other leading churchmen, who concluded not to yet cooperate with the government. They recognized that if they achieved statehood, it could bring them greater protection from federal oppression. But to see polygamy "waived or laid aside" was too great a price. One of them doubted they were dealing with honest brokers. Their experiences in the past had led them to filter even friendly overtures through a lens of suspicion.[17]

It was not just federal officials the LDS leaders distrusted. They

16. Miller to Endicott, Oct. 27, Nov. 9, 1885.
17. Cannon to Miller, Nov. 19, 1885, Cleveland Papers.

considered the *Salt Lake Tribune* their arch-enemy, especially after the two Nevada businessman connected with mining, Patrick Lannan and Charles C. Goodwin, assumed control of the paper as publisher and editor. Even before that, *Tribune* employee William Nelson had promoted the attack on polygamy through his Associated Press dispatches to a nationwide audience. In 1873 Cannon called Nelson "the champion liar of his class. Every day we have a batch of inflammatory and lying dispatches" they had to answer to. John T. Caine deplored the amount of time he spent deflecting and correcting Nelson's press dispatches. Later Caine would say that the distorted news of Christian ministers in Utah was equally irritating.[18]

The warnings of violence came a step closer to reality toward the end of the year. A plural wife, Agnes McMurrin Young, was subpoenaed and cross-examined, perhaps too aggressively, about her relationship with her polygamous husband, Royal B. Young. Deputy marshal Henry F. Collin angered Agnes's brother, future member of the First Council of Seventy Joseph W. McMurrin. When the two met in an alley on November 28, 1885, McMurrin punched the deputy who responded with two shots fired into McMurrin's abdomen. Fleeing the scene, the deputy went to US marshal Ireland, who offered him protection for fear he would be lynched. McMurrin survived. After Collin was placed under the protection of Fort Douglas soldiers, he appeared before US Commissioner William McKay on January 22, 1886, and pled self-defense. After hearing the details, McKay decided to discharge the deputy marshal, who fled the territory. The incident increased the bitterness already in existence, and some of the news stories predicted more trouble as a result.[19]

Another incident occurred on February 10, 1886, when sixty-year-old George Q. Cannon took a train for California, with Mexico as his ultimate destination. Despite being in disguise, he

18. Malmquist, *First 100 Years*, 57–74, 80–137; George Q. Cannon journal, Feb. 11, 1873; *Salt Lake Herald*, Apr. 19, 1889; John T. Caine to Wilford Woodruff et al., Jan. 7–21, 1888, John T. Caine Papers; also Hulse, "C. C. Goodwin," 165–69.

19. Cannon to Cleveland, Mar. 25, 1885; Cannon to Manning, Aug. 7, 1885; Whitney, *History of Utah*, 3:346–57; also Larson, *Americanization of Utah*, 142–45; Baskin, *Reminiscences*, 222–23.

was recognized at Humboldt Station in central Nevada and was transferred to the returning train, accompanied by marshal Ireland. The marshal had rushed to the location to take charge of the situation. As Cannon stretched his legs and stood a while on the car's rear platform, the locomotive slowed to ease down a hill and he jumped or fell off, injuring his right knee, left arm, and side; his lacerated head was bleeding as he staggered, dazed, along the railroad grade. The marshal retrieved him. Governor Murray was notified of this and sent additional marshals from Salt Lake City and a detail of soldiers from Fort Douglas to make sure the prisoner did not fall off the train again. In court an unusually high bond of $45,000 was set for Cannon's scheduled court appearance on March 1, 1886. He posted the bond, but upon direction from President John Taylor fled once again on the underground.[20]

On March 6 the women of Salt Lake City staged a notably fervent demonstration against federal meddling in their marriages. Filling the Salt Lake Theater to the walls, they protested the Edmunds–Tucker Bill then under consideration. Among its provisions was the abolition of women's suffrage. They also objected to the flagrant disrespect of women demonstrated by US deputies and judges. "Ringing speeches" were offered, and the women appointed a committee to draft a memorial to Washington. The committee was composed of Relief Society general secretary Sarah M. Kimball, former president of the LDS Retrenchment Association Mary Isabella Horne, female physician Romania B. Pratt, women's advocate Jane S. Richards, and suffragist Emily S. Richards. The editor of the *Woman's Exponent*, Emmeline B. Wells, and female physician Ellen B. Ferguson were appointed to personally carry the memorial to Washington, where it generated a sometimes positive but limited response.

Wells wrote about the congressional debates over the Edmunds Bill she was able to observe and an acquaintance she struck with Rose Cleveland, the bachelor-president's sister who served as the White House hostess. Wells attempted to explain plural marriage to Miss Cleveland, being herself the seventh wife of Daniel H. Wells, but

20. Bitton, *George Q. Cannon*, 276–80.

the president's sister was unimpressed. However, as Wells traveled home, she received a telegram from Miss Cleveland asking her and Dr. Ferguson to return and personally present the Mormon women's memorial to the president. They did so, and he read it through in their presence. On his recommendation it was introduced in Congress and published in the *Congressional Record.* The women also had the unexpected opportunity to meet with the co-sponsor of the Edmunds–Tucker Act, Congressman J. Randolph Tucker of Virginia. They met the new Utah governor, Caleb W. West, but made headway with neither of these two individuals. They did receive positive newspaper attention during their stay in Washington.

At about the same time, territorial governor Eli Murray was suffering bad publicity for his use of excessive force in escorting Elder Cannon back to the city and losing him again, as well as for his action on March 12 in vetoing the entire appropriations bill for the territory. In the ensuing disagreement, he argued that the treasurer and auditor were not legally recognized officials. For the long-tolerant Cleveland, that was enough to ask for Murray's resignation on March 17, followed shortly afterward by a request for US Attorney William H. Dickson's resignation.[21] Edward Ireland completed his term as US Marshal in June 1886 and was not reappointed. Orlando Powers, who had functioned as Supreme Court judge for a year without having received Senate approval, also had to go when Cleveland withdrew his nomination in April.

The new governor, Caleb West, was a Kentuckian, as was Murray, and had served in the Confederate Army during the Civil War. His appointment was urged by Democratic House Majority Leader John G. Carlisle. It violated Cleveland's pledge to appoint only Utah men to such positions, but West was qualified in every other way and was "broad-minded and unbiased, possessing intelligence, prudence and courage; qualities necessary to fit him for the position peculiar among its class." It was a tactful way to describe the patience and skill necessary to lead strife-torn Utah. To replace Ireland, the president picked the more moderate Eli H. Parsons. Powers was replaced

21. Madsen, *Emmeline B. Wells,* 218–24.

by the moderate Democrat Henry P. Henderson from Michigan, who eventually won respect despite his strictness in following the letter of the law. The loathed US Attorney William Dickson was replaced by George S. Peters, former mayor of Columbus, Ohio.[22]

As soon as Governor West was sworn in on May 6, his first important act was to offer amnesty to polygamists who promised to obey the Edmunds Law. He even visited the penitentiary to meet privately with inmate Lorenzo Snow, a seventy-two-year-old apostle and future Church president. Snow was immovable. He proclaimed "that doctrine is a fundamental principle of our religion, we cannot consent to relinquish it." West replied that he had no intention of asking that the apostle renounce his *belief*, only that he modify his *behavior* in relation to it, since it was "in conflict with the expressed wishes of the nation."[23]

Snow had not resided with his wives for some years and had appealed his arrest to the US Supreme Court, represented by the eminent constitutional lawyer George Ticknor Curtis and prominent LDS attorney Franklin S. Richards. His advocates chose not to challenge the polygamy ban, but simply to question the practice of joining successive shorter sentences into one longer sentence, known as "segregation." Historian Richard Poll observed that the two attorneys gave "probably the most complete and logical explanation and defense ever made of the plural marriage doctrine." The assistant attorney general in Utah, William A. Maury, had recently asserted that "it would have been infinitely better if these people, years ago, had been put to the sword." Curtis found this to be an "atrocious suggestion," even in jest. "What must these people do?" he asked. To that, the court answered on February 7, 1887, that the lower court was in error "to inflict a punishment in respect to more than one of the convictions." With that, Snow was released the next day.[24] He returned three months later to ask inmates being held for cohabitation to sign a note to the governor that they would not

22. Whitney, *History of Utah*, 3:223–24, 499–506.

23. Cannon to Caine, Jan. 6, 1886.

24. Whitney, *History of Utah*, 3:500–515, 537–45; Poll, "Twin Relic," 217–18; Curtis, *A Plea for Religious Liberty*; also *Supreme Court Reporter* 7 (1887), 556–62.

sacrifice their "honor and manhood" through "the repudiation of our wives and children, the violation of sacred covenants. Heaven forbid that we should be guilty of such perfidy," the statement read. He acknowledged that the governor had meant well. Chagrined, West made an about-face and thereafter aligned himself with those who had advocated a harsher course. In his annual report to the Secretary of Interior, written in mid-October 1886, he recommended that the pending Edmunds–Tucker Bill be enacted.[25]

Despite the perception that Cleveland's appointees were of better quality and more considerate than their predecessors, they maintained the intensity of the raid, including a senseless killing in Parowan on December 16. Thirty-four-year-old Edward Dalton, a popular militiaman and husband of two wives, was indicted in the southern Utah town of Beaver. Having appeared before the grand jury, he eluded the court officials and returned home to Parowan thirty miles away. Deputy US Marshal William Thompson Jr. boasted that he would get his man. Anticipating Dalton's participation in a cattle drive, Thompson waited for him at the home of Daniel Page, who was, like the deputy marshal, a former Mormon. Eventually Dalton rode by, unarmed. Thompson emerged from his hideout and shouted for the fugitive to halt, then fired. A neighbor woman had run out to warn Dalton and heard him gasp, "I am killed." Thompson then approached and said, "I thought I would get you after a while." When Thompson was brought to trial for killing a man who had only committed a misdemeanor, he was defended by Charles Varian, the only remaining Republican in the territorial government. The jury, drawn from the mostly non-LDS mining camps in the Beaver area, acquitted him.[26]

During the first week of the new congressional session in December 1886, William Springer of Illinois, the Democratic chairman of the House Committee on Territories, reintroduced an omnibus bill for admitting Dakota, Montana, and Washington Territories as

25. "Report of the Utah Commission," in *Annual Report of the Department of the Interior*, 1886, 2:1063–66.

26. Dix, "Unwilling Martyr," 162–77.

states. John Taylor and George Q. Cannon recognized the possibility of adding Utah to the bill. After a flurry of correspondence on the matter involving delegate Caine; John W. Young, the railroad promoter who operated mainly in New York; and Franklin S. Richards, the leading Church attorney in Washington, the three Church agents met to assess what could be done.[27]

Young occupied the ambiguous position of having been ordained an apostle and served as a counselor to the Quorum of the Twelve and as a counselor in Brigham Young's First Presidency without ever having been invited into the quorum or showing much interest in a lesser calling in the presidency. He had apparently earlier falsely portrayed himself to Democratic leaders in Washington as the heir-apparent to the presidency. He took the initial lead in the lobbying effort for Utah and gave ever-sanguine reports about the close relationships he had established with important party leaders. He had personal problems—questionable business endeavors, lavish spending, and failure to pay debts—but it was true that in this case he had forged a working relationship with members of the Cleveland administration. He referred to them in coded correspondence with Salt Lake City by numbers one through eight to refer to President Cleveland, his private secretary and advisor Daniel Lamont, Congressman William L. Scott from Pennsylvania, Senator Arthur P. Gorman of Maryland, Attorney General Augustus H. Garland, Solicitor General George A. Jenks, and party leader Chauncey Black.[28]

This onetime favored son of Brigham Young met with Cleveland on February 10, 1887, to mutually alleviate the "public clamor over polygamy." Reporting this to John Taylor, Young received a reply with telegraphic brevity: "Cannot change our attitude on main question. No surrender on principle."[29] The curt response hid a

27. Lamar, *Dakota Territory*, 257–73; Taylor to Young, Nov. 29, Dec. 22, 29, 1886; Cannon to Young, Dec. 16, 1886, John W. Young Papers.

28. Lyman, ed., *Candid Insights*, 79, 253–54, 260, 464–65; Young to Taylor and Cannon, June 2, 1887; Compton, "John Willard Young," 111–34; J. Mack [Joseph F. Smith] to Woodruff and Cannon, Apr. 6, 1888, Woodruff General Correspondence; Penrose to Woodruff and Smith, Jan. 23, Dec. 27, 1888; Richards to Woodruff et al., Jan. 23, 1888.

29. John W. Young to James Jack, Feb. 11, 1887; Jack to Young, Feb. 13, 1887, Jack Papers.

growing internal debate about how to proceed with this major public relations challenge. Taylor had probably never previously considered the possibility of cooperating with a president of the United States on such a matter. But such things were changing.

In the first session of the forty-ninth Congress, Representative Tucker of Virginia introduced a revised Edmunds Bill that he, as chair of the House Committee on the Judiciary, had rewritten. The earlier version had been reported to the House floor in May 1885 and had stalled. The Senate version passed the next year, but like its twin bill before it, it had not progressed until Governor West and the Utah Commission reported on how dire the situation was in the territory. That changed the mood in Congress, so that the bill's advocates were poised to pass it early in 1887.[30]

Governor West traveled to Washington to throw his support behind the bill. He had a close connection to fellow Kentuckian John G. Carlisle, Speaker of the House, and was able to secure time to debate the amendments on the House floor, neutralizing the efforts of delegate Caine and his hired lobbyists George Curtis and an attorney from Baltimore, Jefferson Chandler, to get the bill delayed.[31] Also in Washington were Utah's Liberal Party lobbyists Robert N. Baskin and Charles W. Bennett. These two helped Tucker add even more punitive measures to the bill. Caine told a secretary in the Church presidency's office, James Jack, that if the Tucker amendments reached the floor they would likely pass. Carlisle was offering great assistance to the bill's authors. In addition to being Speaker of the House, his position as chair of the House Rules Committee allowed him to control the agenda. Caine looked for help from the large railroad lobby, the same sources and methods that had "held matters [in check] in past years." However, there was a tragic turn of events when Charles H. Sherrill, chief lobbyist for Pacific Railroad tycoon Collis P. Huntington, died suddenly on January 3, leaving

30. Paschal, *Mr. Justice Sutherland*, 9, 28–31, 80, 139; Poll, "Twin Relic," 248–61; "Report of the Governor of Utah," in *Annual Report of the Dept. of the Interior*, 1886, 2:989–1003, 1063–66.

31. *Congressional Record*, Dec. 7, 1886, Jan. 10, 1887; also Fales and Flake, *Mormons and Mormonism*, 152.

the Union Pacific–Central Pacific Railroad lobbying network temporarily paralyzed.[32]

In desperation Caine and his associates drafted what would be designated as the Scott Amendment proposing to delay the Edmunds–Tucker Bill from becoming law for a period of six months. With that as a last resort, Caine hoped for a Utah state constitution prohibiting polygamy, as a way to avoid the legal disestablishment of the LDS Church. It was the best recourse Caine could think of.[33] His assistants, Charles W. Penrose and Franklin S. Richards, were perceptive enough to read the threatening tenor of the legislative activity and lent their support to Caine's plan.

When the House of Representatives debated the Tucker Amendment on January 12, Chandler presented the LDS position, which was that the government had no right to disestablish a Church or interfere with religion at all. It could repeal a charter, if some offense justified that action, but had no right to confiscate property and force a Church to close its doors. The congressmen were unpersuaded. Some of the provisions the Senate Judiciary Committee had added to the amendment were so drastic that Tucker himself withdrew his support of it, although by January 1887 he would change his mind and urge passage of the bill. Some Democratic senators were by nature opposed to the bill. Caine hoped to persuade them by pointing out that even the bill's sponsor had turned his back on its more radical provisions, and now doing another about-face was not to his credit. Caine responded to Baskin's negative rhetoric about Mormons as well. Near the close of the debate on January 13, Representative William L. Scott, a Democrat from Pennsylvania with ties to railroad interests, attempted to get his amendment attached to the bill, but without success. Tucker so strongly objected that other members shied away from it. The bill passed in the House

32. Caine to Jack, Jan. 14, 1887; Journal History, Jan. 12, 1887; obituary, *Louisville Courier-Journal*, Jan. 5, 1887.

33. Caine to Jack, Jan. 14, 1887, Jack Papers; also Scott, "Anti Polygamy Bill"; Wolfinger, "Reexamination of the Woodruff Manifesto," 336–46. Scott, a Democrat who was close to the Pennsylvania Railroad Company, cooperated with Caine, but the Scott Amendment was actually drafted by Mormon attorney Franklin S. Richards

of Representatives on January 12. Senator Edmunds was unhappy with the House version. A conference committee was appointed for January 14 to reconcile the differences. It consisted of three senators, including Edmunds, and three congressmen, including Tucker. Caine wrote to Taylor and Cannon that it was possible the committee could lessen some of the harsher blows of the Edmunds–Tucker Act and incorporate the six-month delay, although he knew he should not count on it.[34] The committee, like the House, considered the Scott Amendment and voted against it.

In another tragic twist, Tucker's daughter was injured in an accident and died, drawing him away from the committee's deliberations. In his absence, Edmunds inserted provisions he preferred from his own bill into the combined version. On February 15, 1887, after more than a week of "protracted and stormy" meetings, the committee reported that it had eliminated some of Tucker's harshest features and incorporated several of Edmunds's own. LDS attorney Franklin S. Richards and associates were relieved to learn, most importantly, that each instance of cohabitation would not be counted as a separate offense. The *Salt Lake Herald* significantly described the compromise bill as having drawn the "fangs ... from the Tucker Bill."[35]

On February 17 the House accepted the conference committee's report, essentially Edmunds's version of the bill, and the Senate passed it the next day. Senator George Vest (D–Missouri) announced that he could not "vote for the bill because in my judgment it violates the fundamental principles of the Constitution of the United States." Another friend of the Church, Senator Wilkinson Call (D–Florida), denounced it for its "wickedness and moral enormity." Grover Cleveland was equally wary of its violation of the Constitution, but he allowed the bill to become law without his signature on March 4.[36]

---

34. *Congressional Record*, Jan. 12, 1886; Jan. 12, 1887; also Whitney, *History of Utah*, 3:560–73; Caine, *Mormon Problem*; Tucker, *Polygamy*.

35. Young to Jack, Feb. 3, 1887; *Salt Lake Herald*, Feb. 5, 12, 13, 20, Mar. 9, 10, 13, 1887; also *Congressional Record*, Feb. 18, 1896.

36. Young to Jack, Mar. 4, 1887; Whitney, *History of Utah*, 3:565–74. Cleveland feared a veto would result in an even more harsh subsequent law.

For complex reasons, as the new law went into effect, the bitterness that preceded it diminished, at least at the highest executive-government levels, and an unlikely confluence took place in the plans of the US president and LDS Church president, as both of them embraced the spirit of the Scott Amendment in allowing a time-out while political priorities were reappraised. Apparently resigned for the moment to what seemed to be a surprisingly fortunate development, President John Taylor dictated a message to John W. Young that the Lord must have some purpose in allowing the law to pass. About the same time in another letter, also to Young, he predicted that outsiders would not be satisfied with anything less than a "complete renunciation" of their doctrine. "Nothing less than complete destruction of our system of plural marriage will appease the popular clamor," he wrote.[37]

Perplexed, but equally determined, Young telegraphed back to explain that it was unnecessary for the Church to surrender anything. These were political questions, not matters of religious belief. The issue on the table was whether the terms of the Scott Amendment, or more precisely the Penrose interpretation of it (Charles W. Penrose was diligently laying out a proposed strategy in a nine-page brief to the Church president) were acceptable. Penrose was a professional newspaperman, who was able to convey the subtle distinctions he wanted the Church president to understand, and he prefaced his arguments by observing that "statehood under the auspices of most citizens [rather than under a few appointees] means deliverance from political bondage and influence in the councils of the nation." If they achieved statehood, they could "protect themselves" from outside meddling, so that if Utahns drafted a state constitution that outlawed plural marriage, it would mainly be up to them, the citizens, to interpret the meaning of it. Those who drafted the constitution and voted for it would be monogamist Latter-day Saints—those who had not been disfranchised. Taylor himself, and

37. John Taylor and George Q. Cannon to John W. Young, Feb. 13, 1887 (cf. Taylor and Cannon to Caine and Franklin S. Richards, Feb. 2, 1887), Taylor Correspondence; also Cannon and Taylor to Young, Nov. 1, 1886, John W. Young Papers

other polygamists, were already disqualified and would not have to swear to abide by the new constitution or to conform to any undesirable interpretation of it.[38]

The letter proved to have a momentous impact. Penrose, on leave as editor of the Church's *Deseret News* in order to assist Caine, well understood the Church leader's usual inflexibility. But a logical presentation of the relevant facts, related by Penrose in person on a short visit to Utah, allowed the venerable Church president to set aside some of his long-standing assumptions. Taylor conceded that "the plan of Brothers Penrose and Richards, if it could be successfully accomplished, might perhaps avert the evils which [were then] impending." His nod toward the reasonableness of the approach loomed in the minds of the Church lobbyists, too, as considerable encouragement. In fact, what was developing proved to be a pivotal transition from persistent fanaticism to a more realistic polity. While they were only beginning to consider the possibilities of the strategy, Taylor added that even though people could not be expected to accomplish any more than was requested in the proposition, the brethren might expressly go that far "toward conciliating public opinion." If they ventured in that direction, they would all need to trust in the Lord to sustain them in such a momentous step.[39]

Taylor asked Cannon's opinion. The former delegate to Congress later explained he was careful not to prejudice the Church president's opinion where a departure from precedent was anticipated and divine inspiration was required. In a private meeting in Taylor's office, but without the president, Cannon later informed four apostles that Taylor had studied the Penrose letter and become "very clear" that it was the proper course for the Latter-day Saints to pursue.[40] Cannon attested that he had not offered his own opinion

38. Young to Jack, Feb. 14, 1887, Jack Papers; Penrose to Smith, Feb. 11, 1887; Penrose and Richards to Taylor and Cannon, Feb. 16, 18, 1887, Taylor Correspondence.

39. Taylor and Cannon to Caine and Young, Feb. 2, 13, 16, 1887; Penrose and Richards to Taylor, Feb. 18, 1887, Taylor Correspondence; Lyman, "Alienation of an Apostle," 69; Grant, *Diaries*, July 7, 1887.

40. George Q. Cannon journal, Feb. 10, 1887; Bitton, *George Q. Cannon,* 312–13; Grant, June 20, 1887.

until after his uncle had arrived at a conclusion, and then he supported the president's decision.

Taylor remained concerned that approval of an anti-polygamy constitutional provision would convey the impression that Latter-day Saints were surrendering an essential principle, and he did not want to see a situation develop where the new state government would become the new zealous enforcer of monogamy. Still, he accepted Penrose's argument that the non-voting LDS authorities themselves would not be committing themselves on the matter. A harbinger of things to come, this was one of the first times LDS leaders would carefully differentiate between a political and religious stand. The implication was that the non-polygamist population could have its own standards, while those who remained aloof from the standards of the world were free to believe in and practice a "higher law." The letter stressed that, at minimum, the officials chosen by the predominantly Mormon electorate after statehood would likely be more lenient in enforcing the law than the adversarial federal appointees had been.[41]

Before receiving Taylor's first full reply, but probably after his first telegram, Penrose and Richards sent a second letter on February 18 reiterating more specifically that the only remedy to their persistent problem was statehood. The next day Taylor and Cannon discussed the matter. They doubted that President Cleveland would agree to the plan, that the "concessions" they had discussed would "not [be] all he would ask [for]." He might "insist on the future discontinuance of plural marriage" entirely.[42] They naturally looked at Washington with skepticism, but they had no other alternatives.

Young was hoping for a swift reply from Taylor because he had scheduled another audience with President Cleveland. The day arrived without an answer, but it did not matter. To his relief, Cleveland expressed himself completely satisfied with the provisions of the Scott Amendment. The need for Church leaders to abandon

41. Penrose and Richards to Taylor, Feb. 16, 1887; Taylor and Cannon to Penrose and Richards, Feb. 16, 1887, Taylor Correspondence.

42. Penrose and Richards to Taylor, Feb. 18, 1887; Taylor and Cannon to Penrose and Richards, Feb. 19, 1887.

plural marriage was virtually not mentioned, only that the Utah constitution would officially prohibit polygamy, and that, Young predicted, it would "make us [Utah] a state."[43] This lenient tactic of viewing the wording of the constitutional concession as a prohibition on future plural marriages, while allowing existing polygamists to continue its practice for the time being, became the basis for the LDS side in accepting the entire plan, particularly statehood.

Young's report of his meeting with Cleveland alleviated Taylor's reservations. In a telegraphic reply on February 27, 1887, Taylor stated that if the Scott Amendment was satisfactory to President Cleveland, it was acceptable to Church leaders. He repeated his determination not to yield any religious principle, pledging he would "recoil from it and emphatically reject" such a statement. Yet as the situation now portended, "[We would] only be punishing ourselves for what our enemies are now punishing us," he said.[44]

As this flurry of communication went on, the Edmunds–Tucker Bill became law. While the Scott Amendment was omitted, it still became the premise for moving forward. This was the first time since President Zachary Taylor's overture in 1850 that such a cordial entreaty had been offered by the executive branch.[45] Both Cleveland and Taylor kept the terms of their understanding vague, knowing that the monogamists in the territory would have no trouble approving a state constitution that prohibited plural marriage, if guided in that direction by the hierarchy, and that those who had been disfranchised for practicing polygamy would not be allowed to vote, and would therefore not be voting against it. After statehood, both presidents understood, the polygamists would be treated more humanely. It might have been implicit in their understanding that new plural marriages might be solemnized beyond US jurisdiction, as they already were being performed in Mexico, and that past and present relationships would continue.

For instance, on January 4, 1887, Abraham H. Cannon, one of the LDS First Council of the Seventy, planned with a woman he

43. Young to Jack, Feb. 2, 25, 1887.
44. Jack to Young, Feb. 27, 1887.
45. Caine to Jack, Mar. 1, 3, 1887; Young to Jack, Mar. 4, 1887.

had become engaged to, Mamie Croxall, to travel to Mexico to be married as his third wife. His associate, Don C. Young (Brigham's son), also had a plural bride-to-be, Marion Hardy, and the four met to finalize their travel plans before setting out together. It was decided that the women would take the train to Provo separately to avoid suspicion. From there they would be joined by the men through Colorado and New Mexico to Colonia Díaz, south of the border, inhabited primarily by LDS polygamists. On January 11 the two couples arrived at their destination and presented their recommends to apostle Erastus Snow, who performed the marriages, with apostle Moses Thatcher as a witness. They returned home with caution, the women remaining in Provo for a day before continuing on to Salt Lake City alone.[46] This was the usual procedure for those entering into new plural marriages at that time.

The Church authorities went out of their way to prohibit new marriages from being contracted in the United States, but the new plural husbands demonstrated no hesitation about having sexual relations with their plural wives within the country, believing that it was not part of the legal definition of polygamy. One aspect of the Penrose approach LDS leaders found comforting was that if things went according to plan, sympathetic juries could interpret a ban on polygamy in that same narrow way, to mean that new weddings were forbidden, but the observance of regular marriage conventions for those already in plural-marriage arrangements would continue. The statute of limitations would absolve those guilty of actual marriage infractions after three years. If juries could be convinced that polygamy applied to the ceremony and not to sex, then polygamists would be free to continue living the way they had prior to the federal raid. For now, they hesitated to get into those kinds of specifics with President Cleveland in case he saw things differently.[47]

At the end of March, the Utah Commission sent a circular letter to voter registrars throughout the territory instructing them to

46. Abraham H. Cannon journal, Jan. 4–14, 1887.

47. Abraham H. Cannon journal, July 1887; also Hardy, *Solemn Covenant*, 84–104. The latter source makes clear that Mexican law did not back the lenient interpretation of polygamy treated above.

allow anyone to vote who could swear, as required by the Edmunds–Tucker Act, that "they will faithfully obey the laws" and "will also obey this act" and "will not, directly or indirectly, aid or abet, counsel or advise, any other person to commit any of said crimes," all stated in future tense. The recent amnesty for past but discontinued cohabitation indicated the Democrats' desire to take a gentler approach. It infuriated the Liberal Party, whose attorneys could not see in the Edmunds–Tucker Act an intent to look the other way.[48] Commissioner Carlton defended the adherence to "the language of the law." If they "depart[ed] from this rule," he wrote, they would find themselves "in a labyrinth of conflicting opinions." This made him the target of ridicule by the *Tribune*, among other foes.[49] Carlton acted in concert with Cleveland, who conveyed a message to President Taylor through the territorial delegate that there would be no vindictiveness in the administration of the new law.[50]

In early April, John W. Young outlined for Church leaders how to frame the desired Utah constitution. Taylor and Cannon affirmed that there should not be even the appearance of the "surrender of any doctrine, however objectionable it may be to the world. ... All the advantages which are likely to flow to us by obtaining a state government, if they were multiplied a million-fold, ought not to have any weight with us in the face of God's commands." They characteristically concluded that if statehood was meant to be, God would open the way and provide the means for it to come about.[51] Into the late spring, the correspondence back and forth probed the possibility of amending the 1882 draft of a constitution, but it was concluded that too many of the key figures at that convention were polygamists now hiding on the underground, and it would not look good to have their names attached to the document. A new convention would have to be held and should be run by delegates who

48. *Salt Lake Tribune*, Apr. 25, 26, 29, June 9, 12, 1887; Whitney, *History of Utah*, 3:580–83; *Salt Lake Herald*, Apr. 8, 20, 23, 29, 1887.

49. A. B. Carlton to Robert N. Baskin and John E. Dooley, Apr. 22, 1887. When I saw this letter in 1972–73, it was in a file of Carlton correspondence that has been misplaced and is not presently cataloged at the Church History Library.

50. Caine to Jack, Mar. 6, 1887.

51. Taylor and Cannon to Young, Apr. 6, 1887, Taylor Correspondence.

were not polygamists. The People's Party central committee would hold mass meetings throughout the territory to select men to do the work. The Liberal Party would be invited to send a proportional number of delegates as well.

The White House asked the Utah Commission to assist wherever it could in adding the ratification of a state constitution to the August ballot. The US Attorney General promised to have an interpretation of the Edmunds–Tucker Act by then, in order to sort out which restrictions applied to Latter-day Saint voters. John W. Young and Charles W. Penrose met with President Cleveland's cabinet secretary, Daniel Lamont, and the US Solicitor General, George A. Jenks, on May 26, 1887. Jenks was the administration's top legal adviser. He had discussed the matter with the president and drafted two paragraphs on plural marriage that needed to be inserted into the Utah constitution, making it "as lenient as we could expect to get through Congress." He said he had considered "every point that might be assailed when the matter should come up for discussion." The administration regarded this "as purely a political settlement of the question" and not an intrusion into religious beliefs.[52]

Within two weeks of this meeting, Penrose traveled to Salt Lake City to be sure that the convention proceeded along the lines that were expected. On June 13 he met with available Church authorities to report on his "interviews with some of the leading men of the nation." He told them the White House had helped rewrite a proposed version of the 1882 constitution to make it politically acceptable. Bigamy would be classified as a misdemeanor that would not be punished by more than $1,000 and three years in prison. Unlawful cohabitation would incur no penalty at all.[53]

If the public had known the extent of the behind-the-scenes activities in June and July, they would have seen the Liberal Party's oft-repeated allegation of Church dominance in Utah politics

52. Cannon to Young, May 9, 25, 1887; Young to Taylor and Cannon, June 2, 1887, Taylor Correspondence; Young to James Jack, June 14, 21, 1887, Jack Papers; also "Letter from the Attorney-General," Dec. 12, 1888, exec. doc. 21, 50th Cong., 2d. sess., referred to Committee on the Judiciary Dec. 17.

53. Abraham H. Cannon journal, June 13, 1887.

confirmed. What's more, they would have seen the Cleveland administration accepting that reality and moving forward on that assumption. On June 1 Church authorities met with stake presidents and the People's Party central committee to consider the "men and measures" the territorial legislature would move forward prior to the constitutional convention. Everything was coordinated so that in mid-month the People's Party could issue a call for mass meetings to be held on June 25, to select delegates for a convention five days later. Special invitations were sent to the chairmen of the local Democratic and Republican Parties, who acted as links to the Liberal Party.

Joseph B. Rosborough, chairman of the territorial Democratic Party, was perturbed by the late notice and cited it as one more example of why Utah did not deserve to become a state—its "spirit of opposition" to fair elections. If the territory became a state, he said, the theocracy would pervert and abuse its powers and make things worse for non-Mormons. Not only that, but calling for mass meetings implied that the legislature was giving the people themselves the authority to draft a state constitution, and he was certain that was not the case. He said he would not wish to convey that erroneous impression.[54]

By June 20 everything else was in place. People's Party mass meetings had been scheduled. Elder Cannon explained to fellow apostles Franklin D. Richards, Heber J. Grant, and Moses Thatcher that President Cleveland "was willing to sign a bill admitting Utah into the union" if its constitution contained the necessary stipulations. Cannon assured his colleagues that President Taylor, whose health was rapidly deteriorating, had fully understood and approved of the plan. He attested this would be "the most important" political development in "his lifetime." That afternoon approximately fifty LDS officers, many occupying both political and ecclesiastical positions, gathered at Church headquarters to further discuss the convention. President Cannon outlined the undertaking without mentioning the encouragement from President Cleveland. John T. Caine expressed confidence that the prohibition of polygamy would

54. Franklin D. Richards journal, June 1, 13, 16, 1887.

clear the way for statehood to become a reality. Elder Grant assured the gathering that the presidency and Twelve favored the proposal.[55]

In the lengthy discussion that followed, longtime People's Party activists emphasized the need to carefully control the nominating conventions in order to assure sympathetic proceedings and delegates. Men like John R. Winder, who was about to become chairman of the People's Party, reflected the old regime of "prearranged" endorsements of "the right men." The primary worry was that delegates would be in full sympathy with the essential provisos that had been hammered out with the White House. To eliminate controversy, it was decided not to allow polygamists to be selected as candidates or to make women's suffrage an issue after being abrogated by the Edmunds–Tucker Act. This carefully choreographed convention convened on June 30 in Salt Lake City, the sixth attempt in the territory's long experience with such gatherings to try to forge a new political entity. It continued until July 7, ending with a vote of support for a document with a provision that stood out starkly, stating that "bigamy and polygamy being considered incompatible with a republican form of government, each of them is hereby forbidden and declared a misdemeanor."[56]

Church leaders may not have fully comprehended where this was headed. They assumed they were giving up control of territorial politics in the short run, but had no intention of abandoning polygamy. Since Brigham Young's death, there had been several significant evidences of a greater degree of individual choice, or "free agency," regarding crucial life choices such as whether to participate in plural marriage. There appeared to no longer be any stigma of unfaithfulness visible for those who chose not to enter into polygamy. What was occurring now, however, was a diminishing of the political status of those who had. Political power was being transferred

55. Grant, *Diaries*, June 20, July 6, 1887; Franklin D. Richards, notes of a meeting, June 20, 1887; Abraham H. Cannon journal, June 20, 1887. Solicitor General Jenks visited Utah to help quietly oversee framing the constitution.

56. Grant, June 20, 1887; Richards, June 20, 1887; Cannon journal, July 8, 1887; "Not in the Constitution," *Salt Lake Tribune*, July 10, 1887; Bernstein, "History of the Constitutional Conventions, 63–73.

to the non-polygamist members of the Church, who would immediately gain increased status in the community as a result of having taken the Edmunds–Tucker-provided oath. The elevation of these participating citizens in the actual governance of Utah Territory, and eventually the state, including the voluntary promise not to aid or abet those continuing to practice plural marriage, added a degree of autonomy previously unimagined in a region where LDS Church authorities had long presumed it their inherent right to dominate in everything, both religious and secular. This represents one of the most momentous political developments in Utah history.[57]

Still following the lead of the *Salt Lake Tribune*'s prominent United Press agent Nelson, the national press doubted the sincerity of the Latter-day Saints in opposing polygamy. Two newspapers in particular picked up and dissected the core of the statehood motives. The *New York Times* mentioned that after statehood, the anti-polygamy law "would be in the hands of Mormon officials, Mormon courts, and Mormon juries." The *New York Evening Post* noticed that cohabitation was not even mentioned in the proposed constitution. That meant that polygamy would be legal for couples who went undiscovered for three years. The nuts and bolts of the quiet compromise thus became, among opponents, an open secret by process of deduction. No one should have expected the loopholes to go unnoticed. They probably anticipated allegations of duplicity but concluded it did not matter, as long as the plan was successful. In early July the territory received a visit from the solicitor general. There were only a few individuals in the inner circle of the Church leadership who knew that Jenks had authored a key section of the constitution. The *Salt Lake Tribune* correctly surmised that his visit signified the Democrats' blessing on "the admission of Utah into the union," that he was probably there to "manage the necessary negotiations."[58] Publicly Jenks demonstrated little interest in the convention, all the

57. Grant, July 7, 1887; Richards journal, June 28, 1887; Larson, *Americanization of Utah*, 217–19; John A. McClernand to Grover Cleveland, June 30, July 5, 9, 1887, Cleveland Papers.

58. *Salt Lake Tribune*, July 1–6, 8, 1887; *New York Evening Post*, July 6, 1887; *New York Times*, July 7, 1887.

while conferring frequently with Franklin S. Richards and offering suggestions on how to assure the success of the proceedings. He was interested in meeting Elders Penrose and Cannon and was disappointed to learn that it was considered too risky to smuggle them out of their hiding places for a meeting. Despite being fugitives, they were near enough to answer questions themselves and offer advice. Penrose had input into the committee meetings, for instance. When the convention adjourned, Cannon met privately with LDS participants to relay the "hearty approval" of the First Presidency. He repeated that this was "the most important [political] move up to date that had been taken by any body of men since he became associated with the church." Apostles Heber J. Grant, Franklin D. Richards, Lorenzo Snow, and Moses Thatcher followed with their own messages of congratulations and encouragement for the delegates to quietly inform friends and neighbors of the need to support the document they had created.[59]

The next day Abraham H. Cannon recorded that the First Presidency "assigned" him to visit Emery and Uintah Counties to "urge upon [stake leaders] the importance of getting every possible vote cast at the coming election in favor of the constitution." He told them that "the head authorities approve[d] the measure." Other Church authorities were similarly engaged in other parts of the territory. In the election of August 1, a week after President Taylor's death, the constitution was ratified, 13,195 to 507. Wilford Woodruff became acting Church president, with George Q. Cannon and the comparatively youthful fifty-year-old Joseph F. Smith retained as close advisors and eventually counselors who assured local and federal officials they would not be abandoning previous commitments.[60]

59. Charles Williams [Penrose] to John W. Young, July 6, 1887, John W. Young Papers; *Salt Lake Herald*, July 31, 1887; Richards journal, July 5, 7, 9–14, 1887. Cannon also confided that John Taylor was then on his deathbed.

60. Abraham H. Cannon journal, July 10, 14, 1887; Grant, *Diaries*, July 12–25, 1887; Alexander, *Things in Heaven and Earth*, 243–46; also Lyman, "Succession by Seniority," 113–138. This last item recounts the efforts of apostles Moses Thatcher and Heber J. Grant to delay actual organization of the new First Presidency two years because of ill feelings toward proposed counselor Cannon.

Most of the highest LDS leaders met on August 4, 1887, to discuss further steps in making Utah a state. Present were Daniel H. Wells and some of the First Council of Seventy and Presiding Bishopric. The gathered Church authorities nominated Cannon and Smith to serve with Woodruff as a committee that would do everything possible to make Utah a state. Over the next two years, this committee would sign relevant correspondence on political and economic matters from their hiding places, with the bracketed word "committee" next to their signatures, meaning the statehood committee. Cannon considered "his position as one of the committee on [the] state move[ment] [to be] the most responsible one of his life."[61]

Despite the rapprochement the Church achieved with the Cleveland administration, and despite the Edmunds–Tucker Act allowing former polygamists to vote if they renounced their former family ties, other aspects of the law encouraged US marshals to step up the pressure on violators to an unprecedented level. Another complication emerged because neither the LDS lobby nor the White House had involved key congressional leaders in their agreements. Members of Congress did not fail to notice that the proposed section of the constitution forbidding polygamy did not forbid cohabitation, or that Church leaders themselves had failed to make public concessions, all of which soured the legislators on taking the proposal seriously. Congress would resolve to withhold the enabling act needed for statehood. In the face of the good will demonstrated by the executive branch, this sixth effort at statehood would falter and die much the same as the others had. It was part of an ongoing learning process. With each failure, the proponents gained experience and learned what else would need to be done to eventually achieve the ultimate goal.

61. Grant, Aug. 4, 12, 13, Oct. 23, 26, 1887; Smith, *Church, State, and Politics,* Aug. 13, 1887; Bitton, *George Q. Cannon*, 335–72. Later lobbyists were more comfortable cooperating with this small committee rather than a much larger group of Church authorities.

6

GENERATING A MORE POSITIVE IMAGE

1887–88

The Latter-day Saint leadership accomplished a crucial step in establishing a good rapport with President Grover Cleveland and the executive branch. Together they had drafted and promoted a provision prohibiting plural marriage in the recently ratified constitution for the proposed state. Nevertheless, the territorial citizenry remained as bitterly divided as ever, as did people elsewhere as they read reports circulated by the Associated Press networks, originating with the *Salt Lake Tribune*, which was itself aligned with many of the non-LDS clergymen of Utah. The *Tribune* deftly documented the fact that, despite passage of the Edmunds–Tucker Act, there had yet been no visible evidence of a retreat by LDS leaders on their commitment to polygamy.

Solicitor General George A. Jenks, when he visited Utah during the constitutional convention in early July 1887, suggested to Mormon authorities that they cease referring to polygamy at all in public addresses. It would go a long way, he advised them, in conveying the idea that the Church was loosening its attachment to the doctrine as a centerpiece in its theology. The LDS hierarchy was anxious enough to retain the good will of the Cleveland administration that it immediately implemented the suggested policy. However, at private gatherings, the leaders continued to promote plural marriage as a necessary element of personal salvation. Speaking at the George Q. Cannon farm on July 31, President Joseph F. Smith, who had recently returned from hiding in Hawaii, stated that "the men who obeyed it [the doctrine of celestial marriage] occupied a higher plane than those who disregarded it," and that the women would be blessed for remaining with their polygamous husbands. Then he added something relatively new—a qualification—by saying that "this celestial law is permissive, just as other laws of the gospel are," meaning that it was ultimately up to each individual to decide whether to pursue that course in life. According to Smith, "those who reject it would be damned"; meaning they would be prevented from reaching the highest level in the three heavenly kingdoms of the LDS afterlife. It was clear that dedicated polygamists continued their intent to ignore the law and seek rather "the general assembly and church of the firstborn, which are written in heaven" (Heb. 12:23).[1]

The entire plural marriage situation had entered a state of flux, at least beyond the elite of the Latter-day Saint community. The number of formerly committed polygamists who had promised to obey the law in exchange for some measure of leniency in prosecution doubtless alarmed the leadership. As stated previously, and from contemporary observers who will be cited herein, many of the LDS generation of young adults were choosing a different course than their parents had on plural marriage. The late Church president, John Taylor, and counselor George Q. Cannon, had probably not anticipated the result when they advised monogamist Church members to submit to the test oath in the Edmunds–Tucker Act so they could continue active participation in elections, which they did. The consequence was the assurance that those who would emerge as leaders of the state, when it was finally formed, would be monogamist Latter-day Saints. It would be LDS candidates who had repeatedly promised not to aid or abet those who continued to live in defiance of the law.

A possible complication that was feared was that approval of the proposed constitution could be thwarted by vocal polygamists

1. Abraham H. Cannon journal, July 8, 1887, Sept. 31, 1889; Franklin S. Richards to John W. Young, July 8, 1887, John W. Young Papers. The flexibility to decide one's own course of salvation was probably not much taught in Brigham Young's time.

who objected to it, especially Church leaders who might be brought to court and compelled to express their views. The earlier defiant responses in court by young polygamy advocates Rudger Clawson and Abraham H. Cannon still rang in people's ears. If such statements were repeated, it could be devastating to the quest for political independence. It predictably led the Church's attorneys and some Democratic party leaders to try to devise a strategy to avoid this potential problem. As they weighed options in September 1887, they summoned the twenty-eight-year-old member of the First Council of Seventy, Abraham Cannon, to solicit his opinion. He recorded in his diary that he was brought into a room where his father, apostle George Q. Cannon; acting Church President Wilford Woodruff; Church attorney LeGrand Young; and one other dignitary asked him, as a matter of strategy, if he would agree to stop living with his three wives if necessary. Would it make a difference to him if he were privately assured that he would not have to renounce polygamy and that the prohibition would certainly no longer be binding after the policy was repealed? The young leader of the Seventy said he could not see his way clear to comply with such a request. He was under divine command, he said, and if he did not increase his family through procreation, he would be in violation of the divine order. He was surprised, he confided to his journal, to be asked such questions by the acting Church president. He knew the implication was that the concession was under consideration as a price tag for statehood.[2]

Twelve days later other apostles listened to a document read to them that was apparently written by someone in the Democratic leadership in Washington, stating that unless those who were brought to court "promise[d] to obey the law against these offenses," Congress would not believe the Church had been "honest in adopting a constitution prohibiting polygamy." In preparing the suggested guidelines for Church members when they appeared in court, Church attorney LeGrand Young had drafted a paper with

2. Abraham H. Cannon journal, Sept. 17, 1887.

similar content—answers to the same questions that had been posed to Abraham Cannon.[3]

After considerable discussion, the acting First Presidency concluded to withhold its endorsement of such an approach. "No Latter-day Saint could make such a promise," they concluded. "If such a promise was necessary as a condition to our securing statehood," they should "give the administration at Washington to understand that we could not accept of it." Thus began their gradual abandonment of the plan for the political deliverance they imagined statehood would bring, although in reality they were only postponing the day when this would become a necessity. In the meantime, their position posed a difficult problem. If they publicly disclosed this decision, it would validate their current critics' allegation that they were insincere in promising to compromise; it would bring their integrity fully into question. At the very least, they would not wish to publicize that they were encouraging new plural marriages, which would be an invitation for the US marshals to again step up their investigations.

This was actually the second time, the other being in 1871–73, when substantial progress toward statehood, with cooperation from friendly outside political figures, led to a late crucial juncture when the Church would stop short of making substantive concessions regarding plural marriage, still deemed going too far. This time the leaders of the People's Party had already issued a call to reconvene the constitutional convention in order to draft a memorial to Congress. The gathering took place on October 8 without interference from the Church. Caine, the convention president, probably wrote the memorial. Now he was appointed to present it himself to President Cleveland. The First Presidency urged him to deliver a handsomely embossed copy of both the constitution and memorial, with the hope that the president might be nudged toward mentioning the matter in his annual state of the union report. When Caine met with the president, Cleveland said he

3. Grant, *Diaries,* Sept. 29, 1887.

thought the Latter-day Saints had done all anyone could reasonably ask of them.[4]

John W. Young followed up with President Cleveland's advisors and ascertained that they were still in support of the statehood effort. The Church's statehood committee had by then distanced itself from Young, but Brigham's son still considered himself to be in charge of the LDS agents working at the nation's capital. A tacit hope of his and the Church statehood committee both was that the president might publicize the topic in his speeches. But as Young learned from Cleveland's chief political lieutenant, Daniel Lamont, at the end of November 1887, the entire presidential message would be devoted to tariff reform, the most divisive political issue of the era.[5]

Cleveland had already angered many of his own Democratic Party professionals by pressing for fuller implementation of the new Civil Service reform law regarding political appointees, including those appointed by previous Republican presidents. Cleveland not only alienated virtually all of his party's experienced election strategists, but party-affiliated businessmen were also unhappy that the president was exclusively focusing his political attention against high protective tariffs. Cleveland's courageous and stubborn action assured that he would not be re-elected at the end of 1888.[6]

One of the crucial flaws in the effort at statehood was that while the executive branch of the national government was fully engaged, there had been little similar involvement or support among the counterpart legislative branch. Although John W. Young had engaged Senator Arthur P. Gorman of Maryland and Congressman William L. Scott of Pennsylvania, these men essentially faded away from supporting Utah by the end of the year. It may have been unrealistic to expect both branches of government to be brought into full cooperation so rapidly, but when the White House came around

4. Grant, Nov. 14, 1887; Roderick, "John T. Caine," 78; Wilford. Woodruff et al. to John T. Caine, Oct. 19, 1887, Woodruff letterbooks.

5. John W. Young to Woodruff et al., Nov. 29, 1887, Woodruff General Correspondence.

6. Nevins, *Grover Cleveland*, 367–79. This biographer concluded that the president made reform a higher priority than reelection.

to backing statehood, there was still virtually no legislative support for it. Generating something like consensus, or at least developing a good measure of positive public support on any issue expected to clear Congress, was an essential prerequisite. After a full four decades of negative press reports regarding Utah and the Mormons, it appeared nearly impossible to generate positive support from a wide range of congressional constituencies. An absolute fact of life was that political figures usually avoided causes that were unpopular with their constituent voters.[7]

There had been a long and extensive barrage of negative publicity generated by the arrests of men caught cohabiting with women they called their celestial wives. Early in 1887 attorney George Ticknor Curtis, a man of long experience in national affairs, observed that he had never seen such a phenomenon as the journalistic fervor over polygamy. As Utah expressed a desire to attain statehood, he explained the odds to his associate, Church attorney Franklin S. Richards: "You are a mere handful of people; 150,000 against 50 or 60 millions, and those millions have made up their minds."[8] A primary source of negative impressions was the *Salt Lake Tribune,* the leading intermountain newspaper and one that catered to the growing body of non-LDS citizens in the territory. It was also engaged in a lively running editorial feud with the other local dailies, the *Deseret Evening News* and *Salt Lake Herald*, both of which targeted LDS audiences. The *Tribune*'s reporter William Nelson was still the region's Associated Press telegraphic correspondent, and his reports reached the entire nation.

While the Edmunds–Tucker bill was pending, an unsigned press dispatch had falsely claimed that a "strong Mormon lobby" was on its way to Washington to work against the bill. Delegate John T. Caine attempted to refute this claim. He advised influential LDS people to visit William Henry Smith in Chicago, manager of the Western Associated Press, regarding "their Salt Lake agent (Nelson)

7. Morgan, *From Hayes to McKinley*, 271.

8. George T. Curtis to Franklin S. Richards, Jan. 23, 1887, George Ticknor Curtis Papers.

on account of rabid partisanship and false telegrams which[,] while it is injuring our people[,] deceive the general public." The *Salt Lake Herald* wondered if "during the last five years there had [been] ... a single Associated Press telegram" from the Salt Lake office "that was not in some sense a lie." Church press agent Penrose soon discovered that William Nelson and William Henry Smith were longtime friends. It appeared there was little chance of having Nelson replaced.[9]

LDS lobbyists had earlier resorted to an arrangement with the *National Republican*, a Washington newspaper, that for a fee it would print articles composed by Church correspondents. In response to Nelson's wire story about the Saints' supposedly bitter reaction to the Edmunds–Tucker Bill, they telegraphed their own story with quotes from the *Deseret News* to show the actual moderate response to the bill. Another telegram from Church headquarters to the *National Republican*, after the bill became a law, reported that Mormons of all stripes were unfairly barred from jury duty by US District Attorney William H. Dickson and Chief Justice Charles S. Zane. Church members willing to take the test oath were sometimes declared ineligible to vote. "This makes [the] test imposed entirely a religious one," the news story concluded.[10] True enough, it would take considerable time to assure that the new law would be fairly administered. The slant of the LDS dispatch leaned as much in one direction as the *Tribune* did in the other.

A breakthrough occurred after the Edmunds–Tucker Act passed and Curtis saw indications that he could "get access to public opinion" in ways previously unavailable to him.[11] He was probably also putting a positive spin on the situation as he sought a substantial legal retainer, but he managed to place two important articles he had written in New York newspapers and magazines. Much less

9. *Salt Lake Herald*, Feb. 9, 10, 1887; C. Williams [Penrose] to Woodruff et al., Oct. 26, 1887, First Presidency Collection; Whitney, *History of Utah*, 3:405, 413, 487C.

10. James Jack to *National Republican*, Feb. 21, Apr. 19, 1887, James Jack Papers.

11. Richards to John Taylor, Feb. 9, 1887. Taylor Correspondence; Curtis to Richards, Mar. 8, 1887;

successful in the image-shaping business was John W. Young. As early as March 1887, he asked Church leaders if he should "begin to create a little public sentiment by gradually introducing friendly articles in the New York papers?" He stressed caution that such items could not be written in a way that showed their hand in trying to influence "the public mind in a manner favorable," and they would need to be careful about their choice of newspapers. However, he proved unable to generate any such influence as he had promised. In June he naively announced that he had managed to get William Nelson replaced, something that he may have thought would happen but did not. He was equally unsuccessful in convincing eastern press outlets to distance themselves from the Associated Press and rely more on the New York City Press Association, which he also failed to noticeably influence.[12]

Significantly, Young offered some good advice to the Church about a practice begun several summers previously of lowering American flags to half staff on the Fourth of July. It was a form of protest against the judicial crusade against polygamy. Young thought they should move in the opposite direction and plan an elaborate celebration to show their loyalty to the country.[13] The First Presidency agreed. Its direction to the People's Party was that in celebrating the Fourth of July "in proper form" it would create an "impression" that would be useful "abroad." Accordingly, such a celebration was arranged for 1887. It was widely publicized as a step toward reconciliation.[14]

After Congress took its Independence Day recess, there was an increase in press commentary about news stories that appeared in the *Salt Lake Tribune* and were carried by the Associated Press. In relying on the *Tribune*, the *New York Times* proved strikingly accurate in its criticism of the Utah constitutional convention. On July 9

12. John W. Young to James Jack, Mar. 16, Apr. 9, May 28, 1887, Jack Papers.

13. Young to Jack, June 17, 20, 29, 1887; Roberts, *Comprehensive History*, 5:359–62; 6:159–62.

14. Young to Jack, June 21, 1887; John Taylor and George Q. Cannon to John R. Winder, June 23, 1887, Jack Papers; also *Salt Lake Herald*, July 6, 1887; *New York World*, July 6, 1887.

the *Times* directly challenged the genuineness of the anti-polygamy provision and questioned why Church leaders, who had so often encouraged their people to stand firm against the war on polygamy, now kept such a strange silence in commenting on the alteration of its position in the proposed constitution.[15]

Young wrote to Taylor and Cannon that Congress would also likely focus on the perceived insincerity of the Church as one of its main questions to the territorial delegation in the approaching session. Young stressed that the *New York Times* editorial had been especially influential. To counteract its effect, he suggested an interview with someone in the First Presidency by a respected newspaperman.[16] No such interview ensued. Taylor was on his deathbed and died two weeks later. It was determined that a statement from his counselors would not carry the same weight as commentary from the Church president, but the nation's curiosity about the absence of public statements from the Church leadership may have been temporarily alleviated by notice of Taylor's death. All the while, the Church hierarchy was becoming increasingly disenchanted with Young's failure to produce results or account for the considerable volume of Church funds that had been sent to him. George Q. Cannon, who had been a newspaper publisher himself, thought it was apparent Young's efforts with the eastern press were not yielding results commensurate with the effort and cost invested in it. Of several articles appearing in six New York newspapers that covered Utah's constitutional convention, only two of the articles were somewhat positive, and a dozen were generally hostile. The *New York Times* raised questions again in July about the deafening silence from the Church, following the *Salt Lake Tribune*'s presumption that the Church had not changed its mind about polygamy.[17]

15. *New* York *Evening Post*, July 6, 1887, tellingly noticed that without mention of cohabitation, polygamists would need to keep their marriages secret for only three years until the statute of limitations took effect.

16. Young to Taylor and Cannon, July 15, 1887, Taylor Correspondence.

17. See, e.g., *New York Herald*, Mar. 22, 1887; *New York Sun*, Aug. 30, 1887; *New York Times*, July 3, 6, 7, 9, 25, 1887; *New York Tribune*, July 11, 1887; *New York World*, July 7, 1887.

By the crucial early summer of 1887, the two Democrats on the US-appointed Utah Commission had already demonstrated marked fairness and helpfulness to LDS people who wanted to assert their rights as full-fledged citizens of the United States. Ambrose B. Carlton of Indiana had recently conferred with US Attorney General Augustus H. Garland, presumably about how to interpret the Edmunds–Tucker Act.[18] In late June the other Democratic commissioner, John McClernand, corresponded with President Grover Cleveland about "the work of reform in this territory." He reported that "the tenacity with which the institution and practice of polygamy was cherished has correspondingly relaxed." His main point, which was most perceptive, was that the constitutional provision against polygamy might not immediately eradicate allegiance to the practice, but "the more often the Mormons commit themselves, whether regularly or irregularly, against polygamy, the more they will have increased the obstacles to a retreat from the path of reform." This astute understanding of the situation accurately predicted the future.[19]

In mid-July McClernand wrote to Senator Shelby M. Cullom, who like McClernand was from Illinois, to explain that the Edmunds–Tucker Act had proven disappointing to the clique of territorial politicians who had become accustomed to federal patronage. The so-called carpetbaggers had become "unsparing in their censure" of congressional leaders for the leniency they had exhibited in their recent reforms. McClernand observed that monogamous Mormons had been persuaded to accept and comply with the test oath required of prospective voters. He enclosed copies of instructions the commission had sent to election precinct judges directing them to facilitate the broadest possible extension of the elective franchise. They wanted "a full vote" of qualified voters in the election later that month. He predicted that if fairly enforced, the law would "conquer polygamy" in the territory.[20]

In a prompt reply, Cullom expressed thanks for the thorough

18. Young to Jack, June 15, 21, 1887, Jack Papers.

19. John M. McClernand to Grover Cleveland, June 30, July 5, 9, 1887; McClernand and A. B. Carlton to Grover Cleveland, July 12, 1887, Grover Cleveland Papers.

20. McClernand to Shelby M. Cullom, July 18, 1887, John A. McClernand Papers.

survey of the Utah situation and agreed that it was right to adhere closely to the law. Without citing Judge McKean explicitly, he mentioned the overzealousness that had been struck down by the US Supreme Court. Cullom was nevertheless unpersuaded that Mormons would abandon polygamy. Less than three years later, he would champion another bill that, if passed, would have forced the LDS Church to cease open operations altogether, backed by decisions of the Supreme Court.[21] The gulf between moderate non-LDS and anti-LDS factions was becoming more pronounced, and McClernand had come to agree that the anti-Mormons in Utah aimed to dominate the region for their own political and economic purposes. Carlton and McClernand encouraged non-polygamist LDS people to become more involved and more independent of the conservative Church hierarchy in order to join the mainstream of American voters, perhaps to break the territory's reliance on bloc voting. Within several years the moderate Republican "half breeds," as that faction of the party opposed to the more blatant types of patronage and corruption were called, would become considerably more supportive of the monogamous part of the LDS population.

In August 1887 Carlton and McClernand asked former Iowa congressman Hadley D. Johnson, who had long resided in Salt Lake City, his impression of the situation. Johnson had been around Church members in Iowa and Utah for over thirty years. He told the commissioners he knew some Latter-day Saints were "sincerely desirous that the system of polygamy shall be eliminated from the practices of the Mormon church." In his opinion it would be impossible to see it "entirely suppressed," but it was a distinct possibility that it would "become so unpopular that the younger members of the Church will repudiate the system and refuse to engage in its practice." He predicted that it would die a natural death, and the government should continue its "effort to enforce existing laws," assuring changes for the better.[22]

21. Shelby M. Cullom to John A. McClernand, July 29, 1887, McClernand Papers. See also chapter 8 herein regarding the Cullom–Struble Bill and *Davis v. Beason* court decision.

22. Johnson to Carlton and McClernand, Sept. 1, 1887, McClernand Papers.

In September a counselor in the Presiding Bishopric and chairman of the People's Party, John R. Winder, encountered some members of the Utah Commission at a local mountain resort. In interacting with General McClernand, he found that the old Civil War veteran was "friendly disposed to the people of Utah" and was "desirous that the forthcoming report of the Utah Commission should be as fair as possible." The First Presidency passed this along to John W. Young in the east, urging that "proper steps should be taken to influence Judge Carlton" in the same direction. Carlton, also of the Utah Commission, told Young he was desirous of a face-to-face interview with Grover Cleveland to "fully advise the president of the condition of affairs" in the territory.[23] The "statehood committee" directed Young to escort former senator Joseph McDonald, often engaged as a lobbyist for LDS interests (also of Indiana), from the East Coast to "meet Carlton of Utah Commission on or before [September] 26 at St. Louis to influence favorable report," suggesting that "the result might be of sufficient importance to repay the trouble and expense." Young could soon confirm there would be a "good report."[24]

McClernand had already finished a minority report suggesting that the constitutional convention had been important in "manifesting in a most solemn manner a disposition on the part of the Mormons in Utah to recede from polygamous practices."[25] When the reports were filed later that autumn, they provided clear evidence of a dramatic split along party lines on the commission. The Republicans continued to display a negative view of circumstances and wanted a theological retraction before they would believe Church leaders were sincere in retreating from polygamy. There needed to be stricter restrictions and more stringent law enforcement, they believed. By contrast, Carlton's and McClernand's minority report

23. Young to Woodruff, Cannon, and Smith, Sept. 17, 1887, Woodruff Letterbooks; Carlton to Young, Aug. 27, John W. Young Papers; McClernand to Cleveland, June 30, 1887.

24. Woodruff et al., to Young, Sept. 17, 1887, Woodruff Letterbooks; Jack to Young, Young to Jack, Sept. 17, 1887, Jack Papers; Caine to Woodruff et al., Dec. 3, 1890, Woodruff General Correspondence; Abraham H. Cannon journal, July 31, 1887. It is probable Carlton did not then confer with Cleveland.

25. Longhand draft of McClernand dissent to majority report in McClernand Papers.

demonstrated no animus or dire predictions. The Democrats found the laws sufficient and the constitution, ratified by at least three-fourths of Latter-day Saint voters, a testimony to change. "We believe the great mass of the Mormon people are determined to go on with the reform," the two commissioners wrote, "and that they will accomplish the work." There would be residual fanaticism, they conceded, but young people ("young Utah") were eager to move forward "regenerated, and disenthralled from the heavy burden that has so long rested upon the people." Carlton and McClernand thought the people were redeemable. Charles Penrose suggested that the Church reprint the upbeat minority report and have it "sent to all prominent men in politics,"[26] which was done— at least to the known friendly members of Congress. Church lobbyists distributed it more generally as well.

Knowing they needed to overcome the devastatingly negative press reports from opponents of the Church, some of the highest LDS authorities became aware of a complex and secret public relations network they decided to avail themselves of. Carefully considering the situation, the statehood committee was encouraged to learn they could tap into the same Associated Press newspaper network that had so long shaped public opinion against them. They decided it would be foolish not to, despite the enormous expense involved in persuading newspapers to publish favorable news reports, the risk of exposure, and some ethical considerations.

It came about partly because of two California businessmen with family ties to Latter-day Saints. One of the two was Alexander Badlam Jr., whose father had been a member of the powerful Nauvoo, Illinois, Council of Fifty, a Church-organized group. Alex headed an insurance company in the San Francisco Bay Area. The other individual was Isaac Trumbo, a colonel in the state national guard and biscuit manufacturer who had investments in mining property. His grandfather John Reese founded the LDS settlement

26. Grow, "Study of the Utah Commission," 100–02; Penrose to Woodruff et al., Oct. 11, 1887, First Presidency Papers; "Report of the Utah Commission," *Executive Documents of the House of Representatives*, 1887–88, 10:1317–43; *Minority Report of Utah Commission*, 1887.

of Mormon Station in Carson Valley, Nevada. His mother was a cousin of Salt Lake City Bishop Hiram B. Clawson, who made contact with them through an influential California company he employed to help resolve a problem with a lucrative silver mine in Eureka, Utah, the Bullion Beck Mine. The mine had become engaged in a conflict with the neighboring Eureka Hill Mine, and the dispute threatened the interests of stockholders such as John Taylor and George Q. Cannon.[27]

Writing to John W. Young on May 9, 1887, Clawson indicated that his associates had powerful financial reasons, along with their personal friendship, for seeing Utah receive just treatment from the federal government. They were anxious to see the railroad receive the same, so they were interested in who might soon be appointed to the territorial supreme court. The Californians preferred Harvey D. Talcott, originally from New York, who they said would be a fair judge. The Californians offered to influence the news coverage of issues related to Utah in the *Salt Lake Tribune* and *San Francisco Chronicle*, and to a limited degree elsewhere, a possibility that was too much to ignore. This initial contact with Badlam and Trumbo would quickly develop into a complex undertaking of remarkable proportions in 1888. As usual, John W. Young was incredulous when told that his lobbying effort could be improved on.[28]

Clawson received a follow-up letter, apparently from Badlam, mentioning a previous success in keeping newspapers quiet about an unrelated matter. In a statement that was extracted and quoted in subsequent letters between Mormon leaders, he proposed that "securing the papers" should be the "keynote" in a serious publicity campaign. That was the "advice from men who have had the experience" to know, the correspondent wrote. The men who had the experience to know were officials with the Central and Southern Pacific Railroads, one of them later specifically identified as

27. *Salt Lake Herald*, May 24, 1887, Mar. 19, 1890; *San Francisco Chronicle*, May 4, 1887; Lyman, "Isaac Trumbo," 129–34; Lyman, *Candid Insights*, 56, 59–60, 81–82.

28. Young to Taylor and Cannon, May 12, 1887, Taylor Correspondence; Young to Jack, July 22, 1887, James Jack Papers. President Cleveland knew Talcott and rejected his application.

Senator Leland Stanford, one of the railroad founders and directors.[29] Enclosed in the letter was a set of handwritten notes headed "memorandum–proposition–etc.," dated July 16, 1887, regarding a potential alignment with railroad lobbyists. The memorandum cautioned that if the Church entered into the agreement, it would need to have realistic expectations. If it thought its position was strong enough to merit help, and that given the neutralization of some of the opposition it had the chance of success, then it should commit funds to accomplishing that goal. If it appeared to be an insurmountable expectation, then the Church should not waste the money necessary to become associated with the railroad syndicate. If the Church decided to proceed, it would need to commit the means outlined in the cover letter. With that, the lobbyists would begin "securing" newspapers connected with the Associated Press.

The notes implied that there was an existing special arrangement with the AP network, representing 307 small daily newspapers, and the National Associated Press, serving twenty-six of the nation's largest papers. It was recommended that if the proposals were carried out, an effort should be authorized to establish a closer relationship with several of the country's principal newspapers: the *Chicago Times, New York Evening Post, New York Times, Philadelphia Times, San Francisco Alta California, San Francisco Chronicle, St. Louis Globe–Democrat,* and "three southern papers." The agents of the "R–Co [Railroad Company] will try and arrange the terms with the papers satisfactorily, also with the Associated Press." Church leaders would need to adhere to "utmost secrecy." In fact, the lobbyists would not let the newspapers know the LDS Church was even connected to the lobby. If it became known, the newspapers would back out or try to obtain separate payment from the Church, amounting

29. [Badlam] to Hiram B. Clawson, July 21, 1887, rough notes of document in First Presidency Political and Contractual Papers, also available in the Edward L. Lyman Papers and Scott G. Kenney Collection. Most of the First Presidency and James Jack material will be cited in the Lyman Papers because it is often restricted at the Church History Library.

to double billing. "S— [Stanford] and party do not want to have to pay them over again."[30]

There were several reasons, according to the memorandum, why officials of Southern Pacific would be interested in a closer relationship with the LDS hierarchy. When Utah became a state, they would acquire the assistance of a "senator not averse to their [railroad's] interests." In the state itself, it would be useful to see judges in office who were "favorable to them," and other sympathetic politicians "where their interests were concerned." Clawson submitted the proposal to the acting First Presidency, and on July 27, 1887, two days after Taylor's death, George Q. Cannon and Joseph F. Smith wrote a letter of introduction for Clawson to act as their representative in negotiations with the railroad lobby. The letter attested to Clawson's discretion and tact.[31] With that, Clawson traveled to San Francisco and met with Stanford and other "principals whose names have been mentioned" to get "a full understanding of the propositions which they make."

In their correspondence with Clawson, Cannon and Smith asked him to determine precisely the "character of the work which they propose to do and the nature of our obligations that they expect us to assume." There was concern about the suggestion that sitting judges would be influenced, but they could see no objection to helping install men who would help the railroad, "as friends should" do. The apostles wanted to know up front the cost of the lobbying so that there would be no grounds for misunderstanding later on. In the papers of the First Presidency are two telegrams Clawson sent from San Francisco in early August 1887. The first reported that Senator Stanford would lend the aid of lobbyists "if press can be secured to help. Thinks that absolutely necessary." The second said, "Answer from East has come. The newspapers we want both East and here will work for us, if the price each names is satisfactory. Everything else alright."[32]

30. Handwritten notes, "memorandum–proposition, etc., July 16, 1887, Lyman Papers, written by Clawson in conversation with Leland Stanford in California.

31. Cannon and Smith to Stanford, July 27, 1887, notes in Lyman Papers.

32. Cannon and Smith to Clawson, July 27, 1887; Clawson to Jack, Aug. 4, 7, 1887, Jack Papers.

Clawson made notes elaborating that the objective would be "fair and reasonable protection." A list of newspapers previously named gave amounts ranging from $500 to $20,000 for each paper's services. The total cost was estimated to be about $140,000.[33] Clawson wrote that Church agents had previously (through J. W. Young) been ineffective, spending too much money for too few results. He had been told that if politicians thought they could "get any amount of money" out of the Church, they would keep up the "pressure" for the Church to do so. It would only get worse as the territory got nearer to statehood. If the Church were "drained" of resources, Stanford had offered, he would contribute funds himself because of their mutual interest. Church leaders expressed appreciation for what they detected to be a lack of pecuniary interest. They were assured by Badlam and Trumbo that the amount of money requested by the newspapers was moderate compared to what they had seen in the past. When the newspapers were told the client was a Church "fighting for existence with comparatively a very small amount of means," they waived their usual higher corporate fees.[34]

Within a week of Clawson's return from San Francisco in early August, the Church sent Charles W. Penrose, who was still editor of the *Deseret News*, to New York, with instructions for Young to give him free access to the newspapermen there. Penrose was told to write copy for dispatches and determine how close Young's relationship actually was with the city newspapers. Penrose quickly ascertained that there was not much of a connection there, but he did confirm that the rapport Young had claimed to have with the Cleveland administration was genuine.[35] As Penrose settled into New York, Clawson returned for a second visit to San Francisco. On August 23 he was told by the statehood committee that since Young was not in a position to effectively influence the New York

33. Clawson's penciled notes, Aug. 4, 7, 1887, copy in Lyman Papers. Grant, *Diaries*, June 20, 1887, mentions a million dollars, and in August John Henry Smith (White, ed., *Church, State, and Politics*, 176–77) cites a half million. The Church appropriated $100,000.

34. Clawson to Jack, Aug. 4, 7, 1887.

35. Woodruff et al. to Young, Aug. 16, 17, 1887; C. Williams to Jack, Aug. 22, 1887, First Presidency Collection; Williams to Woodruff et al., Aug. 24, 27, 1887, Woodruff General Correspondence.

City press, Clawson should go ahead and agree to the best terms possible with the railroad lobby. A coded reply from California indicated that the arrangement with the Stanford group had been finalized by payment in cash.[36] And so began an unlikely alliance between the elaborate railroad lobby and the LDS Church to convince the American people that Mormons were not as licentious or politically rebellious as had been so widely alleged. The arrangement smacked of bribery, yet it was during the Gilded Age when such arrangements were sufficiently common that they were rarely noticed, and likely necessary. Historians have not infrequently discussed the prevalence of payments at the time from the "third house" of Congress, meaning the lobbyists, to "the fourth estate," the press. A letter from railroad tycoon Collis P. Huntington asked a colleague to "get some well written articles published in the S[an] F[rancisco] papers showing up the great value of the [Southern Pacific Railroad]," and to get them republished in eastern newspapers. It was a rather common practice at the time to offer payment for reprints of articles to other newspapers rather than more expensive advertising. To modern ears it may appear questionable, but it was considered an essential business practice during the era of excess.[37]

Not every paper had to be paid. If a story ran in a major publication, because of the common exchange practice, it was often borrowed by smaller papers and printed word for word, so that one can often find the same item reprinted from coast to coast in numerous newspapers. In 1887 particularly, the Central–Southern Pacific Railroad needed to counter customer complaints about unfair freight rates and political manipulation, culminating in passage of the Interstate Commerce Act of 1887. Of even greater concern to the "big four" railroad heads was a special investigation by the Pacific Railway Commission that threatened to generate considerable unfavorable public sentiment.

36. Jack to Clawson, Aug. 22, 27, 1887, Jack Papers. Grant, *Diaries*, Aug. 12, 13, 1887, noted that a total up-front installment of $74,000 had been made, with another $70,000 contingent on actual statehood.

37. Farnham, "Weakened Spring," 662–69; Thompson, *Spider Web*, 1–4, 24–25, 49–50, 65–66, 90, 139–42, 162–63, 213–14; *Chicago Tribune*, Dec. 27, 1883.

Badlam and Trumbo had been working part-time with the railroad lobby before they became involved with the LDS Church's campaign. A letter from Badlam to Wilford Woodruff contained revealing bits of information. Badlam confided that they had "a great and powerful combination" they could draw on for the Church's benefit. The Stanford group claimed to have "friends in the various rings and syndicates which almost sway the councils of the nation [in] ... all of the states and are a small army."[38] When Church leaders wondered if anyone was overseeing their interests in Washington from day to day, Trumbo reassured them. "You need not worry about a single thing as they have, all told, over thirty people to watch their interests, which yours are tied to in every instance and they do it grand." In the same communication, Trumbo divulged that others with interests in the syndicate, besides Huntington and Stanford, were Jay Gould and John D. Rockefeller, adding that together "they are making an enormous pull" in opposing legislation inimical to the interests of their companies.

One of the primary undertakings of the lobby was to nullify the negative influence of the *Salt Lake Tribune*. On December 19 Trumbo sent Clawson a proposal to establish another non-LDS newspaper in Salt Lake City that would have to "appear [to be] strictly a Gentile" paper. In contrast to the *Tribune*, it would favor statehood. It "could be so managed as to become the accepted authority" on Utah affairs at Washington and "paralyze" the *Tribune's* influence. Badlam considered this to be a helpful but not essential innovation. To him it was more important, as he advised Church leaders, that the *Deseret News* and *Salt Lake Herald* stop responding to the *Salt Lake Tribune*. Neither newspaper should mention Utah statehood at all, he advised. Accordingly, the statehood committee told Penrose they had agreed to cooperate with this proposal and privately met with some of the key editorial writers at both papers. Badlam thought the further step of employing a censor was needed—someone who would scrutinize the daily coverage so that every item was precisely what was wanted. "Allow the

38. Maude to Lewis, Nov. 15, 1887; Lewis to Maude, Nov. 28, 1887, Lyman Papers.

name of the *Tribune* never to appear in either of your papers," he insisted. "Don't allow one word to be said in either of your papers in favor of statehood." There should be "no advocates from that quarter" because they do not control votes in Congress, and "every word to be said in either [the *Salt Lake*] *Herald* or [*Deseret*] *News* is an absolute injury." Again, Church leaders heeded this advice until at a later time when just such a crisis virtually dismantled the entire operation. Coincidentally, three years later another newspaper emerged, the *Salt Lake Times*, which functioned mainly in the manner previously suggested.[39]

By October, Charles Goodwin of the *Salt Lake Tribune* had recognized the change in strategy at the rival newspapers and concluded it was time to "sound the alarm that in the movement for statehood for Utah there lies a mighty menace to the future peace of the republic." It was a widespread conspiracy, he wrote, no doubt hatched in Washington. The only way to quash it would be if "the press and pulpit of the country stamp it out."[40] This was a good example of the Goodwin strategy that had been so successful in the past: sound the alarm and conceal the fact that the plot was based mostly on conjecture. On the LDS side, Church leaders and their associates were looking at circulation numbers and costs for various national newspapers to print positive information or remain silent.[41] Clawson referred to two AP organizations and provided the number of small and large daily papers involved with each wire service, along with the regular and discounted costs for positive coverage. When the Church secured the Associated Press's services, it would mainly bypass William Nelson, the AP agent in Salt Lake City, they were told. The lobby recommended that an outside correspondent be engaged for a Utah locale "on the ground," who could write "one or more letters per week to each of the papers secured and also attend to the dispatches."

39. Dellie [Isaac Trumbo] to Lulu [Hiram B. Clawson], Aug. 8, Dec. 19, 1887; Maude to Lewis, Nov. 15, 1887; Clawson–Badlam Notes, Aug. 4, 7, 1887, Lyman Papers.

40. *Salt Lake Tribune*, Oct. 22, 1887.

41. In Clawson's notes of July and August, he listed totals of $74,000 and $70,000 to be paid to eleven newspapers in Chicago, New York City, Philadelphia, San Francisco, and St. Louis.

The best way to examine the effectiveness of this type of campaign is to consider the coverage in two Midwestern newspapers known to have received $8,000 each from the Church, the *Chicago Times* and *St. Louis Globe–Democrat*, before and after being subsidized. In January and February 1887, both papers printed news dispatches, probably from the Associated Press, expressing a negative view of the LDS Church and polygamy. On the day after the Edmunds–Tucker bill passed, both published reports that ran two columns each detailing and praising the law. The next day the *Chicago Times* printed an interview with Governor Caleb West lauding the Edmunds–Tucker Act. The *Globe-Democrat,* a Republican paper, devoted a full-column editorial in praise of the Edmunds-Tucker Act and characterized it as the death knell for the Mormon problem. They interviewed Charles Goodwin, who denounced President Cleveland's lack of courage in signing the bill, having let it pass without his signature. In July each newspaper again published negative dispatches about Utah's statehood effort, with editorials closely resembling those in the *Salt Lake Tribune*. Both papers continued to run such headlines as "The Crafty Mormons" through July and into early August.[42] Then the railroad lobby's influence kicked in.

In August a reporter for the *St. Louis Globe–Democrat*, J. J. Jennings, visited Salt Lake City and had a pleasant conversation with apostle Franklin D. Richards. The interview was reported in the newspaper on August 9. Five days later the *Globe–Democrat* described a worship service in the Tabernacle, with comments about the intelligence, neatness, happiness, and health of the worshipers. The reporter noticed that polygamy was not mentioned in the day's preaching.[43] Similar news items appeared during the remainder of the month under the byline "J. J. J." One article based on interviews with LDS women explained what it was like to share one's husband with other wives, emphasizing the extra dedication and mutual love necessary in these unions. An article considering the viewpoint of

42. *Chicago Times*, Jan. 13, 14, July 3, 8, 13, 19, 21, Aug. 6, 1887; *St. Louis Globe–Democrat*, Jan. 13, 22, 23, 30, Feb. 2, 29, Mar. 6, 8, July 6–11, 22, 23, 1887.

43. Franklin D. Richards journal, Aug. 9, 1887; *St. Louis Globe–Democrat,* Aug. 14, 1887.

younger LDS women who had rejected polygamy concluded that it was possible to be a Church member in good standing without becoming a plural wife.[44] After September 10, the reporting from J. J. J. ceased. It may be, however, that Jennings remained in Salt Lake City to send unsigned correspondence to the syndicated papers.

As for the *Chicago Times*, on October 1, 1887, it made reference to its previous editorials questioning the sincerity of the LDS statehood effort, concluding that the Saints had since changed, to the extent that they had complied with the requirements of the law, as demanded by the American people. On the last day of the month, the paper drew from an interview with an unnamed apostle (possibly Richards) conceding that Utahns needed to show "something more substantial than words" in professing loyalty to the country, a quotation that faithfully expressed the theme the lobby advisors had advocated. The same apostle reportedly predicted that while the practice of polygamy would be discontinued, belief in the principle would continue. It was nevertheless "the first time" a "high churchman" had said that polygamy would cease or had mentioned "the necessity for a law against plural marriage."[45]

Meantime, President Woodruff had been advised that it was sometimes good to throw an opponent off track. One way was, "when you desire to accomplish a particular object, to treat it in the least important manner possible." If Utahns gave the appearance of having capitulated, it might give anti-Mormons a rhetorical victory and the Church a victory in fact. In the *Chicago Times* and other papers, the idea that Utah had gotten over its former trauma and moved on to a more positive outlook was repeatedly expressed.[46]

Penrose continued to labor in the center of the nation's journalism industry, New York City, while Badlam worked behind the scenes in Washington. There is no indication that Penrose coordinated his efforts with the railroad lobby, and the fact that he kept

44. *St. Louis Globe–Democrat*, Aug. 17, 20, 1887.

45. *Chicago Times*, Oct. 1, 31, 1887.

46. Maude to Lewis, Nov. 15, 1887, First Presidency Papers; *Chicago Times*, Dec. 2, 22, 25, 1887; *Louisville Courier–Journal*, Jan. 13, 14, Nov. 18, Dec. 23, 1887.

his knowledge of the lobby's work to himself allows some comparisons. On August 27, 1887, he assessed the coverage in several New York newspapers. The *New York Star* was "alright," the *New York Sun* "favorable," and the *New York Herald* willing to publish an interview Penrose arranged with Curtis Bean, Arizona's former delegate to Congress. Penrose learned that the *New York Herald's* influence "could be had" for somewhere between $25,000 and $50,000. Regarding the *New York Times,* he wrote that "it is understood here that the *Times* cannot be engaged for any amount of money." John W. Young had met with a news editor several times and thought he had found someone who would be sympathetic, but Penrose found this appraisal to be overly optimistic. In October he concluded that "the *New York Times* had remained totally adverse to our cause."[47]

Penrose experienced barricades at every turn in his effort to present the Utah viewpoint to city newspapers. At the *New York Tribune,* he arranged an interview with George Ticknor Curtis, but the paper incorporated only a small amount of the information gleaned from the interview into an editorial, without running a separate feature article. Penrose replied to negative articles in the *New York Tribune* and *New York World,* but found "they don't want anything on our side of the Utah question." Such were his "feeble" attempts to bring "influence ... to bear in our favor."[48]

But the tide was turning, even in New York. A month later he found that "public sentiment seems to have modified considerably and less bitterness appeared in the press references to Utah," no doubt because of the influence of the railroad lobby. In December he struck up an acquaintance with a Colonel Handy, sometimes managing editor of the *New York World.* Handy told him he had approached his publisher, Joseph Pulitzer, about sending a man, possibly himself, to Utah to "write up" the statehood and Mormon questions. It is likely that Handy was unable to get approval for this

47. C. Williams to Woodruff et al., Aug. 24, 27, 1887, First Presidency Collection; Clawson to Jack, Aug. 4, 1887, Jack Papers.

48. Williams to Woodruff et al., Oct. 11, 17, 26, 1887.

assignment from Pulitzer, founder of the "yellow press," who was more interested in scurrilous reports than positive news.[49]

Looking at the leading New York newspapers for November and December, we can see some of the same turn-about that was evident in the midwestern newspapers in August and September. Whether the *New York World* was retained or not, we know it was approached. The *New York Evening Post* was on the original list of papers deemed essential to engage. The *Post's* two-column December 4 article from Salt Lake City shows an abrupt about-face, compared with an editorial of July 6. The *New York Herald*, not on Clawson's list, ran articles in November and December that reflected Badlam's talking points. The *New York Sun* had not been unfriendly toward Utah, but may have been subsidized nevertheless. The *New York Times* remained consistently opposed to the statehood movement. At year's end the *New York Tribune* showed itself to be somewhat resistant to influence, publishing another negative editorial on the subject, but thereafter running nothing about Utah or the Mormons for a year.[50] From any perspective, this amount of coverage in the news capital of America, especially considering how distant and relatively insignificant Utah was, is amazing.

Trumbo wrote, as 1887 came to a close, that "everything looks much better than we ever anticipated at this time of the game." On January 7, 1888, he sent an issue of *Public Opinion,* a journal with excerpts from the nation's press, to show how well his "friends [in the news media] stood up" for Utah. It was true that there was positive coverage for a change, and where negative comments were made they were "not very strong and not very lengthy," in his opinion. The lobbyists considered it a "splendid showing." It is hard to know how he scored the results, since the *Public Opinion* excerpts mentioning Mormons seemingly ranged from predominantly negative to indifferent

49. Williams to Woodruff et al., Dec. 10, 1887; also Juergens, *Joseph Pulitzer*, 351–89.

50. *New York Evening Post*, Dec. 4, 13, 1887; *New York Herald*, Nov. 6, Dec. 4, 21, 1887; *New York Sun*, Nov. 17, 1887; *New York Times*, Nov. 7, 8, Dec. 7, 21, 23, 1887; *New York Tribune*, Nov. 15, Dec. 27, 1887; Weinheimer, comp., *New York Daily Tribune: Index, 1881–90*.

on statehood.[51] But it was true that the tide was turning, if not all at once. However, if the coverage could be considered predominantly positive, there was not yet a discernable change in Congress.

The lobby suggested that what was needed was to further expand the number of newspapers it was subsidizing. Badlam informed Clawson in March 1888 that he was leaving Washington for Boston, by way of New York City, and would visit "four or five other New York and New England cities to see some other newspaper men and pacify them." It was easier, he found, than working with the pillars of news publishing in Manhattan. Midway into the trip, he reported that "the puritanical and sectarian press here have been looked after and their material interest consulted in so handsome and economical a manner that you must pardon me for reference again to it. I have got to put up some more this week, but it will be well spent and in most cases final." The only problem with midsized newspapers was that there "are so many of them and so many different circumstances and men to consult that my head just spins." Yet he believed the effort would bear good fruit, so that "when a certain question comes up properly before Congress I am satisfied it will have strong support, where formerly enmity existed."[52]

One of Trumbo's letters advised the Church to "hurry and make stronger connections with all merchants possible." In January 1888 the First Presidency sent Robert Watson, superintendent of the Church-owned ZCMI department store, to visit company suppliers in the East, asking them to "use their influence with their representatives in Congress in favor of the state movement." In a follow-up letter, the First Presidency summarized its goal and Watson's role in it: "We feel it to be our duty, at this time particularly to do all in our power to disabuse the public men from the prejudices which they have imbibed concerning us. The lies which are so commonly told about us are repeated so often that many people who have no opportunity of hearing the other side, never appear to think for a moment

51. Dellie to Lulu, Jan. 7, 1888, First Presidency Collection, notes in Lyman Papers; presumably *Public Opinion*, Dec. 31, 1887.

52. Alex [Badlam] to Hiram [Clawson], Mar. 5, 1888; Trumbo to Clawson, Mar. 13, 1888, First Presidency Collection, notes in Lyman Papers.

that there can be any other side to our question, and that we are all that we are reported to be."[53] Watson's visits should "awaken the feeling within them that we are not such odious people as we are represented to be," the Church presidency concluded.[54]

In mid-January the First Presidency effused to Caine that "there is such a difference between the spirit which now prevails and that which formerly had sway that we feel great relief."[55] In late February Woodruff and Cannon expressed their opinion to Joseph F. Smith, still supervising Church lobbyists with Congress, that "it has been a great labor to keep the papers in line, and taking everything into consideration, we think the success has been very remarkable. To keep the papers quiet upon a subject of such interest is a wonderful performance in the excited state of feeling which prevailed in the public mind a short time ago." They continued to credit the railroad lobbyists for this success: "We think our friends have had a great labor to perform in accomplishing this, and that they have been so successful is very creditable to their efforts and an evidence to us that the Lord has favored us."[56]

Some of the era's most negative news reports had stemmed from LDS missionaries proselytizing in the southern states. The antagonism reached a peak in 1884 when a handful of missionaries and adherents were killed by an anti-Mormon mob in Tennessee. The LDS agents discovered that southern senators would support Utah's bid for statehood except for a constant stream of letters from constituents opposed to it. After considerable discussion, the acting Church presidency directed the president of the Southern States Mission to withdraw missionaries from districts where their presence could produce unfavorable publicity. Woodruff explained the retreat: "The present appears to be a time when it is wise for us to

53. Caleb [Trumbo] to Hiram [Clawson], Dec. 19, 1887, First Presidency Collection; Woodruff et al., to Robert S. Watson, Jan. 17, Feb. 4, 1888, Woodruff Letterbooks; cf. Woodruff to William Spry, June 15, 1888, Woodruff General Correspondence.

54. Woodruff et al. to Penrose, Dec. 20, 1887, First Presidency Papers; cf. Caine to Woodruff et al., Dec. 2, 1887, Caine Letters.

55. Woodruff et al. to Caine, Jan. 17, 1888, Caine Papers.

56. Woodruff and Cannon to Smith, Feb. 28, 1888, Woodruff Letterbooks.

pursue a conciliatory policy and to do everything in our power to allay prejudice and to quiet down hostility."[57]

In New York and Washington, the lobbyists were not only courting politicians, but also a surprising number of celebrities. Trumbo informed Clawson, "I'm getting acquainted with all of the great big men and some of them seem to be a grand lot. We had a big dinner with [former senator] [Roscoe] Conkling [of New York] and Senator [John P.] Jones of Nevada the day before yesterday." In addition, "yesterday afternoon we were at [writer] Bob [Robert G.] Ingersoll's house with Mark Twain, who is assisting Maude [Alexander Badlam] as regards some of the newspapers. He goes to Washington with us on Thursday and a jolly fellow he is too."

Trumbo thought the new US Attorney General Don M. Dickinson would "have to be looked after, as he is very bitter." President Cleveland had become so sympathetic that they decided to leave the task to himself "of softening [Dickinson] until someone else can reach him." A surprising target of influence was Susan B. Anthony. The lobbyists, and particularly Joseph F. Smith, contributed over $100 toward her expenses as she hosted the International Council of Women in Washington, DC. However, President Smith wanted it known that he and others had contributed "with the express understanding that the Church donors did not want to pay money to be misrepresented and maligned." He was concerned about a speech expected to be delivered by Ruth Woods, director of the Industrial Christian Home in Salt Lake City, a failed halfway house for runaway wives. Her speech was canceled, and the only mention of Latter-day Saints during the proceedings was from the leader of the Utah delegation, Emily S. Richards, wife of Church attorney Franklin S. Richards.[58]

Unquestionably the greatest challenge the lobbyists faced was convincing people that Utah Territory would leave polygamy behind. An examination of the engaged newspapers indicates that care

57. Woodruff and Cannon to Smith, Apr. 5, 1888; Woodruff to Spry, June 15, 1888; also Roberts, *Comprehensive History*, 5:558–67, 6:89–96.

58. Dellie to Lulu, Mar. 13, 1888, First Presidency Collection; Mack [Joseph F. Smith] to Woodruff and Cannon, Mar. 27, 30, Apr. 6, 1888, Woodruff General Correspondence; *New York Times*, Mar. 26–30, 1888.

was taken to emphasize that point. A dispatch from Utah published in November 1887 in the *Louisville Courier–Journal* gave the impression that the older men involved with polygamy had passed political dominance to the younger generation of monogamists. Since the old guard could "neither vote nor hold office," they were "naturally and necessarily forced into the background." Even if the bearded patriarchs tried to keep younger people in line, their "influence over their followers … [was] not strong enough to destroy the ambition of the younger element."[59]

Although this was as much wishful thinking as fact, at that point in time, but it was a reasonably good prediction of the future. For the moment, the apostles were still firmly in charge of everything ocurring in both church and state. The incidence of plural marriage had faded, but was hardly going away. As Wilford Woodruff and George Q. Cannon informed John T. Caine in February 1888, they had been persuaded by the lobbyists to make strategic concessions, but it was difficult "for a people like we are to condescend to ask for a measure of this character when every feeling of our hearts revolts at it." They recognized how necessary it was for attaining full admission into the United States. Still, "to the present we have not been able to bring our mind to that point," meaning the acceptance of a full abandonment of plural marriage.[60] While working behind the scenes to help disseminate positive information and assuring people that polygamy was on its way out, they had not yet accepted the inevitability of that development or relinquished control to the monogamists.

An episode from the spring of 1888 illustrates the problems with this double position. It also points to the lack of unanimity among members of the hierarchy regarding their message and confusion among the public over the conflicting official and private expressions of it. In early April at the Church's general conference, Wilford Woodruff was still on the underground, from where he issued the sixth of the presidency's "epistles" to the Saints. The lobbyists sent out dispatches noting the absence of any reference to polygamy in

59. Maude to Lewis, Nov. 15, 1887; *Louisville Courier–Journal*, Nov. 28, 1887.
60. Woodruff and Cannon to John T. Caine, Feb. 18, 1888, Caine Papers.

his comments. A telegraphed dispatch from Church headquarters to the *National Republican* emphasized that there had been a change in tone when compared to messages from his predecessor, the late president John Taylor. The communications from Taylor had been filled with references to wives and concubines from the Old Testament and apocalyptic revelations. Woodruff's messages were, by contrast, gentle admonitions that cited the New Testament. They were not dissimilar from what might be expected from a Protestant minister's sermon. A dispatch from Church headquarters to the *National Republican* emphasized that the LDS leader's silence about polygamy "may be counted [as a] healthful sign [for] Utah and her future." This "distasteful doctrine is not flaunted in face of public opinion," the news release read. Essentially the same story appeared in the *San Francisco Call.*[61]

Whatever good this public relations effort was supposed to accomplish, it was undermined at the same conference by the sermons of two young polygamists. On the first day of the meetings, Seymour B. Young of the First Council of Seventy alluded so obviously to celestial marriage that one of the lobbyists felt constrained to telegraph from Chicago to complain. On the second day, there was a speech by future apostle Rudger Clawson, the hero of the federal raids who had patiently suffered through the longest prison term yet levied against a Latter-day Saint and had been released only six months earlier.[62] He openly declared that he was going to live with his plural wife again and stated, "It is pleasing to God for men to go to prison under [an] unjust law rather than act contrary to their covenants," as quoted in the *Deseret News*.[63]

The *Salt Lake Tribune* disseminated telegraphic reports of Clawson's speech. The *New York Times* featured it in a front-page article stating that Mormons were digging in their heels and would not

61. Jack to *Washington, D. C. National Republican*, Apr. 7, 1888, Jack Papers; *National Republican*, Apr. 8, 1888; *San Francisco Call*, Apr. 13, 1888.

62. Woodruff and Cannon to F. S. Richards and Penrose, Apr. 11, 1888; Woodruff and Cannon to Penrose, Apr. 20, 1888, First Presidency Collection; Hoopes and Hoopes, *Making of a Mormon Apostle*, 130–31, 289.

63. *Deseret Weekly News*, Apr. 11, 1888.

"abandon their faith" in polygamy.[64] James Jack, the trusted clerk at Church headquarters while the presidency remained in exile, issued the following statement to the *National Republican*: "I understand young Clawson, just released from penitentiary, delivered an address in Tabernacle in which he used some expressions favoring polygamy. But his remarks were viewed with much disfavor by leading elders." A similar dispatch in the *San Francisco Call* declared that after Clawson's address, "deep indignation has been expressed by the public[,] and interviews with leading Mormons prove that the young man's reckless and unauthorized remarks are as deeply chagrined by them as others."

Joseph F. Smith communicated to Woodruff and Cannon in their place of hiding that the report of "remarks on polygamy at conference are reported in several New York papers in proof of the determination of the Church to continue and extend polygamy. Very damaging to our cause. We understood such remarks were discouraged." Woodruff replied that "no one could have been more surprised at these utterances than ourselves ... because it was understood that care would be exercised upon these points." Woodruff and Cannon explained that apostle Lorenzo Snow had been placed in charge of the session because he was a "prudent man" who understood the need to keep controversial subjects out of conference. Woodruff had told Snow "that if anyone attempted to speak about polygamy, to throw his hat at him." But Snow was far too politically naive to understand the extent of the problem.[65] He had also been a prison cellmate of Clawson, so he was disinclined to embarrass his friend by interrupting or contradicting him.

Woodruff and Cannon believed the storm would "blow over and the Lord will overrule all things for good." However, from the perspective of Badlam and Trumbo, the lobbyists had been placed in a position that put their credibility at risk. They commented that "their labors" had been, "to a great extent, nullified." To John

64. *Salt Lake Tribune*, Apr. 7, 8, 1888; *New York Times*, Apr. 7, 1888.

65. Mack to Woodruff and Cannon, Mar. 30, 1888; Mack to Jack, Apr. 10, 11, 1888; Woodruff and Cannon to Penrose and Richards, Apr. 11, 1888; Woodruff to Joseph F. Smith, Apr. 19, 1888, Woodruff General Correspondence.

T. Caine, they wrote that "it is easy to understand how annoyed President Cleveland must have been at hearing about it."[66] Joseph F. Smith sent Woodruff and Cannon clippings of the unfavorable newspaper articles. "It seems that a great change had taken place within a brief period," they acknowledged.

This episode would, in fact, end the complex, expensive, and secret effort that had been launched the previous August with the assistance of the railroad syndicate. Badlam, the key liaison with the Church, who had never fully trusted the more rigid members of the hierarchy, took the opportunity to permanently withdraw from the LDS cause. Fortunately the alteration in press treatment of Latter-day Saints had become sufficiently entrenched to remain pointed in the same direction from then until Utah's admission as a state, in contrast to the barrage of anti-Mormon coverage that preceded the lobbying effort. In the end it had all paid off.[67]

Delegate John T. Caine and Church attorney Franklin S. Richards obtained an audience with the nation's president and informed him that "the people of Utah" were "in harmony with the rest of the nation" except for "the only question of difference between them." The president answered that he did not know what "those fellows at the Capitol" would think if they heard them profess that. It was an expression of flagging confidence in Congress, more than a criticism of Utah. Caine and Richards were aware of how unpopular Utah was with the senators and congressmen. Even their earliest supporters, Senators Gorman and Brice, had retreated because the statehood topic had proved too toxic.[68]

President Cleveland had his own disagreements with Congress. He became so aloof after he was rebuffed over tariff reform, even in a day when presidents were expected to remain independent from

66. Woodruff and Cannon to Caine, May 9, 1888, Caine Papers.

67. Woodruff and Cannon to Smith, May 2, 1888; Young to Woodruff et al., Dec. [8], 1887, Woodruff Papers.

68. Franklin D. Richards journal, Dec. 20, 1887; Richards to Woodruff et al., Dec. 17, 1887, First Presidency Papers; Penrose and Richards to Woodruff and Smith, Dec. 7, 1888, Penrose Papers; Cannon to Woodruff, July 21, 1888, Woodruff Papers; also Lambert, *Arthur Pue Gorman*, 114–44.

the legislative branch he became particularly inaccessible.[69] In Utah Church leaders had followed the same path, entirely withdrawing from all aspects of public notice. The two poles of Church and political interests were no longer in total opposition, but neither expected to see progress on the statehood issue anytime soon. Cleveland would disappear during Benjamin Harrison's four-year term and then take the unprecedented step of running again, and serve another four years. By then the high Church officials would be in the company of a range of powerful, mainly Republican, political allies and closer yet to their fervently held goal, while still in need of significant change prior to that juncture.

In retrospect it is breathtaking to see the speed with which the professional lobbyists were able to change the nation's negative impressions of Latter-day Saints. One would think it would have taken years to see such a transformation in public opinion, and such dramatic change to bring it about that a public pronouncement alone would not be sufficient. There were other obstacles on which progress would hinge prior to Utah's statehood, namely regarding the actual situation with polygamy and longstanding dominance of the LDS hierarchy in political affairs. But to an extent that was likely unprecedented, by the time these issues had been mainly resolved there was no longer sufficient public opinion against the Mormon lifestyle to create a problem in allowing admission of the desert territory into the community of states.

69. Morgan, *From Hayes to McKinley*, 8, 56, 85, 146, 150, 271, 355, 527; Nevins, *Grover Cleveland*, 4–5.

7

HOPE, DISAPPOINTMENT, AND LOSSES

1889

As the push for statehood finally seemed within reach, Utahns shepherded their latest application through the labyrinthine legislative process, even though they knew Congress expected concessions Latter-day Saint authorities were still unwilling to offer. There had been hope of local accommodation between LDS and non-LDS factions, understanding that if statehood were to be granted they would need to be able to assure the national political advisors that the animosities between the groups had been ameliorated. Throughout most of the anti-polygamy raid, the two sides were so divided that people in Utah seldom crossed the lines of separation. Now there would be a few cautious attempts by those on the LDS side to break down the barriers, although without giving up political control; most citizens remained hesitant to fully cooperate. This remained particularly true regarding the requirement to forego plural marriage as an essential element in progressing toward statehood.

The 1887–88 Congress took more time than usual getting organized before taking up its regular business. Those friendly to the Church advised patience in trying to nurse the statehood application through the legislative process. But the Utah delegation that had come east to deliver the constitution and memorial wanted to finish that initial task and return home prior to the next national election when political control could likely change back to the more hostile Republican Party. So on December 17, 1887, John Caine introduced his associates to the president pro tempore of the Senate, John J. Ingalls, and Speaker of the House John G. Carlisle. LDS attorney Franklin S. Richards explained the provisions of the proposed state constitution. Ingalls, a Republican from Kansas, graciously accepted the documents and promised to have them presented to the Senate. In the House, Carlisle, a Democrat from Kentucky, said that because the current lower-house rules prevented him from presenting the proposal himself, he would be pleased to allow Caine to do this. Before the month was out, Caine did so in the House of Representatives, longtime friend of Utah Wilkinson Call of Florida performing the parallel function in the Senate.[1]

Senator Call proposed that the memorial be printed in the *Congressional Record.* Senator Algernon Paddock, a Republican from Nebraska and former member of the Utah Commission, raised an objection. The result was that the motion was tabled. When Call attempted to resurrect it, Paddock delivered a diatribe against the LDS Church. It was endorsed by the man for whom the Edmunds Act was named, Senator George F. Edmunds, who said that based on his experience the memorial from the Utah legislature no doubt would contain "something disrespectful to Congress." Nevada Senator William M. Stewart agreed. To counter their efforts, Call read the full text of the memorial from the floor, thereby accomplishing the same result of getting it included in the *Record* and demonstrating that there was nothing offensive in the document. He then withdrew his motion to print the petition for statehood.[2] This meant that from the start, the Latter-day Saint agents had already promptly failed to achieve a positive initial step necessary in getting the bill through the Senate. John W. Young had naively advised a quick introduction as the best approach to success.[3]

Undaunted, when Caine introduced a bill on January 10, 1888, in

1. John T. Caine to Wilford Woodruff et al., Dec. 31, 1887; Caine to Woodruff et al., Jan. 7–21, 1888, Woodruff General Correspondence. Ingalls had already backed away from any encouragement of statehood for Utah.

2. Whitney, *History of Utah*, 3:607–8.

3. *Congressional Record,* Dec. 19, 20, 1887; John W. Young to Woodruff et al., Nov. 29, 1887, Woodruff General Correspondence.

the friendlier House of Representatives, he proposed the admission of Utah based on the new constitution the people of the territory had recently ratified. The bill was read by title and referred to the House Committee on Territories for consideration. That evening, accompanied by Richards, Caine had a two-hour meeting with the chairman of the committee, William Springer. The Illinois Democrat had not read the proposed constitution, but listened patiently as the two men explained its main points and argued the essentials of Utah's case. The chairman promised a prompt hearing and support in pushing it through. However, from the negative reception in the Senate, he could not see that it looked promising. The Utah delegate mentioned other territories that were seeking statehood and asked if Utah could be added to those later in the year. It was doubtless clear to Caine that they would not otherwise be able to receive a fair hearing.[4]

Although Springer assured Caine and Richards that he would cooperate, they wondered if he was sincere. To find out, they asked a trusted Vermont newspaperman, A. W. Gibson, to interview Springer and ask what he thought of Utah's chances for statehood. In the interview Springer said he was sympathetic but doubted whether the Democrats could "carry Utah," meaning it would be impossible to overcome the Republican opposition, particularly in the Senate. Even if Utah were attached to an omnibus bill with the other territories, there would still be resistance, he added. He predicted that the people of Utah would have to wait a little longer to achieve their goal. This was interpreted by Caine as the true measure of the chairman's support, which was slight.[5]

One essential prerequisite for Utah, even for attracting Democratic congressmen to the statehood measure, was an amendment to the US Constitution outlawing plural marriage.[6] When Caine and Richards met with Springer previously, he had mentioned

4. Caine to Woodruff et al., Jan. 7–21, 1888, Woodruff Correspondence; Franklin S. Richards to Woodruff et al., Jan. 23, 1888; Charles W. Penrose to Woodruff and Smith, Dec. 19, 1888, First Presidency Collection; *Congressional Record,* Jan. 10, 1888; *House Miscellaneous Documents*, 50th Cong., 1st Sess., no. 104.

5. Caine to Woodruff et al., Feb. 4, 1888.

6. *Congressional Record.* SR 3, Dec. 12, 1887; H. Res. 45, Jan. 5, 1888.

that someone was considering taking this kind of action. The person doing so turned out to be Springer himself. He later said he was doing so to remove the primary objection to admitting Utah. It was widely suspected that once Utah had achieved statehood, the LDS population would reinstate plural marriage. In fact, that strategy had been discussed among some Utah advocates. Springer's amendment therefore called for federal enforcement if a state failed to compel compliance with the ban on men taking multiple wives. Springer had discussed his amendment with Speaker Carlisle and Chairman David B. Culberson of the House Judiciary Committee, and they had judged it superior to any other attempt to contain alternative marriage relationships. Some of the territory's best friends in the House agreed that this was also the best way to bring Utah Democrats into the union.[7] Caine and Richards were themselves fully cognizant of the need for concessions on marriage if they were going to obtain an enabling act, although understanding that the Church hierarchy remained adamantly opposed to any such action.

Church agent John W. Young tried to persuade the apostles to consider the question. Visiting the territory just before the US congressional session opened in December 1887, he met with the acting First Presidency to explain his views. The three men admitted that they had been unable to formulate answers for polygamists who asked what to say in court to satisfy both their fellow Mormons and members of Congress. Any such statements, the hierarchy asserted, came too close to renouncing the marriage principle. They were therefore disinclined to follow the advice of Washington as "saying too much."[8] Young had no choice but to accept those conclusions, although he again wrote to them in January that he was being "urged by our friends all the time to put ourselves into the shape that [is needed so] the party can handle us."[9]

7. Caine to Woodruff et al., Jan. 7–21, 1887; also Richards to Woodruff et al., Jan. 23, 1888, Woodruff General Correspondence.

8. Woodruff et al. to Young, Dec. 7, 1887, Woodruff Letterbooks.

9. Young to Woodruff et al., Jan. 18, 1888, Woodruff General Correspondence.

Instead, the Church presidency pulled back even further, informing their agents that they should not even back the enabling act because it would only invite the committee to insert wording into the proposed requirements specifying what was demanded regarding plural marriage. However, recent developments made it clear that Utah would not be admitted without an enabling act, in which such prerequisites would be outlined, including provisions that would be required to be inserted into the proposed constitution. By mid-January John T. Caine, who had distanced himself from Young's manner of lecturing the Church presidency, nevertheless considered it his duty to report that there was a "fixed determination among members of Congress to adopt a constitutional amendment upon the subject of polygamy." He understood, and so stated, that the amendment was getting the most support from those who were most sympathetic to Utah.[10]

At least some Democratic congressional leaders persisted in seeking an acceptable compromise. In early February 1888 the House Judiciary Committee chairman, David Culberson of Texas, reported a substitute to the Springer amendment that omitted mention of unlawful cohabitation. This was expected to be more acceptable to Latter-day Saints. Culberson cautioned Caine about speaking favorably of it. No one in the LDS camp should "give it even a seeming approval" lest it ignite the opposition. Caine acknowledged Culberson's intent to make the amendment "as harmless as he possibly could," but firmly stated being opposed to any such amendment, "no matter how modified." Without the support of the Utah delegation, this and other attempts by friendly legislators had little chance of success. The Utah lobby turned their attention away from statehood to simply blocking hostile legislation. Franklin S. Richards reported that Church agents could probably block most inimical legislation, except possibly "a constitutional amendment, which is much talked about," stating the only thing holding it up was that its advocates had disagreements among themselves. If they

10. Caine to Woodruff et al., Jan. 7–21, 27, 1888; Richards to Woodruff et al., Feb. 11, 1888.

overcame their differences, they might be able to pass it.[11] However, by May the Utah delegate, John Caine, could reassure everyone that the Church's new railroad lobbying associates had, in an unspecified manner, halted all progress on the amendment.[12]

On January 30, 1888, the Senate Committee on Territories considered the proposed Utah bill. Republican sub-committeemen William M. Stewart and Shelby M. Cullom presented a preliminary report that was laced with anti-Church statements, and the two denounced the recent statehood movement as fraud. The Democrats called for a delay until the bill's sponsors could have an opportunity to refute these charges. Granting the request, Orville H. Platt, a Republican from Connecticut and chair of the Senate Territories Committee, asked Caine if any of the Utah agents in Washington desired to speak before his committee.[13]

Caine worried about explaining the complicated position he would be expected to defend, especially since he had had little time to ascertain how the Church presidency wished such questions to be answered. He telegraphed an urgent request for clarification and mentioned his own unenviable position of having to satisfy doubting senators without conceding more than the Church authorities would approve. Replies from Utah were slow. The message received by James Jack in Salt Lake City had to be conveyed to several underground hideouts. When the Church leaders wrote their replies and returned them back to the office, secretary Jack had to prepare them in cipher code for the telegraphic transmission. The answers were similar to those offered in 1887 when the Scott Amendment was under consideration, that ultimately Caine and his assistants should make whatever assurances they deemed necessary. As previously, Caine was reminded that he represented monogamists. His role was to "preserve political as distinct from [religious] attitudes," the presidency had directed.[14]

11. Caine to Woodruff et al., Feb. 4, 1888; Richards to Woodruff et al., Jan. 23, 1888.

12. Woodruff and Cannon to Caine, May 9, 1888, Caine Papers.

13. Caine to Jack, Jan. 31, 1888; Richards and Caine to Jack, Feb. 2, 1888, James Jack Papers.

14. Jack to Caine and Richards, Feb. 2, 1888, Jack Papers; Richards to Woodruff et al., Feb. 11, 1888; also Woodruff and Cannon to Caine, Mar. 9, 1888.

The point the leaders intended to make was that they were not averse to non-polygamists complying with a law against polygamy, but that they themselves and their closest followers would not. If the restrictions were properly interpreted, those taking the "test oath" could vote, even if others conforming to the higher marriage practices remained outside the political process. This view might well accelerate Utah's progress toward statehood. The "statehood committee" (acting First Presidency) in urging Caine and Richards to represent the monogamous class of Utah citizens, conceded that polygamists had been disfranchised anyway and should not be their concern. With this direction in mind, Caine and Richards prepared to face the Senate committee, engaging two prominent capitol-area attorneys to assist them. One was Joseph E. McDonald, a former Democratic senator from Indiana who had represented the LDS Church in the past and was well versed on the statehood question. The other, Jeremiah M. Wilson, was a Republican attorney who, despite conscientious efforts at preparation, requested a postponement to give him time to consider any potential questions. He was granted a reprieve until February 18.[15]

During this period, about a year after launching their sixth statehood attempt, Elders Woodruff and Cannon confided most significantly that "we feel it to be our duty to do everything in our power, consistent with honor, and with the professions we make as Latter-day Saints, to bring about a better condition of feeling." They correctly worried that while they were in hiding, they had neglected their duties as pastors: "Everything that can be done should be done by us to bring about the necessary freedom, that we may be able to go out among the people and magnify our priesthood and callings."[16] They may have finally concluded that they should count the cost of plural marriage on the entire Church community, although they were not yet prepared to make significant compromise.

15. Caine to Woodruff et al., Feb. 11, Mar. 3, 1888.

16. Woodruff et al. to Caine, Jan. 17, 1888, Caine Papers. See also Alexander, *Things in Heaven and Earth*, 236, 250–51, 257–59. As elsewhere stated, this leaderless situation, over an extended period of time, had markedly enhanced the growing antipathy of the younger generation toward plural marriage, which they had seldom heard preached or explained as they approached adulthood.

On February 18 the Senate hearings commenced with Richards making the opening argument. According to Joseph F. Smith and Charles W. Penrose, who were present as observers, Richards's story of outrages performed by marshals under the guise of protecting the territory's law and order impressed some of the committeemen. The first opponent to speak was Idaho delegate Fred T. Dubois, followed by Robert N. Baskin of Utah, who gave the standard arguments about LDS insincerity in promising to follow the law. Smith and Penrose noticed that Baskin's lengthy verbal excursion bored his listeners so much, they finally cut him off and requested that his speech be printed rather than having to listen to the rest. Ostensibly for the purpose of granting the LDS-engaged attorney Jeremiah Wilson still more time to prepare final arguments, the hearing was again postponed, this time to early March.[17]

During that same spring of 1888, John W. Young had attempted another approach to persuading elected officials to support Utah. On February 13 he telegraphed Church headquarters that he needed $15,000 "for [Senators] [Shelby] Cullom and [Cushman] Davis," explaining that it would secure their acquiescence and perhaps cooperation in generating a favorable report on the statehood bill. Another $10,000 would be essential to "make sure of the majority of the committee."[18] Alarmed by this request, Woodruff and Cannon informed Caine that this was "not to be a moneyed fight." They flatly ordered a halt to the plan to "buy up Congress." Young was under scrutiny among the hierarchy already for his free-spending ways. The Church leaders suspected that he had been using Church funds to grant "retainers" to politicians through 1886–88.[19]

17. Jason Mack [Joseph F. Smith] to Woodruff and Cannon, Mar. 13, 1888; Penrose to Woodruff et al., Mar. 20, 1888; Richards to Woodruff and Cannon, Mar. 22, 1888, Woodruff General Correspondence.

18. Young to Jack, Feb. 2, 4, 1888; Jack to Young, Feb. 13, 1888, Jack Papers. Young had advised the presidency to have "at the very least $50,000" on hand in Washington (Young to Taylor and Cannon, July 11, 1887) and requested $25,000 for himself (Woodruff and Cannon to Caine, Feb. 18, 1888; Young to Woodruff et al., Feb. 13, 1888).

19. Young had written to Caine that "ten thousand [was needed] now to check new plans of enemies. Elections must be assisted" (Young to Caine, Sept. 17, 1886, Caine Papers).

Communicating with Caine by telegraph, the presidency instructed him to take no further steps until he had consulted with the other LDS agents. They let him know that President Joseph F. Smith would soon be in Washington. His mission, which they had not yet specified, was to replace Young as head of the LDS lobbying group. The presidency assumed that Young would still be visiting senators and promising them money; they informed him that his actions had been counterproductive and an embarrassment to the Church.[20]

The presidency had already set in motion efforts on the part of their California friends to secure positive treatment without resorting to bribing senators. Along with others of the era, they drew a moral line between paying journalists to write favorable reports and paying elected officials to do so. Beyond the ethics, they understood that bribing members of Congress could rebound with disastrous results. A cash outlay might be occasionally necessary, but they stressed that this was not the right time or place. Even among the railroad lobby, it was considered more corrupt to buy off a senator or congressman than to pay for newspaper coverage. It did not help matters that Young's lifestyle was loose and that he had harbored long-standing ambitions to lead the Church. For those reasons and others, he had been kept out of the Quorum of the Twelve even though his father had ordained him an apostle.[21]

Charles W. Penrose, acting as Caine's secretary in Washington, described Young as "greatly jealous" of anything that was done by the delegation that was outside of his control. Young had learned of the "other agencies" that had been employed, meaning the railroad lobbyists, but did not believe they could be more effective than he was. The clerk for the Church agents, George F. Gibbs, confided to

20. Woodruff and Cannon to Young, Feb. 18, 1888; Smith to Woodruff and Cannon, Feb. 18, 1888, Woodruff General Correspondence. The presidency wanted Caine to "help [government officials] understand" that the Church had no part in the "political doings or obligations of J. W. Young" (Jack to Caine, Oct. 24, 1888, Caine Papers).

21. J. Mack [Smith] to Caine, Apr. 11, 1888, Caine Papers; Compton, "John Willard Young," 111–34; also Grant, *Diaries*, Oct. 23, 1887. It was widely known that Stanford's longtime railroad associate, Collis B. Huntington, had bribed numerous national politicians in his day.

James Jack that Young held himself above Caine and Richards and hardly ever communicated with them. The only reason Young let the Church presidency know he had offered bribes to senators and congressmen was because he needed funds. The presidency also heard from lobbyist Alexander Badlam that Young gave people the impression that the Church had unlimited resources, which had attracted the attention of "sharpers," all at cross purposes with the efforts of other Church agents to portray an image of decency. Young had to be removed from the lobby, it was finally decided.[22]

In the ensuing weeks, Penrose and Richards continued to visit key Democratic senators and representatives. Their pitch was that hardly anyone in Utah practiced polygamy, and what polygamists there were had been barred from political involvement. Therefore, the lack of political rights for the majority of citizens appeared increasingly unfair. The non-polygamists were denied fair consideration. In Utah the anti-polygamy advocates were largely working against the Democratic Party in behalf of a tiny minority of Republicans aimed at gaining political control by disenfranchising Latter-day Saints, including many of the monogamists. If Utah advanced to statehood, it would assure the ascendancy of the Democrats. With the two Dakotas expected to be admitted as Republican states, the need for a Democratic stronghold had never been greater. The Democrats would be helping themselves if they would at least prevent the issuance of an unfavorable committee report and keep future options open, and if there was no chance for admission now, it would be best not to have a report at all. The enabling bill Senator Matthew C. Butler, a Democrat from South Carolina, was writing might be the most workable solution. The response Penrose and Richards received in Washington was that everything they said was well and good, as long as, first and foremost, the Democrats could be "assured that polygamy is destroyed as a practice." That was all that really mattered, since that was the expressed demand of everyone's congressional

22. C. W. Williams [Penrose] to Woodruff et al., Aug. 24, 27, 1887; Woodruff and Cannon to Mack [Smith], Feb. 16, 1888; Mack to Woodruff and Cannon, Apr. 6, 1888, Woodruff Correspondence; George F. Gibbs to James Jack, Feb. 11, 1888, Jack Papers; Woodruff and Cannon to Smith, Feb. 18, Apr. 5, 25, 1888, Woodruff Correspondence.

constituents.[23] The Church lobbyists nodded their understanding but could say nothing, knowing they had to remain noncommittal. This was in speaking with Democrats. They opted not to visit Republicans at all, deeming them to be beyond their reach.

On March 26, likely because Young's promised payoff had not materialized, the Republican Senator Cullom supported the kind of sub-committee report the Church was afraid of, recommending that Utah not be admitted until it was (1) "certain beyond doubt that the practice of plural marriage, bigamy, and polygamy" had been abandoned and (2) "civil affairs of the territory were not controlled by the LDS church hierarchy." These were legitimate concerns, although Joseph F. Smith hardly ever grasped such political realities. He had only considered reports from friendly Democrats, and thus-found this "wholly unexpected." A more astute observer might well have anticipated the logical action from Cullom after his "retainer" was not received. Woodruff and Cannon read into the report something more positive in the realization that a future acceptance of the territory as a state remained a possibility. Since it was but a sub-committee preliminary report, it was generally ignored, and the friendly Utah press published only what the railroad lobbyists advised them to. For instance, the *Salt Lake Herald* editorialized in late March that "there is less desire for a state government today than there was two years, or five years, or ten years ago." The territory had experienced an "improvement" in relations with the federal government, so that the "discontent" is "less pronounced." There were advantages to the territorial system, the *Herald* argued, where the federal government paid the expenses of maintaining the government. It is doubtful the editorial represented the true feelings of the majority of Latter-day Saints, yet in terms of putting the situation in the best possible light for the time being, it was well reasoned.[24]

23. Penrose to Woodruff et al., Dec. 30, 1887, Mar. 20, 1888; Richards to Woodruff et al., Jan. 23, 1888; Richards to Woodruff and Cannon, Feb. 11, Mar. 22, 1888; also *Congressional Record*, Mar. 16, 1888; Lamar, *Dakota Territory*, 244–84.

24. J. Mack [Smith] to James Jack, Mar. 26, 1888, Jack Papers; Mack to Woodruff and Cannon, Mar. 27, 30, Apr. 12, 1888; also Maude [Alexander Badlam] to Allen [Woodruff], Nov. 15, 1887, First Presidency Collection; *Salt Lake Herald*, Mar. 27, 1888. For the committee report, see *Admission of Utah*.

By this juncture there was a stalemate in Congress between opposing forces in favor of or opposed to Utah Territory. Neither side could get enough support to accomplish their aims. Senator Stewart was constrained to admit to a Minnesota clergyman that he could not get his committee to do anything against the Mormons "until the country stirs up Congress" again through negative press comments. With another presidential election approaching, there was little prospect for immediate action either way. John Sharp, of the Union Pacific board, suggested that the Church interests should attempt to accomplish more through the railroad lobby. Following up, Charles Penrose traveled to New York to confer with Sidney Dillon, an executive of the Union Pacific Railroad Company. Dillon suggested that the person most able to influence Church critic Senator Paddock was Paddock's brother-in-law, Cornelius S. Bushnell, who had been an early investor in the railroad. The senator was independently wealthy, so only "moral suasion" would work. Penrose invited Bushnell to Washington at the Church's expense and asked him to inform Paddock, on Dillon's advice, that the railroad wanted a friendly relationship with the Mormons. On hearing that, it became difficult for the senator from Nebraska to oppose the LDS wishes, since the Union Pacific headquarters and a major railroad hub were in Omaha. He thereafter made no further stand against Utah.[25]

Other similar lobbying efforts were less detailed in documentation, but seem to have been equally effective. For instance, there was a similar outcome with Senator Stewart of Nevada. People sometimes referred to him as the third senator from California because of his habitual actions in concert with the interests of the Southern–Central Pacific Railroad out of San Francisco. Almost no one knew that Leland Stanford had offered the assistance of the railroad lobby to the LDS Church. When Stewart learned that Stanford and his associates took a dim view of opposing Mormon interests, he experienced such a sudden "change of heart,"

25. J. Mack [Smith] to Lewis Allen [Wilford Woodruff], Apr. 10, 1888, First Presidency Collection; William M. Stewart to M. W. Montgomery, May 5, 1888, William M. Stewart Papers; Woodruff et al. to John Sharp and LeGrand Young, Jan. 7, 1888, Woodruff General Correspondence.

intentionally of course, that it was a "subject of surprise and comment," even among LDS agents.[26]

At about the same time, Isaac Trumbo informed Hiram Clawson that he and his railroad associates had approached Senator George F. Edmunds, who he reported had ceased to oppose the LDS Church. The senator committed to Leland Stanford, a US senator since 1885, that he would not say anything one way or the other regarding statehood, although adding that he "did not want to chew any dirt," meaning he was not going to make apologies for his previous legislation.[27] Thus, most of the outspoken recent opposition against Utah had been neutralized by the railroad agents' arm twisting. Cullom proved to be the only major critic in Congress who had not been so stifled.

At this crucial time, with helpful actions from business figures on both sides, the first semi-successful venture in Utah toward bridging the gulf between Mormons and Gentiles came from the more moderate members of the business community. Some of them had grown weary of the effect the anti-polygamy crusade was having on trade, property values, and the ability to attract outside investors. People who felt this way got together and formed the Salt Lake City Chamber of Commerce in April 1887, with Governor Caleb W. West a leading figure in its formative phase, along with Gentile banker William S. McCornick and several other LDS businessmen and two LDS churchmen, Heber J. Grant and John W. Young. Recognizing that aside from business concerns, the group was an experiment in harmonious Mormon–Gentile relations, its members adopted the motto of "no politics or religion in the chamber." This was difficult to enforce, but in time the organization served as an important forum even for discussing crucial political matters.[28]

John W. Young found that on the occasions when he met with

26. Mack [Smith] to Jack, Mar. 13, 1888, First Presidency Collection.

27. Penrose to Woodruff et al., Oct. 11, Dec. 10, 1887; Dellie [Isaac Trumbo] to Lulu [Hiram Clawson], Mar. 13, 1888, First Presidency Collection; Mack to Woodruff and Cannon, Apr. 12, 1888, Woodruff General Correspondence; Morgan, *From Hayes to McKinley,* 73; Nevins, *Grover Cleveland*, 178.

28. Whitney, *History of Utah*, 3:609–14.

US President Grover Cleveland, the president indicated a concern about how the non-LDS minority in Utah would be treated if the LDS people gained control of the government. From that question, Young recognized how favorable an impression politicians in the East would have if the LDS and Gentile factions could reconcile. With good insight he suggested to the Church presidency that "we of all people ought to show minorities by a practical demonstration in our policies that we firmly believe in minority representation." Young recommended that in the municipal elections of February 1888, some of the "best non-Mormons" be brought forward to run for seats on the Salt Lake City Council, strictly as a practical matter. However, when these leading Gentiles were approached with this overture, they rejected it for seeming to be blatantly patronizing. When the legislature soon thereafter enacted a uniform system of municipal and county government organization, with representation by ward in cities and by district in rural areas, it made it possible for moderate Gentiles to run where the population mix was sufficiently favorable, and a few of them cooperated with the People's Party in what was called a Citizens' Coalition. The LDS party convention ratified this slate of candidates and Church leaders expressed hope it might "allay the great hostility between the Mormon and gentile elements of the community."[29]

As the merits of this approach were debated in a series of heated meetings, it revealed a division within the Gentile ranks. The anti-Mormon faction of the Liberal Party denounced the moderates, including those in the Chamber of Commerce, as traitorous for cooperating with the other side. Similarly, the Democratic wing of the Liberal Party was chaired by J. B. Rosborough. He saw the overtures from the Church as window dressing for Washington and asserted that he would rather see a "square-toed fight" than pretense. Within two years the Liberals would control Salt Lake City in any case, he said. By contrast, Governor West found the coalition to be a good thing and endorsed the candidates.

29. Young to Woodruff et al., Dec. 8, 1887, Woodruff General Correspondence; Caine to Woodruff et al., Jan. 28, 1888; Woodruff et al. to Caine, Jan. 17, 1888; W. W. Riter to Caine, Feb. 7, 1888, Caine Papers; Abraham H. Cannon journal, Feb. 4, 1888.

As a member of the Chamber of Commerce, he asserted that this thawing in relations would help attract outside capital and new residents. He had already seen the results of cooperation in the Chamber and thought it to be the best means of attaining change and making progress. The anti-fusionists rejected this rhetoric and called West a "traitor," along with the four city council candidates. At an event where the governor was publicly promoting the coalition, he needed to be protected from hecklers when they became too aggressive, so General Patrick E. Connor, an older but still respected Liberal Party founder, climbed the stage to stand at West's side.[30] The general was barely able to restore order. The ill feelings among the non-LDS factions demonstrated how persistent the divisions were among them.

In mid-February 1888, the Citizens' Coalition ticket, including John E. Dooley, W. S. McCornick, Bolivar Roberts, and M. B. Sowels, was elected by a majority of about 860 votes out of 2,700. When the clamor subsided, the Church leadership confided to John T. Caine that they were gratified with the results. Other actions would "soften" the hearts of the respectable element of non-LDS society to establish "a division between the better class of non-Mormons and the howling rabble," they said. This favorable development proved short-lived, though, largely because Governor West became disillusioned with the prospects of cooperation with members of the hierarchy on the important issue of public schools within the territory. Thus, he returned to his previous position: Utah was not ready for statehood.[31]

What Governor West wanted was free public schools—one of the last areas of the country to offer this service if the territorial legislature agreed to it. It was blocked by the LDS majority, which preferred to keep common schools in the hands of the LDS wards. When Governor West spoke to the territorial legislature about it in January 1888, he had the impression that the elected representatives were receptive, just not yet agreed on what exactly the schools would

30. Whitney, *History of Utah*, 3:617–23.

31. Grant, *Diaries*, Jan. 23, 1888; also Woodruff et al. to Caine, Feb. 18, 1888, Woodruff General Correspondence; Woodruff and Cannon to Young, Feb. 28, 1888; *Report of the Governor of Utah*, 1888.

look like. In mid-February lawmakers met with Church authorities and "concede[d] a few points to the governor if he will yield a little." But less than a week later, the Church reconsidered the matter and reversed itself, deciding it would not make any concessions. In early March during the closing days of the session, seven apostles discussed the school issue and reiterated their intent to discomfit the governor by passing a substitute bill for the funding for public education to be shared with denominational and private schools. West vetoed it, saying it was a far cry from what was needed to establish viable public schools. His strongly worded statement revealed a long-term disgust with local politics and the unchanged attitudes the Church harbored regarding good government.[32] He thus reacted to another aspect of Church domination which had probably outlived its legitimate purpose as well.

Another development that was particularly unsettling to non-LDS people was Cleveland's removal of Chief Justice Charles S. Zane, a judge who by then was almost universally respected by all territorial non-Mormons. The president's associates had promised the LDS agents a replacement for one of the Republican judges. Frank J. Cannon, the politically active son of George Q. Cannon, spent two months negotiating a policy that he claimed would allow the government and LDS people to settle their outstanding difficulties. Essential to his plan was the appointment of a judge to "show leniency to every [polygamist] who should come in" voluntarily. This would attract from hiding the polygamists who would "rather go to prison for a short time and then be free than to continue in their present unfavorable circumstances as fugitives."[33]

Mainly through Frank Cannon's efforts, President Cleveland appointed Elliot F. Sandford to be territorial chief justice. Sandford was a New York attorney and state court official who was committed to follow the program of cooperative leniency. He received his

32. Grant, *Diaries*, Jan. 7, 23, Mar. 5–7, 1888; *Message of His Excellency*, 6–11; Smith, *Church, State, and Politics*, 189–91; also Franklin D. Richards journal, Mar. 5, 6, 1888; "Communication from the Governor," *House Journal of the [Utah] Legislative Assembly*, 1888, 342–43.

33. Cannon and O'Higgins, *Under the Prophet in Utah*, 77.

appointment on July 9, 1888.[34] Congress at that time also created a fourth judicial district for Utah Territory and accordingly enlarged its supreme court to four members. John W. Judd was appointed to fill this position. Judd was an attorney from Tennessee. Caine expressed appreciation and recommended to Cleveland and solicitor general Jenks that they advise the new judges of the administration's policy regarding the Mormons, which they did. Caine met personally with Judd and assured the LDS presidency that Judd would be alright. Judd had told Caine he would not "torture the law into an engine of persecution against any people or their religion." He likewise pledged that he would administer the law "in a spirit of moderation and kindness." Cleveland's about-face, yet unknown beyond Mormonism's inner circle, perplexed non-Mormons who preferred Zane's hard-fisted approach to lawbreakers. Before the new justices were appointed, the Salt Lake City Chamber of Commerce, in the process of circulating a petition requesting Zane's reappointment, attracted Governor West among the signers. The petition was still circulating when word came by telegraph of Sandford's and Judd's selections.[35] Even before the two judges arrived in Utah, Frank Cannon reported that Cleveland and his Attorney General had promised an unprecedented degree of leniency for George Q. Cannon if he surrendered. Accordingly, the apostle gave himself over to authorities on September 17 and was quickly brought to trial, where he pleaded guilty and was fined $200 and sentenced to only seventy-five days in the territorial penitentiary. The sentence was so light, the *Tribune* clique was said to be "blue with rage."[36] It was an unwise demonstration of favoritism that set the previous progress toward territorial unity back several additional years.

34. Frank J. Cannon to Woodruff, July 1, 1888, Woodruff General Correspondence; Abraham H. Cannon journal, May 8, 12, 1888; also Larson, *Americanization of Utah for Statehood,* 230–32.

35. Caine to Woodruff et al., July 7, Aug. 10, 1888, Woodruff General Correspondence; Caine to Mack [Smith], July 28, 1888, Caine Letterbooks; Caine to Woodruff et al., Aug. 10, 1888; Abraham H. Cannon journal, July 22, 1888; *Salt Lake Tribune,* July 10, 1888, on the petition originating with a Democrat.

36. Abraham H. Cannon journal, Aug. 2, Sept. 8, 11, 14–17, 1888; L. John Nuttall to J. T. Caine, Sept. 25, 1888, Caine Papers.

Another sign that the division in the community would continue was the development of Democratic Clubs by young LDS men who were mainly educated outside of Utah and wanted the territory to become a state without religious divisions, if possible. These "young Utahns" quietly desired to see the discontinuance of polygamy as well. Many of them attorneys, they demonstrated little sympathy with the idea that its prohibition was unconstitutional.[37] Thus they straddled the divide between their own faith's unusual political position, but certainly without sympathy for most of the Liberal Party's position.

In the late spring of 1888, a Democratic territorial convention was called to elect two delegates to the party's national convention. Members of several of the new clubs sent representatives. It was an open secret that Mormons were not wanted, but the four young LDS men who sought seats representing four different counties ignored the hostility they encountered until a committee on credentials excluded them, backed by the resolutions committee in decreeing that no member of the People's Party would be allowed into the Democratic ranks. At first the four refused to relinquish their seats, and a disorderly effort to force them out reached such a high pitch, they had to withdraw. There would be more demonstrations of that type during the later fall 1888 election campaign.[38]

Some of the LDS leadership had been watching the convention proceedings with interest—two members of the presidency and six apostles deciding in a meeting with the People's Party Chairman John R. Winder that the Church should withdraw from any involvement in national political parties. On the Republican side, a national convention that met on June 20 pledged to "divorce the political from the ecclesiastical power" in Utah and stamp out polygamy. Caine's predictable reaction was that such a strong statement would "frighten the Democrats" away from their support of statehood, which was already beyond the grasp of the Utah delegation. Nevertheless, LDS leaders continued to support Cleveland's

37. Grant, *Diaries*, Sept. 15, 17, 1888; Jensen, *Unfavored Few*, 154–59, 166–70; Whitney, *History of Utah*, 3:632–36; Roberts, *Comprehensive History*, 6:278–81.

38. Kenner, *Utah as It Is*, 137–141, 144–47; *Salt Lake Herald*, May 6, 1888.

candidacy. In late July Caine commented that Cleveland's "reelection will bring us some deliverance," quickly adding the caution that it would not do the president's campaign any good if LDS leaders backed him too loudly. But upon request, the Church contributed $25,000 to the national campaign.[39]

In the territories, where citizens were not allowed to vote for the US president, the most they could do was hold a convention and voice their approval of a candidacy. The non-LDS Democrats held such a territorial convention in Provo to ratify Cleveland's candidacy. The statement the delegates approved warned against admitting Utah as a state, which would be "a lasting disgrace to the republic, because it would fortify behind state lines an ecclesiastical hierarchy whose principles are in favor of the domination of the Church in the temporal, as well as spiritual affairs of men." The delegates further predictably resolved to give their continued local support to the Liberal Party.

The *Herald's* account of the proceedings was headlined "Democrats Desert their Colors and Become Liberals." It contained an announcement about a People's Party convention scheduled for October 8. Prior to that, taking advantage of reduced railroad rates during LDS general conference, the young Democrats attracted about 100 people to a twelve-hour convocation.[40] Samuel R. Thurman, a young attorney from Provo, was nominated to run for delegate to Congress. Fervent pledges were made to support him in the race against the Liberal and People's Party nominees. For several days the press showed considerable interest in this independent political movement that aligned itself with a national party. The *Salt Lake Tribune* called them "Sagebrush Democrats." They accepted the epithet, with a comment that they had never known sagebrush to "grow on unfruitful soil." The *Herald* offered supportive words

39. Caine to C. Williams [Penrose], June 21, 1888; Caine to Mack [Smith], June 23, 1888, Caine Letters; Mack to Caine, Oct. 19, 1888, Caine Papers; William H. Barnum et al. to John W. Young, Sept. 1, 1888; Barnum to Young, Sept. 6, 1888, Young Papers; Grant, *Diaries*, Oct. 15, 23, 24, 1888; Porter and Johnson, *National Party Platforms*, 79–81.

40. Hadley D. Johnson to John T. Caine, Sept. 22, 1888, Caine Papers; *Salt Lake Herald*, Oct. 3–9, 1888.

until John Caine, one of the newspaper's shareholders, was re-nominated by the People's Party as its delegate candidate.

Two weeks after Thurman's nomination, he and a few supporters met with Church and People's Party leaders to clear up what they thought had been a misunderstanding about why they had organized the party. They had intended to bring a truer version of the Democratic Party to Utah and thereby divide the Liberal Party. It was not their intent to harm the People's Party. Woodruff and the others could not find fault with this logic, except to point out the damage that would be done if they "draw votes from the People's Party." They advised the young men to "get out of the mistake" they had created "as best they could." Thurman's circle of friends ignored this advice and garnered a respectable 511 votes in the election.[41] Although they would subside somewhat in visibility, they were in fact the predecessor of a regular Democratic Party that would soon be organized in the territory.

Another obstacle for statehood in 1888 was a general disinclination to interfere with the electoral college balance prior to Dakota Territory applying for admission as a state. Its people were expected to vote Republican, and it was anticipated that it would split in two, more than doubling Utah's possible electoral vote. As John W. Young had reminded Church leaders, the Democratic Party had not forgotten Samuel J. Tilden's loss to Republican Rutherford B. Hayes in 1876, which occurred largely because Colorado had been admitted that year and cast its electoral votes for the Republican.[42]

That being the case, Utah Territory was a potential liability for Democrats in an election year. John W. Young had warned the LDS presidency of the "disinclination to disturb that political status this side of the presidential election. The idea [had been] well received [that] we do not want to embarrass the [Democratic] party with [our] case" during the campaign season.[43] In late January 1888, Young admitted that the Republicans were prepared and "anxiously

41. Grant, *Diaries*, Oct. 8, 22, 1888; *Salt Lake Herald*, Nov. 1, 1888.
42. Young to Woodruff et al., Dec. 8, 1887.
43. Penrose to Woodruff et al., Dec. 30, 1887, First Presidency Collection.

waiting for the opportunity to charge the Democratic Party of admitting the Mormon church into the union." He advised working quietly to prepare Democrats for action in the post-election congressional session.[44]

Another factor that later loomed as a significant hindrance to the people was that when the territory had attempted to avoid some of the harshness of the Edmunds–Tucker Act of 1887 by supporting the Scott Amendment, that approach, with a constitution generated solely by the citizens of Utah Territory, had roused the antipathy of Congress because it seemingly attempted to bypass a usually mandatory step in the admission process. Franklin S. Richards later confided to Church headquarters in mid-February 1888 that "none of the senators and representatives, not even among the Democrats, are willing to admit us on the [1887] constitution. They all say we must come in under an enabling act," with its usual congressionally prescribed steps, including some likely provisions in the proposed constitution.[45]

The 1888 election also stood as crucial because it pointed to the temporary demise of the Democrats as the dominant party. The Republicans were at that point firmly backed by industrial interests that approved of the high tariffs the party advocated rather than with Cleveland's advocacy of lower tariffs. With money from wealthy backers, the party was able to bombard voters with pamphlets warning them of economic depression, wage cutting, unemployment, and even starvation if they voted for Democrats. Hoping not to be outmaneuvered, the Democrats chose as their national chairman, William H. Barnum of Connecticut, to run their presidential campaign. Barnum owned extensive iron mines in Michigan and was himself quietly pro-tariff. Even Cleveland's running mate, Allen G. Thurman, appeared to be ambivalent on the issue. At the national party convention, Senator Gorman led the platform subcommittee to oppose Cleveland's tariff reformation and reaffirm the party's 1884 pro-tariff position.[46] This virtually assured party defeat.

44. Young to Woodruff et al., Jan. 23, 1888.
45. Richards to Woodruff et al., Feb. 11, 1888.
46. Nevins, *Grover Cleveland*, 400, 415.

Most Latter-day Saints were devastated by Cleveland's loss to Benjamin Harrison. Not only did the Democrats lose the presidency, they lost both houses of Congress. One of the LDS presidents of the Seventy, Abraham H. Cannon, asked in his journal if this would "mean great oppression for the saints?" Anti-Mormons in Salt Lake City held victory celebrations. It was clear what they thought of the election results. When John T. Caine was asked about it, he fended off questions by saying he would need to consult with national leaders at the beginning of Congress's new session in December before answering. The LDS leadership concluded that it was essential to make one last hasty bid for statehood during Cleveland's lame duck term that ended in March 1889, before the Republicans diminished the prospects during the subsequent session.[47]

Charles Penrose and Franklin Richards returned to the nation's capital in early December 1888 for the last-ditch fight, conveying their regrets directly to Cleveland and, in an hour-long interview, explaining that they may have to turn to the Republicans for help. The Church agents informed the president that there was a growing number in Utah that believed the Republicans "would be more likely to accord them political freedom than the Democratic Party." Cleveland expressed preference for the idea of combining Utah's effort with other territories seeking statehood during the current congressional session. He promised to see House Speaker John Carlisle on the matter and advised the two LDS men to visit with some northern Democrats he thought might be of assistance. Following the president's advice, they met with William S. Holman, an experienced Democrat from Indiana who was willing to help. S. S. Cox, an equally seasoned Democratic congressman from New York, was less encouraging. He was committed to seeing the Dakotas admitted as two states. If Utah were added to the omnibus bill involving the Dakotas, he knew the Republicans would oppose it. It was well known that there were already Republicans who wanted to call a special session after taking majority

47. Abraham H. Cannon journal, Nov. 7, 10, 1888; Grant, *Diaries*, Nov. 13, 1888; also Smith, *Church, State, and Politics*, 212–14. Young Cannon would become a member of the Quorum of Twelve Apostles in October 1889.

control of the House in March to pass the omnibus bill. Cox nevertheless stated that he would follow his party's priorities when they were discussed at the approaching party caucus.

The LDS team next met with Congressman William Springer, sponsor of the omnibus bill and chairman of the Committee on Territories. He was aware that the LDS Church had not made any concessions to the fair-minded members of his party, and therefore, as he informed Penrose and Richards, he thought their action stood little chance of success. They countered that Utah could be of help to the party by not only bringing in votes from Utah but also generating "probable political influence in other territories" neighboring Utah. Springer said that since the Democrats were making a concession to the Republicans in allowing in the two Republican-leaning Dakotas anyway, there might be a chance for reciprocity on that count. He promised to keep an open mind at the upcoming caucus.[48]

The outcome of the caucus proved disappointing enough that John T. Caine delayed reporting the results to Church headquarters until two days after Christmas, explaining that there was a general feeling of kindness toward Utah but hesitancy to act in its defense. It was "evident from the first" that they would not get behind the statehood effort.[49] Caine had presented the case for Utah being accepted along with the Dakotas, to which Speaker Carlisle stood and replied that he opposed "complicating the omnibus bill with any matter that would give the Republican Senate a semblance of an excuse for rejecting it." They had the other territories to think about, where people would think poorly of the Democrats if they encumbered the bill with a provision for Utah that would all but guarantee its defeat. In addition, the representatives were aware, through Governor West's report, that Mormons had blocked universal education. That, as much as any other factor, was decisive for Carlisle, who was a long-time friend of West.

As the congressmen were preparing to leave the hall, J. H. Blount of Georgia moved that the caucus recommend a separate

48. Penrose and Richards to Woodruff and Smith, Dec. 7, 1888, First Presidency Collection.

49. *Washington Post*, Dec. 14, 1888; Penrose to Woodruff and Smith, Dec. 19, 1888; Caine to Woodruff et al., Dec. 27, 1888.

bill for Utah's admission. J. H. Outhwaite of Ohio endorsed it, but "Sunset" Cox immediately interjected that it would be an unnecessary "fly in a pot of ointment." All the same, the motion passed. Afterward Penrose continued to visit with congressmen who were friendly toward Utah. Many of them "recognize[d] the value of our influence to the party" in the Great Basin. "They could [still] not afford to vote for Utah … because of the prejudices of their constituents." Representative Call thought it would be ten times more difficult to admit Utah alone than in conjunction with other territories. Springer shared a copy of the omnibus bill with the Utahns, showing that one of its proposed amendments was a condemnation of polygamy in Utah. Caine, Penrose, and Richards suggested adding the words "and Utah" throughout, but that idea went nowhere since the Utah agents also wanted to leave out the polygamy amendment.

The LDS leaders received a lengthy plea from its "friends in the East," meaning lobbyists, about the obligation of church members to conform to civil law. The plea was filled with quotations from Joseph Smith and the Doctrine and Covenants, indicating that it was probably written by John W. Young. The presidency gave it to members of the Quorum of the Twelve, where Heber J. Grant complained that the author had incorrectly interpreted his sources. A few of the apostles appeared willing to consider the merits of the case, while others said they would accept such a proposal only if it came as "the Word of the Lord through the servant of God whose right it is to speak," meaning Wilford Woodruff. In four months Woodruff would be formally installed as Church president, but he was already recognized as the current prophet. As the discussion concluded, Woodruff proclaimed that "the Lord never will give a revelation to abandon plural marriage" and therefore "we cannot deny [the] principle." What is most noteworthy about his statement is that in a little over a year, he would be the one to announce the end of the practice, after being essentially forced to by unavoidable circumstances.[50]

50. Grant, *Diaries*, Dec. 20, 1888; also Franklin D. Richards journal, Dec. 20, 1888. Actually, Woodruff's commitment to plural marriage already appeared to waver more than that of his counselors, George Q. Cannon and Joseph F. Smith, during the next year and a half.

When the Church sent its response eastward, the Democratic Party became even more inclined toward keeping Utah at arm's length. John T. Caine asked whether he, in his official position, should continue pressing for a statehood bill at all. His instinct was to continue, but he was disheartened. Springer scheduled Utah's agents to speak to the House committee the week of January 12, 1889, along with leaders of the Liberal Party. Caine and Richards led the remarks for the proponents, followed by those speaking against the measure: Robert Baskin, Idaho delegate Fred T. Dubois, and Governor Caleb West. As the prolonged debate made its way to the congressional floor during consideration of the omnibus bill, Charles Dougherty of Florida presented an amendment that would have added Arizona and Utah to the bill, saying he did not see why a proposal originating with the Democrats should admit solely Republican territories and keep out the Democratic ones. The reaction, according to the *Congressional Record*, was applause and laughter. "It is bad politics," he continued, "for any party to admit territories in such a way as to increase the strength of their opponents and keep out territories which would add to their own strength." The party should do "all that is honest and fair to strengthen" itself. "Let in Arizona and Utah," he said. "They will both be Democratic States. New Mexico will also be Democratic." The amendment was quickly killed.[51]

The subcommittee reporting on the separate Utah proposal explained that due to being late in the session, it would not be able to secure its passage. The bill was quietly ignored, and then the Democrats went out of power. The House passed a statehood bill for Dakota, Montana, New Mexico, and Washington. The Senate version dropped New Mexico because of suspicions about the loyalty of Spanish-speaking people, who the *Chicago Tribune* editorialized were "not American." The representatives in Congress simply said that the territory was not prepared for being received as a state. A deadlock ensued, but eventually a bill advanced that provided enabling acts for four territories, all Republican-leaning, including

51. Caine to Joseph F. Smith, Apr. 13, 1889, Caine Letterbooks; *Congressional Record*, Jan. 18, 1889; also *House Reports*, 50th Cong., 2nd sess., no. 4156.

North and South Dakota.[52] Each was subsequently admitted into the fraternity of states, marking the close of Utah's sixth unsuccessful attempt to join them.

Though the struggle was temporarily over, it was not forgotten or abandoned, as Caine wrote to George L. Miller in Nebraska, reviewing what had occurred, his disbelief that Democrats would rather give up four states to the Republicans than include the Latter-day Saints. He recalled Congressman Cox's quip about a fly in the ointment. In Caine's opinion, the party had "lost the ointment, pot and all. In rejecting the only certainly Democratic territory[,] they lost all the new states and the control of the government, for many years to come." It was actually the beginning of a slow transformation in Utah itself, away from the Democrats, into the lap of the Republicans. Utah's party friends in Congress had been less than courageous in standing up for the Latter-day Saints when the time came. Congressman William L. Scott was not even in Washington when the Utah bill was considered, and Senator Arthur P. Gorman, who wielded considerable influence in the Senate, remained silent.[53] In reality, however, Carlisle and Cox were probably correct about Utah sinking an omnibus bill if attached to it, at least in the Senate.

John W. Young wrote to his friend Charles W. Nibley, who would later become a high Latter-day Saint official, that the "campaign for statehood tapered out to a rather small point."[54] Young had himself contributed to the problem by entertaining the suggestion that the Church might give up polygamy, setting it up as something of an expectation, then often telling LDS leaders only what they wanted to hear, which was that they might achieve statehood without making such a concession. The ultimate responsibility rested with the Church leadership, of course, in seeming to make promises they were not

52. Abraham H. Cannon journal, Feb. 7, 1889; Larson, *New Mexico's Quest for Statehood*, 147–55.

53. Caine to George L. Miller, Oct. 26, 1890, Caine Letters; Penrose to Woodruff, undated fragment filed with Dec. 1889 papers, Woodruff Correspondence; Penrose and Richards to Woodruff and Smith, Dec. 7, 1888.

54. John W. Young to Charles W. Nibley, Mar. 5, 1889, John W. Young Papers.

prepared to keep. The Democratic leadership, particularly later in the executive branch, in wanting to add a state to the Democratic side of the ledger, had probably been too lenient with Church emissaries. As will be seen, the Republican Party would wield a far heavier hand and threaten dire outcomes for noncompliance, yet exact far greater concessions and win rather firm LDS allegiance all at the same time.

Elder George Q. Cannon had been the first to explain to politicians how strategically LDS political power was distributed throughout the Intermountain West. The person in Washington to fully appreciate the implication was Republican James G. Blaine, who with his key lieutenant, James S. Clarkson, recognized the possible benefit of friendship with this long-beleaguered people. The LDS population was increasing every year due to the constant flow of convert immigrants, but for the first time LDS members would lose control of municipal elections in the two most populous cities in the territory: Ogden and Salt Lake City. There were several reasons. For instance, the influx of outsiders into Ogden, as the most important railroad center in the territory, had been significant. Also, a large number of LDS polygamists had been removed from voting lists through the Edmunds–Tucker Act, as had all women and even many legitimately qualified Church members who were barred by election registrars. The People's Party was also apparently uncertain how to effectively proceed. At the same time, particularly in Ogden, there was some independent agitation among LDS people for more democratically selected candidates, although this did not yet appreciably lessen the party's influence.[55]

The major reason for the Liberal Party advantage proved to be voter fraud, backed by intervention by the courts in favor of the Liberals and against the same practices allegedly committed or contemplated by the People's Party. LDS residents who appealed to the courts mostly had their appeals rejected. All of these factors being in play, the outcome of both elections was nearly inevitable. When the results in Ogden were announced, the *Ogden Standard*,

55. Cannon to Daniel Manning, Aug. 7, 1885, Cleveland Papers; Kotter, "Examination," 100–10; Middleton, "Life of Charles Franklin Middleton," 81.

the People's Party newspaper, reported that poll watchers had been unable to prevent non-resident Gentiles from voting: "Challenges were rapidly made and as rapidly over-ruled." The party spokesmen minced no words in alleging "there was every appearance of fraud being practiced" by throngs of illegally registered miners and railroad workers who materialized on the streets on election day. One of the "masterminds" of this insidious endeavor, H. W. "Kentucky" Smith, was heard by a reputable witness to say that "one man voted twelve times at the Ogden election."[56]

When the new mayor, Fred Kiesel, took office, the liquor laws and municipal supervision of vices were relaxed. The notorious 25th Street red-light district flourished to the point that many people on either side of the political spectrum were alarmed. Others were not, as indicated by a grand jury ignoring federal district judge Henry P. Henderson's explanation that gambling and prostitution were illegal, that the owners of some establishments on 25th Street were openly flaunting the law. Arthur Pratt, the US marshal in the Ogden region, threatened to arrest the suspects on his own authority since the vested officials appeared unable to get indictments. The *Salt Lake Herald* enjoyed keeping tabs on these developments to the discredit of the Liberal Party.

Although the Salt Lake City elections were held later, the matter of choosing school trustees attracted the attention of the non-LDS electorate, less so the LDS voters. Church leaders belatedly commenced trying to rally the membership behind the issues and laid the political groundwork for one of the most bitter elections in Utah history. They appointed two popular young apostles, Abraham H. Cannon and Heber J. Grant, to deliver speeches across the county to motivate LDS voters.[57] Their encouragement prompted people to register to vote. In addition, at the close of the Church's semi-annual general conference on October 7, 1889, some of the hierarchy met with local stake presidents to

56. Franklin D. Richards journal, Mar. 13, 1888; *Ogden Standard*, Feb. 12, 1889; Kotter, "Examination," 152–53; Lyman, ed., *Candid Insights*, 15–16; also Stegner, *Uneasy Chair*, 60–66.

57. Caine to Cannon, Aug. 15, 1889, Caine Papers; Grant, *Diaries*, Aug. 6, 1889; *Salt Lake Herald*, July 9–10, Aug. 3, 6, 1889.

describe the situation in Ogden where Liberals had brought in miners and railroad graders. According to Abraham H. Cannon, "It was proposed that those stakes who could spare young men to come to [Salt Lake City] and acquire residence so as to be able to vote, do so, and that we here provide employment and pay for such." Individual Church members were asked to assist in similar ways. For example, John W. Young consented to furnish work for one hundred men hauling rock from his quarries. George Q. Cannon and others considered building a Church college and fine hotel in the downtown area.

Several days later the Quorum of the Twelve Apostles suggested that members of the city council should be asked to give employment to new voters. Abraham Cannon and other Church officials met the next day with some councilmen, who agreed to employ large numbers of workmen on city projects. This marked the beginning of construction on the long-afterward famous joint city-and-county building. There were already some 330 men employed installing sewer lines and related water projects, so Mayor Francis Armstrong was reluctant to add more until it was pointed out that if the party lost control of the city's reserve of some $75,000, the money would fall into the hands of the supposedly unscrupulous Gentiles. Suddenly street-paving projects were given approval, and a water line from City Creek Canyon was installed. The city quietly doubled its workforce "on public improvements until after the election." Simultaneously, the Church took the opportunity to demolish the Endowment House, where polygamous marriages had been solemnized in the absence of a completed temple.[58]

Apparently it was not just assumed that the workers hired from the hinterlands would register to vote and support the right party. As Joseph Christensen of Gunnison, a young man recently back from his LDS mission to Sweden, confirmed in his diary, he was "called on a political mission" to work and help prevent anti-Mormons from obtaining control of the city.[59] The scheme was technically legal but more

58. Lyman, ed., *Candid Insights*, 6–15; Grant, *Diaries*, Oct. 12, 17, 18, 1889.

59. Joseph Christensen, "Life and Ancestry of Joseph Christensen," *Utah Genealogical and Historical Magazine*, Oct. 1937, 148.

effectively thwarted by voter registrars, most of whom were committed instruments of the Liberal Party, in effectively barring many temporary residents from the polls, whether or not they were qualified to register.

Church leaders took the additional step of encouraging a substantial number of male converts who had not yet been naturalized to apply for citizenship. This resulted in a questionable "investigation" of whether LDS immigrants were suitable for naturalization. Associate Justice Thomas J. Anderson, a Democrat appointed to the Utah Supreme Court during the last days of the Cleveland administration, concluded that ultimately most LDS people were unfit for citizenship, regardless of whether they professed belief in plural marriage or not. The aims and practices of the Church were "antagonistic to the government of the United States, [and] utterly subversive of good morals and the well being of society," he wrote.[60]

On the Sunday prior to Judge Anderson's decision, President Woodruff met with Church attorneys LeGrand Young and James H. Moyle, who reportedly urged him toward "some concession in court on polygamy and other questions." John W. Young had made another visit and offered his own advice and chiding in the same direction. Woodruff dictated a statement, "the word of the Lord," that brought his counselor Joseph F. Smith to tears when he read it later that evening. Woodruff's secretary L. John Nuttall recorded it verbatim in his journal three days later and referred to it as a revelation. If so, it was rather fully in the direction the attorneys had desired. Instead, Woodruff announced that celestial marriage was part of God's word for man's salvation, and there should be no "further pledges from the Priesthood" to the contrary.[61]

Also at that time, there was an appeal to the Utah Commission by two members of the People's Party central committee, Heber M. Wells and Richard W. Young, to challenge the political interference by voter registrars. To that point in time, the Utah Commission had

60. *Salt Lake Herald*, Nov. 1, 8, Dec. 1, 1889. This decision was markedly different than the earlier ones during the time of commissioners Carlton and McClernand, when the Utah Commission appeared to be less biased against Latter-day Saints.

61. Alexander, *Things in Heaven and Earth*, 256; Lyman, ed., *Candid Insights*, 38; Rogers, ed., *In the President's Office*, 393–96.

seldom become directly involved in questions of whether one given individual was qualified to vote or not. Earlier in the year the commission had appointed a new chief registrar and five deputies for the city, all men the commission considered to be competent and reputable (all non-LDS). The commission had further reminded all registrars in a detailed circular to carefully follow proper procedures. Upon receiving allegations that the appointees had acted in a partisan way, Chairman G. L. Godfrey consented to a special meeting, at which Wells and Young were invited to present their accusations.[62]

On the appointed day, attorneys for the People's Party, Young and Moyle, claimed the registrars had allowed Liberals to enroll with ease, while blocking the registration of People's Party applicants. When the commission pressed for substantiation, witnesses who were brought in and asked to answer the charges were unable to sufficiently substantiate their allegations. The matter thus appeared to be only serious enough to require the registrars to be reminded on December 19 to treat all applicants fairly. A few weeks later, the commissioners should have been nonplussed with the Liberal Party announcement that four of the recently appointed registrars had been nominated to run for office. The *Deseret News* labeled this a blatant payoff for "notoriously unfair manipulation" of the vote. During the Liberal Party convention, a question arose about E. R. Clute's qualification to be city assessor, but when reference was made to his heroic party service as a registrar, the opposition melted away. The newspaper denounced the obvious: the one trusted to ensure a fair election would personally benefit from his own shady actions.[63]

During the commission hearing, the registrars discussed the LDS plan to "colonize" the city with temporary residents. Even though it did not seem right, they admitted that such applicants were technically qualified after they had lived a minimum of six months in the area and it could not be proved that they intended to abandon the area immediately after the election. The *Herald* admitted

62. Minutebook D, Utah Commission Minute Books, 302–04, 307–11; *House Executive Documents*, 51st US Cong., 2nd sess., 13:398–406.

63. Minutebook D, 313–21, 323–28; *Deseret Weekly News*, Dec. 28, 1889, Jan. 25, 1890.

that the newcomers might be temporary, but were legal. The People's Party conceded that this was their response to the known Liberal scheme of bringing people into town on election day. It was known that Liberal agents had visited the mining areas and traveled along railroad construction lines, "drumming up men" to spend a day in Salt Lake City and vote, which was clearly illegal. The party set up an employment bureau to provide temporary work for some of the Gentile recruits. The *Salt Lake Herald* intercepted a note from John Whitbeck in Nephi to the Liberal campaign chairman Orlando W. Powers. Pleased to be able to broadcast the message of the short note, the paper printed it under its masthead for the subsequent few weeks: "The bearer of this wants to vote, look after a job for him."[64] This was precisely the practice the registrars were rejecting among temporary LDS residents.

The *Herald* noticed something equally interesting in an obituary from the *Salt Lake Tribune*. It was for Ernst F. Warner, a young tuba player who had died suddenly, whose name was on the voter registration list. He had arrived in the city a few months earlier, shorter than the requisite length of time to be eligible to vote, to play in the Liberal Party campaign band. The *Tribune* had no answer other than to denounce the *Herald* for defaming the dead.[65] Even more significantly, the People's Party was suspicious enough of occasional evidence of wrongdoing that it employed a nationally known private detective to investigate voter registration more thoroughly. John Bonfield had recently retired from the Chicago police department. He and eight men working closely with him heard about a small train that had been chartered from the Denver and Rio Grande Railroad to transport a deer hunting party. They discovered that the train included a car with a voter registration table and registration book of E. R. Clute. At each point along the track where workmen were engaged in grading, the train stopped and the men were invited inside. The car with the voter registration

64. *Salt Lake Herald*, Dec. 15, 21, 1889; Jan. 24, 1890.
65. *Salt Lake Tribune*, Jan. 25, 1890.

table was a saloon, and registrants who promised to vote were rewarded with abundant liquid refreshment.

There was a decline in questionable registrations after the *Herald* ran a January 31 exposé informing readers that there were detectives on the watch. Agents of the Liberal Party were apparently unwilling to risk jail time for their shenanigans. The *Herald* predicted that fewer illegal voters would probably travel into the city from the outlying areas on election day either. It reprinted the warning Orlando Powers had directed at the People's Party colonizers that those who were not permanent residents should not vote. Powers responded that if evidence could be shown of "packing the registration books," he would strike out any names that had been illegally entered. The People's Party decided not to accommodate his request because it would indicate which voters the LDS party had evidence on, making it safe for the remaining non-residents to vote.[66]

The Liberals nominated a less-than-impressive slate of candidates for Salt Lake City offices led by a local hardware merchant, George M. Scott, for mayor, and Louis Hyams and E. R. Clute, both election registrars, for recorder and assessor/collector. Their platform stated that the party was for "the lowest rate of taxation compatible with proper administration of municipal affairs, including free schools." The People's Party candidates, by contrast, were better qualified. Yet the party scheduled very little in the way of campaign events. It did invest in uniforms for its marching bands, which performed on a handful of occasions. The Liberals regularly held smaller rallies and torchlight parades. For the largest People's Party campaign exercise, despite a rainstorm, 3,350 members of nine bands and drum corps marched for several blocks down Main Street on January 10 to converge on the Salt Lake Theater, demonstrating thoroughly drilled routines, accompanied by a huge fireworks display. Even Chief Justice Zane, who admired few things Mormon, was impressed.[67]

66. *Salt Lake Herald*, Jan. 31, Feb. 2, 1890; *Deseret Weekly News*, Jan. 18, Feb. 8, 15, 1890.

67. Grant, *Diaries*, Feb. 8, 10, 1891; Zane diaries, Jan. 25, 1890. The parade took place despite intermittent rain.

On election day, February 10, 1890, Elder Grant observed that he had never seen "a livelier day in our city." Both parties placed monitors at the polling places. Throughout the day, people on both sides were ruled ineligible and barred from voting. The Liberal Party had bondsmen available to assist party members when they were arrested. By midday it was certain the Liberals would sweep almost every office. LDS leaders concluded that if the margin of victory was less than 500, the People's Party would contest the results. The opposing candidates, with only one exception, won over 500 more votes than their opponents, up to 808 more votes in one case. The Liberal celebration was spectacular. Charles Penrose of the *Deseret News* predictably editorialized that "it was not a victory gained, but a robbery consummated, which has given to the Liberals the majority they claim." The *Salt Lake Herald* wondered if there had ever been "a more crooked election." Some of the Gentiles expected a mass exodus of Mormons from the city after the overthrow of the LDS-run government. Doing their overzealous best to prevent LDS candidates from holding office, election commissioners disqualified several of the People's Party candidates who actually won their city council seats in predominantly LDS neighborhoods. The candidates appealed to the court of Charles Zane, but their terms were three-quarters done before they were seated.[68]

The Utah Commission's annual report took note of the high-pitched partisan spirit of the contest and accusations of fraud, for which the commission excused itself of further involvement by stating that it "did not deem it proper to pay heed to articles appearing in partisan newspapers" until specific charges of dishonesty were brought to them.[69] Then they inquired, for instance, of Charles Penrose of the *Deseret News* if he had further information about the train that allegedly had a voter registration book and saloon. The editor responded that he had no first-hand knowledge of it. The Church dispatched Heber J. Grant to Colorado to examine the Denver and

68. *Salt Lake Herald*, Feb. 11, 1890; *Deseret Weekly News*, Feb. 22, 1890; Grant, *Diaries*, Feb. 3–10, 1889; Lyman, ed., *Candid Insights*, 63–64; Whitney, *History of Utah*, 3:705–08; Roberts, *Comprehensive History*, 6:207–09.

69. *House Executive Documents*, 51st Cong., 2nd sess., 13:409–12.

Rio Grande Railroad employment records, to discover people as far away as Grand Junction, Colorado, on the Salt Lake City voter registration rolls. However, they appeared in the registration books of Hyams and McCullom rather than Clute—although some of these discoveries were not made until after the election had been won. For the commission's part, it declared the matter closed. To whatever degree there had been dishonest practices, they were not deemed widespread enough to alter the results, and they were alleged to have been committed by both sides. The elections created a sense of alienation among LDS people, who worried about the future of their municipal governments, about which they could do little.

That was the situation faced by LDS President Woodruff as the year 1889 came to an end. All he could see at the time was to call for fasting and prayers for divine assistance. The result of that supplication the next year was inspiration regarding "exactly what would come to pass if there was not something done." The vision that opened to his mind was not a hopeful one. Therefore, he would do in 1890 what he had long resisted. He felt compelled, saying he "should have let all the temples go out of our hands; I should have gone to prison myself, and let every other man go there, had not the God of heaven commanded me to do what I did do; and when the hour came that I was commanded to do that, it was all clear to me."[70]

70. Alexander, *Things in Heaven and Earth*, 248–49, 252, 257–59, 287; Bitton, *George Q. Cannon*, 301; Official Declaration 1, Doctrine and Covenants.

8

THE CRUCIAL YEAR

1890

Even though plural marriage was less visible and no longer publicly discussed, LDS leaders still resisted pressure to consider halting the practice. Then came the shock of the devastating Supreme Court decision, *Davis v. Beason*, and the realistic threat of the Church becoming a legal pariah in all the states, its members deprived of citizenship. Soon Church President Wilford Woodruff recognized that it was time to issue a statement, popularly called the Manifesto, that polygamy would no longer be the practice of the Church. It has been widely understood that the political situation in the region changed at that moment, but less attention has been paid to the background of what happened in Salt Lake City and Washington immediately prior to and after the announcement. By the time the manifesto was issued, the Republican Party had become fully entrenched again in Washington. Quite surprisingly some of the Grand Old Party were already seeing Mormons differently, based on shared economic interests in the region and possibly because of the quiet political negotiations going on behind the scenes. The series of severe blows the government had landed to that point had the Church on the proverbial ropes, its existence threatened, and Congress preparing a knockout punch, forcing LDS leaders to recognize the need for change. With change came an unexpected broadening of political options.

As the Republicans resumed control of the national government in the spring of 1889, John T. Caine, then in his eighth year of service as the territorial delegate, acknowledged that he lacked sufficient influence with the Republican administration under US President Benjamin Harrison to be effective. He thus queried Latter-day Saint leaders: "Can you not ask your San Francisco friends [railroad lobbyists] to aid you with this administration?"[1] President Harrison replaced a few territorial officials with party loyalists beginning in March 1889, then called for the resignation of the Utah Commission's chairman, Ambrose B. Carlton, his replacement bringing the number of Republicans on the five-member commission to four. The president dismissed Governor Caleb W. West in favor of Arthur L. Thomas, a former Utah commissioner and member of the *Tribune* ring. He also replaced the controversial Chief Justice Elliott F. Sanford with Charles S. Zane, who had formerly occupied the same position. These officials were less bitter than a majority of their party fellows had been in times past, but they were not altogether sympathetic either.

Some of the Utah Democrats directed their frustration at recent national party leaders. In January 1889 the editor of the *Salt Lake Herald*, Byron Groo, lay blame on them for not earlier granting the territory statehood. Then the paper denounced the party for "sneaking about and dodging the question," while the Republicans at least had been open and direct about what their position was in opposing it. He stopped short of placing any blame on the LDS leadership for failing to compromise, asserting only that the Democrats had betrayed them. Groo continued to say that even when they professed to be allies, the Democrats' antipathy showed through more vividly than among the Republicans. This was evident in Idaho Territory where a Democrat authored the anti-Mormon test oath in 1884 that prevented Latter-day Saints from voting. The regional Democratic Party endorsed the oath, it was upheld by a Democratic territorial judge, and Democratic Governor Edward A. Stevenson added it to the territory's proposed statehood documents.[2]

1. John T. Caine to Joseph F. Smith, Apr. 13, 1889; Caine to Woodruff et al., Mar. 20, 1889, Caine Letters.

2. *Salt Lake Herald*, Jan. 25, Feb. 7, 1889; Lyman, "Mormon Transition in Idaho Politics," 6–11, 24–25; Wells, *Anti-Mormonism in Idaho*, 85–98, 133–54; also *Idaho*

National Democratic leaders had assured the LDS people that they would be lenient in carrying out the economic mandates of the Edmunds–Tucker Act. But during much of Grover Cleveland's administration, it had been difficult to detect the fulfillment of those expectations. Instead, the courts seized Church property and placed it in the hands of receiver Frank H. Dyer, a Democrat, who probably mismanaged it. The escheatment case and the Idaho test oath were both appealed to the US Supreme Court.[3] As Latter-day Saints waited with apprehension, a decision was announced on February 3, 1890, in *Davis v. Beason*, upholding the test oath. It was written by Justice Stephen J. Field, who had sometimes shown friendliness to the Church. His view was that bigamy and polygamy were such egregious "crimes against civilization," they "tended to destroy the purity of marriage while degrading and debasing men and women." The ruling not only confirmed the criminalization of plural marriage as a practice but constrained even the belief in the practice or teaching of it as religious doctrine.

Field had no sympathy for the idea that such a deviation from traditional marriage could be a religious tenet. "Crime is not the less odious because sanctioned by what any particular sect may designate as religion," he wrote. The test oath was constitutional and "not open to any valid legal objection to which our attention has been called." It excluded from voting or holding office anyone either convicted of a violation or who had condoned someone else's support of it. It meant that either the Church had to change its teachings or allow its members in Idaho Territory to be permanently prohibited from active citizenship. A bill would soon make its way through Congress, the Cullom–Struble Bill, that if passed would universalize these restrictions for all states and territories.

From the point of John Taylor's death in August 1887, the new senior apostle, Wilford Woodruff (not actually sustained as president for another year and a half), demonstrated a more realistic

---

Reports, Mar. 6, 1888; Larson, *Americanization of Utah*, 247–48; Lyman, ed., *Candid Insights*, 23–24, 60–61, 109–10, 231.

3. William Budge to Jeremiah Wilson, Oct. 21, 1890; Linford, "Mormons and the Law," 397–412; Firmage and Mangrum, *Zion in the Courts*, 232–36.

outlook in dealing with government coercion than either Brigham Young or John Taylor had ever displayed. Biographer Thomas Alexander observed that even while himself a fugitive from anti-polygamy deputies, Woodruff had "mellowed" in his attitude and showed far less resentment of the government or need to remain detached from American society than Latter-day Saint leaders had previously demonstrated. Indeed, with hindsight this stands as an important step toward resolving the dilemma. Woodruff recognized, again more than either predecessor, that statehood would be the best avenue possible for achieving political freedom from undue federal interference. He affirmed this change in attitude to his protector, William Atkin, while on the polygamy underground near Bloomington, Utah, southwest of St. George, at the end of January 1889.[4]

In September that same year, Woodruff answered an inquiry from a Davis County stake president about whether to encourage or allow new plural marriages. The senior Church leader answered, "I feel that it is not proper for any marriages of this kind to be performed in the territory at the present time." This reply, accepted by the inquirer, probably perplexed Woodruff's counselors George Q. Cannon and Joseph F. Smith. The former confessed that he was "not prepared to fully acquiesce [to Woodruff's] expressions," this being the "first time that anything of this kind had ever been uttered by one who holds the keys," meaning the authority to make such a change if inspired to do so. Woodruff mentioned the command to Joseph Smith to build a temple in Jackson County, Missouri, which Smith considered void when hostile outsiders sufficiently blocked their progress that it was impossible to complete the assignment. After Cannon and Smith had come to fully conform to their leader's views, the same justification would be repeated to the Latter-day Saints assembled at general conference when the Church ratified Woodruff's manifesto ending polygamy.

In a candid interview with a *St. Louis Globe–Democrat* reporter in October 1889 regarding the federal law banning polygamy,

4. Alexander, *Things in Heaven and Earth*, 236, 251, 256–57, 259; Lyman, "Succession by Seniority," 113–14.

Woodruff replied, "We have no thought of evading or ignoring this or any other law of the United Sates," saying "we recognize its laws as binding on us." He assured the reporter that he had "refused to give any recommendation for performance of plural marriages since [he had] been president" of the church.[5] The interview, part of a series of ten articles, triggered a barrage of negative dispatches from William Nelson of the *Salt Lake Tribune*, one quoting Governor Thomas about the Church's stranglehold on territorial politics, another regarding the steady influx of LDS immigrants which had increased the LDS population 16 percent in that decade.[6] The governor explained that the rank-and-file Latter-day Saints wanted to evade federal officials and statutes wherever they could, due to their "complete and immovable" loyalty to their Church. Nelson wrote articles for the Associated Press about oaths sworn in LDS temples to obey only the priesthood and to "avenge the blood of the prophets," meaning Church founders Joseph and Hyrum Smith, whose murders were allegedly due to government negligence.[7]

In an interesting contrast, Ambrose Carlton, who had recently been replaced on the Utah Commission, granted a frank interview with the St. Louis newspaper about the anti-LDS critics, some of whom were "so bitterly hostile that they cannot do justice to the Mormons even if they were inclined" to. He asserted this to be particularly true of Nelson in writing his AP dispatches. What Carlton had experienced during his time in Utah was that "the nearer the Mormons come to being in rapport with the public sentiment of the country, the more [certain "*Tribune* ring"] gentiles of Utah want to push [the Mormons' backs] to the wall." No matter how far Mormons retreated and made concessions for this or that, their opponents consistently stepped up their charges to provide "an excuse for Congress to utterly destroy local self-government and to disenfranchise all

5. Bitton, *George Q. Cannon*, 300–01; Doctrine and Covenants 84:2–5; 124:49–54.

6. *St. Louis Globe–Democrat*, Oct. 3, 4, 8, 13 (Woodruff's interview), 17, 18, 22, 23, 24, 1889; also Quinn, "LDS Church Authority," 32, 36–38; Whitney, *History of Utah*, 3:687–704.

7. *St. Louis Globe–Democrat*, Nov. 11, 21, 22, Dec. 2, 1889; Lyman, ed., *Candid Insights*, 38–39.

Mormons." He alleged that no one would be more disappointed to see the abandonment of polygamy in Utah than those non-Mormon opponents for whom that peculiar practice was used as a weapon to arouse hostility against the Church. This perceptive newspaper interviewee hinted that the anticipated drastic Supreme Court decision that occurred at precisely the time when Church members were beginning to pay more attention to public opinion.

Utah was not the only territory seeking statehood. There was Democratic concern about Idaho and Wyoming increasing the Republicans' hold on Congress if they were admitted. The same had been the result of four other territories that had recently been made states: North and South Dakota, Montana, and Washington. The Democrats wanted to see the simultaneous admission of all the remaining territories, including New Mexico, but the Republicans, as Democratic spokesman William Springer expressed it, were unwilling to do as the Democrats had done and "treat all these territories fairly."[8]

John T. Caine and one of the attorneys the Church had hired, Jeremiah Wilson, along with LDS political organizer William Budge, continued working to prevent admission of Idaho with its test oath. There was little realistic hope of accomplishing their purpose, even before the Supreme Court cut the ground from under their feet in February 1890. With Republicans in control of both houses of Congress, Idaho delegate Fred T. Dubois was more confident than ever. Budge decided it was pointless to even remain in Washington long enough to see the outcome of the tug-of-war over the territories. As Caine concluded in disgust, it had become "a party necessity" to punish the Latter-day Saints.[9]

For their part the Democrats continued to oppose the test oath, as they also opposed woman suffrage in Wyoming. Congressman Springer asked why the Republicans were opposed to Mormons voting in Idaho and unconcerned about their significant presence in Wyoming. The difference, he knew, was that LDS people in

8. Lyman, "Mormon Transition in Idaho Politics," 24–29; also Wells, *Anti-Mormonism in Idaho*, 133–54; Gould, *Wyoming*, 113–22, 159–215.

9. Caine to William Budge, Apr. 1, 1890, Caine Papers.

Wyoming tended to vote Republican. "It appears that Mormonism is objectionable only when the person entertaining that belief is suspected of a desire to vote the Democratic ticket," he offered.[10] Caine wrote to LDS attorney Franklin S. Richards that Republicans were agitating to have the test oath applied in every territory where there was a significant LDS population and a Democratic majority. There had previously been oaths to weed out undesirable voters in Arizona and Nevada. Caine was afraid of the potential to "saddle that outrage" on Mormons "for all time," and it seemed to partisan observers, at least, that the Republicans would "resort to any means" to gain more Senate seats for their party.[11]

Even more ominously, on April 10 Senator Shelby M. Cullom of Illinois introduced in the Senate a bill that was the logical result of the recent Supreme Court ruling on the Idaho test oath. It read that "no person belonging to a Church organization teaching or practicing polygamy shall be permitted to vote," hold political office, or sit on juries. The next day a similar bill was introduced in the House of Representatives by Isaac N. Struble, a Republican congressman from Iowa. Caine conferred with Church-employed attorney Wilson about how to counter this, and decided that, for all practical purposes, there was nothing they could do. The Supreme Court had already upheld the legality of it. They could only hope the Cullom–Struble measure might meet the same fate as a similar proposal introduced earlier in the session. That one was authored by Robert N. Baskin, who had also written the Cullom and Struble Bills, and quietly died in committee. Unfortunately for the Utah delegation, that was not the trajectory of the current set of bills.[12] Caine suggested that LDS businessmen "make a strong and earnest appeal to the firms from whom they purchase goods, to ... use their

10. *Congressional Record*, Mar. 26, 1890; also *House Reports*, 51st Cong., 1st sess., 1, no. 39, part 2, 1–7.

11. Caine to Franklin S. Richards, Mar. 26, 28, 1890, Caine Papers; also Lyman, "Elimination of the Mormon Issue," 207–08; Moody, "Nevada's Anti-Mormon Legislation," 21–30.

12. *Congressional Record*, Apr. 10, 11, 29, June 28, Sept. 19, 1890; Caine to Woodruff et al., Apr. 12, 30, 1890, Woodruff General Correspondence; Franklin D. Richards journal, Apr. 26, 1890; Baskin, *Reminiscences of Early Utah,* 184.

influence with the members of Congress from their respective districts to defeat this measure." Representatives from a dozen Utah merchandising and professional enterprises were sent east to generate letters in protest of removing civil rights from a group, however odious one might find their marriage practices.[13] Petitions arrived from non-LDS businessmen in Salt Lake City and Ogden who were clearly concerned about the adverse economic effects of the measure. Their entreaties were soon countered by Utah businessmen in favor of passage.

On April 22 a group of about one hundred men, described as "mostly newcomers" to the territory, met in Salt Lake City to organize a Democratic club. Colonel T. B. O'Brien had been in the territory only a few months but emerged as the group's leader. He stated that though it was "something out of the routine" to have a local Democratic organization where there were no regular national parties, he and others present found themselves at odds with the LDS-dominated People's Party and with the Republican-leaning Liberal Party. One of the concerns voiced at the initial meeting was that the Cullom–Struble Bills might pass. "We don't propose to have this great state of Utah pocketed by the Republican thieves," was their position. There were a few Latter-day Saints present, including the original "Sagebrush Democrat" Scipio Kenner, but most in attendance were non-LDS. The former Iowa Congressman Hadley D. Johnson wrote a letter to the *Salt Lake Herald* encouraging them to persevere.[14]

Three nights after their initial meeting, the men gathered again, this time to formalize their bylaws, affirming that the "abnormal political distinctions which exist in Utah should be obliterated." The best interests of the territory would be served by "Democratic doctrine," they stated, and therefore proceeded to establish

13. Cannon to Woodruff and Smith, May 21, 1890; Spencer Clawson to Woodruff and Smith, June 11, 1890, Woodruff Correspondence; William Lowe et al. to Caine, May 23; George T. Odell to Caine, June 12; Caine to Junius F. Wells, June 20; E. C. Simmons to Charles H. Mansur, May 16, 18, 1890, Caine Papers.

14. *Salt Lake Herald*, Apr. 23, 25, 26, 29, 1890; *Salt Lake Times*, Apr. 23, 26, 1890; *Salt Lake Tribune*, Apr. 23, 24, 1890.

a party structure allowing any male citizen of Salt Lake County whose secular allegiance was to the United States to enroll "without any other or further test," as long as they paid dues. At the same meeting, Colonel O'Brien introduced a resolution protesting the draconian measures of the Cullom Bill and Idaho's bid to become a state. According to the Republican-run *Salt Lake Times*, these would-be Democrats were not initially unanimous in approving O'Brien's resolution, and some heated debate ensued. The bylaws were tabled for a week. By the time they met again, the Struble Bill had been favorably reported out of committee in Washington.[15] Representative Springer tried to amend the Struble Bill so "that no person shall be deprived of the right to vote, hold office or sit on a jury on account of his religious belief or opinions," but this was voted down. The Committee on Territories reported that in the past, Mormon leaders had thwarted the Edmunds statutes by simply advising their people to take the oaths and continue to participate in elections.[16]

While the bills were being discussed, Governor Arthur L. Thomas and former governor Caleb W. West arrived in Washington, supposedly to promote federal allocations of funds for government construction in Utah. Their expenses were being underwritten by the Salt Lake Chamber of Commerce. When it was learned that they were involved in supporting the Cullom–Struble Bills, the chamber disavowed its involvement, having eschewed the use of its facilities or organization for political or religious purposes.[17] At a public meeting of the chamber on May 5, 1890, Elias Morris, a respected LDS manufacturer, suggested that the chamber raise its voice against disfranchisement of a significant segment of the population, for the good of the economic advancement in the territory. Vice President Fred Simon, a clothing merchant, called the speaker out of order for infringing on the rule against political talk. Morris ignored him and continued on, alluding to West's and Thomas's

15. Caine to Woodruff et al., Apr. 30, 1890.

16. *Congressional Record*, Apr. 29, 1890; "Hearings before the House Committee on Territories," *House Reports*, 51st Cong., 1st sess., 6, no. 1811, 1–24.

17. *Salt Lake Times*, Apr. 29, 30, 1890; also *Deseret Weekly News*, May 31, 1890.

suspected promotion of the Cullom–Struble Bills. When Simon insisted that "the gentleman shall confine his remarks to manufactories or take his seat," the others applauded, so Morris took his seat.[18]

However, embarrassed by its missteps, the Chamber of Commerce began trying to distance itself from the Cullom–Struble bills. Even Fred Simon, whose name was already on a petition favoring passage, co-sponsored a large list of businessmen opposing the bills. Simon apologized to Caine for his earlier action and pledged that the chamber would circulate a resolution denouncing the bills. The non-LDS division over the topic grew as time went on, the *Salt Lake Herald* warned that if the law passed, "the commercial unity" of the territory would disappear. The *Herald* applauded the Liberal Party mayor of Ogden for speaking against the bills.[19]

Franklin S. Richards wrote to Caine and Cannon at the nation's capital, after overseeing the preparation of an anti-Cullom–Struble petition, that it was more important to secure "remonstrance from non-Mormons" than from Church members. He had found, even among those whom he termed their fairest friends, hostility toward the Church's political methods and little sentiment against the disfranchisement measures. However, when he patiently explained how these laws would retard the economic growth of the territory, it struck a responsive chord with these men. Soon there were several of them, representing different elements of the Liberal Party, trying to convince their friends that they needed to oppose the Cullom–Struble assault. Much of Richards's initial success was in Ogden, but Salt Lake City Democrat Thomas O'Brien and others were equally receptive.[20]

Earlier in 1890, Wilford Woodruff had sent George Cannon to Washington to help John Caine delay or diffuse the Cullom–Struble Bills. While there, Cannon became profoundly disappointed with the lack of assistance from leading Democrats and with the solidarity of the Republicans. This alignment of interests against Utah was almost insurmountable. He invited Budge to join him in conferring

18. Whitney, *History of Utah*, 3:734–35.

19. Fred Simon to Caine, Mar. 6, 1890, Caine Papers; *Senate Miscellaneous Documents*, 51st Cong., 1st sess., 2, no. 156, 1–3; *Salt Lake Herald*, May 11, 1890.

20. Franklin S. Richards to Caine and Cannon, May 22, 1890, Caine Papers.

with Senator Arthur P. Gorman (D–Maryland), still leader of the Democrats in Congress, and later with Calvin Brice in New York, chairman of the Democratic National Committee. Brice would dispassionately compare Latter-day Saints to early Christians and predict that "until they assimilated to the world," they would continue to be fed to the lions. He said they needed to abandon plural marriage, that was all there was to it. Cannon briefed him on the mistreatment of LDS people at the hand of Democratic officials in Idaho and suggested he could at least try to put a stop to that. In fact, the Democratic chairman offered no real assistance at all.[21] Cannon was surprised by this, because he had become accustomed to a more solicitous reception from Democrats. By the time he arrived back in Utah, he was convinced the Church would need to look elsewhere for help. That conclusion looms large in Utah political history. Two months later, when he returned east in mid-April, he turned his attention to prominent Republicans through the aid of Isaac Trumbo, the California lobbyist. His goal was still primarily to defuse the disfranchisement that would result from the pending bills being passed.

The Cullom–Struble Bills were probably the most ominous threat the LDS Church had ever faced, with the distinct prospect that the entire Church could be disbanded as a legal entity, its members denied citizenship, and their legal powers removed. There were other challenges as well, as the *Deseret News* reported on other legislative threats—more, the newspaper claimed, than faced by any other group in the nation. They included the suggestion that convert immigrants be sent back to Europe, children of polygamous marriages be prohibited from receiving inheritances, and the permanent loss of previously confiscated Church property and funds. The situation was certainly worse than it had been at the end of the previous year when Church members went on a fast to petition for divine assistance.[22]

21. Rogers, ed., *In the President's Office*, 407; also Grant, *Diaries*, Jan. 1, 1890; Franklin D. Richards journal, Jan. 9, 1890; Bitton, *George Q. Cannon*, 304–09.

22. Caine to Richards, Mar. 26, 1890; Woodruff et al. to William Spry, Sept. 29, 1890, First Presidency Letterbooks; *Deseret Weekly News*, July 12, 26, 1890; *Salt Lake Herald*, July 15, 1890; *Salt Lake Tribune*, July 15, 1890; *Salt Lake Times*, July 16, 1890; Lyman, ed., *Candid Insights*, 99–101; Cannon and O'Higgins, *Under the Prophet in Utah*, 85–88; Roberts, *Comprehensive History*, 6:193–97.

Yet amid this flood of negative developments for LDS members, an apparently sympathetic agent of the US Justice Department, E. C. Foster, arrived in Salt Lake City on April 7, 1890. According to an interested observer, Judge C. S. Zane, one of the nation's ranking law officials was assigned to look into "law enforcement in the territory," particularly in the office of US Attorney C. S. Varian and his assistants. There was a significant indication in this that some in the often hostile federal agency had the Saints' best interests in mind. Through other positive gestures through the still-troublous succeeding years, the justice department sometimes demonstrated good concern and even cooperation.[23]

For some time, Isaac Trumbo had been engaged enlisting the cooperation of several prominent politicians, and during his intermittent service to the Church he urged his sometime employer, Leland Stanford, to discuss Utah with Benjamin Harrison, the intolerant Protestant who demonstrated no sympathy for heretics. Morris M. Estee, also of California, chairman of the national convention that nominated Harrison, became involved in lobbying for the Latter-day Saints, as well, after being enlisted by Trumbo. While the Cullom–Struble Bills were being discussed in congressional committees in April, Trumbo appealed for assistance from the chairman of the Republican National Committee, James S. Clarkson, of Iowa.

Clarkson thereafter proved to be a longtime consistent champion of the LDS cause. Together with Trumbo, he approached Secretary of State James G. Blaine, who was the most influential of all Republicans at the time. In an obsequious way, Clarkson later wrote to Wilford Woodruff that he and Blaine "learned of the magnitude of the Mormon people, the greatness of their development in many states besides Utah, and the large part that they were sure to bear, for good or evil, in the destiny of this republic." He explained that Trumbo "came upon the scene and gave to Mr. Blaine and me such a practical and accurate knowledge" of the situation that they

23. Zane diary, Apr. 7, 1890; John T. Caine to James Jack, Apr. 6, 1890, Caine Papers; Caine to Woodruff et al., June 17, 1890, Caine Letters; Woodruff to E. C. Foster, Oct. 23, 1890, First Presidency Letterbooks.

easily recognized potential for a strategy involving the Mormons' political deliverance that would greatly enhance Republican membership in the region.[24]

Blaine was the only political figure of the era who could, almost singlehandedly, halt a popular piece of legislation such as the Cullom–Struble Bill. Blaine possessed "magnetism," or what we now call charisma, and had nearly received the 1880 Republican nomination for president. When he and Ulysses S. Grant deadlocked at the convention, the party settled on compromise candidate James A. Garfield,[25] who chose Blaine as Secretary of State. Four years later Blaine won the nomination for president, but his assistants alienated some voters, primarily Irish emigrants, causing him to lose the election. It would have been still possible for him to run again in 1888, if he had not lost interest by then. He was a hypochondriac, more concerned with his health than political prominence. Benjamin Harrison filled the void and basked in Blaine's endorsement; the new president then again appointed him Secretary of State.[26]

Virtually all national elections of that age were hotly contested. Often the winner had a razor-thin margin over his opponent. Neither party was completely united either. The Stalwarts, as the Grant Republicans were called, espoused the spoils system, despite the damage that caused to the party's reputation. They labeled Blaine and his followers "half-breeds" for their unwillingness to embrace the appointment of party loyalists to offices they may not have been entirely qualified for. However, Blaine's people were not averse to combining politics with business interests. That kind of conflict of interest was a hallmark of the times. As the 1880s arrived, disagreements over cultural heritage and economic status boiled over. The Stalwarts had long been intolerant of Roman Catholics, German-language schools, Mormon polygamists, and the availability of alcoholic beverages on Sunday. Politicians like Clarkson realistically

---

24. James S. Clarkson to Woodruff, July 11, 1894, Volwiler Papers (appendix).

25. Garfield was born in Ohio, may have attended school for a while in the Kirtland Temple, and was familiar with some Latter Day Saint teachings. It is possible that he conveyed his impression of the Church to Blaine. Cannon, "Mormon Issue in Congress," 68.

26. Marcus, *Grand Old Party*, 7–9, 24–31, 59, 96–107, 114–15, 124–25.

worried that these biases would eventually backfire on the Republicans. Clarkson was also aware that in the spring of 1890, only Blaine's influence was able to stem the anti-Mormon furor for the moment. Before Blaine became involved in the matter, it was assumed the combined Cullom–Struble Bill would easily pass. Caine requested that his former assistant, Frank J. Cannon, appear before the Senate Committee on Territories and testify against the Cullom version. Cannon was one of the then-rare LDS Republicans who had the necessary background for this assignment.

It was at that precise moment that Blaine too opposed the Cullom Bill, through comments in the committee and, to a greater extent, behind the scenes. Clarkson later prompted President Woodruff to remember how Blaine had appealed to the Senate committee, "protesting against such an outrage upon any portion of a free people, [and] asserting that no republic of free men could tolerate such a wrong and live." In his effusive style, Clarkson concluded that "the summit and sublimity of all was reached when [Blaine] stood in this small committee room and smote down with the great strength of his indignant wrath this further attempt, in a free government[,] to degrade further a people already wronged too much."[27]

Following the powerful message by the Republican whose oratorical ability was unquestioned, a thirty-one-year-old Frank J. Cannon, who at the time was an Ogden newspaperman (later Utah's first US senator), appeared before the well-prepared committee and bluntly pointed out that the Cullom–Struble Bill was intended to punish and disfranchise the "class of [young] people [in Utah] who have obeyed the laws, and who swear that they will not aid or abet anybody else" who defied the law, and who had demonstrated a willingness to reaffirm this each time they took the test oath. The young journalist reminded the committee that those who had more than one wife had been disfranchised already, so it was only the remaining innocent people, who had no sympathy for

27. J. S. Clarkson to E. W. Halford, Dec. 5, 1891, Harrison Papers, Clarkson to Woodruff, July 11, 1894 (see appendix); Woodruff journal, Apr. 16–24, 1889; also Jensen, *Winning of the Midwest*; Kleppner, *Cross of Culture*; Kleppner, *Third Electoral System*; Whitney, *History of Utah*, 3:743.

the "dying institution" of polygamy, who stood to suffer from the proposed law. Making clear that he personally preferred the Republican Party, he expressed regret that since they presumed they could not win Utah by conventional means, they were stooping to other methods to assure election victories.

As effective as this testimony may have been, it was what Cannon stated next, in the question-and-answer segment, on the heels of leading comments by friendly Senator Matthew Butler of South Carolina, that likely proved the most persuasive:

> SENATOR HENRY B. PAYNE (D. OHIO): One question more, if in your opinion the young Mormons of whom you have spoken ... would have [polygamy] disavowed by the church if they had the power?"
> MR. CANNON: "They do disavow it two or three times a year, usually. Every time they take this oath they disavow it."
> SENATOR PAYNE: "I understand you; but would they have the power to amend the creed of the church?"
> MR. CANNON: "They have not the power."
> SENATOR PAYNE: "If they had the power would they do it?"
> MR. CANNON: "I think so."
> THE CHAIRMAN, ORVILLE H. PLATT (R. CONN.): "They have not the power because it is a revelation."[28]

Although Caine introduced Cannon as being in the area by chance, he had made his appearance at the behest of his father, the second-highest official in the LDS Church, George Q. Cannon. Caine would not have known of the behind-the-scenes arrangements to get him there. However, Caine was pleased with the young Cannon's skill in answering questions, concluding to the LDS presidency that Frank "did much to defeat the ... friends of the bill in the senate." Frank had previously met with Blaine, a friend of his father from their congressional years together. Blaine had advised the young advocate to follow up his testimony with personal visits to individual congressmen, saying he would do the same to bolster the hesitant ones. He cautioned Cannon to see this as a temporary

28. *Hearings before the [Senate] Committee on Territories,* May 19, 1890.

fix only. "This time" Utah would not be harmed, he assured Cannon, but for the permanent solution it would be necessary to "get into line" on polygamy.

George Q. made another appearance in Washington in late May 1890 and wrote back in code to other members of the Church presidency that "we shall have time to get in some work and I favor the proposition which Tobias [Trumbo] submitted to you, and which you referred to me, if the party [Republicans] will now accept the business on those terms." He affirmed he would do all he could, "and I feel that the Lord has been with us, and that our efforts have been blessed. Tobias has seen Basil [Blaine] today and he feels all right."[29] Scott G. Kenney, a longtime knowledgeable scholar of this period, was the first to recognize the significance of this proposition by Trumbo, and no one has since questioned that this was the moment when both sides would come to an agreement to halt plural marriage in exchange for halting passage of the Cullom–Struble legislation. When Frank pressed the matter with his father, George Q. informed him that "President Woodruff has been praying. … He thinks he sees some light. … You are authorized to say that something will be done." Frank lost no time visiting members of the congressional committees to inform them in confidence that the desired concessions were now pending.[30] This is what prevented the Cullom and Struble Bills from progressing any further, as Frank himself would later claim.

Robert N. Baskin, the person who drafted and helped sponsor the disfranchisement bills, corroborated Cannon's account. He wrote in his memoirs that when the Senate committee had decided to report the bill favorably to the floor, Cullom informed him "he had been assured by a delegation of prominent Mormons, that if further action on the bill was delayed for a reasonable time, the practice of polygamy

29. Cannon to Woodruff and Smith, May 24, 1890, Woodruff Papers. Sometimes clerks wrote translations for coded letters above the lines, and in some instances the cipher books have survived. In this case "Basil" seems to be Blaine and "party" implies Republicans. See also Ardis E. Parshall, "The Qmlbwpnygax Eujugec Have Not the Power," *Keepapitchinin*, Dec. 9–11, 2008, www.keepapitchinin.org.

30. Caine to Woodruff et al., June 17, 1890; Cannon and O'Higgins, *Under the Prophet in Utah*, 85–91.

would be prohibited by the Mormon church." It was understood that if this did not happen soon, the bills would be revived. The legislation was not the only thing on the minds of Church leaders. In May 1890 Joseph F. Smith confided to secretary John Nuttall that "we are making a strong effort to *do something* in defense of the rights of our '*monog*' [monogamous] brethren. I hope we can do as much in their behalf as they have done in ours." In other words, the leadership wanted to be absolved of responsibility for the persecution of the monogamous members for the sake of those who were not monogamous. These actions would at least partially correct the imbalance.[31]

Just over a month after the Senate hearings, another son of George Q. Cannon, apostle Abraham H. Cannon, was in New York City for medical treatment. While George Q. visited with him, he asked his son to sign a statement Secretary Blaine had drafted. The alarmed Abraham recognized it as "a virtual renunciation of plural marriage," and the fearless defender of "the principle" recorded that his "feelings revolt at signing such a document," although he clearly eventually did sign it.[32]

George Q. Cannon's interaction with legislators had a strong impact on the decisions made in a private Church council meeting on July 31, 1890, when Woodruff and Cannon discussed politics with four prominent LDS Democrats: apostle Heber J. Grant, Church attorney Franklin S. Richards, *Deseret News* editor Charles W. Penrose, and a little later Brigadier General Richard W. Young. These men reported that Democrats in Idaho, Montana, and Wyoming were seeking to "get Mormon votes." Could they be assured of that? No, the First Presidency replied. It was a better strategy now for Church members to throw their support behind the Republicans "as a reward to Delegate [Joseph] Carey and his party for getting Wyoming admitted as a state without anti-Mormon legislation." The Democrats "had the power to do us good" and had done little. They were "afraid, and betrayed us[,] so that now we

31. Smith to Nuttall, May 7, 1890, Smith Letterbooks; Paulos, *Mormon Church on Trial*, 52–59; Baskin, *Reminiscences of Early Utah*, 183–86.

32. Lyman, ed., *Candid Insights*, 98, 109–10.

feel as though the Republican Party should be tried[,] to see if they will be fair to us." The contrast between Idaho, where the Saints were disfranchised by the Democrats they voted for, and Wyoming, where they leaned toward Republicans and were included in civic life, was on the minds of all those present.[33]

It was probably during the same meeting that George Q. Cannon affirmed to the four men that the prospects for statehood had taken an unexpected upswing. According to Richard W. Young, Cannon said Congress would doubtless have disfranchised them if party leaders had not recognized "there were Republicans in Utah and that a wise course on the part of the Republicans would doubtless make more."[34] Cannon had recently privately observed that "the Democratic Party today is helpless. They can be of no benefit to us." The foremost political strategist in the Church had thus turned decisively anti-Democrat,[35] asserting that at least it would be unwise not to allow the other party to explain its principles to young Latter-day Saints. It is clear in hindsight that by the time the policy change regarding plural marriage was announced, the decision had been made some months earlier. Other clarifying developments occurred that summer. Joseph F. Smith was asked privately by fellow Church leader Charles W. Nibley if a friend (probably himself) could marry a plural wife, and Smith's response was that he approved of it in principle but that "times have changed, the conditions are not propitious and ... the decree now is that there shall be no p[lural] m[arriage]s in the United States, and that there should be none anywhere else" unless at least the woman remained in that country. Nibley was directed to convince "his friend" to be satisfied with what wives he had for now.

Probably a more important historical development occurred on July 10, 1890, when according to A. H. Cannon, the First Presidency and Quorum of the Twelve had a private reading of a resolution stating that no plural marriages would be permitted "even in Mexico unless the contracting parties, or at least the female," intended

33. Joseph Carey to John T. Caine, Aug. 6, 1890, Caine Papers.

34. Richard W. Young to John Henry Smith, Feb. 6, 1892, and Young's accompanying notarized statement, John Henry Smith Papers.

35. George Q. Cannon journal, June 17, 26, July 21, 31, 1890.

to remain a resident of that country. This was the first disclosure that the Church was extending the prohibition somewhat beyond the US boundaries. It makes the Woodruff Manifesto issued three months later a public announcement of a policy adopted the previous June and July; the proximity to the time when George Q. and Frank J. Cannon promised James G. Blaine that they would do so makes it an even more significant event.[36]

While word of the new position quietly spread through Mormon circles, it was accompanied by confusion and dismay. Since territorial officials had not been informed of these plans, they continued to pressure the Church to conform. The Utah Commission assigned a new member, former lieutenant governor of Indiana Robert S. Robertson, to draft the annual report to the US Secretary of the Interior and instructed him to include a full and accurate statement of the "existing status of the polygamous question, including such facts and statistics as may show, or tend to show the increase or decline of the practice." Robertson charged that forty-one males had contracted plural marriages since the previous year's report. He included evidence for one well-publicized case. The others were based on hearsay that had come from voter registration officers who may have confused new marriages with older polygamous relationships, with details gleaned from obituaries. There were probably but few new sealings performed that year—anywhere.[37] LDS leaders said the allegations were blatantly false. Because they made these remarks in private and recorded them in their diaries as spontaneous expressions of frustration, one has to believe that they had done their best to put a stop to new plural marriages. Caine demanded documentary evidence from the commission, but was ignored. Joseph F. Smith was so angry, he charged the commission with "falsifying the statements of the presidency" with the intent to

36. Lyman, ed., *Candid Insights*, 103–04; Franklin D. Richards journal, July 10, 1890; Joseph F. Smith to Charles W. Nibley, June 20, 1890, Smith Papers; cf. Whitney, *History of Utah*, 3: 734–35.

37. Minutebook D–E, Utah Commission Minute Books, 461–81; also "Annual Report of the Utah Commission," *Annual Report of the Department of the Interior, 1890*, 397–428; *House Executive Documents*, 51st Cong., 2d sess., 13:414–20; Caine to Charles W. Penrose, Dec. 9, 1890, Caine Letters; Caine to Penrose, Dec. 19, 1890, Caine Papers.

"create a furor." Cannon was quoted in the *St. Louis Globe–Democrat*, for instance, saying the Church was prepared to "bow to the law," but the commission had detected in his choice of words a lack of enthusiasm or commitment, belying the opposite.[38]

As the summer wore on, the Church presidency left Utah and visited other LDS leaders in Colorado, New Mexico, and Arizona, and then embarked for San Francisco. Abraham H. Cannon, now a member of the Quorum of the Twelve, wrote in his diary that their purpose was to avoid being subpoenaed as witnesses in Church property suits. While in California they consulted with a friendly legal advisor, Morris Estee, about the Church's confiscated property. Their friend pointed out that Latter-day Saints numbered some two hundred thousand people facing about sixty-five million Americans; the Mormons could no longer "hope to stand out against them. You simply must make an announcement that you are laying aside polygamy," he warned. Cannon was still thinking in terms of a statement they could live with, without conceding anything permanently. He explained the difficulty in drafting a document that would serve the purpose of satisfying both Church members and opponents. Estee's response: "It is going to have to be done sooner or later anyway," meaning the necessity of a clean break that would not be popular at home.[39] President Woodruff clearly found Estee's advice persuasive.

Perhaps the final blow came when Frank Dyer, receiver of Church property, was replaced by apostate and Church critic Henry W. Lawrence. Dyer informed John R. Winder of the Presiding Bishopric that "an attempt would soon be made on the part of the government to confiscate the Logan, Manti and St. George temples on the grounds that they are not used for public worship." The Salt Lake Temple was still three years away from completion but

38. Joseph F. Smith to L. John Nuttall, Sept. 22, 1890, Joseph F. Smith Papers; Caine to George L. Godfrey, Nov. 11, 1890, Caine Papers.

39. Bitton, *George Q. Cannon*, 311, 312–13; also Woodruff journal, Sept. 16, 17, 1890; Lyman, ed., *Candid Insights*, 124–25; Franklin D. Richards journal, Sept. 23, 1890; Woodruff et al. to J. A. Fillmore, Sept. 23, 1890; Woodruff et al. to A. N. Towne, Sept. 23, 1890, First Presidency Letterbooks.

might have been endangered as well. Hearings regarding the original disposition of the temple properties were being re-examined by a commissioner appointed by the Utah Supreme Court, Colonel M. N. Stone, who was reviewing Dyer's accounts and the earlier compromise negotiated by the former receiver as to whether there was an avenue through which such property might yet be placed under Lawrence's control.[40]

US Attorney C. S. Varian attempted to deliver a subpoena to President Woodruff but could not find him. The entire First Presidency adopted a policy of trying to out-wait Stone and Varian in California. They returned in late September after the subpoena crisis had passed, but were warned on arrival by Church attorneys that the temples were in imminent danger. Woodruff was "stirred up in his feelings" by this and "felt that it was his duty to get out some kind of manifesto," Cannon wrote.[41] The president dictated the essence of what he desired to say to secretary George F. Gibbs. When Cannon was consulted, he said he supported the president's judgment but wondered if it was too soon to disseminate such a statement publicly. The next day the First Presidency invited three men to the Gardo House office to read the draft to them and ask *Deseret News* editor Charles W. Penrose, second counselor in the Presiding Bishopric John R. Winder, and George Reynolds if they would polish the document for publication. They agreed to do so. When they brought it back to the presidency, Cannon made several more emendations, and that afternoon the First Presidency read the document to apostles Franklin D. Richards, Moses Thatcher, and Marriner W. Merrill. Again "slight alterations" were made.

Apostle Marriner W. Merrill, then president of the Logan Temple, discussed the document with Woodruff on September 24, the day before it was released. Merrill's journal entry observes that the manifesto was "the only way to retain the possession of our temples and continue the ordinance work for the living and dead which was

40. Cf. Alexander, *Things in Heaven and Earth*, 264.

41. George Q. Cannon journal, Sept. 23, 1890; *Deseret Weekly News*, Sept. 13, 20, 27, 1890.

considered of more importance than continuing the practice of plural marriage for the present." Moses Thatcher, another Logan apostle, who also spoke with Woodruff beforehand, commented on how upset the president was with the false statements that had been published by the Utah Commission. Woodruff feared "great trouble was coming unless something was done to offset their publication." Thatcher also found Woodruff particularly apprehensive about Congress enacting further legislation against the Church. Thatcher was not specific, but likely meant a threatened revival of the Cullom–Struble Bills.[42]

The Church president's emphasis on saving the temples was corroborated by other statements, including his own over the next year. At the Cache Stake conference in Logan on November 1, 1891, Woodruff declared, "The Lord showed me by vision and revelation exactly what would take place if we did not stop this practice [plural marriage]." He explained that the brethren who officiated at the local temple would be cast out and probably "made prisoners," and "all ordinances would be stopped throughout the land of Zion." He added stirringly that he would not have taken the action he did "had not the God of heaven commanded me ... I went before the Lord, and I wrote what the Lord told me to write." Heber J. Grant echoed in his journal a year after the declaration that "if it had not been for the manifesto, all the work for the living and the dead in our temples would have had to stop."[43]

Church attorney Franklin S. Richards was also at the president's office the morning of September 25 "when President Woodruff came in and stated that the Lord had made manifest to him, after much prayer and supplication, that our people must submit to the law, inasmuch as they had exhausted every legal means of showing its unconstitutionality."[44] None of the issues cited by Woodruff were necessarily new. However, the pressure had continued mounting from many directions. Whereas in the past, the Church had found

42. Marriner W. Merrill journal, Sept. 24, 1890; Grant, *Diaries*, Sept. 30, 1890.

43. Official Declaration 1; *Deseret Weekly News*, Nov. 14, 1891; Durham, *Discourses of Wilford Woodruff*, 213–16; Grant, *Diaries*, Apr. 2, 1891.

44. Grant, Sept. 30, 1890; also Richards address, Nov. 13, 1932, in Richards Papers.

a way around obstacles, the difference this time was that Woodruff said his action was dictated by God.

On September 25 Woodruff penned in his diary his oft-quoted observation:

> I have arrived at a point in the history of the Church of Jesus Christ of Latter-day Saints when I am under the necessity of acting for the temporal salvation of the church. The United States government has taken a plan and passed laws to destroy the Latter-day Saints upon the subject of polygamy or patriarchal order of marriage. And after praying to the Lord and feeling inspired by His Spirit, I have issued the following proclamation which is sustained by my counselors and the twelve apostles.[45]

The Church telegraphed the document to the territorial delegate, John T. Caine. With some earlier warning that it was coming, he lost little time in having it printed for distribution. It appeared in the *Washington Evening Star* the same day, headlined "An Official Declaration," accompanied by Caine's message that he hoped this would put to rest the false accusations of the Utah Commission and quash the Cullom–Struble Bills. He was likely acting on previous instructions from the First Presidency, suggesting some motivation for the content and timing of the manifesto being a response to the report of the Utah Commission and Congress's reading of it.[46]

The opening paragraph of Woodruff's message itself reinforced concern about the Utah Commission's statements. The second paragraph denied the specific charge that "either forty or any other number of plural marriages" had been solemnized during the previous year "in our Temples or in any other place in the Territory." After acknowledging that "the court of last resort" had declared Congress's suppressive laws constitutional, the Church president

45. Woodruff journal, Sept. 25, 1890. For the text of the manifesto, see Official Declaration 1, Doctrine and Covenants. Temporal salvation might well include preserving the temples in Church possession.

46. *Washington Evening Star*, Sept. 25, 1890; W. B. Dougall to John T. Caine, Sept. 24, 1890; Caine to Woodruff, Sept. 26, 1890, in Caine Papers.

affirmed his intention "to submit to those laws, and to use my influence with members of the church over which I preside to have them do likewise." He pointed out that nothing in his recent teachings "or those of my associates ... can be reasonably construed to inculcate or encourage polygamy." In conclusion he wrote, "I now publicly declare that my advice to the Latter-day Saints is to refrain from contracting any marriage forbidden by the law of the land."[47]

Press coverage of this announcement was extensive. The *Salt Lake Tribune* questioned why it had not come "in the authoritative manner in which orders of the church are generally clothed," why Woodruff spoke "merely as an individual." Placing emphasis on the term "advice," the paper noted that the Church president had not spoken "as though that advice had come authoritatively by revelation." When the *Salt Lake Herald* retorted that it was because it was a policy statement, not a revelation, the *Tribune* rebutted that "if the saints do not understand it as a revelation, but simply as the words of a weak old man[,] then it will not count as against the former declaration which all saints have been taught to understand was a revelation."[48] There was probably no explanation for the statement that would convince *Tribune* supporters of the genuineness of the Church president's intent.

People on all sides were scrutinizing the wording and intent of the manifesto when Utah Governor Arthur Thomas, in an interview with the *San Francisco Chronicle*, mentioned that the declaration "in no way asserts that polygamy is wrong or the law right." The *Deseret Weekly News* replied that "there is nothing in President Woodruff's declaration in regard to faith, or doctrine, or tenets, but it contains a volume in a few words as to practice." This was because the Supreme Court had originally drawn a distinction between tenets and practices and upheld the government's right to impose conformity of action, not of belief. The *News* editor, Penrose, was unhappy to

47. Official Declaration 1; also Lyman, "Political Background of the Woodruff Manifesto," 21–39.

48. *Salt Lake Tribune*, Sept. 26, Oct. 10, 1890; *Salt Lake Herald*, Oct. 9, 1890.

see the Church criticized after having met the level of compliance demanded of them.[49]

The fact is that Penrose was incorrect about where the legality stood after US Supreme Court Justice Stephen J. Field's majority decision in *Davis v. Beason*, issued on February 3, 1890, that there could be no distinction between belief and behavior either. Those who condoned polygamy without participating in it were thereafter to be excluded from voting and holding office in Idaho, so the decision went. Since the Supreme Court had the final word, there was no longer a possibility for all Latter-day Saints within the United States to interpret the law otherwise.

As word of the manifesto filtered through the isolated settlements of Mormondom, LDS people awaited further direction. Most of the leaders withheld public comment until the approaching semi-annual pre-conference leadership meetings beginning September 30. There the apostles expressed their feelings among themselves. Apostle Heber J. Grant suggested that realistically "President Woodruff had simply told the world what we had been doing[,] and if there were any advantages to secure by the manifesto[,] I feel that we should have them."[50] The most striking aspect of this and similar comments by members of the Twelve was the assumption that the declaration did not mean much to them individually, that it was a legal matter and not a theological one. Several stated that their intention was to continue living with their current wives. John Henry Smith pledged that only jail would prevent him from continuing his living arrangements with all his wives. Francis M. Lyman agreed: "I design to live with and have children by my wives, using the wisdom which God gives me to avoid being captured by the officers of the law." He realized that in so doing, he would be acting as an individual rather than a Church official.

President Joseph F. Smith wrote to his plural wife Sarah, residing in the central-Utah town of Nephi, that she would hear of a "pronunciamento by Prest. Woodruff in relation to our political

49. *San Francisco Chronicle*, Sept. 27, 1890; *Deseret Weekly News*, Oct. 18, 1890.
50. Lyman, ed., *Candid Insights*, 135–41; Grant, *Diaries*, Sept. 30, Oct. 1, 1890.

and domestic status." It would "no doubt startle some folks," but he hoped "it will not startle *you*, neither will you be worried about it[,] for you and the rest of us are all right."[51] Those already married considered themselves beyond the sweep of Woodruff's declaration. Others who had not previously availed themselves of the opportunity to take plural wives had by then procrastinated too long and could no longer do so, was the thinking. The leaders had not even planned to discuss the manifesto in general conference, except that Secretary of the Interior John W. Noble insisted on it. As he informed J. T. Caine, the government would not accept the manifesto as a valid statement of official policy unless it was sustained by a vote of those attending the Church conference. The matter was therefore introduced on October 6 by Bishop Orson F. Whitney after reading the Church's Articles of Faith to the throng in the Tabernacle, probably with emphasis on the eleventh: "We believe in being subject to kings, presidents, rulers and magistrates, in obeying, honoring and sustaining the law." Whitney read the text of President Woodruff's statement, after which Lorenzo Snow, president of the Quorum of the Twelve, made the motion that "we accept his declaration concerning plural marriages as authoritative and binding" upon Church members. The vote to sustain was nearly unanimous.[52]

George Q. Cannon followed by reminding the congregation of their difficult earlier times in Missouri when the Church was prevented from constructing a temple at Jackson County because of opposition from older settlers, when God, through Joseph Smith, relieved the Church of that assignment. Cannon stated that current Church members had been similarly absolved of this former responsibility, and also significantly explained the reason it had taken so long to resolve the matter of polygamy, because "we have waited for the Lord to move on the matter." Cannon further explained that the delay in the widely anticipated announcement was so that adherents could demonstrate their commitment, even

51. Joseph F. Smith to Sarah E. Smith, Sept. 24, 1890, Joseph F. Smith Papers.

52. John T. Caine to Warren [Woodruff], Oct. 4, 1890, Caine Papers; Lyman, ed., *Candid Insights*, Oct. 5, 6, 1890; Quinn, "LDS Church Authority and New Plural Marriages," 47–48.

through incarceration, while they "waited for the Lord to move on the matter." The counselor attested that when President Woodruff commenced composing his statement on September 24, it was because "at that time the spirit came upon him, and the document that has been read in your hearing was the result."[53] President Woodruff then spoke. Given his age, he assumed he was not long for this world, he said. He would soon stand before his predecessors and the God of heaven to answer for his actions. His intent had not been to "undertake to please the world," and rather than simply concede to the federal government, "I would rather have gone out and been shot," he confided. Then he testified that God had spoken to him, saying that because the way forward had been blocked, there was nothing else to do but retreat, adding tellingly, "The Lord does not require at our hands things that we cannot do."[54]

On October 7, 1890, the day after the sustaining vote for the manifesto in general conference, there was already an indication that some government officials would accept the manifesto as an authentic statement of intent and alter their policies accordingly. On that day Utah's Chief Justice Charles Zane granted citizenship to a number of LDS applicants; he also said he recognized Woodruff's statement as sincere and binding and affirmed he would recognize the manifesto as the legitimate Church position in the future, contrary to the rest of the territorial administration.[55] It was a courageous act of leadership on his part, especially given how vehement the opposition was among other territorial officials.

Less than a month later, Woodruff privately asked the Department of Justice investigator E. C. Foster, who had visited Salt Lake City in April, to clarify the claim of the Utah Commission that the Church was out of compliance with federal statutes. He referenced Foster's earlier-expressed concern for the humane treatment of men still imprisoned for cohabitation and explained that polygamists had hesitated in court about doing what would seem "dishonorable in

53. Bitton, *George Q. Cannon*, 315; also Doctrine and Covenants 124:51–53; *New York Herald*, Oct. 7, 1890.

54. *Deseret Weekly News*, Oct. 18, 1890.

55. Roberts, *Comprehensive History*, 6:290–91; Charles S. Zane journal, Oct. 7, 1890.

them, and would amount to an entire repudiation of past obligations" to wives and children, giving as an example a man who had visited a sick child and had been sent to prison for being found at the home of a plural wife. Woodruff now stated, "Having acceded to the requirements of the law, it has seemed to us that a more lenient interpretation of what constituted unlawful cohabitation might now be rendered and enforced." There was no response from Foster, but two weeks later Woodruff received a message through J. S. Clarkson that US Attorney General William H. H. Miller had directed prosecutors to be certain they were fair and careful "not [to] alienate Mormon citizens."[56] This proved to at least be a sign of concern, if not of any general or concrete manner of improving the situation.

Thus, at the next general conference in April 1891, counselor George Q. Cannon referenced whether plural wives should be considered still bound to their husbands or should be seen as separated. He predicted that when the government became "convinced of our sincerity," the status of existing relationships would be clarified. He testified that his faith in the doctrine of eternal celestial marriage was embedded in his very being, and appealed to each concerned member to seek spiritual guidance to reconcile the seeming contradiction of formerly held ideas with the new reality of acceptance of US law, and to "trust in our God for the results." As he advised the congregation, "I say now publicly that it is the intention of the Latter-day Saints to obey the law and leave the results with the God of Heaven."[57] This would not have comforted anyone, and offered no direction on existing plural-wife relationships, but it was all that could be said at that time.

The Utah Commission issued another negative report in 1891. A minority dissent was written by the sole friend of the Church still on the commission, General John A. McClernand. It was the

56. Woodruff to E. C. Foster, Oct. 23, 1890, First Presidency Letterbooks; Caine to Woodruff et al., June 17, 1890; Zane journal, Apr. 7, 13, 1890; W. H. H. Miller to James S. Clarkson, Nov. 7, 1890, Miller Papers.

57. *Deseret Weekly News,* Apr. 11, 1891. Cannon was convinced that more leniency regarding husband/fathers' direct involvement with wives and children would occur when there was a thaw in the relationship with the government.

position of the majority that there had been eighteen new plural marriages solemnized that year, something the Church denied at the ensuing October general conference. In fact, the large congregation was asked to publicly endorse the denial, which it did. Certainly none of the opponents were convinced by the theatrics of the vote.[58]

In mid-November 1891, Woodruff unintentionally took another step toward defining the manifesto as the end of all existing plural-marriage relationships. The Church had thought there might be a chance to recover the confiscated property held by the federal receiver. The escheatment had been processed through a chancery court under the direction of Master in Chancery Charles F. Loofbourow. He needed to be convinced that the Church would not use its resources for the promulgation of polygamy. As early as October 12, 1891, Church attorneys coached Woodruff, Cannon, and others on how to answer questions. So far their explanations had indicated that the manifesto was not meant to end all polygamous relationships. They expected to see the day when they could once again demonstrate open concern and care for their plural families, the victims of the prohibition. They were convinced that public sentiment would change and statehood would be achieved, and the law would perhaps be interpreted more leniently so that they could be engaged in some manner with their plural families.[59]

When the Church president was finally questioned in the chancery court, the inquiries were worded in such a way that essentially compelled him to say he was not sure if "the manifesto applies to the cohabitation of men and women in plural marriage where it already exists." He finally stated that "the effect of it is so," and that he could "not see how it can be otherwise." A Church attorney, W. H. Dickson, tried to establish that the law did not intend to prevent a man from providing for his family, but US Attorney C. S. Varian pushed in the other direction, asking whether the manifesto applied to foreign

58. Alexander, *Things in Heaven and Earth*, 271–73, 415n50; George Q. Cannon journal, Sept. 8, 21, 27, Oct. 4, 1891; Brigham Young Jr. journal, Dec. 24, 1892; Franklin. D. Richards journal, Jan. 11, 1892.

59. Firmage and Mangrum, *Zion in the Courts*, 164–86, 252–59; also Lyman, ed., *Candid Insights*, 263, 268; Whitney, *History of Utah*, 3:661–63.

countries. Feeling his back against the wall, Woodruff said it did. Other Church officials were more equivocal in their testimonies.[60] Many of them later admitted they were startled by the president's answers. It was not in Woodruff's nature to be disingenuous. More likely he was himself still struggling with the implications. Within the confines of a later quorum meeting with the apostles, he asserted that if a man deserted or neglected his plural families he would be liable to lose his fellowship in the Church. The apostles would continue to advocate what George Q. Cannon enunciated about the need for men to "be careful to avoid exposing themselves to arrest or conviction for violation of the law, and yet they must not break their covenants with their wives." They were still charged with overseeing their families' well being.[61]

During the master-in-chancery proceedings, President Cannon attempted to extract some clarification about occasional contact with family members, privately explaining to Varian that he too had a son who was ill and felt unable to visit him because of the "great danger" it would place him in. Unsympathetic, Varian stated that personal visits were not required in giving financial support, and his officers "intended to prevent the semblance of criminal intercourse." Some apostles, notably John W. Taylor, took a more defiant position on this, eventually defying Church authorities as well as the government. Others resigned themselves to the new normal. Elder Abraham Cannon said, "As the opposition to it increased, … we became convinced that it was useless to further oppose public sentiment." Whatever determination they had felt at first dissipated when "the manifesto was issued and we [were] relieved of further obedience to this principle." Yet his own diary indicates extensive further visits with his plural wives.[62]

Despite these dramatic and, to many, heartbreaking indications

60. Alexander, *Things in Heaven and Earth,* 272–73, 414–15.

61. Lyman, ed., *Candid Insights*, 265–70.

62. Bitton, *George Q. Cannon*, 316; Jorgensen and Hardy, "Taylor–Cowley Affair," 4–36; Lyman, ed., *Candid Insights*, 334, 351, 372, 432, 562, 572–77, 701; also Taylor, *Rocky Mountain Empire*, 92–100; Gordon, *Mormon Question*, 198–208, 214–15, 571.

of decline of existing marital bonds,[63] Loofbourow's ruling was that the Church could not have its property back.[64] He was aware of the ruling in *Davis v. Beason*. To whatever extent the LDS leaders were advocating conformity to the letter of the law, it was clear that they believed plural marriage to be a God-given principle. Thus he recommended that the Church funds be devoted to a fledgling public school system. It was a bitter disappointment to the old guard, but to some of the younger generation of Latter-day Saints this may have been a step toward a more normalized Utah than had existed before.

Two letters thereafter penned by First Presidency counselor Joseph F. Smith reveal what the situation inside the Church was officially interpreted to be. Smith wrote that God did not want men to put away their plural wives, and neither did the law say that they could not support their families. "What the Lord requires is that we shall not bring upon ourselves the destruction intended by our enemies, by persisting in a course in opposition to the law." Smith saw it as a case of contrasting commandments, wherein every man would have to determine for himself how best to proceed in keeping families secure without violating the law. To a brother residing in Mexico, he stressed that the manifesto did not apply "anywhere except where the law applies. ... The US laws do not apply in Mexico: there you must be governed by the Mexican law," likely unaware that polygamy, although rarely prosecuted, was also illegal there.

Over the span of the decade of the 1880s, the anti-polygamy momentum mounted toward an almost inevitable result, even gaining some support from monogamists within the Church. A true irony emerged, that the Republicans, consistently wielding a sword against polygamy, emerged as the preferred political party among Latter-day Saints. One perceptive Democrat, Utah Commissioner Gen. J. A. McClernand, recognized what eventually emerged as the primary forecast for the institution of plural marriage: the more often Church leaders declared they were backing away from

63. Allen et al., *Studies in Mormon History*, 856–57.

64. Joseph F. Smith to Warren M. Johnson, Dec. 15, 1891; Smith to I. E. D. Zundel, Dec. 21, 1891, Joseph F. Smith Papers; also Hardy, *Solemn Covenant*, 307–78; Jorgensen and Hardy, "Taylor–Cowley Affair," 4–36.

practicing it, the more difficult it would be for them to ever fully resume the status quo ante. A careful review of relevant actions previously treated herein shows three instances of varying time spans when such retrocessions may be inferred, and to that extent probably help indict the Church's political strategists for the ultimate demise of this widespread institution of marriage.

9

DEMOCRATS AND REPUBLICANS

1891–92

Utah's unique political divisions were incompatible with typical American politics. Previous efforts to organize national parties in the territory, based on religious fault lines, had failed. The year 1891 saw the permanent rise of local organizations affiliated with national parties and the demise of the LDS-controlled People's Party, if not yet the non-LDS Liberal Party. This helped alleviate the impression, and eventually the reality, that the Church controlled the political scene in the territory. The change was prompted by the experience LDS people had of seeing their beloved capital city pass into the hands of the Liberal men, widely thought to be enemies of the Church, in the first of a series of shocks subsequent to the election of 1890. Liberals had predicted a real estate boom in Salt Lake City if they were elected, and that, in fact, happened as non-LDS people swarmed in and established businesses. Property that had sold for $300 per acre three years earlier was soon selling for $2,000 or more. Spring arrived, and the total sales of real estate in the Salt Lake Valley reportedly reached a million dollars per week. Construction thrived, supply lagging behind demand. The face of Zion was being transformed by people who had not been there during the colonizing period, and the old timers became increasingly frustrated.

There was little oversight either to control or plan the growth. City officials had paid attention to the infrastructure, however, to support the growth, in contrast to the previous administrations, that had let public utility projects lapse, bordering on negligence. Even the friendly *Herald* and the new *Salt Lake Times* had published editorials about the neglect of sidewalks and street paving, the need for improved water quality, the limited reach of the sewer system, insufficient street sprinkling to eliminate dust, and the scarcity of street signs. In these areas the new city council made a real effort to implement necessary programs, even knowing it would cost taxpayers more than they were probably willing to pay. The property assessments conducted by the new assessor, E. R. Clute, who had doubled as an election registrar, involved an incentive of 2.5 percent of all funds collected as the assessor's compensation for the work, meaning that he was less inclined to balk at new rates than the taxpayers themselves. People knew the rates would go up, but no one expected a 400 percent increase. The *Herald* and *Deseret News* both assumed that there had been a mistake.[1] Taxpayers from all classes complained, and a massive petition was presented to the city council, which proceeded to ignore it. The LDS portion of the citizenry bemoaned their new position of helplessness.[2]

As the economy grew, so did the city's gambling, prostitution, saloons, and business on Sundays. Non-LDS clergy started meeting with parishioners to consider how to restrain this spread of sin. At one gathering Judge Orlando W. Powers attempted to justify the leniency of law enforcement of these areas, and the *Tribune* backed him up editorially, but with the fleshpots came lawlessness—an increase in assault, burglary, robbery. The *Herald* warned that there had "never [been] a time when" criminals were "more numerous, more vicious, more daring[,] or more desperate." The *Tribune* labeled it a "crisis" and praised the doubling of the ranks of policemen.

The prominent Republican leader from California who had befriended the Latter-day Saints, Morris M. Estee, advised Church

1. *Salt Lake Times*, Mar. 6, 22, May 6, July 17, 1890; *Salt Lake Tribune*, May 2, 1890; *Salt Lake Herald*, July 20, 1890. This would be about $28 million in 2020.

2. Baskin, *Reminiscences*, 26–27; Lyman, ed., *Candid Insights*, 124–25, 178–80; *Salt Lake Herald*, May 10, June 18, 27, Aug. 9, 31, Sept. 2, 1890; *Salt Lake Times*, May 6, 12–14, 21, 23, 28, 30, June 7, July 16, 1890; *Deseret Weekly News*, May 3, July 5, 26, Aug. 16, Sept. 6, 1890.

officials to demonstrate their cooperation with former opponents by showing that "Mormons are at liberty to vote according to their political convictions and not according to the dictates of the priesthood." Church leaders took this to heart and resolved to "establish greater harmony between Mormons and gentiles in Utah," although without initiating any immediate action in that regard. Contemporary Utah historian Edward Tullidge predicted that after recovering from the surprise of having the Liberal Party win the election in the two largest municipal areas of the territory, local politics would "become reconstructed under the regular organizations of Democrats and Republicans." It was a perceptive prediction.[3]

Even before Estee suggested it, about a hundred outraged non-LDS voters in Ogden organized themselves to fight the incumbent Liberal clique with what they called the Citizens' Party. On January 16, 1891, they discussed strategies for winning the local election in the ensuing month. The *Ogden Standard*, representing the People's Party, praised what it saw as a rebuke of the recent Liberal city government. Not that they "loved liberalism less, but [they cherished] good government more," the editorial read. A fair number of non-LDS people had become dissatisfied with the undemocratic way the Liberal Party was run by its inner ring of influence peddlers. An example was the choice of pharmacist and alleged liquor dealer J. W. McNutt, who was also the city treasurer, to be the mayoral candidate for the Liberals. It would not have been the choice of those who were concerned about the city's moral direction.[4]

In late January another faction calling itself the "Anti-Ring Liberals" held a small convention in Ogden to discuss the election. It included current city officials who had been excluded from the new Liberal ticket, forming yet another political group, this one called the Citizens' Party, although they discussed joining forces with the other group of discontented voters. The two groups got together,

3. Tullidge, *Histories*, 2:112–13, 249, 319; *Salt Lake Tribune*, Apr. 14, July 15, 1890; *Salt Lake Herald*, July 15, 1890; Wilford Woodruff journal, Oct. 14, 1890; Woodruff et al. to Morris M. Estee, Dec. 3, 5, 9, 1890, First Presidency Letterbooks.

4. *Ogden Standard*, Jan. 15, 1891; *Salt Lake Herald*, Feb. 11, 1891; *Ogden Daily Commercial*, Jan. 15, 1891.

and after negotiations produced a slate of candidates that included popular non-LDS individuals and two who were LDS; Frank J. Cannon and Thomas Dee, both of whom were vying for spots on the city council. With that, the People's Party, at its convention, also chose to support the "fusion party," leaving the Liberal Party's *Ogden Daily Commercial* to assume, erroneously, that the movement had been organized by the LDS Church to lure in some of the non-LDS electorate. The *Tribune* reached the same conclusion and suggested that it was still "the People's Party with a change of name." Both newspapers predicted that the Liberal ticket, McNutt and colleagues, would win.[5]

The separate groups comprising the fusion ticket had put forward possible candidates for mayor, who stepped aside to combine their support for a well-liked incumbent city councilman, W. H. Turner, who himself agreed to run on the fusion ticket. Everyone acknowledged his qualifications and honesty. In the end, Turner emerged triumphant, although unable to lift most of the other coalition candidates to victory. They won only seven of twenty city offices. However, among the seven were the most prominent and popular individuals, including Dee and Cannon, of whom much more would be heard in the future. The *Standard* saw the possibility of a new era being ushered in, when "religious prejudice will cease." It boasted that Ogden was the "first to avail herself of the disposition" of diverse factions that would cooperate with each other.

The anti-ring Gentiles saw things similarly, although through the eyes of the erratic editor of the *Ogden Daily Union*, Charles S. King. On election day he wrote to the rival *Standard* that McNutt was just a "sneaking Copperhead," meaning a Democrat who was half Confederate rebel. King himself then joined the Republican Party at its organization in Ogden, complaining that the city's affairs "had been too long dictated ... by a bad Democratic ring." He considered the Republicans to have been too timid and allowed themselves to be imposed upon.

5. *Ogden Standard*, Jan. 29, 31, Feb. 9–11, 17, 1891; *Salt Lake Tribune*, Jan. 28–29, 1891; *Ogden Daily Commercial*, Jan. 30, Feb. 3–4, 1891.

Just two days after the February 9, 1891, election, a petition was circulated calling for Republicans to meet "for the purpose of consultation and organization." Fifty men signed the petition to commit to attend, almost none of them LDS. In the keynote address, Judge Allen Miller remarked that Utah was the only place in the union where national politics were not the rule, and they should organize because of the benefits of a national affiliation. Other speakers voiced distrust of LDS voters taking over the local party, but the consensus was that if that happened, they could regroup. They were somewhat reassured by an LDS participant, English immigrant David Kay, who told them Mormons were not "dictated to in politics," that at least in his experience this had not been the case. The meeting adjourned with a general summons for all interested Weber County residents to attend a mass meeting on February 16.

On the appointed day, activist D. H. Baldridge was elected permanent chairman of a Republican auxiliary club. Mormons were tacitly welcomed by the acceptance of the nominal Church member Frank J. Cannon as vice-president. Completing the club organization, those present adopted a series of traditional Republican resolutions, including a motion by Cannon's LDS friend Ben E. Rich to encourage people throughout the territory to similarly organize themselves as Republicans. Prodded by editorials in the *Standard* and talk of possible success when the Republicans stood as candidates for election, there was soon a response from those in Ogden who favored the Democrats. A meeting was held in the Grand Opera House on February 21, where the Democrats selected recently retired Utah Supreme Court Judge H. P. Henderson as their president. Not to be outdone by the Republicans, they approved Charles C. Richards, son of LDS apostle Franklin D. Richards, as vice-president. Among the speakers, H. W. "Kentucky" Smith, who had authored the Idaho test oath and had been one of the strategists for the initial Liberal victory in Ogden, suggested that it was time to forgive and forget, and no one disagreed. Their comments foreshadowed the transition from sectarian politics to the intra-Church battles that would soon divide the Latter-day Saints themselves.

An LDS visitor from Salt Lake City, Scipio A. Kenner, objected to an editorial by Frank Cannon lauding the achievements of the Republican Party, substantiating what the *Salt Lake Herald* observed, that people were overlooking past religious differences and dividing along Democratic and Republican lines.[6]

The ecumenical development began with non-Mormons. LDS political activists came on board after the movement was underway. On the morning after the Republican mass meeting, two of the LDS Weber Stake presidency, L. W. Shurtliff and H. H. Rolapp, accompanied Frank Cannon to Salt Lake City to brief the First Presidency and ask for their advice. They explained that they were being encouraged by non-LDS friends to break up the People's Party, to let their members do as the Liberals were doing in Ogden and choose between national parties. The First Presidency considered this for two days before concluding to allow Latter-day Saints in Ogden to combine with the national parties, but limited their decision to Ogden for the time being as a test case.[7]

Within a week a new concern emerged that would define the transition over the next few years. The Church legitimately worried about what would happen nationally if the parties in Utah did not end up being numerically equal. For now the Church would treat Weber County as an experiment. George Q. Cannon emphasized that nothing should be done anywhere else by local Church leaders unless they were in a clear minority and had been invited to join with non-LDS voters. At the same time, he acknowledged that the "Lord's Hand" was in this.[8] If not so, the movement could be easily contained, being that the Liberals were the ones who had taken the initiative. Already in Salt Lake County there was talk of following the same path, resisted by the *Tribune* but hard pressed to prevent it, and the Weber County counterpart to the *Tribune*, the *Ogden Commercial*, was reporting that LDS people in Ogden were sincere about letting bygones be bygones; the skeptical *Tribune* suspected a ploy

6. *Ogden Daily Commercial*, Feb. 13, 17, 22, 1891; *Ogden Standard*, Feb. 20, 1891; *Salt Lake Herald*, Feb. 21, 1891.

7. Rogers, ed., *In the President's Office*, 441–46.

8. Lyman, ed., *Candid Insights*, 196, 202; Grant, *Diaries*, Apr. 2–7, 1891.

by the Mormons to split the non-LDS vote and capture both parties. As spring 1892 approached, the *Tribune* found itself answering letters from non-LDS readers telling them that Latter-day Saints wanted to cooperate with them. A longtime non-Mormon resident of Payson, Calvin Reasoner, accused Liberal Party members of being unable to think independently when the *Tribune* made assertions to the contrary. The *Tribune* often talked about the need for reform, and here was an opportunity. In his opinion the reformers needed to reform themselves. The opposing *Salt Lake Herald* liked the idea and encouraged it in a way that seemed to heap coals on the fire by calling on citizens to repudiate the "disfranchisement and robbery doctrine" of the Liberals and join in harmony with those of the majority faith.[9]

The alignment of the parties with specific newspapers was part of the political landscape at the time, so it was a consideration for the LDS presidency. Joseph F. Smith argued that since the *Herald* was so influential in supporting the Democrats, "the Republicans should have the [Ogden] *Standard*." Sure enough, within a few days Frank J. Cannon resumed editorship of the *Standard* and turned it into a Republican organ. At the request of Democratic Club President H. P. Henderson, Church leaders agreed that John Q. Cannon, Frank's brother, an experienced editor, should take a similar post with the Democratic *Commercial*.[10] There was even more concern about the newspapers in Salt Lake City. As mentioned, the *Herald* was the major outlet for the Democrats. In January 1890 apostle Heber J. Grant admitted privately that he wrote articles (and probably editorials) for that paper. When President Woodruff complained about the newspaper being unduly critical of Republican President Benjamin Harrison and Secretary of State James G. Blaine, Grant asked the editor, Byron Groo, to tone down the partisan attacks.[11]

The Church leadership heard on March 16 that a significant volume of stock in the relatively new Republican-affiliated *Salt Lake Times* was available. The sellers had incorporated with $30,000. They

9. *Ogden Daily Commercial*, Feb. 18–19, 1891; *Salt Lake Tribune*, Feb. 18, 20, Mar. 4, 6, 9, 16, 1891; *Salt Lake Herald*, Feb. 26, Mar. 18, Apr. 7, 9, 1891.

10. Alter, *Early Utah Journalism*, 177.

11. Grant, *Diaries*, Jan. 25, 1890, May 31, 1891.

were now offering the Church investors shares worth $12,000 and an additional $3,500 in escrow to guarantee the new investors editorial control of the paper. The aim of the Church, they knew, would be to "work against the *Tribune* and try to break its influence, and to sustain Republicanism." Church leaders confirmed that it was important to do if it could be kept quiet, so that the *Times* would appear to remain independent from the Church.[12]

In April investors in the *Ogden Standard* asked to have apostle John Henry Smith assume the presidency of the board of directors. Even though the Quorum of the Twelve warned that the apostles should "hold themselves aloof from politics," the First Presidency overruled them and gave Smith a green light, President George Q. Cannon appearing to be the leading proponent of this decision. The involvement of the young apostle, who was forty-two years of age, would be his first step toward an extensive amount of personal political activity over the next year. His activism would become controversial enough, particularly among his fellow apostles who had Democratic leanings, that it would ultimately help end in the dismissal of one of the Democrats from the quorum. Smith was soon meeting with leading Gentiles to organize the Republican Party on a broader scale and wrote in his diary that Presidents Cannon and Woodruff, while not explicitly endorsing his further involvement, had at least given him their tacit approval.[13]

There were several reasons why he was permitted to do so. One was the fact that Utah Democrats had freely opened their party organization to LDS participation, in contrast to the continued opposition by Liberal voters who veered toward the Republicans. When President Benjamin Harrison visited the territory in May 1891, the Liberal Party hosted him, to the exclusion of LDS Church leaders. It was clear that if the Latter-day Saints were going to join the national parties, someone was going to have to lead out in courting and promoting the Republicans among LDS people, otherwise there would

12. Lyman, ed., *Candid Insights*, 187–88, 194–97.

13. John Henry Smith to Ben E. Rich, Apr. 8, 1891, John Henry Smith Papers; John Henry Smith journal, Apr. 3, May 5, 1891; White, ed., *Church, State, and Politics*, 250–51. See also note 34 herein.

be a lopsided affiliation. Anticipating the visit of President Harrison, Church officials wanted to demonstrate their patriotism despite being shunned by the non-LDS organizers and assigned people in the small communities along the railroad route to line the tracks and wave flags and decorate buildings to indicate a welcoming spirit. The Liberals took conspicuous steps to keep Harrison from seeing much of this. One morning in Salt Lake City, on May 9, 1891, the visitors were treated to a parade and patriotic songs by schoolchildren in just-greening Liberty Park. While there, the Harrisons asked about the Tabernacle, which was not on the itinerary. The *Deseret News* concluded that there had been an effort "to keep the virtues and progress of the Mormon people as far as practicable in the shade."[14]

Even before the presidential visit, the political redistribution in Utah gained impetus from the revival of the Salt Lake Central Democratic Club when its organizers met on May 5 in the offices of club president Frank Dyer. It was proposed that local political parties organize "upon the lines of national politics" and leave "each individual citizen to choose for himself." The Gentiles declared themselves to be "unalterably opposed to the disfranchisement of any citizen except for crime, whereof he shall have been first duly convicted." As news of the party rejuvenation spread in Salt Lake City, prominent Democrats and People's Party leaders together voiced hearty approval. The *Tribune*, on the other hand, suspected that the Democrats had come to some sort of "secret understanding" with the LDS Church and that Mormons would still vote as instructed by their leaders. The *Tribune* said it would celebrate when Church members actually participated freely and independently. The *Deseret News* editor, Charles Penrose, offered encouragement for people to at least study the issues from the perspective of the national party. The *Salt Lake Times* prodded Republicans to act more aggressively to boost their membership, asserting that with statehood on the horizon "it would be almost criminal on the part of the

14. Bitton, *George Q. Cannon*, 307, 318–19; George Q. Cannon journal, June 26, 1890; *New York Times*, Apr. 22, May 5–6, 1891; *Deseret Weekly News*, May 16, 1891; *Salt Lake Herald*, May 10, 1891.

Republicans" if they did not encourage especially young LDS men to investigate their party as well.[15]

Those who would be instrumental in bringing forth a straight Republican organization in Salt Lake City were already quietly preparing to do so. They included non-LDS and Mormon organizers after John Henry Smith met with the most highly respected local Republican, territorial Chief Justice Charles S. Zane, on May 12. After Smith announced his preference for the Republicans and referenced the fact that the Democrats had already organized, he said that "if the Republican Party does not [become established soon], it will be in a minority when it does." He said there were other LDS people who were Republicans at heart. Zane reminded him that a judge could not actively be involved in politics, but that he would like to see the party get set up and running. The apostle said that if they worked together, he was sure they could "mak[e] Utah Republican." On the assumption that Smith was acting privately, Zane wrote in his diary that "Mormons have abandoned politics as an organization" and were leaving to the people the ability to "hereafter cooperate with the other political parties."[16]

Smith and some others, including William S. McCornick, a prominent Gentile banker and former city councilman, met with Wilford Woodruff and George Q. Cannon on May 14. Woodruff stated his own preference for the Republican Party and encouraged them to go "ahead and organize." Smith "spent most of the [next] day buttonholing men to find out what their politics were, if they had any," having been told by the Church president "to select such men as I wanted to go with me in this work." The Democrats staged their mass meeting that same day, May 15, at the Salt Lake Theater, with some 1,500 enthusiastic attendees, the *Herald* reported. Dyer announced their purpose and nominated Samuel A. Merritt, a former Liberal Party leader and former Idaho delegate to Congress, as

15. *Salt Lake Tribune*, May 7–8, 10–11, 13, 1891; *Deseret Evening News*, May 8–9, 13, 1891; *Salt Lake Times*, May 13, 15, 1891.

16. White, ed., *Church, State, and Politics*, 253; John Henry Smith to Joseph Smith III, Jan. 14, 1892, copy in John Henry Smith Papers; Charles S. Zane journal, May 12, 15, 1891.

chairman. When Merritt was accepted, he spoke to the crowd about Democratic principles, self-consciously ingratiating himself to the Latter-day Saints who were present. A former Territorial Supreme Court judge, John W. Judd, took a similar tack in his remarks. Dyer requested that someone from the People's Party speak, so John T. Caine addressed the crowd and enthusiastically endorsed the platform, giving his pledge to the party. Following him were the LDS party's former chairman John R. Winder, along with Judge Elias A. Smith and other LDS participants. There were enough Church members in attendance that the *Tribune* called it "the marriage of the Democratic Party of Utah and the Church of Jesus Christ of Latter-day Saints."[17]

The success of the Democrats provided the promised motivation for the city's Republicans to step up their attempts to divert the tide of People's Party members rushing into the arms of the Democrats. The very next day, the Republicans gathered at the Mining Exchange and selected McCornick as chairman, then voted in favor of a motion by Judge Charles W. Bennett to organize the party. There were objections from members of the Liberal Party, on the basis that the People's Party still existed, so the probable result if they split their vote and the People's Party remained united was defeat in the next election. Arthur Brown, of the Liberal Party central committee, countered that the LDS party would not disband if "there was no place for it to go. It is waiting to be swallowed up, and the Republican Party should swallow its share." John M. Zane, the judge's son, observed that "the Democrats were organized, ready to take the People's Party in, and the Republicans were in duty bound to meet them on their ground." The president of the Young Men's Liberal Club, Edward B. Critchlow, proclaimed the Liberal organization obsolete—a "bastard" that should be disinherited. When the vote was taken on whether to organize, the ayes held a clear majority. A committee was designated to determine the details and schedule a general meeting.[18]

17. *Salt Lake Herald*, May 16–17, 1891; *Salt Lake Tribune*, May 16–17, 1891.
18. *Deseret Evening News*, May 18, 1891.

They suggested beginning by forming a Republican club, based on a suggestion by Mormon-friendly James S. Clarkson of the national party leadership. Learning of this, the *Tribune* called on backers of the Liberal Party to attend the first club meeting to disrupt it. It was held on May 18, the audience packed with Liberals who wanted to push their anti-Mormon agenda. Chairman Nick Treweek opened the proceedings, called for a postponement, and promptly adjourned the meeting. The audience stayed to hold its own meeting and hear from the first Liberal Party chairman, US Army General Patrick Edward Connor. He was followed by the future congressional candidate Clarence E. Allen. Edward Critchlow was asked to come forward to defend his support of the Republicans. Facing the hostile audience, the alleged traitor calmly laid out his view that the Democrats had gotten a head start and were not going to retreat, so the Republicans, "masquerading under the name of the Liberal Party," needed to quickly reorganize in the same manner, under the national banner. He was denounced by subsequent speakers who claimed he had deludedly jumped into the arms of the LDS-run Republicans. The Liberal Party faction would stay independent of the Latter-day Saints, they promised.[19]

The mass meeting for the Republicans was held May 20 in the Salt Lake Theater. Despite bad weather, there was a large crowd in attendance, the *Tribune* having again encouraged Liberals to attend. John M. Zane of the arrangements committee opened by recommending C. W. Bennett as chair and asking for a voice vote. The Liberals roared their opposition, but Zane declared Bennett confirmed anyway, over the objections of the Liberals. The proponents of organizing a party took to the floor first: Zane, followed by Critchlow. Clarence Allen stated his belief that political enlightenment had not extended beyond the two urban counties in Utah Territory, so they should not yet fragment their political strength, especially not in LDS-dominated "cow counties." This was seconded by William Dickson, the former territorial prosecuting attorney. In his view the Democratic organization was not yet formidable

19. *Salt Lake Herald*, May 19, 21, 1891; *Salt Lake Times*, May 19, 1891.

enough to be a legitimate threat. Mormons would still vote as their leaders dictated, so it did not matter if they were voting as members of the People's Party or as Democrats.

The decisive moment came when Bennett invited John Henry Smith to the rostrum. Apostle Heber J. Grant, in the audience as a spectator, wrote that he thought Smith was making a mistake to accept the invitation. But surprisingly enough, the group settled down and paid attention to his explanation of how the People's Party had become more democratic of its own accord. He declared that no one had told him how to vote, and while he could not speak for the preference of LDS people as a whole, he himself would cast his lot with the Republicans. A *Times* reporter stated that this "cleared away doubt from the mind of every man who was at all inclined to be just."[20]

Judge Bennett read the resolutions containing the meeting's real purpose, "that political parties in Utah should be organized with reference to the national questions and politics" and that as chairman, he should appoint a committee to establish Republican cells throughout the county. Weber County representatives Frank Cannon and Ben E. Rich spoke in favor. The voice vote was again interspersed with hoots and hollers from the opposition, but the motion was declared carried. According to the *Tribune*, it failed, but the *Times* reporter called this a "shame-faced falsehood." The *Herald* defended the chairman's acknowledgement of a clear two-to-one advantage of those in favor of the party. The Liberals grumbled that they had won the municipal elections on their own, and only they could capture the legislature. *Tribune* editor C. C. Goodwin declared an end of the effort to become Republicans and called people back to the barricades.[21]

Charles Penrose used the *Deseret News* to advocate support for the national parties as a way to keep the Liberals from winning statewide elections for seats in the territorial legislature, where he

20. Grant, *Diaries*, May 20, 1891; White, ed., *Church, State, and Politics*, 25; *Salt Lake Times*, May 21, 1891.

21. *Salt Lake Tribune*, May 20–23, 1891.

suspected they would try to "pass laws to disfranchise all Mormons." Church authorities came to agree that they could not stand "aloof" from the political fight. Abraham Cannon claimed that after the defeat of the Liberal Party at the Republican mass meeting, its adherents hatched plans ("vile schemes") to block further efforts at accommodation. On May 25 the First Presidency discussed what to do as their next step.[22] Three days later they met with the territorial chairman of the People's Party, Franklin S. Richards, his predecessor, John R. Winder, and other party officials to recommend that they disband the old Mormon party and allow their adherents to "ally themselves with the respective national parties, according to their individual preferences." The *Deseret News* published this resolution and opined that it only made sense, given the Liberal Party's determination to dissolve its "unnatural union" with the Republicans.[23]

The Church sent word to John W. Young, long-time contact with the national Democratic leaders, asking him to relay their message that the political field in Utah was "ripe[,] ready to harvest." Also, for Young's information, they were going to take necessary steps to prevent "a general rush into the Democratic ranks." They were looking for an honest "struggle for territorial supremacy" and hoped for "a close and interesting one." It would be best if the two parties were "evenly balanced," securing the citizenry in its liberties regardless of who was in power in Washington.[24]

One logical base for spreading the party organization was the network of Republican clubs organized throughout the territory by apostle John Henry Smith and two young men in their twenties, George M. Cannon and John M. Zane, both of whom had prominent fathers: Salt Lake Stake president Angus M. Cannon and territorial chief justice Charles S. Zane. Between May 26, when they received their assignment, and August 3 when the legislative election was held, Smith participated in setting up Republican

22. Lyman, ed., *Candid Insights*, 202, 209, 211, 214–15; Roberts, *Comprehensive History*, 6:300–01.

23. *Salt Lake Herald*, May 26, 31, 1891; *Deseret Evening News*, May 28–29, June 1, 1891; Franklin D. Richards Journal, May 28, 1891.

24. Woodruff et al. to John W. Young, May 29, 1891, First Presidency Letterbooks.

groups in more than thirty locations, and his younger associates were similarly successful.[25]

A typical example of their efforts entailed a call to meet in a courtroom in Provo on May 28, 1891. The participants elected an LDS chairman and Gentile secretary. Smith rehearsed a partisan version of local and national history, showing the need for his listeners to put Utah County alongside Salt Lake and Weber Counties as examples of Republican strongholds. They immediately enlisted several dozen members, among them Provo's mayor and LDS bishop John E. Booth. A week later Booth was the featured speaker at a club rally, where the editor of the *Provo Enquirer*, John C. Graham, noticed how orderly and dignified the people were, and how instructive the proceedings were. He admitted having long been opposed to the party's policies. Only four months earlier he had editorialized about the "Evils of High Tariff," but it took him less than two months to write his first editorial on the "Benefits of a High Tariff," an about-face that did not go unnoticed by the *Tribune*. Undaunted, Graham became an evangelist for the party. In some localities, such as the sugar-factory town of Lehi, he found people needing little convincing regarding the importance of tariffs.[26]

The *Salt Lake Herald* had been a People's Party newspaper. As that party folded up, the *Herald* encouraged its readers to join the Democrats. A June 3 editorial suggested that one could switch parties without having to "abandon or modify a single [political] doctrine." Conversely, the editor tried to show that the Liberal and Republican parties shared similar planks, making them essentially "identical." When subsequently asked why Mormons were being encouraged to join both parties, he was hard pressed to say why it would be a bad thing for them all to join the Democrats.[27]

Abraham Cannon privately expressed concern that it would

25. *Salt Lake Times*, May 22–23, 25–26, 30, 1891; White, ed., *Church, State, and Politics*, 254; J. H. Smith journal, July 31, 1891.

26. *Deseret Evening News*, June 2, 1891; *Provo Enquirer*, Jan. 29, Aug. 5, 1890, May 18, June 4–5, 10–11, 16, 18, 1891; *Salt Lake Tribune*, June 26, 1891; Anderson, "History of the *Provo Times*," 83–88, 90–91.

27. Salt Lake *Herald*, June 3–4, 1891; Grant, *Diaries*, May 1, 4, 1891; *Deseret Evening News*, May 25, 1891.

indeed happen. There was a "danger [in] our people all becoming Democrats," he wrote. If it happened, it would no doubt be "through the influence of the *Herald*." The First Presidency thought that result would "prove ... disastrous," because they had already observed what had happened to their leverage with members of Congress when the electorate had backed only the other party. The Quorum of the Twelve decided someone should "instruct our people in Republicanism ... thus winning them to that party" as well. Once the negative influence of the *Tribune* was broken, there would thus be a more equitable political division of the people, they believed.[28] The Salt Lake newspapers carried Franklin S. Richards's summons to fellow People's Party board members for a June 10, 1891, meeting. In a letter Richards wrote to San Juan County committeeman Francis A. Hammond, who was also the LDS stake president, he divulged that the aim of disbanding the party was to force the breakup of the Liberal Party and reduce the influence of the *Salt Lake Tribune*'s editor C. C. Goodwin and his "small clic of anti-Mormon fanatics."[29]

At the June meeting, it was clear that M. M. Estee's advice had fallen on fallow ground. Church leaders by then had come to recognize the need to be connected nationally and to get along with leaders of both parties. The dismantling of the territorial party had been announced in advance, so the meeting was a formality. That afternoon at the Gardo House, the First Presidency addressed former party leaders to explain the reasoning behind "the present political move," and the information was cheerfully accepted by all, wrote Franklin D. Richards. The presidency "desired the saints to join the different [national] parties" and "did not want them to go en masse into either side," according to Abraham H. Cannon's notes. John Morgan, one of the First Council of the Seventy and soon a Republican enthusiast, recorded that "the present Democratic tendency was not what it should be." They were "advised" to seek an equilibrium between the major parties.[30]

---

28. Lyman, ed., *Candid Insights*, 218–19.
29. Francis A. Hammond journal, June 3, 1891.
30. Richards journal, June 10, 1891; John Morgan journal, June 10, 1891.

The attorney James H. Moyle found George Q. Cannon's insight impressive regarding the effect of a stampede to the Democrats, which would drive non-LDS people to the Republicans and perpetuate the division along religious lines. Asking about his own long-standing preference for the Democrats, he was assured by Cannon that it was fine to ally with that party, that only those without a strong preference should be encouraged to consider the Republicans. Moyle emphasized that there was no "Church fiat" to dissolve the People's Party either, or to join the Republicans. The Church was simply helping facilitate what had become a groundswell of public support.[31]

Alma Eldredge, a counselor to the Summit Stake president in Coalville, returned from the June 10 meetings to find Democrats fully organized and actively campaigning. One of those making stump speeches was his stake president, W. W. Cluff, accompanied by the congressional delegate, John T. Caine. Another month would go by before Eldredge and others would be ready to issue a call for a Republican county convention, by which time the legislative elections were weeks away.[32] More than two hundred miles to the south, a new counselor in the Beaver Stake presidency, John F. Tolton, observed that "the people who are afflicted with [a] political itch in any manner are almost unanimously Democrats. No move has yet been made by the Republicans to organize, and encouraging and flattering reports come from the lower settlements [Cedar City and St. George] that the masses of people are there Democrats as well as in Beaver." Apostle Francis M. Lyman, a Republican, made a similar observation.

In late May the *Salt Lake Herald* criticized the lobbying and alleged distortions of John Henry Smith. William King, Charles Penrose, and Franklin S. Richards were soon "getting concerned" that Smith had been too successful at recruiting Republicans. A month later, as the Republican apostle began a six-day tour of Weber County, Richards's brother Charles, an Ogden party leader, went to Church

31. Sessions, *James H. Moyle*, 178–81.
32. Eldredge diary, June 10, 12–13, 15, July 10, 1891.

headquarters to insist that some Democratic apostle be allowed to lecture there for a week too, but this was apparently not done.[33]

In early July the apostles gathered for their quarterly meeting under the direction of the senior member of the quorum, Lorenzo Snow. An ardent seeker of group harmony, Snow was displeased to find tension in the quorum over these issues, or outside criticisms that had found their way to him regarding John Henry Smith. At first he had been upset with Smith, but concluded that because the First Presidency had approved his activities, they were "all right." He encouraged the other apostles, while accepting Smith's mission, to express their views openly about the cause of the division in the quorum.

Moses Thatcher, the fervent Democrat from Cache Valley, complained that at a previous meeting they had been "united in saying John Henry Smith should not actively engage in politics," and despite that he had done so, although "doubtless with the sanction of the Presidency." If he "goes into politics," Thatcher argued, "I do not know why other apostles should not seek to make converts to their [political] principle[s]." Thatcher would become increasingly outspoken on this point and would finally be dropped from the quorum in 1896 for insubordination, mainly over politics.[34] Elder Grant said he felt awkward about not being able to do his part to support the Democrats. He had been active in the People's Party campaigns, so "his Democratic friends could not understand" why he had not "come out and work[ed] for them." Likely correct in their assumptions, the Gentiles had said the Church had restrained him in order to let the Republicans get a better foothold. It would be better, he suggested, if he and Thatcher could make some speeches for the Democrats, but the quorum was undecided.[35]

Two days later several apostles, including John Henry Smith, met with George Q. Cannon and Joseph F. Smith to try to clarify the situation. The younger Smith apologized for having been absent on the speaking circuit, explaining that after John T. Caine

33. *Salt Lake Herald*, May 27, 29, 1891; *Salt Lake Times*, May 27, 1891; White, ed., *Church, State, and Politics*, 255; Richards journal, July 2, 1891.

34. Lyman, "Alienation of an Apostle," 74–82.

35. Lyman, ed., *Candid Insights*, 227–30.

and others, including John Winder and Franklin S. Richards, had declared themselves Democrats, he felt it was "necessary for him" to balance the scale. "I have tried to disprove the theory that this territory belonged to the Democrats by divine right." He said he felt good about eliminating the prevalent notion "that it would be a crime to become a Republican."

President Joseph F. Smith admitted that the First Presidency had been less than clear in their instructions. Their intent was to prevent the Saints "from going overwhelmingly in either direction," not "to influence or coerce them contrary to their desires." It was because "the leanings of the people seemed to be to join the Democrats" that it was "absolutely necessary to have some one high in authority" campaign for the other side. John Henry Smith had appeared to be that person. Cannon added that while the presidency had not specifically singled him out or asked him to be as fully involved as he had become, "at the same time they had felt that what he had done ... was for the best interests of the people and he had had their full approval."[36]

Smith and Cannon suspected that the majority of Mormons did not have party preferences at all, so there was still a good chance for an equitable division, except for "the impression all over the land that it was almost a crime [for a Latter-day Saint] to be a Republican."[37] The presidency had been advised by "friends" to manage their "political affairs" so that "we would have friendship if possible of both the political parties." The "friends" who had advised them were the Republican leaders Morris Estee and James Clarkson. Abraham Cannon recorded that President Smith had "received the strongest admonition from our Republican friends that we must not allow this territory to go strongly Democratic." The Republicans "today [are] our friends and are working in our interests," said Joseph F. Smith. He did "not know a single Democrat who is helping us." Among the Republicans mentioned were Leland Stanford, James

36. Grant, *Diaries*, July 7–9, 1891.

37. Those present were G. Q. Cannon, H. J. Grant, F. M. Lyman, M. W. Merrill, J. F. Smith, J. H. Smith, L. Snow, and J. W. Taylor (Lyman, *Candid Insights*, 230–33, 264).

G. Blaine, and others who were "deeply interested in [our] affairs and desirous of doing [us] good."

The ultimate benefit the First Presidency anticipated from its friendship with Republicans was amnesty for polygamists. President Smith knew that such a gift was attainable only through the party in power, and in that regard Smith and Cannon lavishly praised Estee and Trumbo. Isaac Trumbo had "done more in time and in money for us than any man among the outsiders," Cannon stated, and the people were "under deep obligations" to him and his associates. Estee too, who was then in Salt Lake City, was gathering support for a petition to Washington that would grant amnesty to Latter-day Saint polygamists.

Church authorities were only partially aware of the size of their debt to Clarkson. George Q. Cannon read a copy of a letter from Estee to Clarkson in which the former reminded Clarkson that "if the Mormons are now properly handled they will make of Utah a Republican state." In light of the close balance between the two parties in Congress, gaining additional Republican states was the motivation for courting Utah's favor. In spite of the First Presidency's attempt to balance the scales in the summer of 1891, the question of how much the division of loyalties was pushed toward the Republicans is more complex. Shortly after the dissolution of the People's Party, the *Salt Lake Times* submitted a series of questions to Woodruff and Cannon, to which the leaders carefully phrased their answers, and the editor's headnote revealed warm sympathy for the LDS Church, although without divulging the financial support that had helped in influencing his affections. Hardly a day went by between April and August 1891 that the *Times* did not battle the *Salt Lake Tribune* in its editorial columns.

The interview was intended to put to rest the *Tribune*'s contention that Church authorities were puppet masters determining the outcome of the elections. In the view of the *Times*, the accusation was not relevant in light of the dissolution of the People's Party. Questions like "Does the Church claim the right to dictate to its members in political matters?" and "Is it your wish that the Republican and

Democratic parties should organize and present their principles to the Mormon people?" were vague enough to be unthreatening. Yet the answers were so explicit that one could doubt the leaders were "deeply interested in securing the establishment of conditions that would forever remove" the Church from politics.[38] They believed themselves to be creating a fair playing field. Beyond that, it was a complicated issue, because to shift their global influence in territorial politics to a more limited involvement would not be something that would happen overnight. It would be difficult to suddenly give up temporal political power after wielding it for so long.

Historian D. Michael Quinn commented on the dilemma represented by the *Times* interview: "On the one hand, political issues that were regarded as crucial to the Church's interests could fail without active support of the hierarchy. On the other hand, any time the hierarchy became involved in a political issue, both Mormon and non-Mormon partisans of the contrary view would become alienated and accuse the hierarchy of violating promises concerning the separation of Church and state." Scholar Jan Shipps explained the outcome by writing that "a vacillating course between [abstinence and involvement] was pursued. Denials of the use of ecclesiastical influence followed hard upon decisions announcing the Will of the Lord concerning political matters. The consequent confusion gave credence to the earlier charges of duplicity."[39]

In other words, there were no intentional falsehoods in the questions and answers published in the *Times*. The division into Democrats and Republicans and disbandment of the People's Party were underway before the Church became involved. The leadership never denied its involvement after the changes were in progress. There is some indication they were not happy with the outcome of the 1891 campaign and wanted things to be handled differently in the future, because as with anything, there were unexpected complications. In this instance they had to do with the People's Party accelerating their activities in Salt Lake County when the Liberals refused to break up,

38. *Salt Lake Times*, June 23, 1891.
39. Quinn, "Mormon Hierarchy," 240; Shipps, "Mormons in Politics," 215.

leading to second thoughts among LDS voters about the wisdom of dividing their vote. On the evening of June 30, 1891, over a dozen leading political activists met at the office of Franklin S. Richards to discuss a return to some kind of cooperative ticket. Heber J. Grant, who had been in favor of a coalition, concluded that "if we were to have a fusion ticket it would give our enemies a chance to say that we were not really Democratic or Republican in our politics." Maintaining the straight party division would produce good results in the long run to offset the short-term success of the Liberals, but a continuing commitment to that principle required discipline.[40]

Other Latter-day Saints, with less experience and prestige, got involved in opposing the Liberals in another school board election, calling their Salt Lake County candidates a citizens' ticket. It was a mostly disorganized venture that allowed the Liberal candidates to emerge victorious. According to the *Times*, there was a silver lining in the smaller margin of victory, indicating an erosion of party strength. More realistic observers conceded that the regular elections attracted a larger turnout and would produce a significantly different outcome. While the campaign for territorial legislative seats was building to a crescendo, the *Herald* detected a resistance to joining the Republicans. A letter from a prominent Salt Laker who wanted to align with the Republicans concluded that, since the Liberal Party was a foe of both Democrats and Republicans, and since "his vote would be most effective in killing that enemy if cast for the Democratic ticket," he would defer his support for the weaker party until after the immediate crisis had passed. As a Democratic paper, the *Herald* interpreted this to be an expression of a broader public sentiment and portent for coming party success.

Two days before the August 3 election, the *Tribune* charged that, in case of emergency, Church members were being asked to be available to shore up the Salt Lake County Democratic ticket. Such an emergency, the paper alleged, was developing because the Liberal Party had not yet fallen apart. In an adjoining column, the *Tribune* claimed that even Frank J. Cannon had been told by the Church to

40. Grant, *Diaries*, June 30, July 9, 1891.

stop opposing the Democrats for the moment. This should be taken with a grain of salt, but it is true that there was disappointment and consternation over the Liberals failing to follow the lead of the People's Party and closing ranks instead of closing down.

The outcome of the election gave the Democrats two-thirds of the seats in each house of the legislature, the Liberals garnering the other third. The Republicans were unable to capture a single seat, even though their support (a total of 6,397 votes) was not far behind that of the Liberals (7,411), even so too little to win in any individual contest, so that the divided LDS vote helped the Liberals tie up the legislature with people who were mostly committed to opposing whatever the Mormons wanted. The *Times* explained that "human nature led [LDS voters] to cooperate in the election with the party that promised to make the greatest headway against Liberalism and their votes went to the Democracy." The Republican paper criticized the *Herald* for its attempts to link Liberalism with Republicans, which wrongly caused people to shy away from the Republicans.[41]

The *Salt Lake Tribune*'s view was polar opposite. It considered the whole affair to be a dirty trick on the part of the LDS Church. In one precinct before the election, 700 Republicans, of which 150 were Gentiles, had pledged support for the Republican ticket. Since only 365 votes were ultimately cast for the Republicans, it seemed to imply defections from the LDS side. Naturally the *Herald* countered that LDS support for Republicans could be detected by straight-ticket votes, and it was the non-LDS voters who stayed with the "Liberal fold," "almost to a man."[42] Whatever the case, the Republicans ended up with no representation. Scipio A. Kenner, who was one of the first to break with the People's Party in favor of the Democrats, understood the Democrats and Republicans to have united together against a common foe. It was the Liberal "wolf" who needed to be kept from the door, so the impulse was to go with the more familiar Democratic Party.[43]

41. *Salt Lake Times*, July 14, Aug. 4, 1891.
42. *Salt Lake Tribune*, Aug. 1, 5, 1891; *Salt Lake Herald*, July 11, Aug. 9, 1891.
43. Kenner, *Practical Politician*, 148.

Apostle Anthon H. Lund ran as a Republican in Sanpete County. He was defeated by the Democratic candidate from adjacent Millard County. President Cannon found it appalling that an apostle could not be elected to the legislature. Joseph F. Smith considered the problem generally to have been that more apostles had not campaigned for the Republicans to show the Church was "in earnest" in freeing up the vote. Only three—Anthon H. Lund, Francis M. Lyman, and John Henry Smith—had exhibited noticeable preferences in that direction. Cannon suspected that Church members were still wary of the "twin relics of barbarism" party. In early October, as the Church continued to be accused of having directed the members' votes, President Woodruff commented that it was a strange allegation, since they had "very much desired to see some Republicans sent to the legislature, but not one had been elected."[44]

The Republicans thought they could solve their deficiencies before the next election by forming a territory-wide organization, approved by the individual clubs. A convention was called to order in September by the territorial president of the Republican League of Clubs, Arthur Brown. His idea was to organize a territorial committee that was independent of the anti-Mormons. Committeemen were selected to represent nineteen of the territory's twenty-five counties. Resolutions were passed reflecting strong opposition to the Liberal Party, with an eye to establishing credentials to pass muster with the Republican National Committee. The national chairman, James S. Clarkson, who had advised the LDS Church, accepted their application in November. When the Liberals complained, they were told to seek party harmony rather than division with the non-Liberals.[45]

In late August 1891, on assignment from the First Presidency, Francis M. Lyman and Anthon H. Lund had embarked on a tour of LDS congregations in the south-central portion of the territory. They went by train as far as Salina, in Sevier County, then switched

44. Anthon H. Lund journal, July 9, Aug. 3, 1891.

45. J. S. Clarkson to Woodruff, July 11, 1894 (see appendix); *Salt Lake Times*, Sept. 2–3, Nov. 24–25, 1891; *Salt Lake Herald*, Nov. 25, 1891.

to horse-drawn conveyances into the principal communities in Garfield and Kane Counties, accompanied by local Church authorities. They would typically spend a full day conferring with ward and stake leaders on Church matters and would deliver sermons almost every night. By the second week of September, reaching Washington County, they added a political theme to their preaching. There was not yet a Republican Party presence there. At a priesthood meeting on Sunday, September 11, in St. George, Lyman said, "There are too many Democrats here. We were told to divide[,] but here in St. George you have turned in a body from People's Party to Democracy." The Republicans dominated the national government, he said, and "they can do something for us the Democrats can't[,] at least not until the fourth of March next!" He advised those who had not yet taken sides to consider affiliating with the Republicans to "court the side that is in power." This was in harmony with the policy the First Presidency enunciated in the summer of 1891.[46]

As they journeyed back north, Lyman's actions mid-territory in the small community of Beaver would become the basis of legend about Church authorities arbitrarily dividing congregations into Republicans and Democrats, according to which side of the meetinghouse they sat on. It is not recorded to have happened, however. What was related several years later by John F. Tolton was that while Lyman was in town, he approached Tolton and others about becoming Republicans. Tolton said he "was surprised to see such a political craze as had apparently struck us." He recalled that the apostle "desired us to divide about equally on national party lines in order that we could receive favors from whichever party was in power."[47] Lyman wanted "those who had not already declared themselves Democrats and could conscientiously do so" to "ally themselves with the Republicans."

Tolton attended a meeting where Lyman addressed the presidencies of several stakes: Beaver, Kanab, Millard, Panguitch, and Parowan. They were told the message from the First Presidency

46. Lund journal, Aug. 25, Sept. 8, 11, 18, 1891.

47. Tolton, "Memories," June 18, 20, 1891; also Williams, "Separation of Church and State," 37.

was "that it was not wrong to be a Republican." Much later Tolton objected to this form of coercion, compelling Lyman to gather confirmation from those in attendance that he had not exerted overt pressure. Lyman had also advised the presidencies to keep the source of their counsel secret, to give the impression that the division into political clans had been a local initiative. Four years later, during the heated campaign of 1895, Tolton let it be known that Elder Lyman had crossed a line.[48] By then there was a general Democratic undercurrent of discontent throughout the Church over having been counseled to "divide about equally on national party lines."

When the Utah Commission made its annual report to the Secretary of the Interior during the first week of October 1891, it was the first report since Woodruff's manifesto of 1890. Once again the commission alleged the Church had countenanced new plural marriages and interfered in politics. The leadership discussed the report at length and decided to present an objection during general conference in the Tabernacle. Charles W. Penrose drafted resolutions "deny[ing] most emphatically the assertion of the commission that the Church dominates its members in political matters and that Church and state were united."[49]

Gentiles received this statement with the same dubiousness as the one that had appeared in the *Salt Lake Times* interview a few months earlier. If anything, little attention was paid to it. The opposite was true of the commission report. President Benjamin Harrison borrowed from it in his State of the Union message to say that the only barrier to the continued practice polygamy was the US Congress's passage of laws suppressing it. He expressed skepticism regarding the LDS Church's sincerity. As the *Times* observed, the nation had not been convinced that Mormons could keep a promise. To those outside of Utah, little of what Estee had advised at the beginning of the year had been fulfilled.[50]

48. Francis M. Lyman journal, Nov. 1, 1895; Lyman, ed., *Candid Insights*, 222–23; Gibbs, *Lights and Shadows of Mormonism*, 337–45.

49. Utah Commission Reports, 1891, *House Executive Documents*, 52nd Cong., 1st sess., 16:422–29; Lyman, ed., *Candid Insights*, 258–261.

50. Richardson, *Compilation of Messages*, 12:5641; *Salt Lake Times*, Dec. 10, 11, 1891.

Those who observed Utah's political developments more closely could see that great strides had been made. Individual political independence was being promoted where it had not previously existed. The ensuing election would show that LDS people were spreading their wings, opposing each other along national party lines with the intensity they had previously shown toward their Liberal rivals. This was true even among those in the highest Church councils, who were themselves finding it difficult to refrain from partisan involvement. In March 1892 a seemingly insignificant municipal election in Logan became a case in point. For one of the first times, a predominantly LDS electorate chose between the national parties. The Democrats assumed that after carrying the legislative election seven months earlier by a hundred votes, they would win this time around, even though the *Salt Lake Herald* urged them not to be complacent.

After the ballots were tallied, the Republicans had won by seventy-seven votes. At first there was "puzzlement" and blame laid at the feet of the voter registrar, C. C. Goodwin Jr., who had run the Liberal Party in Logan. Goodwin countered that of eighty voters who had supported the Gentile ticket the previous year (ballots were not yet secret in Utah Territory), all but two had voted Republican. The *Herald* found it "mysterious and unaccountable" that the Republican vote had increased from 207 to 400, especially since "no open campaign was made by the Republicans." The result was traced back to "some kind of still hunt on the part of" George F. Gibbs, a clerk in the LDS First Presidency's office.[51]

On March 16 Democratic leaders, both LDS and Gentile, met with President Woodruff to see if this was true, having heard that Gibbs told people the First Presidency wanted the Republicans to win. Abraham Cannon was present. "All denounced the using of Church influence in political matters," he wrote, adding that "some of these remarks were not mild." One outspoken critic of this kind of activity was Church attorney Franklin S. Richards, son of

51. Salt Lake *Herald,* Mar. 3, 8–9, 17, 1892. A "still hunt" involved small meetings and inconspicuous canvassing "to reach wavering voters without arousing partisan feelings or inviting vigorous counter-moves."

apostle Franklin D. Richards, who predicted bad results from such "far-reaching mischief." In his experience even "Congress admits we are honest and sincere in our religion, but in politics we are harlots." Another Mormon attorney, LeGrand Young, seconded that sentiment. President Woodruff denied having told anyone to go to Logan and pointed out that his own sons were divided on political affiliation, about half one way and half the other. Joseph F. Smith similarly denied having given permission for his name to be used in promoting the Republicans. Before the three-and-a-half-hour meeting ended, Gibbs was called in to answer for himself. He said he had conveyed the presidency's unspoken wish, not their explicit instructions, to see the Republicans "gain ground and preponderance." Under questioning by Salt Lake attorney Joseph L. Rawlins, Gibbs admitted he had not received permission to represent the Church.[52] The presidency, without George Q. Cannon, who was in Washington, drafted a notice for the *Deseret News* denying involvement in the election.

Incredulous, the *Tribune* wondered, if that was the case, how this miracle had occurred. "Logan, which was Democrat last summer, [became] Republican this spring," the paper pointed out. It only made sense if one knew "the workings of George Q. Cannon's mind," the paper asserted, that the electorate was subtly nudged in that direction. In fact, the accusation that Cannon was the one behind the campaigning for the Republicans was probably correct. His son Abraham wrote that "Geo F. Gibbs and Robt. Campbell were selected to go quietly to Logan and work to make the Republican ticket successful in the approaching city election, which takes place on the 1st of March." Whether Gibbs had been formally "called" or not, he and others knew they were carrying out Cannon's wishes.[53]

The election furor exhausted the patience of the Democrats, who learned how clearly biased the First Presidency was in favor of the Republicans. If the Church remained technically consistent with

52. Lyman, ed., *Candid Insights*, 311–12; Richards journal, Mar. 16, 1892; notes of meeting, Mar. 16, 1892, Richards Family Papers.

53. *Salt Lake Herald*, Mar. 16, 1892, Nov. 3–4, 1895; *Deseret Evening News*, Mar. 17, 1892; *Salt Lake Tribune*, Mar. 19, 1892, Nov. 2–3, 5, 1895; Lyman, ed., *Candid Insights*, 302.

its statement to the *Times* in 1891, by next fall Joseph F. Smith's partisan activities would surprise everyone. One of the apostles, Moses Thatcher, who lived in Logan, was livid when he found out the Church had meddled in their election. Instead of bringing unity to the community, "politics have so divided the people that one can scarcely tell saints from sinners," he wrote, "and we are calling each other all the vile names we can think of." He protested the way the Church had stirred things up and warned that continued involvement would "bring irretrievable trouble upon ourselves." What was needed was a separation of church and state, he suggested, even though this was not a principle he himself always adhered to. His role in promoting the Democrats in Logan had already become a controversy all of its own.[54]

On May 14 Thatcher spoke in Ogden to the Territorial Democratic Convention. In a lengthy speech packed with sensational statements, one of its most controversial assertions was that Jesus would have been a Democrat and Lucifer a Republican. Later he claimed he was misquoted in both newspapers. In the meantime, some of his fellow general authorities reacted badly to this effrontery. John Henry Smith told the First Presidency that the "satanic part" was beyond the pale. Smith and Frank Cannon were given permission to draft a response for the *Ogden Standard*. Their position was that connecting Jesus to the Democrats would implicate him in the murders of Joseph and Hyrum Smith in Carthage, Illinois, by assassins who were predominantly Democrats, at least based on the fact that they were in a Democratic region.[55]

In the refutation Thatcher wrote for the *Salt Lake Herald*, in which he claimed he had been misquoted, he found the "intense partisan feeling" of Cannon and Smith regrettable, because he wanted to feel united with his brethren. "In reference to the fundamental

54. Lyman, ed., *Candid Insights*, 316–19, 344–46, 348–51; Lyman, "Alienation of an Apostle," 73–75.

55. *Salt Lake Herald*, May 15, 28–29, 1892; *Salt Lake Tribune*, May 15, 1892; *Ogden Standard*, May 23, 24, 1892; J. H. Smith journal, May 23, 1892; F. Lyman journal, June 16, 1892; also typed notes for 1891–95, Lyman Papers; White, ed., *Church, State, and Politics*, 275–76.

principles dividing Democracy and Republicanism," though, he announced that he would keep his own counsel and not be dictated to, especially regarding the recent Republican promotion of tariffs and bounties, which were "oppressive and harmful to the masses." He and others were free to express their opinions, he wrote, and as long as that was true he would continue to express his. This elicited a rebuttal from some of the Republican churchmen.

After the exchanges died down, Lorenzo Snow suggested a halt to politicking by members of the Quorum of the Twelve. Elder Heber J. Grant correctly thought "the little tilt of Bros. Smith and Moses Thatcher in the papers will do more towards satisfying the people of the world that we are sincere [in allowing political freedom] than a great amount of talk would do."[56] On the other hand, it was not conducive of good feelings within the quorum. LDS people had a lot to learn about separating politics from religion. They were not altogether different from people elsewhere in the country where people of common religious leanings tended to favor one party or another. What one saw in Utah of Catholics and Protestants working so closely together was unusual. They did so only by subordinating their differences for the good of their united front against Mormons. Through the process of normalizing party alignments, strife within the Liberal Party along predictable Catholic and Protestant fault lines would soon become more noticeable. Elsewhere political independence had long been a matter of personal choice. However, in LDS circles this was absolutely new.

The political division that occurred in Utah Territory in 1891 was artificial enough, it would not be possible to differentiate between the ethno-cultural background of Church members who remained Democrats and those who became Republican. All that can be determined is that some went one direction and others the opposite way. The Republicans found ideological compatibility once the party stopped its hostility toward Mormons. The real impetus for this attraction, however, aside from the tariffs that appealed to

56. Abraham H. Cannon journal, July 12, 1892; also Grant, *Diaries*, July 12, 1892; F. Lyman journal, July 12, 1892; Lyman, ed., *Candid Insights*, 342–43.

self-sufficiency, was the pragmatic reality that the Republicans were in power in Washington and were able to deliver statehood. The men in high Church positions who had been politically active in the 1880s remained Democrats. Those who had been active with the Democrats and switched parties, such as George Q. Cannon, were small in number. It was primarily with prompting from the First Presidency that anything approaching an equitable division was even possible in that generation, which proved to be a truly notable accomplishment. As time went on, the movement toward the Republicans would accelerate.

10

THE DEATH OF THE LIBERAL PARTY

1892–93

As polygamy faded from public view, and the major national political parties became organized in Utah Territory, the main obstacles to statehood began to fade. Intermittent opposition from anti-Mormons still persisted but had been weakened by closer ties to the major political parties. Yet before statehood could be realized, there were additional changes that needed to occur, including the capitulation of the Liberal party, more extensive enrollment in the national parties in relatively equal numbers, and success in getting an enabling act passed by Congress. There was still a need for major assistance from high-level lobbyists. Finally in December 1893, the House of Representatives would approve an enabling bill.

About a month after Wilford Woodruff's 1890 manifesto, Joseph F. Smith expressed his conviction that it had prevented additional Edmunds-like bills from being passed. Frank J. Cannon reported from Washington that the feeling toward the Church had become noticeably friendlier, and even though President Benjamin Harrison remained cool toward the suggestion of giving the Saints more voice in government, even he was against any further anti-polygamy legislation.[1] The influence of friends high in Presbyterian Church circles continued to make him apprehensive. Realizing this, LDS agents arranged for his secretary, Elijah Halford, to keep some sensitive

1. Lyman, ed., *Candid Insights,* 153–54 (Oct. 22, 1890). Smith was probably referring to the Cullom–Struble Bill.

matters away from his view. George Q. Cannon reassured Morris M. Estee, former chairman of the Republican National Convention, in early December 1890, there was no foundation for reports on the Church not fully conforming with the law regarding polygamy. There were certainly still some men living with their plural wives, but supposedly not new plural marriages. Cannon explained that the allegations were a smear by those who were determined to prevent the Latter-day Saints from benefitting from their conformity. Cannon reiterated that the manifesto was "a truthful and sincere expression of our willingness to conform to the requirements of the law." For Estee and his associates, that was good enough.[2]

The Republican supporters asked Church leaders for information that would show the LDS people in a favorable light, so the First Presidency put assistants to work soliciting data from outlying stakes that compared the business interests of non-LDS people who owned gambling houses and saloons to businesses conducted by LDS entrepreneurs building irrigation canals and roads. They compiled literacy rates, school statistics, and relative crime rates to document that the moral environment was "equal to if not superior to that of the older states of the union." The purpose was to put LDS morality in a more positive light. Even more important in the long run were the population statistics requested by Isaac Trumbo, James Clarkson, and Morris Estee that would eventually win over the most Republicans. The Church wrote to stake presidents in surrounding states to determine how many members there were in Arizona, Colorado, Idaho, Nevada, New Mexico, and Wyoming, specifically asking William W. Cluff, a stake president with considerable jurisdiction in the new state of Wyoming, for the current Church population there, including members who were isolated from the organized wards and branches and may not have appeared on the semi-annual reports. Requesting a prompt response, the First Presidency advised Cluff not to underestimate the numerical strength of his stake.[3]

---

2. George Q. Cannon to M. M. Estee, Dec. 9, 1890; Wilford Woodruff et al. to M. M. Estee, Dec. 2, 1890, First Presidency Letterbooks.

3. Woodruff et al. to Amos M. Musser, Nov. 28, 1890; Woodruff et al. to W. W. Cluff, Nov. 28, 1890, First Presidency Letterbooks. Even so, the figure for Wyoming

During the first week of December, the Church leaders informed Estee that the approximate number of Mormons in the adjacent states, in descending order, was for Idaho, 25,000; Arizona, 10,000; Colorado, 4,000; Nevada, 1,500; New Mexico, 1,000; and Wyoming, 300. Within a month the California political adviser, who was being considered for a cabinet position in the Harrison administration, met with the US president and passed on the figures. Harrison's reaction was one of alarm: "Such people should be checked," he told Estee. The last thing he wanted to see was the spread of LDS influence into other areas of the West. A rigid Protestant, his view was that the Mormons should "be disfranchised for thirty years."[4] Despite his negative reaction, the argument concerning the LDS voting potential in neighboring states and territories would take hold within the Republican Party and become a persuasive argument for acceptance of Utah as a state.

Harrison's reaction was illustrative of the difficulty Republican leaders were experiencing with him in other areas as well. The congressional and state elections of the previous year (1890) had been disastrous—among the worst in American history for the party in power. The president of the Republican National Committee and Republican League, James Clarkson, labored tirelessly to bolster the party's fortunes by pushing enrollment in the Republican clubs. In that capacity he corresponded often with the president's secretary, Elijah Halford, and with Harrison himself, freely giving and soliciting advice and information. The elections at year's end were better than those of the year before, but still disturbing. The party was losing ground in states that had recently been considered impregnable bastions of Republicanism. The party had essentially given up on any realistic possibility of winning electoral support below the Mason–Dixon line.[5] The alternative strategies of angling for the allegiance

neglected the primarily LDS Star Valley, part of an Idaho stake that had a large number of polygamists across the state line and would have added about 1,000 more LDS people to the Wyoming count.

4. Woodruff et al. to Estee, Dec. 2, 1890; Lyman, ed., *Candid Insights*, 178–81.

5. Benjamin Harrison to Clarkson, July 27, 1891, James S. Clarkson to Harrison, July 22, Aug. 7, 1891, Harrison Papers; also DeSantis, *Republicans Face Southern Question*; Hirshson, *Farewell Bloody Shirt*.

and support from the newly admitted western states had paid large dividends, including eleven out of twelve seats in the Senate. There too, there was enough instability that it was decided to schedule the next year's national convention in Minneapolis. The flood of immigration to the West and growth of the Farmers' Alliance in the Midwest made those areas of major electoral concern.

The party was coming around slowly to an awareness of regional differences and cultural sensitivities. Clarkson was especially cognizant of these considerations and was trying to undo the damage done in his own home state of Iowa, where the party had backed prohibition and turned its back on the farmers, leading to an unprecedented Republican defeat.[6] There was similar trouble in Illinois and Wisconsin when the party supported the elimination of foreign languages in the public schools, especially German. Clarkson generally blamed the recent electoral defeat on the "moral spasms which periodically come over the Republican party. … The trouble is that as a party we are too missionary and too sympathetic and take up with too many isms and hobbies." Among the "hobbies" he wanted to jettison were the animus toward liquor, foreign languages in schools, lotteries, and moral issues. Polygamy was not mentioned, but it fell within the category of moral evils the party leadership had formerly denounced. He warned, "If we try to carry an ism in one state, and a hobby in another, and a moral idea in some other place, we are constantly sheared of our strength locally and left without a majority nationally."

He agued in a letter to President Harrison's secretary that the "police" mentality was too large a burden to carry. He was looking for new methods for winning voters. Otherwise, he warned, the Republicans would "get whipped" in next year's election, and they probably would not recover in his lifetime. Harrison brushed off the suggestion that they give up the party's moral direction, so Clarkson worked around him and made headway with party leadership in other states, as well as with the national committee. The

6. Marcus, *Grand Old Party*, 160; Jensen, *Winning the Midwest*; Kleppner, *Cross of Culture* and *Third Electoral System*.

old Half-breed faction of the party came to see Utah in a different light, for its potential political strength rather than for its polygamy. As Clarkson later recalled, "It took a year of patient effort, of direct personal appeal to almost every member" of the national committee to win them over to a neutral attitude toward Utah. The fear was that by allowing the Mormons political power, the party would reap the indignation of the country's electorate. In time Clarkson convinced most of the committeemen that the LDS people considered themselves true Americans and agreed with the party's promotion of American products, the "protection of American interests and industries," including tariffs. Clarkson was most persuasive when he explained that "this was not merely a Utah question" but concerned the fact that "the Mormon people were spread through the valleys of eight or ten western states, and that sooner or later they would hold the balance of power in the election of every senator and of every electoral vote for president in these states."[7] This was an overstatement, and it became more embellished with every telling, but it caught the attention of many of the party's movers and shakers.

Besides holding out the prospect for statehood, Republicans courted Mormon favor by promising to restore full-fledged citizenship to onetime polygamists through amnesty. Despite Harrison's continued coolness toward Latter-day Saints, Estee and others argued that the president should pardon those who had once engaged in illegal marriage practices but no longer did so. In mid-July 1891, Estee was in Salt Lake City to solicit support for this from the non-LDS Republican leadership. There were a few, notably attorney Charles W. Bennett, who agreed to cooperate with LDS people, especially after, having worked with some of them, finding them to be less fanatical than he expected. As observer, Abraham H. Cannon, understood what Estee had in mind. He came to Utah and circulated petitions for consideration by President Harrison and the Republican National Committee, with the impression that these had been generated locally as a home-grown initiative. His campaign

7. Clarkson to E. W. Halford, Dec. 5, 1891, Harrison Papers; Clarkson to Woodruff, July 11, 1894, Volwiler Papers (appendix herein).

experienced a setback in mid-summer when the Liberal Party experienced a resurgence. After the elections, Estee urged Clarkson to use his influence to convince the Liberals to stand down.[8]

Progress on the amnesty petition was slow. Toward the end of 1891 the petitions had been circulated and were ready for presentation. On December 19 George Q. Cannon, John Henry Smith, and Joseph F. Smith met with Judge Charles S. Zane and Governor Arthur L. Thomas at the governor's residence. Amazingly, the judge and governor said they would compose a cover letter to President Harrison. This meant that the two highest-ranking presidential appointees in the territory were vouching for the sincerity of President Woodruff's call to end polygamy. On December 22 the documents were given to the once more bitter opponent, Charles C. Goodwin, who forwarded them to his friend George B. Williams at the nation's capital. General Williams was close to Harrison.[9]

As other Church leaders were informed of the endorsement they had received from several former adversaries in favor of their "emancipation," they expressed astonishment. Not only the chief justice and governor, but the editor of the *Tribune,* too, were weighing in on their behalf. Copies of the correspondence between Estee and Governor Thomas convinced LDS authorities that the California lobbyist–attorney had been their most influential advocate. These developments necessitated some quick changes in strategy. John Morgan, a member of the First Council of Seventy, and attorney Edward B. Critchlow were in Washington seeking to have Governor Thomas and US Attorney Charles Varian removed from office. Those efforts were abruptly halted. John Henry Smith observed the amazing reversals of the Church's former detractors, all of whom were now asking for statehood when they had previously argued against it. The once anti-Mormon mainstays would soon withdraw their support of the Liberal Party, then waver, and finally recommit to its disestablishment.[10] By February 1892 the *Tribune*

8. Lyman, ed., *Candid Insights*, 230–33, 264.

9. White, ed., *Church, State, and Politics*, 264–66; Lyman, 291–93..

10. George Q. Cannon journal, Dec. 14–21, 1891; John Morgan journal, Jan. 5, 1892; White, 267–68.

had established a consistent editorial policy in support of amnesty for Mormon polygamists. Another surprise came when the former Mormon opponent from Nebraska, Republican Senator Algernon Paddock, introduced a bill repealing portions of the Edmunds Act that might stand in the way of the president pardoning polygamists, even though Attorney General William Miller told Harrison he already possessed the authority one way or the other.[11] Harrison remained notably indecisive. Paddock and others conferred with the president and predicted that an amnesty proclamation would be made within a few days. They were wrong. What gave the president pause was the thought that perhaps adulterers from other areas of the country would be forgiven, along with polygamists. As he hesitated, the *Herald* and other Democratic voices alleged that amnesty was an unfounded rumor promoted to help the Republicans in Utah. On March 23 the newspaper editorialized that Harrison would not dare carry out the plan he was said to be considering. There were later reports that he might pardon a few individuals based on the merits of their particular cases.[12]

Loosely connected to the decision on whether to issue a general amnesty was a plan by the Democrats, introduced to the House of Representatives by Utah's delegate, John T. Caine, early in 1892 and by Charles J. Faulkner of West Virginia in the Senate (Faulkner was the ranking Democrat on the Senate Committee on Territories). The point of the legislation was not statehood, but the abolishment of the Utah Commission and enhancement of the ability of the territory to vote for its own governor and territorial judges. Caine confided to Franklin S. Richards that it was partly a "political move" to put the Republicans on their heels, to see if they would choose to defeat it because it was a Democratic suggestion.[13] Contrary to his expectation, the Home Rule Bill became the impetus to unite undecided Utahns in supporting the Republicans. The *Salt Lake*

11. *Salt Lake Tribune*, Feb. 14–16, 18, Mar. 1, 7, 23, 1892.

12. *Salt Lake Herald*, Mar. 23, May 10, 25, 1892.

13. Franklin S. Richards to John T. Caine, Dec. 21, 1891; Caine to S. A. Merritt, Jan. 23, 1892; H. P. Henderson to Caine, Feb. 7, 16, 1892, Caine to James Wallis, Jan. 26, 1892, Caine Papers; *Congressional Record*, Jan. 5, 7, 1892.

Tribune dismissed the bill as a "stupid document." If Utah was to act like a state, it may as well have the name, the paper insisted. It also noticed that the bill would not allow for the popular election of the territory's congressional delegate, a position the LDS Church knew it could still control because of its members in the legislature. It did not take long for the Republicans and their Liberal sympathizers in Utah to send Frank J. Cannon and John M. Zane to Congress to argue that Utah be admitted as a state rather than accept the disingenuous home-rule bill. That prompted the Church to send one of its men, John Morgan, to the nation's capital with a hastily drafted statehood bill, which Republicans Clarence D. Clarke of Wyoming and Henry M. Teller of Colorado presented in the House and Senate respectively. The response from Orville Platt of Connecticut, Republican chairman of the Senate Territorial Committee, was that it was premature.[14] That did not matter. It had accomplished its goal of neutralizing the Democratic initiative, which the opposing party feared would delay actual statehood.

Caine was incredulous as he watched Senator Teller and the Utah Republicans push for statehood, after having stonewalled him in the past. He suspected it was a trap to lure Democrats into opposing statehood, not genuine support on the part of Republicans. In fact, Democrats in Congress were now opposing the bill, chiding their Republican colleagues for proposing something before its time, so obviously rushed and incomplete. If they came up with a real enabling bill instead of "a skin and bones affair like the Teller Bill," they would consider it, they promised. Caine's hope was that Congress would pass both bills, for home rule to give the territory immediate relief and an enabling act that would, in the absence of the Utah Commission, move the territory more fairly and gradually toward statehood. He saw the possibility of the Republicans being caught in their own trap if they opposed the Democratic home-rule bill.[15]

The Utah Republicans sent two more spokesmen to Washington in mid-February, party chairman Charles W. Bennett and

14. *Salt Lake Tribune*, Jan. 7, 20, 1892; John Morgan journal, Jan. 17, 18, 1892.
15. Caine to William H. King, Feb. 13, 1892, Caine Papers.

apostle John Henry Smith, with the specific intent of opposing anything that would delay statehood. The unexpected consequence of the hearings was the evidence on display for all to see of Utah's maturation, as representatives of opposing parties took either side of the issue, demonstrating the political diversity that now existed in Utah. The Republican view voiced by Smith and Bennett against home rule and in favor of statehood was matched by the Liberal Republicans' opinion that the territory was not yet prepared to accept statehood, expressed by Clarence E. Allen and backed by the Liberal Democratic spokesman Orlando W. Powers. By far the largest contingent, the Democrats, supported home rule, voiced by Gentiles Frank Dyer, Caleb West, John W. Judd, Joseph Rawlins, and H. W. Smith, and Mormons Franklin S. Richards and Charles C. Richards. The home rule advocates occupied most of the time. That was unfortunate because the results were not entirely favorable, due to their inability to avoid criticizing present and former territorial officials who had been approved by Congress and had friends there. Some otherwise receptive lawmakers thus sensed a persistent disloyalty to the federal government in the Democratic position and concluded that Utah, while making progress, was not yet ready for self-government.[16]

The *Salt Lake Herald* remained optimistic that the home-rule bill would pass. In late March the Committee on Territories favorably reported it to the House, against the promise of Orville Platt in the Senate that he would not allow it to be discussed in his committee. The bill was passed in the House and languished in the Senate.[17] Back in Utah predictions of harmony within the Republican ranks, which had grown after both factions opposed home rule, went unfulfilled. The Church's interference in the election campaign in Logan sparked renewed doubts about the motives of the LDS hierarchy. Possibly President Harrison's failure to grant general amnesty, too, convinced the Liberal ring that their tenuous hold on the

16. Pusey, *Builders of the Kingdom*, 167–68.

17. *Salt Lake Herald*, Mar. 19, 31, Apr. 1, 17, 23, May 19, July 9, 1892; *Salt Lake Tribune*, Mar. 23, Apr. 1, 29, May 5, 20, 1892.

territory and its appointees was more secure than they had assumed. Feeling thus emboldened, the Liberals decided to attend the 1892 Republican national convention and challenge the credentials of what they called the "bogus Republican party" of Utah.

By then President Harrison had alienated national committeemen and state bosses, the very people who were most able to guide the Republicans to victory in November. Aside from the president's personal iciness, there was concern that his policy positions would sink everyone else's chances of being elected or re-elected with him as the party's standard bearer. Some people turned almost by reflex to James G. Blaine, still the most popular Republican in the country. Blaine was ambivalent about jumping back into the fray after the abuse he endured in his 1884 presidential campaign. He was recuperating from an illness out of the country when he announced he would not be a candidate for the presidency. That did not stop some Republicans from assuming he could still be drafted at the convention.[18] Clarkson played a prominent role in the movement to draft Blaine, he and the national committee being well aware of the deep-seated dissatisfaction in the Midwest, which was a problem for the party if Harrison stood for re-election. That dissatisfaction would lead to the formation of the Populist Party later in the year. The committee concluded that "any Republican candidate who cannot carry the western states cannot be elected," and they were convinced that Harrison could not win in Illinois, Indiana, and Ohio. Clarkson, as party chairman, wrote to Blaine in January 1892 to try to change his mind for the good of the party. They needed someone "who can draw from the Farmers' Alliance the necessary votes to keep the party in power in the northwestern states." By late spring, the sentiment in Blaine's favor in the Rocky Mountain and Pacific Coast states had reached a frenzied proportion.

In Utah the Republicans convened in Provo on the first day of April 1892 for their territorial convention. Amid the noise of

18. Morgan, *From Hayes to McKinley*, 324–25; Williams, *Years of Decision*, 59–66; Muzzey, *James G. Blaine*, 467–80; also Morgan, "Decline of Agriculture"; Hamilton, *Biography of James G. Blaine.*

electioneering and celebration, Frank Cannon and Orange J. Salisbury were selected as delegates to the national convention. Cannon was a logical choice, carrying the support of Weber County. Salisbury, who was not LDS, was liked even by those in the *Tribune* ring for his political positions and for being the husband of one of Blaine's nieces. Even so, the Liberal Republicans had their own convention and selected another pair of delegates to the national meetings, Charles C. Goodwin and Clarence E. Allen.[19] Aware of that, Cannon and Salisbury went to some trouble to establish their legitimacy, probably with help from Clarkson and Trumbo. For instance, they received an endorsement from Idaho's attorney general, George H. Roberts, who published a supportive pamphlet. Roberts argued that Utah's regular Republicans represented not only Utah but the region, giving an exaggerated figure of "about 200,000 Mormon voters in the United States." Drawing on what he had heard from Clarkson, he claimed the Latter-day Saints held "the balance of power in California, Colorado, Montana, Arizona, and possibly in Illinois and Missouri." The Liberal challengers, by comparison, comprised "the still life of a Dead Sea," not a thriving group that could legitimately claim to represent the territory.[20]

On June 1 Cannon, Salisbury, and over thirty regular Republicans took a special Union Pacific Railroad car to Minnesota and embarked on an itinerary of contacting other delegations for their support, giving them a copy of Roberts's fifteen-page pamphlet. Back in Utah the *Salt Lake Tribune* reported with astonishment that the Mormon Republicans were telling delegates that they represented an LDS population of 460,000, all of whom, the pamphlet asserted, "will feel aggrieved if the Liberal Republicans are accorded full or even partial recognition." The Liberals arrived to find that the party secretary had already entered Cannon's and Salisbury's names

19. *Salt Lake Herald*, Apr. 2, 1892; *Salt Lake Tribune*, Apr. 2, 1892.

20. George H. Roberts to John Henry Smith and John Morgan, May 19, 1892, John Henry Smith Papers; Norman B. Willey to Willis Sweet, May 11, 1892, Willey Gubernatorial Papers. No copy of the pamphlet has been located. As Clarkson would have known, Reorganized Latter Day Saints in Illinois and Missouri were mostly unsympathetic with the Church headquartered in Salt Lake City.

on the roster. That was not entirely unexpected, and they soon convinced the leadership to appoint a subcommittee to hear their challenge. The committee consisted of Garrett A. Hobart of New Jersey, Cyrus Leland Jr. of Kansas, and Charles Warren of Montana. On June 5 the committee listened to both sides. They were taken aback by the animosity demonstrated by the Liberal group, and persuaded, when Hobart questioned Cannon, that the Liberal Party had earlier prevented him from joining their group because he was Mormon. The subcommittee ruled unanimously in favor of the LDS-aligned representatives.[21]

The next day the national committee accepted the subcommittee report. It remained to be seen if the credentials committee would agree. The *Salt Lake Tribune* found it unimaginable that the party would act "so irresponsibly" as to accept the Mormon Church as an ally and refuse to recognize the representatives of Utah's longstanding Liberal affiliate. In fact, the *Tribune* proved to be right. The boom faded on the effort to draft Blaine, damaging the prestige of Clarkson and his associates. Harrison's people looked for areas of support. Nor were they in a mood for delays. A recommendation was made and approved to divide the Utah delegation, letting each group have half representation. With more important business pressing, the regular Utah Republicans were forced to accept the compromise or nothing, thereby catching them in the backwash of half recognition.[22]

Another aspect of the feud, as it unfolded in Minneapolis, occurred when Frank Cannon proposed the name of Arthur Brown to represent Utah on the national committee. The outgoing member was no longer a resident of the territory. Charles Goodwin let it be known that the Liberals would fight to prevent Brown's appointment, and they objected to Judge John R. McBride, the previous committeeman, as well. In an unexpected twist, a representative of the regular Republicans, O. J. Salisbury, ended up receiving the appointment. The delegations on both sides claimed Salisbury was a

21. *Salt Lake Tribune*, June 4, 1892; *Salt Lake Herald*, June 7, 1892; Morgan journal, June 5, 6, 1892.

22. *Salt Lake Tribune*, June 2, 7–8, 11–12, 14, 18, 22, 1892.

victory for their faction. When the *Herald* asked Brown what had happened, he claimed credit as well, responding that he had withdrawn his name and suggested Salisbury in order "to unite the party," which he believed he had done.[23]

A similar contest occurred at the Democratic convention in Chicago. In that instance, it signaled the final days of the Liberal Party's influence. Calling themselves the Tuscarora Club, the Liberals were handicapped by having traditionally leaned toward the Republican Party. That meant they had few friends among the Democrats serving in national positions. Unlike the Republicans, the Democrats knew their nominee would be Grover Cleveland, and seemed to have all the time in the world to consider the disputed claims from Utah's representatives. The Tuscaroras had arrived early and brought a uniformed marching corps with over a hundred members in order to attract attention. But the regular Democrats were connected to Senator Charles Faulkner and the president of the national network of Democratic clubs, Chauncey F. Black, both of whom had visited Utah the previous year and had gotten to know the regularly organized Democrats, whom they now endorsed, recommending that Henry P. Henderson and John T. Caine be seated over the Tuscaroras.[24]

Similarly, Congressman William D. Bynum (D–Indiana) warned that if the forces working against the regular delegation were recognized, it would take years for the party in Utah to recover from that "blunder." Not only that, the impact would be "felt in the adjoining states and territories," he said, drawing on a now familiar theme.[25] The Liberal Democrats stood little chance against supposedly a half-million Mormons in half a dozen states. But rather than admit defeat, the *Salt Lake Tribune* persistently complained about the injustice of it, since the Tuscaroras were true Americans and the

23. *Salt Lake Herald*, June 10–11, 14, 16, 1892.

24. The group facetiously joked that they could trace their genealogy to a Native American tribe that rivaled the Book of Mormon Lamanites. *Salt Lake Tribune*, Jan. 9, June 19, 25, 28, 1892; *Salt Lake Herald*, June 17, 19, 21–22, 24, 1892

25. *Facts in the Utah Case*, 5–23; paper dated Jan. 12, 1892, signed by S. A. Merritt, chairman, and Elias A. Smith, secretary, Democratic Territorial Central Committee, Caine Papers.

Mormons had sworn allegiance "not to the United States but to an alien [LDS] power."

The Liberal Party tried to regroup after the conventions, Powers as chairman and Allen as secretary. However, when a territory-wide convention was called in mid-July, there were representatives from only eight of Utah's twenty-five counties. Charles S. Varian proposed that, in view of the recent rejection at the national meetings, they should disband and direct their energies toward reforming Utah from within the national parties. His associate, William H. Dickson, said in a *Herald* interview, "We might as well accept the inevitable and make the best of the situation." Other Liberals continued for another year, but as the *Herald* observed in August the party was "going to pieces" everywhere but in Salt Lake and Summit Counties. Governor Arthur Thomas was pulling in the other direction to reconcile the rival branches of his party. He appeared on the same speaker's platform with Frank Cannon at one event. He called on apostle Francis M. Lyman at the Church offices and confided that it was the *Deseret News*'s promotion of home rule and statehood that kept the Liberal Party alive. He suggested that if the Church newspaper backed off, the Gentiles would join the national parties, and affirmed his own personal intention to work within the Republican Party. Before the campaign was over, however, he had drifted back into the anti-Mormon ranks, probably through the influence of his close associate, Patrick Lannan, publisher of the *Tribune*.[26]

The Republican territorial convention held in mid-September proved to be a stumbling block to party unification. Bitterness surfaced early on in a dispute over whether proxy delegates could represent counties in which they had never resided. Rival delegations were determined not to allow Salt Lake City to dominate matters any more than its superior population merited. A ruling against the Salt Lakers meant that their preferred candidate for territorial delegate, Charles Bennett, would not win the nomination.

26. Charles Crane to George Veile, Feb. 6, 1892; Francis M. Lyman journal, Aug. 5, 1892; Francis M. Lyman to Woodruff, Aug. 6, 1892, Lyman Papers; *Salt Lake Herald*, June 17, July 9–11, Aug. 10, 16, 18, 1892.

The Weber County contingent supporting Frank Cannon was overjoyed, seeing that their man had earlier stood but a slim chance. After a third indecisive ballot, it was clear to Bennett that he would not prevail. When he withdrew his name and shifted his support to Utah County's George Sutherland, a future justice of the US Supreme Court, it was not enough to beat Frank Cannon, who ended up being chosen because of better-organized supporters who were more unified than the others.

Newspaper accounts told of resentment over Cannon's nomination by Gentiles who had recently been with the Liberal Party. As the *Tribune* reported with ill-disguised glee, Mormons had dominated the convention. The *Herald* quoted Judge Powers's opinion that Cannon's nomination gave votes to the other party. The reality was more complicated. A significant number of LDS delegates had favored Bennett. Even the winner's cousin, George M. Cannon, had worked for Bennett, and apostle John Henry Smith had been active as a campaign manager for him. Nor was the First Presidency entirely sold on Cannon due to his young age, electability, and for some, the fact that he was less than a model Church member.[27]

Seeking to capitalize on the growing dissension in the Republican ranks, some Democratic leaders were determined to nominate a Gentile for territorial delegate instead of a "scion of a royal family of the Mormons." John T. Caine wanted to retire after having been in office ten years. In what appeared to be a harmonious association between Gentiles and Saints, Joseph L. Rawlins, the son of a Mormon bishop, though not affiliated with the Church himself, was chosen as the Democratic Party candidate for Caine's seat. True to their promises, the Liberals held a competing convention to nominate the LDS apostate Henry W. Lawrence and non-Mormon Orlando W. Powers, but in both cases the men declined to have their names considered, and the group settled on Clarence E. Allen for what would be the last Liberal candidate to run for Congress. He received little attention from the press or electorate, who were

27. John Henry Smith to Frank J. Cannon, Aug. 30, 1892, John Henry Smith Papers.

focused on what this time would be a head-to-head contest between the Democrats and Republicans.[28]

The most notable feature of the campaign was the barrage of negative assertions about opposing candidates in pamphlet form, beginning with a twelve-page booklet titled *Nuggets of Truth* that was anonymously prepared by the Republican Territorial Committee. Its purpose, through citing statements by Joseph Smith and three other Church presidents, was to prove that the Church leaders' political views put them squarely in the Republican camp. "A more miserable demagogic attempt than is made in this scandalous pamphlet has never been known in politics," the *Herald* wrote. The Democratic paper pointed to Frank Cannon as the chief beneficiary of the pamphlet's message. Whatever involvement Cannon had, he ordered the pamphlet withdrawn from circulation and later commented on his abhorrence of such exploitation of religious sentiments, although Democrats alleged he stopped the pamphlet only when it became a detriment to him.[29]

This attempt to introduce religion into the campaign was surpassed only by Joseph F. Smith's own partisan booklet that soon appeared, *Another Plain Talk: Reasons Why the People of Utah Should Be Republican*. It was an answer to a *Herald* column by the *Deseret News* editor Charles Penrose. Smith maintained, in a slanted rehearsal of territorial history, that the administrations of US Presidents Buchanan and Cleveland "stand out as the blackest pages in American history, so far as the treatment of the people of Utah was concerned." He emphasized that both presidents were Democrats. The pamphlet elicited opposing broadsides filled with overwrought complaints, including one by Penrose himself. If Smith had paid more attention to basic facts and less to rhetoric, he would have provided Democrats with a smaller target for pointing out his "errors and misstatements."[30]

---

28. *Salt Lake Herald*, Sept. 16, 17, Oct. 6, 11, 13, 17, 25, 27, 30, 1892; *Salt Lake Tribune*, Sept. 17, 20–21, Oct. 6, 13, 1892.

29. Cannon and O'Higgins, *Under the Prophet in Utah*, 124; *Nuggets of Truth and Gems*, 1–14.

30. Smith, *Another Plain Talk*, 2–16; "Jonathan," *Joseph F. Smith Answered*, 1–4; Penrose, *C. W. Penrose Replies*, 1–4; *Nuggets of Truth: Hear Ye the Whole Truth*, 1–3.

Another feature of the campaign involving President Smith was the so-called bishop's recommend for Frank Cannon. Democrats had spread the rumor that Cannon was guilty of serious moral indiscretions. In response, Smith secured a letter from his bishop, Thomas J. Stevens of Ogden's fifth ward, conceding that Cannon had transgressed but had been disciplined, assuring voters that he had made complete amends and was considered a member of the Church in good standing, aside from a spotty attendance record. As the campaign reached its final week in late November, the *Herald* took satisfaction in how disclosures from the LDS side had "boomeranged" back as an indictment of Church involvement in politics. The *Tribune* found it "delicious" to follow the back-and-forth between so-called Democrats and Republicans in what, at essence, was an attempt to defend the Church's political involvement.[31]

Even in the more ordinary aspects of the contest between Cannon and Rawlins, including a series of debates, people noticed a frequent appeal to Church authority. Cannon's backing of tariff protection included the claim that Brigham Young had been a supporter of tariffs. For the present, Rawlins and his party were able to blame the economic downturn on legislation introduced by Republican Congressman William McKinley. But in the October general conference four weeks earlier, both Joseph F. Smith and George Q. Cannon had spoken in defense of home industries and the need to protect them from foreign competition, coded language for support of the Republicans' key issue. Smith called it "the gospel of temporal salvation," to which Cannon ignored even a façade of political neutrality in voicing his agreement, and again in the semi-private priesthood session on October 10 when the presidency again asked for local leaders to ensure an equitable division of their people among the two parties, possibly meaning that more Republicans were needed. If they would do so, they were promised "a bright day … dawn[ing] upon Utah." Abraham H. Cannon overheard his father firmly tell a member of the Presiding Bishopric, John R.

31. Cannon, "Wives and Other Women," 83–95; *Salt Lake Herald*, October 30, Nov. 2, 8, 1892; *Salt Lake Tribune*, Oct. 9, 31, Nov. 6, 1892; *Voters of Utah, Beware!* 1–3.

Winder, at the conference that the Church's safety and prosperity depended on voting Republican.[32]

In the final days of the campaign, a committee of prominent non-LDS Democrats—including past governor Caleb West and territorial judges Henry Henderson and J. W. Judd—complained to the First Presidency about its promotion of the Republican Party. They wanted to be reassured that the intent was not to control people's votes. Several days later, just days before the election, the *Salt Lake Herald* published the presidency's disavowal of political preference. Why had it taken so long for this clarification to be made? They considered their public statements to have been appropriately broad, and partisan only in private conversation, but the *Herald* found that not to be entirely true. When addressing a quarterly stake conference in Logan, Joseph F. Smith had insisted that he would not be limited to spiritual concerns in his sermons. He claimed it was his right to talk about temporal matters. The *Herald* denied only that Smith had backed Frank Cannon in his address. In the end the presidency had obviously not placed enough weight on the scale to tip the balance of the election. Rawlins won a decisive victory, along with the overwhelming national landslide in favor of the Democrats who won the White House (Cleveland again) and both chambers of Congress. Cannon's *Ogden Standard* frankly observed that it was too soon to realistically expect a Republican victory in Utah.[33]

Prior to election day, the First Presidency asserted some political influence behind the scenes when US marshal Eli H. Parsons announced his intent to step down. Concerned that Parsons, who had been relatively lenient, would by replaced by someone who would rejuvenate the anti-polygamy crusade, the Church called John Morgan, a decorated Civil War veteran, to undertake a lobbying effort. The reasoning was that because Morgan and US President Harrison harked from the same state of Indiana and had served in the war, they might find some commonality. Morgan and a Utah Gentile, Willey

32. Abraham H. Cannon journal, Oct. 31, 1892; also excerpted in Lyman, ed., *Candid Insights*, 366.

33. *Salt Lake Herald*, Aug. 31, Sept. 1, 2, Nov. 3, 6, 8, 10, 1892; *Ogden Standard*, Nov. 13, 1892.

H. Brown, with the blessing of Utah party leader C. W. Bennett, traveled together to Indiana to meet people and gather letters from people who knew Harrison. In Washington they followed the same strategy, conferring with men from Indiana: Attorney General William Miller, White House secretary Elijah Halford, advisor Lewis T. Michener, and treasurer Enos Nebeker. Throughout September and into October, Morgan, at least, kept up an intensive round of high-level interviews. In his reports by telegram to Utah, he expressed his satisfaction with the progress he was making and announced that the president would appoint Irving A. Benton, formerly Salt Lake City postmaster, as US marshal. George Q. Cannon privately commented that the new marshal was "instructed from Washington that he must do as he was directed by the heads of the Mormon church if he desired to retain the position." The marshal sent word to the First Presidency that he was willing to comply with those terms.[34]

Church leaders were lobbying the president through other avenues as well, to have him issue a general pardon for polygamists. Estee and others explained that the president was "afraid of injuring his chances for re-nomination," or he would have already issued the pardon. The *Herald* correctly mentioned "the President's course … suggest[ed] that his heart is [not] in the matter." It became an issue of leverage with Democrats to point out the failed expectations and promise of the Republican administration. Even when Harrison saw it would benefit his party, he still hesitated to sign the order for fear it would seem like a desperate act by a losing candidate. He requested that Clarkson gain assurances, especially from the nations' churches, that they would not ridicule him for this action. With the aid of Isaac Trumbo, Clarkson secured a promise of "favorable expression" from numerous church newspapers. Still Harrison refrained from making an announcement prior to the election.[35]

A key western senator also became engaged seeking the president's attention. In August 1892 Senator Francis E. Warren of Wyoming

34. Morgan journal, Sep. 1, 11–12, 15–17, 22–30, Oct. 3–6, 1892; also C. W. Bennett to Benjamin Harrison, Sep. 2, 1892; George F. Gibbs to John Morgan, Oct. 5, 1892, Harrison Papers; Lyman, ed., *Candid Insights*, 366.

35. James S. Clarkson to Wilford Woodruff, July 11, 1894 (see appendix).

explained to Harrison's secretary that LDS voters held the balance of power in western Wyoming. The coming election would be crucial in determining the make-up of the next state legislature, and that would determine whether Warren would be returned to the Senate for another term. The Gentiles in Wyoming wanted the promised amnesty to "hasten the entire solution and settlement of troubles growing out of Mormonism in the past." A rumor had spread about Warren being the reason the amnesty had been held up. If President Woodruff could be disabused of this misconception, Warren said, his position would be strengthened. Word of Woodruff's assumption probably reached Warren through Isaac Trumbo or Morris Estee, with whom Warren was in regular communication. No one came to Warren's aid, probably because Harrison blamed Warren for the president's involvement in Wyoming's Johnson County war, when a militia supported by large livestock companies attacked settlers north of Casper.[36]

In the early autumn, George Q. Cannon learned that the *Tribune* crowd had made their own attempt to influence Harrison's appointment of the US marshal, convincing Cannon and others of the necessity of Morgan's continued rapport with the president's inner circle. As evidence this increased cordiality had developed, Harrison told Estee and Trumbo in mid-October that amnesty for the Mormons would be forthcoming in about a week and they could inform the Church presidency of that fact. This was accompanied by Harrison's request that the presidency pray for his wife, who had consumption (tuberculosis). Sadly, Mrs. Harrison died a week later on October 25. The grief-stricken president lost interest in political matters for a time, postponing the pardon until during the lame-duck period after his defeat. When it was announced, Church leaders were surprised to find that it was less than promised, forgiving only those who had abandoned their wives. As Brigham H. Roberts, one of the polygamists in the hierarchy, reflected, the announcement did little other than improve the public opinion of the Church.[37]

---

36. Francis E. Warren to E. W. Halford, Aug. 29, 1892, Warren Papers; Smith, *War on Powder River*, 183, 260–62, 275.

37. Lyman, ed., *Candid Insights*, 360–62, 350, 378–81; Sievers, *Benjamin Harrison*, 242–43; Roberts, *Comprehensive History* 6:289.

The *Salt Lake Tribune* publisher, Patrick Lannan, wanted to interview the First Presidency about where they stood on various political issues of the day. He stopped by without an appointment and found them away, so he questioned senior apostles Francis M. Lyman and John Henry Smith about the "Kingdom of God," which the Church had previously stated it intended to build in the desert. Lannan wanted to know if they still looked toward the establishment of a separate kingdom or wanted to see Utah become a state within the federal union. The apostles said they wanted statehood. Another question had to do with the treatment of non-LDS people. The apostles stated they could assure the newspaper editor unequivocally that "no non-Mormon … shall ever be disturbed in his person or business in any way whatever in the event of our territory being admitted into the Union." Lannan suggested that he formulate a list of specific questions they could prepare written responses to, and they agreed.[38]

One of the questions he submitted to them was whether the Church would continue to "influence voters through the obedience of the rank and file to their priestly superiors." Another was, again, whether all Utah citizens would be treated equally before the law. The inquiries were carefully considered by a half-dozen ecclesiastical leaders, including the later Church Historian B. H. Roberts and attorney Franklin S. Richards. The answers indicated that conditions had changed to the point that LDS people could be counted on to conform to national standards. There was one significant exception. The Church reserved the right to impose restraints on the political activities of its general officers, a qualification that would be the basis for future controversy, as already somewhat existed regarding Moses Thatcher's speech at the Democratic convention in mid-1892. Joseph F. Smith informed Thatcher in July "that the day would come when he would regret the stand he had taken" in defiance of the presidency. Soon afterward Smith berated him for opposing subsidies for sugar beet farmers.[39]

38. Francis M. Lyman journal, Jan. 13, 26–27, 1893. The questions are filed under Jan. 1893 in the Woodruff Papers.

39. F. Lyman journal, July 12, 17, 28, 30, Aug. 4, 1892; Abraham H. Cannon journal, July 12, 13, Aug. 4, 1892; Grant, *Diaries*, July 12, Aug. 4, 1892.

On October 11, 1892, less than a month before the election, Thatcher and Roberts asked President Woodruff what he would allow them to do for the Democratic Party. They were told to continue their efforts, but to do so "very mildly." That was before Joseph F. Smith's pamphlet hit the streets. Charles Penrose, B. H. Roberts, and Moses Thatcher responded to it. They were soon reprimanded for being "out of harmony" with the Church authorities. In conversation with apostles Lyman and Grant, Thatcher argued that this was backward, that Joseph F. Smith was the one who was out of line, who had violated the rule about unsanctioned political involvement. Lyman and Grant saw it otherwise, that Thatcher was "in error," they said. He had caught himself "on his own hook." In late March, after Thatcher had missed several quorum meetings, the apostles summoned him to explain why he was "working against the policy of the presidency … and bringing them to disgrace in the eyes of the Saints." Unless he traveled to Salt Lake City and answered these charges, he would not be given a place at the dedication of the Salt Lake Temple, he was told. Similar rulings were delivered to Roberts and Penrose, with specific authorities assigned to help them see the error of their ways. All three retreated from their resistance to political control, at least for the time being.[40]

During the second session of the Fifty-Second US Congress in December 1892, several enabling bills were introduced on Utah's behalf. One of them, sponsored by lame-duck John T. Caine, received a favorable report on January 24, 1893, but its progress was hampered by the absence of the committee chairman, Joseph Washington (D–Tennessee). Caine convinced Charles J. Faulkner (D–West Virginia) to raise the matter in the upper house, knowing that time was short. James Clarkson and his associates fervently wished to have the Republican-dominated Senate resolve the issue before the elected Democrats took their seats in early 1893. He said they could count on practically a unanimous vote of the Senate, except for one

40. F. M. Lyman journal, Oct. 11, 1892, Mar.–Apr. 1893. Grant had previously sided with Thatcher as a fellow party member, but had finally recognized him as too defiant of the presidency.

persistent opponent, Orville H. Platt (R–Connecticut), chairman of the Committee on Territories. When a bill was proposed and Platt found himself virtually alone in opposing it, he took the unexpected further step of threatening to resign if the majority overruled him, even going so far as to invoke senatorial courtesy, something usually reserved for a senator whose home state was at issue.[41] William B. Allison (R–Iowa), chairman of the Senate Committee on Appropriations and one of Clarkson's political friends, tried to bring the bill to the Senate floor when Platt was absent, but was unsuccessful.

Clarkson had reported to Allison that their success in the next election "may lie in the action of the Mormon vote," stating the now familiar refrain that the church held "the probable balance of power in 8 or 10 states." It was partly true that when the populists and advocates of silver coinage were gaining popularity in the western states, the Latter-day Saints were a reliable conservative check on that drift to the left. Clarkson wanted to show senators who "may not understand the power of the Mormon vote" how vital Utah statehood was "to the future of the [Republican] party."[42] He knew Platt had been influenced by a man connected to the *Salt Lake Tribune* clique of Goodwin, Lannan, Thomas, and their close ally from Idaho Fred T. Dubois. He never questioned Platt's integrity, but in his mind he saw the senator as someone who represented the past rather than the future of the party. Platt's son had been a roommate of Dubois at Yale, and that was another primary source of negative influence in the matter.

When Joseph Rawlins took his seat in the House of Representatives in September 1893, one of his first acts was to introduce a joint resolution providing that LDS property in the federal receiver's hands be returned to its rightful owner. The Church "no longer encourages or gives countenance in any manner to practices in violation of law," he explained. The bill breezed through the judiciary committees and passed both houses with impressive speed. Grover

41. Caine to J. E. Washington, Dec. 7, 1892, Caine to Charles C. Richards, Dec. 5, 1892, Jan. 31, 1893, Caine Papers.

42. J. S. Clarkson to William B. Allison, n.d., filed under Aug. 1893, Allison Papers; also Lyman, "Politicians' Perceptions."

Cleveland signed the resolution on October 25. A week later Franklin S. Richards, representing the Church, petitioned the Supreme Court to remand the property to the Utah Territorial Supreme Court for disposition, which Chief Justice Melville Fuller did on November 6. The support of the Cleveland administration generated political capital for the Democrats in Utah.[43]

When the Democrats moved into the White House and took control of Congress, the nation was in the thrall of the financial Panic of '93. President Cleveland called Congress to a special session to repeal the Sherman Silver Purchase Act, a devastating blow to Utah's silver mining industry. The president clearly still saw his mandate to be tariff reform, to the harm of three of Utah's main industries, exposing them to foreign competition regarding lead, sugar, and wool, as the Republicans constantly reminded voters. The *Herald*, on the other hand, reminded people of the importance of staying in harmony with the party in power. The return of Cleveland also meant that the popular Caleb W. West would be reappointed.

Utah voters were unimpressed by that argument, and for the first time in the territory's history turned to the Republicans, giving them the upper house of the legislature by a ratio of seven to five, the lower house fourteen to ten. The victorious congressional delegate, Frank Cannon, called the results a "great rebuke" of the Cleveland administration. The former Democratic delegate, Joseph L. Rawlins, could only agree that the party's policies had not been favorable to Utah. In private at the University Club, in a speech he delivered in November, Rawlins criticized President Cleveland over his silver policy and cheered the western Democrats for opposing him.[44] The *Salt Lake Tribune* had difficulty reconciling the Republican victory in Utah after claiming that the party had no chance of winning, due to the Democrats' close cooperation with the LDS Church. The *Herald* consoled its Democratic following by arguing

43. Clarkson to Woodruff, July 11, 1894; *Congressional Record*, Sept. 9, 1893; *Salt Lake Herald*, Sep. 19, Oct. 6, 22, 26, 31, Nov. 7, 1893; *Salt Lake Tribune*, Oct. 28, 1893; Harrow, "Joseph L. Rawlins," 82–83.

44. Nevins, *Grover Cleveland*, 523–48; *Ogden Standard* Aug. 22, 31, Oct. 14, Nov. 8, 9, 11–12, 1893.

that at least the allegation of a conspiracy with the Church had been proven false. That week the *Tribune* significantly began supporting the dissolution of the Liberal Party. The Liberals had already faded almost everywhere anyway, except in the largest urban center and a few mining districts. Since 1891 they had not fared well in Ogden, but they still held sway in Salt Lake City. However, in the November 1893 municipal elections, voters in Salt Lake City accepted the *Herald*'s characterization of the "malodorous" Liberals on the city council being the "exact antipodes" of honesty and capability. At a citizens meeting, people excoriated the council for its financial "extravagance" during a period of economic hardship. Both LDS and Gentiles alike supported the idea of a nonpartisan citizens' party, which the *Tribune* dismissively called a revival of the People's Party, nine of its candidates turning out to be Latter-day Saints. But the ticket also contained six Gentiles, all of whom had been Liberals.[45]

Besides the threat posed by the coalition ticket, Liberals faced a much more formidable problem within its own ranks. During the summer of 1893, a branch of the nativist American Protective Association (APA) was established in Salt Lake City. Reportedly some six hundred members in Utah, referred to as Amorines, united to oppose the influence of the Catholic Church. The press listed about twenty elected and appointed city officials who joined this movement. The *Salt Lake Tribune*'s Catholic publisher, Patrick Lannan, was outraged by the boast that they would remove all public officials who belonged to the Roman institution. Despite their incompatibility with "Lannan Liberals," the Amorines were able to place three candidates on the Liberal ticket in 1893. It put the Liberal mayoral candidate, Jeremiah C. Conklin, in a quandary. By not taking a stand one way or the other, he probably alienated both factions of the party and lost to the formerly fervent anti-Mormon, Robert N. Baskin. It is ironic that the downfall of the anti-Mormon party would be caused by an anti-Catholic group that split the old membership, the mayor's race going to a defector from the

45. *Salt Lake Herald*, Aug. 20, 29–31, Sept. 23, 28, Oct. 22, Nov. 3, 5, 11, 15, 26, 1893; *Salt Lake Tribune*, Aug.–Dec. 1893.

Liberal Party who ran with LDS candidates on a coalition ticket. The tide had turned, and Liberals lost all but a minority of city council seats and the treasurer's office.[46] In post-election interviews, former anti-Mormon activists agreed with Orlando W. Powers that statehood was the inevitable future of Utah. At a mass meeting in mid-December, the Liberals finally voted to disband. First they correctly congratulated themselves on having contributed to the Americanization of Utah. Equally important on the path to statehood was their demise.

Prior to the 1893 elections, the outgoing territorial delegate, John T. Caine, sent his successor, Joseph L. Rawlins, a draft of an enabling act for Utah. It was based on something that had been favorably critiqued by the House Committee on Territories the previous session, copied mostly from Arizona and New Mexico bills that had cleared the committee. Rawlins introduced his bill on September 6, 1893, and it was countered by a bill from Joseph Wheeler (D–New York), the new chairman of the House Committee on Territories, giving the people of the territory less generous terms—less land for school funding, for instance. A bill from William C. Oates (D–Alabama) revived the old idea of annexing Utah to Nevada. In the end, it was Rawlins's bill that was favorably accepted, just before the special session of Congress adjourned after the first week of November. It was expected to be placed high on the calendar of topics to debate in the approaching new session.[47]

In the intervening few weeks, Utah held its election and the voters opted for the territorial Republican legislative majority, showing disregard for the support the Democrats had given their statehood initiative. The message was not lost on the Democrats, nor on the Republicans. When Congress reconvened in the first week of December, Representative Constantine Kilgore, the second-ranking Democrat on the House Committee on Territories,

46. Kinzer, *Episode in Anti-Catholicism*, 93–139; Journal History, Aug. 25, 28, 30–31, Oct. 5, 13, 27, 1893; *Deseret Evening News*, Oct. 13, 27, Nov. 4, 1893.

47. Caine to Joseph L. Rawlins, Aug. 18, 1893, Caine Papers; *Ogden Standard*, Sept. 1, 1893; *Salt Lake Herald*, Sept. 16, 19, Oct. 28, 31, Nov. 1, 1893; *Congressional Record*, Sept. 6, 14, Nov. 2–3, 1893; *House Reports*, 53rd Cong., 1st sess.

called up the Rawlins bill early in the morning before many key committee members had arrived, thinking it would be easily dispensed with. However, the Republicans, including some who had previously opposed Utah statehood, wanted an opportunity to voice support of it, especially in order to explain to constituents why they were changing their minds.[48] James Clarkson recounted entering the committee room in the middle of some unfriendly words from the former Speaker of the House Thomas B. Reed (R–Maine). Clarkson spoke to Reed afterward to inform him of how well the Mormons lined up with Republicans on nearly every contemporary national issue. Unconvinced, the congressman accepted an invitation to discuss the matter in Clarkson's hotel room, where they were joined by Hiram Clawson. After talking for three hours, including more candid answers from Clawson than had been forthcoming from the non-LDS lobbyists Trumbo and Clarkson, Reed agreed to withdraw his opposition.

The bill made it to the floor of the full House of Representatives on December 12, 1893. It was met with an even-tempered response. Rawlins answered questions. One of only two opponents who spoke, Elijah A. Morse, a Republican from Massachusetts, was so ill informed he elicited laughter, aided by Rawlins's goading. The other opponent was Michael D. Harter, a longtime anti-silver Democrat from Ohio who only pointed out that Utah still had a small population. This lackluster attempt to block the bill was an impressive indication of how changed Congress was in its attitude toward Utah. When it came to a final voice vote, no more than a half-dozen Congressmen said nay.[49]

It had taken more than forty years, over the same period of time as the construction of the Church's great temple in Salt Lake City, for a Utah Enabling Act to pass the House of Representatives. There were political developments that year that had been necessary in clearing the way for acceptance by the Senate later in 1894.

48. *Salt Lake Herald*, Nov. 15, Dec. 9, 12–14, 1893; *Salt Lake Tribune*, Nov. 22, Dec. 9–10, 12–14, 1893; *Congressional Record*, Dec. 8, 11, 1893.

49. *Congressional Record*, Dec. 12, 18, 1893.

Those included amnesty for rehabilitated polygamists, the return of a good portion of the Church's property, the demise of the Liberal Party and People's Party, the rise of national political parties in Utah, and especially the balance of support for Democrats and Republicans, all pivotal elements in preparing the ground both in Utah and Washington for what was about to transpire. There were still a few remaining obstacles, but what previously seemed to be an insurmountable hurdle now appeared possible.

11

STATEHOOD FINALLY

1894-96

After the enabling act cleared the House of Representatives, Republican support for Utah statehood increased considerably, even while support from the Democratic majority side of Congress tended in the opposite direction. Many long-time champions of Utah had left advocacy for the territory to a small core of supporters within the party. Then through a series of unique circumstances, the process was accelerated to the point that it appeared the enabling act might be approved by the Senate more quickly than anticipated. The *Salt Lake Tribune* predicted this at the beginning of 1894 after hearing of support from several Republican senators. In mid-January the executive board of the Republican National Committee passed a resolution favoring it. Later in the month the Republican Senate steering committee recommended that the party support the bill. Senator Orville Platt said he would not object to it being considered in committee but might still oppose it when it came to the Senate floor. These were nevertheless decisive hurdles that had never before been cleared by a Utah statehood bill. The *Tribune* observed correctly that any obstruction "now can be charged fairly to the Democratic majority, who have the matter in charge."[1]

Back home in Utah, the Republican press chided the rival party for its lack of interest in the progress of the statehood bill. The *Tribune* republished a comment apparently from the *Washington Star*

1. *Salt Lake Tribune*, Nov. 22, 1893; Jan. 13, 22, 28; *Washington Post*, Jan. 11, 1894.

about President Cleveland, a Democrat, being "opposed to the admission of any more states at present." Another dispatch charged that Senator Arthur Gorman of the Democratic steering committee was behind the delay in the Senate Committee on Territories. Interviews with Republican committee members led the *Tribune* to suggest there was a Democratic plot to stall the bill, claiming deliberation on the Wilson–Gorman Tariff was more important and so complicated that it was consuming everyone's attention. Utah's House delegate Joseph L. Rawlins was increasingly alarmed by his party's inaction. In late January 1893, John T. Caine returned to Washington to assist his successor, both of whom were "greatly perturbed" by their party's failure to support the admission bill. They decided to focus their lobbying on the chairman of the Senate committee, Charles J. Faulkner (D–West Virginia), with the message that further delays might well cost the party major voter support in Utah Territory in future elections, as well as that of LDS people in "all the adjoining states."[2]

Faulkner had thus far prevented the subcommittee from considering the bill. He told the *Herald* to have no fear because it would all happen "in due course of time," saying the Senate was a slow-moving body and could not be rushed. The holdup, as Rawlins confided to Orlando W. Powers, the Democratic Party leader in Utah, was that based on the recent election loss, "Democratic senators are in some doubt as to whether Utah might conclude to do the foolish thing of sending two Republicans to the Senate." Therefore the party leaders had decided to delay Utah's admission until after the current congressional term had expired. The *Herald* explained that if the party lost two Senate seats, it would imperil the Democrats' ambitious legislative agenda, submissively asking whether the party's policies were not "of much wider concern to the nation than the immediate admission of one new state?" Most Utahns would have been unpersuaded by such a lame defense.[3] It became clear that

2. *Salt Lake Tribune*, Jan. 23, 25–28, 30, Feb. 1–4, 1894; *Salt Lake Herald*, Feb. 1, 4, 1894; also Jenson, *Latter-day Saint Biographical Encyclopedia*, 1:737.

3. *Salt Lake Herald*, Jan. 15, Mar. 2, 1894; *Salt Lake Tribune*, Feb. 6, 8, 26, 1894.

a few eastern Democrats were behind the stalling tactic, despite the willingness of other senators to proceed.

James S. Clarkson and his Republican associates remained active but unable to accomplish much, now that the party was in the minority in both houses. Rawlins considered the situation hopeless, correctly interpreting the holdup to be over the fear of admitting to statehood "a territory whose two senators would be Republican and change the balance of power in the Senate." It was at that point in time that an unusual opportunity arose out of the factionalism that had developed among the Democrats and enabled the Republicans to play a greater role.[4] The divisiveness stemmed from persistent rivalries in New York, where Grover Cleveland and his supporters stood at odds with Democratic Senator David B. Hill. It stemmed from growing differences over the pending tariff law, but Hill and Gorman came to also resent much of what the president did politically, including his disregard for senatorial courtesy, and that pushed them into a position of favoring whatever he opposed.[5]

It came to a head when Cleveland nominated William B. Hornblower to a vacancy on the US Supreme Court without consulting the New York senator, in disregard of the longtime prerogative of senators to accept or veto appointments from their home states. Hornblower was a respected New York attorney and had long opposed the corruption of the Tammany Hall political machine with which Senator Hill was allied. The senator reminded colleagues that if they allowed the president to violate such established protocol, there would be dire future consequences.[6] Most in the Senate agreed, declining to confirm the nominee. But some of the Democrats who sympathized with Hill hesitated to openly oppose Cleveland, revealing a split in the party. According to Clarkson, Isaac Trumbo saw an opportunity to be exploited in a deal he cut with Senator Hill, in which he provided enough Republican support to defeat Hornblower if Hill would generate sufficient Democratic backing

4. James S. Clarkson to Wilford Woodruff, July 11, 1894 (appendix).

5. Nevins, *Grover Cleveland*, 563–72; Bass, *"I Am Democrat,"* 161–62, 189, 207, 244.

6. "Memorials of William B. Hornblower"; also Rothman, *Politics and Power*, 180–81, utilizing the Hill–Cleveland controversy as an example of senatorial courtesy.

to enact a measure of importance to the Republicans. That measure would be the admission of Utah as a state. When Cleveland's nominee was defeated, the president stubbornly designated another New Yorker who was even more objectionable to Hill than Hornblower. The *Times* predicted that Hill would be hard-pressed to line up enough opponents to defeat the new nominee, Wheeler H. Peckham. That challenge offered lobbyist Trumbo and his cohorts opportunity for one of their most impressive accomplishments.[7]

An observer at *Harper's Weekly* alleged that Senators Hill and Edward Murphy had gained Republican support in exchange for "a vote against any tariff bill." This may have been true, because there were Republicans who joined Gorman, Stephen M. White (D-California), and other Democrats in voting down a portion of tariff reform. On the other side of the aisle, more Democrats were suddenly eager to take a stand for Utah statehood, Senate territorial committee members Hill and White playing a crucial role in finally pressing Faulkner to take action on the bill.[8] This was fully assisted by three Republican members of the same committee: George L. Shoup of Idaho, Joseph Carey of Wyoming, and Henry L. Hansbrough of North Dakota. In fact, they pushed to place Faulkner's opposition on record so it could be discerned by voters as a flaw in the position of the Democrats.

Senator White asked Faulker why the bill had been pigeonholed. Faulkner said it was because of its too-generous allocation of federal land and general disregard for precedent. William B. Bate of Tennessee suggested that the proposal be investigated (delayed), which confirmed, at least to White and Hill, that their party leaders had political reasons for dragging their feet. That all turned around when the Republican electoral potential of western Mormons was confessed by Democratic leaders to be the cause for delay and the rival party conceded to an amendment preventing Utah from sending senators to Washington during the present term. Thus, that obstacle

7. *New York Tribune*, Jan. 9, 16, Feb. 17, 18, 1894; *New York Times*, Jan. 16, Feb. 13, 15, 17, 1894.

8. *Harper's Weekly*, Feb. 10, Apr. 7, 1894; John E. Osborne to David B. Hill, Mar. 26, 1894, Hill Papers.

was removed. But the still inexperienced Rawlins could see only that a quick granting of statehood was an improbability. Faulkner and Bate put barriers in the way to debating anything that would distract from the tariff deliberations, which had been the main order of business for over three months. The debates were themselves so disruptive to the Democrats that the *New York Tribune* wrote about the "disorganized state of the party" due to the tariff question. With no resolution in sight on that front, Rawlins amazingly decided to abandon Washington and return home to spend time with his family.[9]

Republican advocates, hoping for some kind of breakthrough, concluded to resolve the persistent opposition of Senator Platt. When the senator agreed to meet Frank J. Cannon and another Utah promoter in a private meeting, Cannon showed himself to be less guarded and more forthcoming than his fellow lobbyists. During their conversation Platt asked him pointedly if what Clarkson and Trumbo had said was true, that there was not even a semblance of polygamy left in the territory. Cannon admitted that conditions were not exactly as they had described (something Clarkson and Trumbo would scold Cannon for conceding), because it was still being practiced in secret, with some lingering disregard for the law, but the problem was dissipating as fast as could be expected. That candor overcame the powerful Republican senator's longtime hesitance, as both his and Cannon's later reminiscences/biographies attested.[10]

At the same time, there was equally crucial maneuvering to overcome Faulkner's stalling. Bishop Hiram B. Clawson explained how this came about. The mainstream Democrats were demoralized over the tariff bill, thinking there was little hope of bringing up the Utah bill. Senator Faulkner revealed in a quiet way that he intended to leave the capital for two weeks, as Rawlins had, for a short vacation. This was precisely when the Republicans had intended to hold

9. *Washington Post*, Apr. 15, 1894; *New York Tribune*, May 4, 1894; *Deseret Evening News*, May 19, 1894; Harrow, "Joseph L. Rawlins," 88–91. While Rawlins did well in his early congressional efforts for Utah, his absence from the nation's capital during the time the statehood bill was dislodged and passed prevents considering him the father of statehood.

10. Coolidge, *Orville H. Platt*, 1:135–36; Cannon and O'Higgins, *Under the Prophet in Utah*, 91–93, 130–34.

the committee hearings on Utah. It occurred to Clawson that this was an opportunity, not a setback. Trumbo agreed and consulted with the powerful Republican National Committee chairman, Joseph H. Manley, who joined him in calling on Senator Platt. To their surprise, Platt said he was in favor of resolving the stalemate. In fact, he was resentful of Faulkner and other obstructionists, especially because the blame for the delays had been credited to him. He said he would write to Faulkner and tell him he intended to publish their correspondence, to counter the impression people had that he was the laggard. This struck a vulnerable chord with the committee chairman, who authorized his fellow senators to proceed. Faulkner and his subcommittee took only a day to announce that they had a bill to report to the Senate for the admission of Utah.[11]

The *Tribune* pointed out that this had happened partially through Republican action, without the involvement of Rawlins, and grudgingly credited Trumbo, although not without belittling the mysterious man who was said to be "representing something or somebody" in Washington. The *Herald* was more charitable in reporting that "Isaac Trumbo, of California, a native of Utah, has worked hard for the bill[,] and no happier man was in town today than he when the committee decided to report the bill." Senator Faulkner continued to emphasize that his party's top priority remained the tariff, but at a time when most were tired of arguing over a single issue, the Utah measure had made its way to the calendar so quickly that, unless someone desired an open fight—which could risk alienating the Utah electorate—the bill was set to pass. Because no one was any longer vehemently opposed to it, it would, in fact, be enacted.[12] When it was debated on the Senate floor in early July, some Republicans considered taking a stand against a provision the Democrats had added to delay the bill going into effect until 1896, but then they decided to let the earlier compromise

11. Hiram B. Clawson to Woodruff, May 16, 1894, Clawson Papers; *Salt Lake Tribune*, May 17, 18, 25, 1894; *Salt Lake Herald*, May 17–18, 1894.

12. *Congressional Record*, May 17, 1894; *Senate Reports*, 53rd Cong., 2nd sess., no. 414, 1–29.

remain intact. It passed the Senate with almost no discussion and only a few Democrats opposing it.[13]

The *Tribune* described a jubilant Trumbo shaking hands with half the chamber and Clawson standing smilingly nearby. The colonel received congratulatory telegrams from legislators who knew of his work to bring this about. Senator Henry M. Teller wrote, "You have made the best fight ever before the American Congress[,] and all sing your praises." Skeptics joined in, among them Senator Julius C. Burrows writing, "You have been the peacemaker between a misunderstood people and this government, and I am sure the American people all join in praise to you." Platt himself remarked that Trumbo had done much to his own credit, presenting himself "in good faith before the country" the way he defended an outcast people. Clarkson, Clawson, and Trumbo sent the LDS First Presidency a telegram reading, "Statehood bill signed, your people are free and this ends our hard labor." The reply was: "We rejoice with, and congratulate you on the successful termination of your labor, which has resulted in Utah's enfranchisement, and political deliverance to her people." The presidency acknowledged that "while your hand has not been seen, and others claim all the honor, those who know the facts fully appreciate your efforts, and fully accord to you their heartfelt gratitude for the deep interest you have taken in the matter." Even the long-time anti-Mormon lecturer and Washington commentator Kate Field offered a complimentary summation: "In all probability statehood would have been delayed but for the untiring vigilance of one man. Early and late, in season and out of season, Isaac Trumbo labored in behalf of immediate admission." She had "never seen so well-managed a campaign as the still hunt of Isaac Trumbo and Bishop Clawson during the last six months."

The lobbyists' skill had been most evident when politicians became vulnerable "because of hard times or specific local irritations," according to political historian Robert D. Marcus. The fact that there was none of the bitterness formerly elicited by Utah indicates

13. *Congressional Record*, July 10, 12, 1894.

that most officials had accepted the LDS claim to have moved on.[14] The Democrats had been the traditional champions of the territory's interests, but that ardor had markedly dissipated. When the Democrats split over another matter, the Wilson–Gorman Tariff, it provided an opening for Utah, and the shifting allegiances continued. Neither party could openly oppose the territory without risking the Utah electorate's long-range alienation.[15] Whatever the subsequent political outcomes, the role of the resourceful lobbyists loomed greater than it had ever been in accomplishing statehood in the nation's history.

It remained for the House to ratify the amended bill and send it to the president. With difficulty Rawlins located vice president Adlai Stevenson and acting speaker James D. Richardson to attest to the fact that the bill had been duly passed. Before bedtime on the evening of July 15, 1894, President Cleveland signed the bill, making it official.[16] Perhaps because the struggle had been so long and often disappointing, the most tortuous of any territory to date, in Utah the news was received with striking calmness, with none of the spontaneity and noisy celebrations characteristic of other new states. What enthusiasm there was, was likely blunted by the fact that the act would not go into effect for another year and a half. The *Salt Lake Herald* announced that there would be a celebration at a resort on the shores of the Great Salt Lake on August 1. The program of high-profile speakers proved to be appropriately nonpartisan and nondenominational. Rawlins was acknowledged for his role in securing the enabling act. Prominent Republicans took to the speakers' stand and were warmly received. A short history of the previous half-dozen attempts at statehood, written, but not delivered by, George Q. Cannon, put in context the enormity of the accomplishment.[17]

---

14. Clara, Tobias, and Clio [Clarkson, Trumbo, Clawson], July 17, 1894, Woodruff Papers; Rawlins to First Presidency, Dec. 9, 1895; *Salt Lake Tribune*, July 11–12, 29, 1894; *To the People of Utah*, 1–2, 6–8; *Kate Field's Washington*, July 25, 1894. For "still hunt," see Marcus, *Grand Old Party*, 186–87.

15. *Ogden Standard*, July 11, 1894; Lyman, *Political Deliverance*, 232–48.

16. *Congressional Record*, July 13, 16, 24, 1894.

17. *Salt Lake Tribune*, July 13, 17, 18, Aug. 1, 1894; *Salt Lake Herald*, Aug. 2, 1894.

During the uniquely lengthy interim, the territory had to select delegates to its most significant constitutional convention, decide on a government structure and fundamental laws, and plan and slate an election for the first state officers, including a legislature that would choose two US senators. Most significantly during the continued crucial political episodes of the final territorial year, the most heated partisan controversy in Utah history erupted in the autumn, near the time of admission. There was briefly talk of rejuvenating the Liberal Party due to alleged evidence of Church interference in the electoral process. Yet despite Democratic reports to the contrary, the Cleveland administration was intent on seeing the process through to completion. Remarkably, when the time came for the state to choose its officers, LDS and non-LDS debated real issues and put religion aside. They had themselves decided to enjoy their new status as full-fledged citizens of the United States and act accordingly.

Following the dissolution of the Liberal Party, a representative to the territorial legislature from Salt Lake City, Clarence Hall, died in December 1893. That created the need for an election to replace him. The Democrats chose his uncle and long-time Liberal, W. C. Hall, as their candidate. The Republicans nominated C. S. Varian, also a former Liberal. The *Herald* pointed out that a vote for the Democrat would be an indirect endorsement of the Cleveland administration. The *Tribune* countered that a vote for Varian was the best way to protest the wrongs heaped upon Utah by the nation's Democrats. The election on January 4, 1894, resulted in a Republican victory, this one by a margin of almost 1,000 votes. The *Tribune* called it a "stamp of disapproval on Cleveland's ways." Others saw it as a sign of the Liberal migration to the Republican Party.[18]

The campaign pointed to how some future contests might be conducted, when the *Herald* dug up an old letter in which Varian had criticized Governor Arthur L. Thomas. The *Tribune* brushed it off as unimportant, but the Democrats assumed they had found a potential weak link in their opponent's armor, the existence of rival factions within the Republican Party. During the ensuing months,

18. *Salt Lake Herald*, Dec. 27, 30, 1893; *Salt Lake Tribune*, Jan. 3–5, 1894.

the schisms became more apparent, partly because the *Tribune* ring continued to wield considerable influence. The Liberals who had become Republicans were more fanatical than the faction led by the territorial party chairman, Charles Crane, who was becoming allied with Isaac Trumbo and other moderates. At stake were the governorship and US Senate seats. It was clear that Crane and Trumbo had set their sights on these positions. It soon became equally evident that *Tribune* editor Charles C. Goodwin and former territorial governor Arthur Thomas were rival aspirants for the same offices, respectively.[19]

Another intra-party rivalry bubbled up between urban and rural Republicans. In his position as party chairman, Crane had garnered sympathy and support from less populated areas of the territory. He was a resident of Millard County (4,000 residents) and had support in Weber County (23,000), the rival urban center to Salt Lake County (59,000). The *Tribune* editorialized against him, accusing him of using his position to advance Trumbo, calling for his resignation if he was considering running for office himself. During the territorial party convention at Provo in September 1894, an attempt was made to install Samuel Kenyon, a Salt Lake City banker, in Crane's place, with the argument that Salt Lake City was being ignored. The insurgents made the mistake of not informing Varian in advance of this "scheme of a few designing and self-asserting [Salt Lake City] office seekers" to dethrone Crane, the party chief, and Varian's objection to it was enough to quiet the attempted coup.[20]

The more important development at the convention was the unanimous nomination of Frank J. Cannon for congressional delegate. The Democrats decided to stick with the incumbent, Joseph L. Rawlins, making the contest a repeat of the previous congressional election, this time without the interference of a Liberal Party candidate. The *Tribune* confidently predicted a different outcome, based on Cannon needing no more than to maintain his former strength in the outer counties to put him over the top. This assumed that

19. *Ogden Standard*, Jan. 5, 1894; *Salt Lake Herald*, Apr. 12, 1895.

20. *Salt Lake Tribune*, July 1, 21, 25, 30, 1895; Lyman, ed., *Candid Insights*, 542–43; Salt Lake *Argus*, Sept. 15, 1894.

three-fourths of the 4,000 men in Salt Lake County who voted for Clarence E. Allen two years earlier when he was the Liberal candidate would now vote Republican. The Hall–Allen contest at the end of 1893 had cut heavily into the Democratic lead, even in the party's inner-city strongholds and in mining communities such as Bingham, which gave 244 of its 300 votes to Allen, a former resident. It was assumed that those votes would be solidly behind Cannon.[21]

Rawlins was praised for his "unexampled achievements" on behalf of Utah. In his acceptance speech, he boasted of having enacted almost twice as many bills as any other territorial delegate. "From start to finish the Republican representatives and senators obstructed the passage of the [enabling] bill," until he had persuaded them of how destructive it would be for their future to oppose it. Late in the campaign, on October 10, 1894, Joseph F. Smith gave what he called his "first political speech" ever, to answer Rawlins's claim that Democrats had brought about statehood, when in fact they had dragged their feet and opposed it as it was nearing being passed. Smith concluded that for taking credit where it was not due, Rawlins showed himself to be "not worthy of the honor" of continuing in Congress. Despite the harshness of Smith's rebuke, the campaign was otherwise not acrimonious. At one event John Henry Smith and Moses Thatcher appeared on stage together, arm-in-arm, in an appeal for partisan civility.[22]

The candidates' stump speeches centered on financial issues. Rawlins and Cannon blamed each other's party for the economic stagnation. Rawlins asserted it was due to Republican monetary policies and trusts, rather than the revised tariffs. It did not matter. The party in power always received credit for the current economic situation. Frank Cannon began asking in a dramatic rhetorical style, "Who will give back the work, the wages, the prosperity, the dignity, and the hope to the mightiest nation under the sun?" The applauding audiences learned to shout back positive answers. As any

21. *Salt Lake Tribune*, Sept. 12, 13, 1894; *Ogden Standard*, Sept. 12, 1894.

22. *Salt Lake Herald*, Sept. 15, 16, Oct. 17, 1894; *Salt Lake Tribune*, Sept. 16, Oct. 11, 20, 21, 1894; Francis M. Lyman journal, July 26, Aug. 25, Sept. 19, 1894.

politician in a silver-producing state knew to do, Cannon supported silver coinage, while his national party objected to it. The Republican Party's unqualified support of tariffs appealed to Utahns, and nothing the Democrats offered could overcome the territory's support of that one issue alone.

The *Herald* was optimistic on election eve that the state would back a Democratic victory. For Cannon to win, 75 percent of the former Liberals would have to back the GOP, and the paper could not see that happening. But it did. The Republicans were victorious. The *Herald*, when it finally acknowledged this, attributed it to a larger percentage of ex-Liberals defecting to the Republicans than it had predicted. The Democrats did well in the inner city and fairly well in many of the outlying areas. There were sections of Salt Lake City that needed greater "organization" and care, as Charles Goodwin had predicted, and this was where Frank Cannon acquired his needed margin of victory.[23]

Another aspect of the November 1894 campaign was the contest for seats at the convention the enabling act had decreed would be held the following March, involving 107 delegates. In mid-September a group of LDS Democrats reflected on the LDS ban on participation by Church leaders, which would deprive the convention of some of the territory's most capable citizens. Apostles Moses Thatcher and Franklin D. Richards discussed this with two members of the First Presidency, President Wilford Woodruff and Joseph F. Smith, who asserted that Church authorities were free to "make all proper efforts on both sides to carry their parties, only not [to] slander, throw dirt and demean each other."[24]

With that permission, Thatcher and Richards sat on the speakers' stand the next day, along with a third apostle, Heber J. Grant, during the Democratic territorial convention. Grant was surprised to be called upon to speak. He did so briefly, and to his dismay his remarks were printed and circulated as a campaign tract. He asked Richards if he had violated anything the presidency had specified

23. *Salt Lake Herald*, Oct. 3, 30, Nov. 6, 8, 10, 1894.
24. Franklin D. Richards journal, Sept. 14, 1894.

and was assured by his colleague that, as he understood it, "the brethren" were free to do "any political work that they might think best ... that all were at perfect liberty to do what they pleased as to making speeches for either party." This was not only a relief to Grant's mind, it apparently convinced other churchmen that the restrictions no longer applied. The presidency soon clarified that they had only meant this to apply to the constitutional convention, not to "ordinary politics." The hasty change was not sufficiently clarified to prevent more trouble in the coming months.[25]

In the contest for convention delegates, the Republicans proved strongest. Of 107 seats, they won 59, to the Democrats' 48. Of those, 79 were LDS, 4 of them high Church leaders: Republican John Henry Smith (apostle) and three Democrats, William B. Preston (presiding bishopric), B. H. Roberts (seventy), and Moses Thatcher (apostle). There were ten members of stake presidencies and fifteen members of LDS bishoprics.[26] The Democrats challenged the election results, but the Republicans countered with the allegation of irregularities in Sanpete County. As the matter was being investigated throughout the month of January 1895, the *Tribune* claimed that Democrats had forged signatures in registration books and possibly tampered with ballot boxes.

The Church leadership took an interest in the accusations. Elder Abraham H. Cannon referred to "the present effort of the Democrats to steal the control of the constitutional convention," in conjunction with (an unfounded) rumor about the Cleveland administration planning another investigation of cohabitation to pack the convention with people of their choosing. Eventually the Democrats tried to prevent Republicans in the third precinct from taking their places at the convention, including apostle John Henry Smith. This backfired when court testimony showed a ballot box disappearing and resurfacing in a Democratic refreshment tent. J. R. Letcher, chairman of the Utah Commission, disqualified the

25. Grant, *Diaries*, Sept. 15–17, 27, 1894; Grant, *Speech of Hon. H. J. Grant*; Lyman journal, Sept. 27, 1894.

26. Ivins, "Constitution for Utah," 100.

precinct altogether, proclaiming it would not be represented at the convention at all. The *Tribune* called this an "outrageous" attempt to "disfranchise" the Republicans, which did not make sense, the newspaper asserted, since the Democrats were at fault.[27]

At the pre-convention Republican caucus, John Henry Smith and George R. Emery, a fellow delegate from the third precinct, showed their intent to participate at the convention without certification and ignore the discredited Utah Commission. So they did, and the convention elected Smith chairman of the entire convention proceedings. The Democrats withheld their objections and failed to even put up a challenger for the position because it would be awkward for LDS delegates to have to vote against an apostle. The *Herald* questioned Smith's competence as well as legitimacy, but he proceeded to handle the task reasonably well.[28] It took nearly two months for the convention to draft a constitution, section by section, since delegates were naturally divided and wanted to debate the issues. With all of that, C. S. Varian, who was a respected member of the convention, complimented his fellow delegates on their fraternity and patience in accomplishing their task despite differences.

Behind the scenes, the most controversial subject was woman's suffrage. It threatened to derail the proceedings, even though both parties had declared themselves in favor of it. David Evans of Ogden, a prominent Democrat, introduced a simple sentence to the proposed constitution about people "not be[ing] denied or abridged on account of sex." The committee on elections gave it a favorable report, and then opposition developed among non-LDS Republicans and spread to others, including LDS Democrat B. H. Roberts, whose impressive oratorical skill was put to use in telling delegates there was reason for concern if President Cleveland were against it, since the Edmunds–Tucker Act, which had invalidated it, was still in force, and because acceptance of women in the elections might prove troublesome

27. *Salt Lake Tribune*, Jan. 9, 10, Feb. 27, Mar. 1–3, 1895; Lyman, ed., *Candid Insights*, 582–84

28. *Salt Lake Herald*, Mar. 16, 1895; Ivins, "Constitution for Utah," 101, 113, 115; also White, *Charter for Statehood*.

enough to delay admission as a state.[29] He had personal feelings, too, against suffrage, but kept those in the background. His position nettled other Church authorities who were in favor of woman's suffrage, in part because it gave LDS people an advantage in the elections.

At an April 4 meeting of the Church leadership, John Henry Smith explained that members of the exclusive non-LDS Alta Club, which admitted only men, had determined to use its influence to defeat suffrage. If it were included in the constitution, the group would work to defeat the constitution, they said. John Henry Smith said he favored suffrage, but under the circumstances it would be better to avoid complications and leave it out. He was alarmed a week later to hear that this position had encouraged a movement "to resuscitate the Liberal Party in order to defeat statehood" rather than allow women to vote. George Q. Cannon and John Henry Smith thought it wise to let it go, over the wish of Wilford Woodruff and his counselor Joseph F. Smith, who wanted LDS delegates to stand firmly by the women. Cannon soon joined them and showed a united front.[30]

Roberts held fast to a compromise position to submit suffrage separately as an amendment, to be decided by the general public. With the help of nationally prominent proponents of female suffrage, including a founder of the Republican Party, Henry Blackwell, Roberts appealed to territorial women to wait until after admission as a state and the matter would then be resolved.[31] The ill will generated by this controversy was lasting, although soon surpassed by disagreements engendered by Roberts's Democratic associate Moses Thatcher.[32] The Logan apostle was ill and missed the beginning sessions of the constitutional convention. His letter of apology, laced with partisan barbs, provoked the first major clash of the convention. After the apostle had recovered sufficiently to participate, he was given "a mild reproof" by President Woodruff "for his failure to

29. *Official Report*, 1:459–63; Roberts, "Life Story"; White, "Woman's Place," 344–69; Madsen, *B. H. Roberts*, 217–20.

30. Lyman, ed., *Candid Insights*, 627–30, 642–44; Grant, *Diaries*, Apr. 4, 11, 1895; Ivins, "Constitution for Utah," 1, 12–13; *Salt Lake Tribune*, Jan. 7, Feb. 23, Apr. 25, 1895.

31. Beeton, "Woman Suffrage," 137–48; *Salt Lake Herald*, Apr. 30, 1895; Richards journal, Aug. 8, 1895; also Van Wagenen, *Sister-Wives and Suffragists*, 6–8.

32. B. H. Roberts to Woodruff et al., Oct. 8, 1895, copy in Roberts Papers.

seek counsel of the presidency in regard to his partisan comments and actions at the constitutional convention and other matters."[33] The presidency was obviously not satisfied with Thatcher's current belligerent direction in politics.

There were significant challenges still to overcome before statehood would be realized. Utahns wrestled with whether to send George Q. Cannon to the Senate after being such a steadfast advocate for it. He was clearly qualified and had perhaps earned the spot. He confided to John Henry Smith that he was undecided about whether to accept the consideration, if offered to him. Abraham Cannon, a politically blind supporter of his half-brother, Frank, denied that his father was politically ambitious.[34] The young apostle said as much to strategist James Devine, a backer of Frank Cannon. Devine had found a way to enhance Frank's political support by offering him backing from the *Tribune* in exchange for support for the *Tribune*'s Goodwin. The rival *Herald* recognized the marriage of convenience and expressed surprise, while conceding that Cannon was seeking wider political support in Salt Lake City where the *Tribune* held sway, and Goodwin supporters needed help in the outlying communities where their new associate was stronger.

A month later *Tribune* publisher Patrick Lannan alleged to Abraham Cannon that Utah's Republican party chairman, Charles Crane, was "playing false to Frank in a political sense." While it is unlikely that Crane would have exchanged confidential information with the publisher of the *Tribune*, the naive Abraham Cannon believed it, and it clearly planted a wedge between Trumbo and George Q. Cannon. According to Trumbo's wife, her husband went out of his way to travel to Utah on a Sunday after the enabling act had passed, to avoid the crowds and brass band he assumed would be assembled to greet him.[35] He could have spared himself the precaution, because people remained essentially unaware of his contributions. They had heard of him through the *Tribune*'s portrayal

33. Lyman journal, July 26, 1894; Lyman, ed., *Candid Insights*, 651–52.

34. Grant, *Diaries*, Apr. 13, 1895.

35. Lyman, ed., *Candid Insights*, 623, 654, 658–60; George Q. Cannon journal, Feb. 1, 1898; White, ed., *Church, State, and Politics*, 328; Lyman, "Isaac Trumbo," 135–37.

of him as an interloper who presumed to be worthy of the honor. When Trumbo moved to Utah, with the senatorial seat in mind, the *Tribune* tried to ignore him at first. Then in May 1895, Utah Republicans chose Trumbo as their representative to the Republican League Clubs convention in Cleveland.

Trumbo went to Ohio primarily determined to promote the silver issue that continued to be so important in the West. Emerging as one of the convention spokesmen, he presided over several caucuses considering silver resolutions. This was his way of preparing for greater regional influence. The problem was that easterners were as committed to passing resolutions rejecting silver as westerners were in promoting it, and they canceled out each other. What he did accomplish was to boost his reputation in the West. Outside of the mountain region, too, he garnered extensive press coverage, partly through his and Clarkson's relationship with the syndicated news services. He was hailed in New York City, where he subsequently traveled, as the new "silver champion of the West." The newspapers called him one of the presumptive senators for the forthcoming state of Utah, and he promptly became the best-known Utahn outside of the territory. The *Salt Lake Herald* candidly asked whether he had assumed this notoriety by arrangement with the Associated Press.[36] However, the *Herald* acknowledged that he had "scooped Goodwin pretty badly" through these activities.

In an era of high political participation, the best means of disseminating campaign information was through partisan newspapers. It was not considered a breach of acceptable practice for financially strapped editors to accept money from favored candidates to include mention of them in their columns during a campaign. In this crucial 1895 election process for selecting Utah's first state officials, a perceptive small-town newspaper proprietor, Josiah F. Gibbs, publisher of the Millard County *Blade* in Nephi, Juab County (population 6,000), and sent by railroad into adjacent Millard County (4,000) for distribution to subscribers, played a formative role in the

36. *Salt Lake Herald*, May 15, 24, June 10, 17, 20, 29, 1895; newspaper clippings, Trumbo scrapbook.

downfall of Trumbo and Crane. In July 1895 the editor predicted that half a dozen new newspapers would soon be established by the Crane–Trumbo campaign as an adjunct to their other campaign activities. It was an absolutely essential part of the process in that day.

However, the often-combative Gibbs, independent from the much-despised (in central and southern Utah) *Tribune* editor, Goodwin, whether with actual evidence or supposition, proceeded to launch a sensationalistic attack on the campaign partners with a headline: "For Sale: One of the Utah Senatorships." He alleged that Trumbo had pledged "a hundred thousand dollars [in subsidies] for suborning the country press of Utah" with "boodle," the era's term for bribery. Within a few weeks, the *Provo Enquirer* editor, J. C. Graham, alleged having observed "so many evidences of boodle that we wonder sometimes what the people think of the newspapermen." As one county delegate to the convention reportedly boasted, "You cannot buy my vote for all the money in Utah County." Even the staid *Salt Lake Herald* was suspected of having taken money from Trumbo. Gibbs questioned whether there was "a self-respecting Republican in Utah" who would approve of this. He imagined a "future history record[ing] that Isaac Trumbo purchased a seat in the US Senate."[37]

The *Salt Lake Tribune* would have done better to remain apart from this attack on Trumbo's qualifications and methods, except that the Californian had made sufficient inroads with the electorate that Goodwin felt it necessary to join in. Trumbo had not previously served in a public office and had something of an elitist air about him. It was easy enough to turn that into a smear, but it mainly only convinced people that the unscrupulous *Tribune* editor wanted to demean a rival. "He came not only with the intention of debauching the people," Goodwin wrote, building on the foundation of the central Utah *Blade*, "but so oblivious are his moral sensibilities that he actually sees no especial wrong and no particular impudence in attempting such a game."[38]

---

37. Nephi *Blade*, July 13, 27, Aug. 3, 10, 24, 1895; *Provo Enquirer*, Aug. 21, 1895; *Springville Independent*, June 21, 1895; *Salt Lake Herald*, June–Aug. 1895; *San Francisco Call*, Aug. 25, 26, Sept. 1, 12, 1895.

38. *Salt Lake Tribune*, June 14, 30, July 1, 21, 25, 30, Aug. 3, 10, 1895.

A major result of this controversy was that the Provo delegation traveled to the convention unpledged for a gubernatorial candidate. As Crane added a bloc of Salt Lake City delegates to his growing ranks from Davis, Millard, Tooele, and Weber Counties, he felt confident of success. However, some innovative rivals adopted the strategy of having delegates propose the names of "favorite sons" from Gentile-dominated Beaver and Summit Counties to block a first-ballot win. They suspected that this would lessen the feeling of obligation people had to Crane for having successfully led the party through its crucial inception period. After the obligatory first ballot, some delegates would feel free to support another candidate who would not prolong the Trumbo–Goodwin controversy. The new gubernatorial candidates presented were Philo T. Farnsworth (1849–1920), who had mining interests in Beaver County, and George A. Lowe, a Park City, Summit County, businessman, along with Heber M. Wells, a Salt Lake City banker and city government official. The latter candidate had not actively sought such a nomination but made it clear he would accept the party compromise mandate if it were thrust upon him. The Crane supporters assumed that their man, the most deserving candidate, did not need much energy or strategy to become the first chief executive of the state.[39]

When the party convention opened on August 28, the gubernatorial race took center stage. The first speech touched on the detrimental effect of the warring factions within the party, which suggested that a third option might be beneficial. On the first ballot, Crane showed 200 votes to Wells's 172, Thomas coming in at a surprisingly weak third. Since 269 votes were necessary for the nomination, a second ballot was called. In the hectic interim, Crane's supporters "used every art to keep their forces from breaking and to add to their strength," but the second ballot was decisive. Relieved from their initial pledges, delegates who wanted to avoid division went with Wells. Crane attributed this to a feeling

39. *Provo Enquirer*, Aug. 22, 1895; Lyman, ed., *Candid Insights*, 717; *Salt Lake Herald*, Aug. 25–27, 1895. For more on Wells, see Lyman, "Heber M. Wells."

that a Latter-day Saint should head the ticket. The *Tribune* blamed Crane's partnership with Trumbo.[40]

Whatever else it was, the frontrunner's defeat was a blow to Trumbo's chances of success. If Trumbo could have toured the territory alongside the gubernatorial candidate, it would have enhanced his own prestige. Despite the setback, Crane retained his commitment to campaign with Trumbo. The two men engaged a good speaker, the journalist William Glassman, to accompany them, as well as entertainment: a popular quartet of African–American singers and a professional humorist. They competed for attention with the regular Republican ticket consisting of Wells, congressional candidate Clarence E. Allen, and one of the candidates for the US Senate, Frank J. Cannon. The latter group received support from new party chairman George M. Cannon, Frank's cousin. The party gave no assistance to the Trumbo–Crane group. One factor in the electioneering was a pamphlet written by Crane to the future state legislature that would select the first two senators. He denied that Trumbo had ever been guilty of bribery or ballot-purchasing, or that if he was, it was during the time he was the chief financial supporter of Frank Cannon. This elaborate document was widely disseminated throughout the territory.[41]

Democrats like Orlando W. Powers continued to push claims of bribery and backroom dealings. Early in 1894 the Democrats' *Salt Lake Herald* and *New York Times* pointed a finger at George Q. Cannon for having been involved with the railroad lobby and otherwise having appropriated Church funds for projects that benefitted his family. Frank J. Cannon's opponent, Joseph L. Rawlins, stressed that there was a "powerful and corrupt corporation" pushing for statehood in order to extract favors for the railroad. As such accusations were slung back and forth, and George Q. Cannon was increasingly mentioned in connection with the railroad lobby, Cannon sought to distance himself from Trumbo.

During the severe financial depression in the years following

40. *Salt Lake Herald*, Aug. 29, 30, 1895; *Salt Lake Tribune*, Aug. 29, 30, 1895.
41. *Ogden Standard*, Nov. 14, 1895; Crane, *To Members of the Utah Legislature*.

the panic of '93, LDS leaders sought to promote the territory's native industries involving coal, iron, hydro-electric power, and salt and the railroad connections to these mines and dams. James Clarkson boasted that he could get outside financing to help local companies meet their potential, and Trumbo promoted the idea of extending the railroad from Salt Lake City to Los Angeles. On October 3, 1893, Clarkson and Trumbo signed a contract with various groups to act as their agents on the East Coast. However, when George Q. Cannon journeyed east and learned that the interested companies expected control of the enterprises, Cannon persuaded his Church associates back home to cancel their contracts with Trumbo and Clarkson.[42] Cannon continued to stay in touch with Trumbo on matters pertaining to statehood but probably never again fully trusted him.

Meanwhile, the *Herald* concluded that the Republican convention was so riddled by factionalism, the outlook for Democrats had never been brighter. The party conventions were a study in contrasts. For the Democrats, the former territorial delegate to Congress, John T. Caine, was unchallenged in his nomination for governor. B. H. Roberts was briefly considered for the same honor, but he had his eye on a congressional seat. The delegates chose Roberts for Congress and Joseph Rawlins and Moses Thatcher for the US Senate, should the party secure the necessary majority in the state legislature where the senators were chosen.[43] Immediately following the convention, except for predictable comment from the *Tribune*, there was little said about the Church wanting its people chosen or any other aspects of the race. It was the calm before the storm, with considerable private talk, from, for instance, apostle Heber J. Grant, who had hoped to be nominated for governor. When he mentioned the possibility to Wilford Woodruff, he was not encouraged. The quietly ambitious apostle well understood that his associates, Roberts and

42. Lyman, *Political Deliverance*, 232–39.

43. *Salt Lake Herald*, Sept. 1–7, 1895. Senators would not be popularly elected until the Sixteenth Amendment was ratified in 1917.

Thatcher, had not asked for permission at all, leaving him more critical of the two than he might have otherwise been.[44]

On October 1, apostle Brigham Young Jr. encountered Moses Thatcher on a Salt Lake City street and advised him that it was not too late to confer with President Woodruff about his nomination. In response, the Logan apostle alleged that other members of their quorum had demonstrated too much "pliability," or submissiveness, with the First Presidency. Young must have passed this on to other Church authorities, as well as the apostle's subsequent comments about his colleagues in the quorum lacking "manhood" and "backbone." He did meet with the elderly Church president, however, and in the ensuing exchange the increasingly defiant Thatcher offered as his position that the president had no right to "dictate" to the other brethren regarding politics, thus depriving them of their "agency," a word loaded with import in LDS theology. Accounts of these brash statements circulated among the other members of the hierarchy and created such resentment that a week later in the priesthood session of general conference, Joseph F. Smith told local leaders assembled there that it was their duty to obey the president, that it had been "wrong" for individuals recently to accept secular "obligations without first consulting and obtaining the consent of those who presided over them. ... No man surrenders his manhood by seeking the advice of his superiors," he said, in obvious response to Thatcher's insult.[45] These public comments proved to be a serious lapse of political good judgment.

Democrats interpreted Smith's comments to be a challenge to their right to put forth the candidates of their choosing, to the detriment of the party in the eyes of the electorate. At a meeting of the First Presidency and apostles the next week, Joseph F. Smith denied that he had intended his address to be taken politically. Woodruff had a statement published asserting that no church influence had

44. *Salt Lake Tribune,* Sept. 7, 1896; Grant, *Diaries,* Sept. 5, 26, 1895.

45. Young Jr. journal, Oct. 1–2, 1895; Lyman, ed., *Candid Insights,* 735–36, 740–42; Grant, *Diaries,* Oct. 7, 10, 1895. This and similar episodes would eventually cause virtually all other apostles, in their quorum meeting, to withhold their sustaining vote from Thatcher as a continuing member of the quorum. See Lyman, "Alienation of an Apostle," 78–86.

been applied politically, their intent having been the opposite, to keep its highest officers out of politics. In a subsequent sermon at an Ogden stake conference, Elder Smith elaborated by saying he was not trying to unite church and state, but, he unwisely added, he wanted to end the state's interference with matters involving the Church. Several days later the presidency and half the apostles discussed this further and resolved to "stand absolutely firm in maintaining church discipline, no matter how much political capital was attempted to be made out of the position."[46]

Still, a week later, a front-page article in the *Argus* elaborated on how the Church presidency had allegedly determined to "wield the rod of discipline on the political anatomies of some of their subordinates." The reporter rehearsed what had been whispered about George Q. Cannon's back-room deals in Washington and what it had just learned about an emergency meeting of the Utah Democratic Party leaders following the LDS general conference, where it was decided to reconvene the territorial convention. The party needed statements condemning the co-mingling of church and state, and Judge Orlando Powers said in a related interview that the party chairman would not "procrastinate ... taking some step that will save the party from defeat ... if the impression remains that we are under the ban of the First Presidency." He conceded the Church's right to direct the political activities of its apostles, but pointed out that John Henry Smith had been openly campaigning for the Republicans and giving advice to local Church leaders about politics. "Why should a Democrat be called upon to counsel with Joseph F. Smith, a Republican?" Powers asked.[47] These remarks intentionally fanned the flames of this explosive situation into the most bitter political fight in Utah's history.

The *Herald* followed the *Argus* with an interview of B. H. Roberts, who said he did not consider his recent actions a breach of Church protocol. What he thought was unfortunate was the timing of the

46. *Salt Lake Tribune*, Oct. 13, 14, 18, 1895; *Deseret Evening News*, Oct. 14, 1895; *Candid Insights*, 746, 748–49.

47. *Salt Lake Herald*, Oct. 11–14, 1895; *Argus*, Oct. 12, 1895.

presidency's intercession right before the election, making the claim that it was non-partisan ring hollow to him. The *Salt Lake Tribune* expressed amazement that a member of the Council of Seventy would criticize the Church president when it appeared to be in the best interests of the Democrats to do so. The equally biased Republican newspaper alleged that the Democrats were desperate in the wake of their declining numbers. Powers was a master of stirring up controversy, the *Herald* proclaimed. Readers were reminded that he had previously asked President Cleveland to reject Utah's petition to be admitted as a state. Cleveland himself ignored the local quarrel. A *New York Times* correspondent accurately reported that the Democratic convention "was not summoned a second time simply because of the actions at the recent priesthood meeting. This was only the culminating challenge to a long series of hostile" exchanges and "unfair influences" involving officers of the Church promoting the Republicans.[48]

At their second convention, the Utah Democrats enumerated the most egregious past violations of the vow of neutrality by the LDS hierarchy. They discussed George Gibbs's letter to Cache Valley Mormons, Joseph F. Smith's speeches, his *Nuggets of Truth* pamphlet, and disclosure of the bishop's recommend in behalf of Frank J. Cannon. They somewhat ironically accused the First Presidency of aiding Frank Cannon. They denounced Francis M. Lyman's participation in the 1894 campaign, although that too had no real basis. The convention heard about the telegram to Trumbo congratulating him for his role in securing statehood, a matter that was especially embarrassing to Rawlins. And they cited the First Presidency's support of tariffs, which the Church officers called protection of home industry.[49] Whatever the accuracy of the list of grievances, it did nothing to generate more positive political results.

Not without reason, the *Salt Lake Tribune* called the second Democratic convention a "grandstand play." The way apostle Lorenzo Snow described the convention, there had not been so "terrible [a] spirit" among LDS participants at an event since the 1837–38

48. *New York Times*, Nov. 3, 1895.
49. *Salt Lake Herald*, Oct. 23, 24, 1895.

apostasy of about 15 percent of the Church membership in Ohio due to a failed attempt to assist persecuted Latter-day Saints there and failure of a Church bank. The Democrats had more appealing candidates and should have been able to overcome the pressure from the LDS authorities to defeat some Republicans. They had gubernatorial hopeful John T. Caine, who had been the territorial delegate to Congress. His Republican opponent, Heber Wells, was only thirty-six years old and had less experience in public life. Brigham Roberts, running for Congress, was perhaps the most popular LDS orator of the day. His opponent, Clarence Allen, was best remembered as a former foe of the Church. In candidacies for other offices, both parties presented a preponderance of LDS office-seekers, with the Democrats seemingly better known and more qualified. However, the fact stood that it was a contest centered more on issues than personalities, which played to the Republicans' favor.[50]

As usual, the most widely discussed clash was over the restraint of foreign competition regarding domestic goods. The Republicans espoused the idea that if production could be carried on in the United Stated, it should be. New and growing industries should be protected. This aligned with the Church's long history of encouraging self-reliance, cooperation, and distrust of outsiders. Democrats attempted to show the difference between the Republican plank and Republican tariffs, but in the eyes of the voter the Republicans held the advantage here. The Democratic argument that if industries could not thrive on their own, they should not be encouraged, was unpopular.[51]

Early in the campaign, the *Tribune* chided the Democrats for wanting to switch the conversation to silver currency. Both parties in the state had advocated the re-monetization of silver at a value with gold of 16:1. There was some doubt whether either national party would commit itself to silver. On the Democratic side was William Jennings Bryan, whose view would be expressed often in the *Salt Lake Herald*. A segment of Utah voters had "come to the conclusion

50. *Salt Lake Tribune*, Sept.3, Oct. 24, Nov. 5, 1895; Lyman journal, Oct. 14, 23–25, Nov. 6, 1895; Young Jr. journal, Nov. 14, 1895.

51. *Salt Lake Herald*, Aug. 24, Sept. 7, 1895; also Arrington, *Great Basin Kingdom*, 380–412.

that there is absolutely no hope for silver in the Republican Party." But instead of switching to the Democrats, they had gravitated to the new Populist Party movement and nominated candidates for a few state offices, including the respected Henry W. Lawrence for governor. It was predicted that he and the silver issue would divert votes away from Wells, who as a banker was suspected of being a closet "goldbug." The *Herald* assumed that the third-party issues would be devastating for Wells. He would "wake up on election day and find that he has simply been cut to pieces by the third party man."[52]

The ballots proved otherwise. Wells received fewer votes than other Republicans in Salt Lake City, then gained strength in the rural areas. When the returns were in, he had 20,833 votes to 18,519 for Caine and 2,051 for Lawrence. The combined total for Caine and Lawrence was 264 short of the number for Wells. Many analysts credited the preference for Republican tariffs, as John Codman wrote in the *New York Times*: "The fact is that the Republican victory dates way back to the days of Brigham Young, whose policy was absolute protection, not only against foreign nations, but against the whole United States outside of Utah." He asserted that Young had often preached against imports, that "there was not a single article of necessity, and scarcely one of luxury, that could not be produced or manufactured in his domain." The reporter, who had long followed the Latter-day Saints, concluded that "the whole Mormon people were imbued with this idea."[53]

In an accompanying negative note, the *Times* editor alluded to a George Q. Cannon bargain with business and party officials. A few days later an anonymous letter from the territory credited "the defeat of Democracy in Utah" to "church influence." That was objected to by no less an authority than Democratic Governor Caleb W. West, who understood how dangerous, or at least counterproductive, it was to say the Church had tried to suppress the Democratic vote. It was at least partly due to the conduct of the party chairman

52. *Salt Lake Tribune*, Sept. 16, 1895; *Salt Lake Herald*, Sept. 4, Oct. 29, 1895. For more, see Cihak, "Bryan, Populism, and Utah," 60, 66–67.

53. Poll, "Political Reconstruction," 125–26; Codman, *Mormon Country*, 7–8; *New York Times*, Nov. 9, 1895.

running the campaign, the governor suggested. The *Deseret News* editor seized on another idea, that it had been a bad year for Democrats nationally. In Utah the party had given as good an account of itself, "if not better … than in any other state of the union." The paper could not resist adding that "truly this appears to be 'a Democratic year'—for defeat."[54] It was true, and in Utah it took almost twenty years thereafter for the party to recover.

The entire slate of Republican state executive officers, including the congressional delegation, won their elections. They came from across the state: three from Salt Lake City—Governor-elect Wells, Congressman Allen, and education superintendent John R. Park—and the others from American Fork (James Chipman, state treasurer), Logan (James Hammond, secretary of state), Ogden (A. C. Bishop, attorney general), and Parowan (Morgan Richards, state auditor). All but Allen and Bishop were LDS. The state legislature would be in the hands of a Republican majority, frustrating the senatorial aspirations of Rawlins and Thatcher, at least for that time. The Republican judicial candidates were also elected, headed by Chief Justice Charles S. Zane and flanked by associate justices George C. Bartch and James A. Miner.[55]

Exhausted by it all, many people hoped that with the election over, the political strife would subside. That could occur only after the infighting among Republican contestants for seats in the US Senate was completed. That Frank Cannon prevailed was due to a combination of farsightedness by his campaign managers; help from his cousin George M. Cannon, who ran the territorial Republican election machinery; and the widespread assumption that the last delegate to Congress was entitled to consideration for a more elevated position, all working to Cannon's advantage. The major obstacle was the still-possible candidacy of his father, the only other serious Latter-day Saint under consideration. At a meeting of Church authorities just after the general election, Grant, Lyman, and Woodruff

54. *New York Times*, Nov. 25, 27, 1895; *Deseret Evening News*, Nov. 6, 1895; also *Lucifer's Lantern*, June 1899.

55. *Salt Lake Herald*, Nov. 8, 10, 11, 18, 19, Dec. 5, 1895.

expressed their desire to see George Q. Cannon elected. Abraham Cannon dissented, saying his father's services were needed at home more than in the nation's capital. In a private conversation the next day, President Cannon confided to his son that he did not much desire to be in Washington, but if he were selected, he hoped his son Frank would not be disappointed. Abraham privately suspected that, despite his father's denials, he would enjoy being returned in triumph to the Senate.[56]

The *Tribune* had no difficulty perceiving the danger that President Cannon's ambition presented to Charles Goodwin, still running for the seat that was generally conceded to belong to a Gentile. If the older Cannon were considered, it would enhance Isaac Trumbo's chances, since the two were linked together in the popular mind, due mostly to Trumbo's efforts to make it so. In the ensuing weeks, the *Tribune* portrayed George Q. in a bad light. Goodwin supporter and US Senator Fred T. Dubois (R–Idaho) assured friends at the paper that, according to Abraham Cannon, George Q. "had declared himself unequivocally out of the senate race under all circumstances." Supposedly no public announcement would be made of this shift, so that Trumbo would not have time to change his strategy and undermine Frank J. Cannon.[57] Throughout this period, Trumbo had continued to decline in George Q.'s eyes. The latter was weary of the constant mention of his close partnership, supposedly, with Trumbo. The resulting inuendo about Cannon had helped create much of the unfavorable image of the Church in recent times.

At a council meeting held on November 21, where some of the apostles and presidency again discussed the senatorial question, President Woodruff reiterated his wish that George Q. go to the Senate. He directed his fellow church leaders to adopt it as their policy to support him. There was apparently no objection from Cannon, except to say he hoped they would not similarly support Trumbo. "He is not a person whose manner and characteristics we

56. Lyman, ed., *Candid Insights*, 705–07.

57. Fred T. Dubois to Abraham H. Cannon, Dec. 6, 1895; Dubois to P. H. Lannon, Dec. 31, 1895; Cannon to Dubois, received Dec. 11, 1895, Dubois Collection; *Candid Insights*, 770–71.

desire to represent us," he observed, "for he is very ignorant, and then he would be, no doubt, a boodler, accepting bribes for services which he would have the power to render." Cannon suggested that Trumbo represented the interests of the Spreckels sugar trust and retained his standing with the Southern Pacific Railroad. His "money barrel" had been at work persuading Republicans who were elected to the Utah legislature on how to vote, Cannon alleged. Simon Bamberger, a business associate of the Cannons and future Utah governor, alleged much the same thing in a different setting. Bamberger reported, and Cannon had doubtless heard it before, that Trumbo claimed "some kind of pull" on Cannon.[58]

Trumbo's associate James S. Clarkson admitted that the dedicated lobbyist could be impetuous and overanxious. At the same time, Trumbo had never seemed to place his personal ambition above the needs of the LDS people, the national Republican leader recalled. In addition, Isaac Trumbo had "established such relations with every prominent man in public life … that it puts him where no other new man from Utah could possibly be if he should serve twenty years in the senate." In his letter on the topic to President Woodruff, Clarkson undertook the delicate task of also discounting Frank Cannon and Charles Goodwin as candidates. Though fond of the young Cannon, he wrote, Frank obviously lacked the stature of his father. As for Goodwin, editor of the *Tribune*, the LDS public would certainly consider him to be a thorn in their side.

Abraham Cannon noted that in President Woodruff's support of his father, George Q., the Church president had not stated that it was the "will of the Lord." It was not alleged that God had spoken to him, and when Woodruff answered Clarkson he wrote that it would not be possible to express a preference for any political candidate, given the hostility generated recently over what people considered interference in politics of the sort Clarkson was requesting. Woodruff

58. Richards journal, Nov. 21, 1895; *Candid Insights*, 762–65. Two years after statehood, George Q. Cannon commented that the Church presidency had never understood they were expected to repay Trumbo with a Senate seat (G. Cannon journal, Feb. 1, 1898). However, that is contradicted by James Clarkson's Dec. 14, 1895, letter to President Woodruff calling in the favor.

acknowledged Trumbo's service, as well as the obstacles he faced, especially among Gentiles who assumed he had "come to the territory merely for the sake of office" and that he secretly represented either the Southern Pacific Corporation or the LDS Church. Aside from the political backlash that could ensue from trying to influence the state legislature, Woodruff and his colleagues lacked the power over the legislature outsiders credited them with, he insisted.[59]

In early December 1895, congressional delegate Frank Cannon heard from President Cleveland that he wanted to see the statehood matter taken care of quickly. A few days later, an official delegation headed by Governor West arrived to present Cleveland with a handsomely bound copy of the proposed Utah constitution. The chairman of the Utah Commission, J. R. Letcher, attested that it had been properly approved by the electorate the previous month. The president congratulated them and said he would have the Attorney General examine it as soon as possible. On December 21 attorney general Judson Harmon approved the constitution, removing that last possible impediment to the president issuing a proclamation announcing a new state.[60]

The announcement was set for Saturday, January 4, 1896, with the state's representatives to be installed the following Monday. LDS and non-LDS dignitaries cooperated in preparing the celebration that convened at midday on Saturday in Salt Lake City to hear the fire of a shotgun in front of the office of the Western Union Telegraph when the president signed the proclamation. At that moment Utah became the forty-fifth state admitted to the union. There was a deafening clamor in the city involving bells, cannon salutes, fireworks, and shouts, and a gigantic steam whistle sounded incessantly for two hours from the Salt Lake City and County Building. Despite a recent snowstorm, people gathered on the streets to express their elation. Two days later there was a more formal gathering

59. Lyman, ed., *Candid Insights,* 775–76; White, "Utah State Elections," 95–109; Woodruff to Clarkson, Dec. 30, 1895, Woodruff Letterbooks. Probably in desperation, Trumbo reached out to railroad baron Collis P. Huntington, who had instead unexpectedly given financial backing to a rival candidate, Arthur Brown.

60. Lyman, "Statehood, Political Allegiance," 354–56.

at the Salt Lake Tabernacle, festooned with a large star above the famous organ, the pipes draped with a gigantic flag, and a full house of about 10,000 observers who packed inside the building, others standing outside on the temple grounds. The outgoing territorial leaders and the officers-elect were seated prominently at the front of the historic building. Because Governor West had not returned yet from the East, Territorial Secretary Charles C. Richards conducted the proceedings. After an invocation written by Wilford Woodruff and read by George Q. Cannon, a musical number was performed by a military band and a children's chorus sang the national anthem. Joseph Rawlins read the admission proclamation, eliciting a natural cheer with the line that declared "the hour has arrived when the federal government is to withdraw from the control of the affairs of the territory, and surrender it up to the people; and to the native son of Utah, who has been chosen to be the governor of the state of Utah." Chief Justice Charles S. Zane administered the oath of office to Governor Wells. In the distance a cannon at Fort Douglas could be heard. The Tabernacle Choir sang a hymn that was composed for the occasion, "Utah, We Love Thee." Then Governor Wells delivered his inaugural address, which reviewed the long struggle looking forward to that day.[61]

In the afternoon at the City and County Building a few blocks away, the governor addressed the new state legislature regarding an array of matters he felt were in need of immediate legislative attention. The executive and legislative branches of the new state government would cooperate in an impressive way through this essential transition period. One of the legislature's major duties was to select two US senators. That automatically elicited partisan attacks once more. The *Herald* mentioned George Q. Cannon as a possible candidate. Others under consideration were Arthur Brown, Charles Bennett, O. J. Salisbury, and Isaac Trumbo, one name being conspicuously absent from its list, that of rival editor Charles Goodwin. Frank J. Cannon returned from Washington, DC, several days later

61. *Salt Lake Tribune*, Dec. 6, 12, 17, 22, 1894, Jan. 5, 6, 1895; *Salt Lake Herald*, Dec. 12, 14, 16–18, 22, 24, 1895; *Deseret Evening News*, Jan. 6, 1896.

and declined to comment on his father's candidacy, while Goodwin felt under no such restraint and used the *Tribune* to launch what the *Herald* called "the use of every sort of innuendo, covert and open threats, to create a sentiment against Hon. George Q. Cannon." The apostle's selection might signal a revival of the old theocracy, the *Tribune* suggested. Other newspapers reported that he was a favorite among legislators of both parties.[62] However, that would not prove to be entirely true.

The Church quietly created a committee to investigate Cannon's popularity. It was comprised of Abraham H. Cannon, John Henry Smith, and stake president Angus M. Cannon, a brother of George Q. The three made inquiries among members of the state legislature to see what President Cannon's chances were, and to their surprise most of the elected gentlemen would not consider voting for him for fear of the repercussions it would produce. Cannon found this intelligence devastating. On the day before the party caucus of January 14, he published a notice in the *Deseret News*, "I can't contribute to division by allowing my name to appear as a candidate." This may have taken some of the party leadership by surprise. It left only one other LDS candidate in the running, and that was Frank Cannon. At the caucus Frank was chosen by acclamation. For the second senatorial seat, Goodwin's supporters knew he lacked enough votes to win if there were several men in the running, so they encouraged legislators to support the presumably weaker Brown in the first ballot. They had not imagined that Brown, having well-organized floor agents, had sufficient support to win in the first round of voting. It was just a straw vote, but with the majority in the legislature being Republican it guaranteed that the same outcome would follow in the actual vote, most of the legislators committing to honor what was decided in the caucus.[63]

A *Tribune* reporter unfairly wrote that Trumbo's name "was not presented because no one could be found to nominate him." The

62. Lyman, "Heber M. Wells," 30–90; *Washington Post*, Dec. 11, 1895; *Salt Lake Herald*, Jan. 9, 12, 13, 16, 1896; *Salt Lake Tribune*, Jan. 10, 11, 1896; *Argus*, Jan. 11, 1896.

63. Cannon and O'Higgins, *Under the Prophet in Utah*, 165–67; *Deseret Evening News*, Jan. 14, 1896; *Ogden Standard*, Jan. 16, 18, 1896.

Standard more accurately elaborated that by then, Trumbo had withdrawn his name. A week earlier he had written to the First Presidency asking for their confirmation of support for his nomination. As he worded it, "Statehood as an accomplished fact has been the dream of eight years of my life ... and at last the consummation so devoutly sought for has become a reality." Since the "complete and perfect fulfillment of all promises will be determined in a few days ... I wish to rest with the satisfaction of being one of Utah's first senators." The First Presidency apparently did not answer the letter, leaving Trumbo helpless. He visited the presidency on the day of the caucus, coming on the heels of President Cannon's withdrawal from consideration. The reaction from the Church must have crushed his senatorial hopes once and for all.[64] He was incapable of mustering enough support on his own, so there would have been no reason to prolong his inevitable defeat.

When the state legislature cast its votes on January 21, 1896, and confirmed Arthur Brown and Frank Cannon as its first US senators, news of the selection provoked considerable discussion among members of Congress who knew Frank Cannon but not Brown. As one news dispatch from Washington to the *Herald* reported, "the impression prevailed ... that Colonel Trumbo would be selected as one of the senators. Some of his friends declare Trumbo's defeat to be a piece of rank ingratitude." Utah had either forgotten or had never known of his impressive service, but in Washington he had not yet been forgotten. It was "expected that he would be rewarded for his loyalty to the Mormons," one senator remarked. The defeated candidate remained in Utah for a short while, meeting a few times with Woodruff, probably considering his political and business options, and then moved back to San Francisco. He was thereafter infrequently heard from in Utah's newspapers. His eight-year contribution to statehood was not exaggerated, nor were his

64. Journal History, Jan. 6, 14, 1896. Trumbo's situation was sadly reminiscent of the experience of the earlier non-Mormon lobbyist, Thomas Fitch, who had done so much to mount the first serious Utah attempt at statehood in the early 1870s (see chapters 2–3). On both occasions Cannon had legitimate reasons for changing his mind about supporting their promised senatorial candidacies, but it is doubtful either man ever forgave him.

shadowy tactics. In the venality of his approach, particularly when he linked George Cannon to it, he alienated his former friend and relinquished any chance for his own election.[65] Instead of Cannon and Trumbo in the Senate, the state chose men who had as yet not proved themselves. Within a year Frank Cannon would walk out of the Republican Party and become an outspoken opponent of the LDS Church. Not long after his senatorial term ended, Brown would be shot and killed by a discarded mistress. Trumbo would stay in touch with Woodruff, who in 1898 would die in Trumbo's home while on a visit to San Francisco.[66]

The continued assimilation of Utah into the nation was enhanced by Utah's acceptance as a state. No territory had struggled as long or experienced nearly as many disappointments along the way as Utah had. After defying the US government over a long period of time, setting itself against federal officials politically, militarily, and economically, the territory entered a dramatic period of social and political acclimation, the people of Utah coming to see themselves as fully American for the first time. It would probably take at least as long for the population to develop true independence from the kind of political dominance they had expected from their ecclesiastical leaders, but progress in that direction was visible from the moment of admission. People came into statehood mainly perceiving themselves as law-abiding and patriotic, in marked contrast to the rough-and-tumble iconoclasts of the frontier period. Their acceptance of other Americans, and vice versa, was the result of a long gestation period, and one that turned out to be mutually advantageous in the end.

---

65. *Salt Lake Herald*, Jan. 16, 1896; Lyman, "Trumbo and Statehood," 146–49.

66. Cannon, "Wives and Other Women," 74; Thatcher "Gentile Polygamist," 231–45; Roberts, *Comprehensive History,* 6:341–44.

EPILOGUE

Wilford Woodruff went to great pains to announce the end of polygamy as the required sacrifice to achieve statehood. He was afraid the government would otherwise continue to seize the Church's assets, including the temples, which it was at that moment considering doing. However, his manifesto was more of a policy statement than a theological resolution of the issue. He said it was based on revelation, but it was not the revelation itself, more of a public relations effort. The meaning was therefore subject to speculation rather than scriptural interpretation. For instance, it did not repudiate the belief that polygamy was God-ordained as the only proper form of marriage, as had been taught. Internally the statement was interpreted to mean that the Church would scale back new marriages only in the United States. Those who were already polygamists assumed they could continue to live as such. In fact, many of the men who had stopped living with plural wives resumed their former lifestyle on the assumption that they would not be prosecuted under the new understanding, especially if statehood were achieved. What was unexpected was that when younger Latter-day Saints took the public pronouncement at face value, they left polygamy behind. Many already had a desire to fit into the modern world and were less convinced that their parents' struggles were a necessary part of their own current faith.

Several days after the manifesto was publicized, Church authorities privately confirmed that it did not apply to men who were already residing with more than one family.[1] In fact, within a few years, there would be hints about plural marriage being revived in the future. In the wake of the manifesto, the federal threat softened, and for that reason the manifesto itself was seldom referred to. This added to the result of men returning to live with their plural wives and more talk of the need to restore the practice. On January 22, 1894, at a public conference in Grantsville, west of Salt Lake City and away from *Salt Lake Tribune* reporters, senior apostle Francis M. Lyman stated that "no man will attain to the godhood as Abraham, Isaac and Jacob have done unless they do the works of Abraham as plainly taught in the law on celestial marriage, either in time or in eternity."[2]

Less than three months later at a private meeting held on April 3 in connection with general conference, George Q. Cannon lamented that his own daughters would not be able to enjoy the privilege of "marrying some good men, even if they were not the first wife," having to settle for younger men who were single and less spiritually worthy. Polygamists were the staunchest believers within the Church, the backbone of the priesthood organization, according to Cannon's view. The leaders privately even spoke of restoring the Old Testament practice of concubinage as an alternative to plural marriage. Wilford Woodruff said, "If men enter into some practice of this character [acquiring concubines] to raise a righteous posterity, they will be justified in it." George Q. Cannon wanted to see "some plan" instituted "whereby men and women can live together under sacred ordinances and vows until they can be married." The president of the Quorum of the Twelve Apostles, Lorenzo Snow, predicted that "concubinage will yet be practiced in this church."[3]

After his son David died in Europe while serving a Church mission, George Q. Cannon worried that David had not married and lacked posterity. After thinking about it, the elder Cannon's remedy, inspired by the Old Testament, was to persuade another son, Abraham, to acquire one of his brother's former girlfriends

1. Lyman, ed., *Candid Insights,* 135–41; Grant, *Diaries*, Sep. 30–Oct. 1, 1890.
2. Francis M. Lyman journal, Jan. 22, 1894; also Hardy, *Solemn Covenant.*
3. Grant, *Diaries*, Apr. 3, 5, 1894.

as a plural wife. The young woman chosen for this honor was Ann Mousley Cannon, who was a first cousin. Like other plural marriages after the manifesto, the documentary evidence is less than one would like, but it seems that Abraham and Annie married in October 1894, four years after the manifesto. In a strange twist, she would end up bearing no children. So Abraham courted David's last fiancée, Lillian Hamlin, probably marrying her in 1896 off the coast of California in a ceremony likely performed by Joseph F. Smith. Abraham became ill not long after and died at age thirty-seven. Lillian nevertheless gave birth to a daughter she named Marba, or Abram spelled backward.[4]

During this same time, Church authorities demonstrated they were not yet inclined to abandon political domination either, as they had promised they would do. Charles W. Penrose, editor of the *Deseret News* and frequent advisor to the First Presidency, confided that he had been appointed to a "regular committee to confer on legislative matters." Two apostles, Francis M. Lyman and John Henry Smith, were also assigned to the committee, along with Church attorney Franklin S. Richards and Salt Lake City businessmen/legislators James Sharp and W. W. Riter. Meetings with LDS legislators were held in Richards's office, where the politicians learned the LDS position on pending bills. For a time Penrose consulted with George Q. Cannon and sometimes with the entire First Presidency, as for instance on March 16, 1896, in consideration of "legislative matters," as he wrote in his diary. That same month the Church committee and First Presidency met with George M. Cannon, president of the Utah Senate, to convey their wishes to him.[5]

Early in the first state legislative session, new governor Heber M. Wells vetoed a controversial bill expanding the agricultural college at Logan. The president of that institution, William J. Kerr, called on Penrose, who took Kerr and Richards to meet with the

4. Lyman, ed., *Candid Insights*, xx–xxii; Hardy, *Solemn Covenant*, 219–22; *Goodwin's Weekly* May 7, 1904; Cannon, "Wives and Other Women"; Quinn, "New Plural Marriages."

5. Charles W. Penrose journal, Mar. 6–10, 30–31, Apr. 1, 1896; also Lyman, "Mormon Leaders in Politics."

First Presidency, which was reportedly in agreement with the governor's veto. Kerr then met with the review committee, trying to convince it that the proposed legislation was essential; but they, too, concluded that it was "unnecessary." He recalled being told that "the committee was acting under the direction of the church authorities and its action was such that it must be obeyed." He told them there were enough votes in the house to override the veto, and he would encourage the legislators to do that. The Church committee, in particular Penrose, conferred with a dozen members of both houses, men who were considered good Latter-day Saints, and came away chagrined that the men felt under no obligation to regard his directive as anything more than advice. It was ample evidence that the legislators were going to act independently in their law-making capacities. Their position was clear: they had been taught that such independence was a religious and political right, and they would vote and act according to conscience. Immediately thereafter, Kerr confided his experience to two Salt Lake city attorneys, who apparently spread the account farther.[6]

The Salt Lake City weekly *Argus* was the first to discuss the existence of the lobbyists with the Church legislative committee. All the reporter knew was that the committee was comprised of five prominent Mormons who sat in judgement on "all important questions" before the legislature, especially matters the governor was asked to pass. The committee considered itself to have "controlling weight," the reporter had been told. Governor Wells denied meeting with a Church committee or deferring to anyone's judgment, but a prominent non-LDS legislator from Salt Lake City, Edward B. Critchlow, published a letter to the *Salt Lake Tribune* confirming that there was a committee legislators had told him about. The *Deseret News* and *Ogden Standard* quickly denounced this as illusory.[7]

Critchlow, as the Republican leader of the House of Representatives, could not be easily brushed aside. His intent, he said, was to reassure voters that his LDS associates held their ground against

6. Lyman, "Heber M. Wells," 69–77; *Salt Lake Tribune*, Apr. 18, 1896.

7. *Argus*, Apr. 11, 1896; *Deseret News*, Apr. 13, 1896; *Ogden Standard*, Apr. 12, 1896.

attempts to influence them. They were sincere in fulfilling their civic responsibilities "in letter and in spirit" and would not succumb to secret oversight. To do so would be a "betrayal of the people," he wrote.[8] The *Salt Lake Herald* took up the gauntlet and asked for interviews with the men who had been identified as members of the committee, all of whom found ways to deny the committee's existence while confirming that they had been involved in the activities ascribed to it. Penrose wrote in his diary that he had admitted the "facts as far as I thought proper and denied Critchlow's falsehoods." He said "there was no committee appointed by the church that I knew of," then said that he and several others, including Richards, often met with legislators when the Church's input was requested. The accounts in Penrose's journal show that meetings were called by the Church, and Church authorities set the agenda. Riter, prior to his interview, asked Penrose how to answer the press. He was warned against full disclosure and told it was more important to protect the Church. Following this advice, Riter told the newspaper the rumors about an alleged committee were complete "bosh."[9]

The First Presidency stated on the record that it had no knowledge of a committee tasked with supervising legislation. President Cannon went so far as to say "the church did not attempt in any way to influence" the government, while he, like the others, were sometimes sought out by legislators for counsel. Even then, he said, since he was unfamiliar with local issues, he sent the elected representatives to "other men in the city who had experience in Utah law-making." Richards admitted that he had conferred on the college bill with Penrose and others. Kerr would have contradicted him if he said otherwise.[10] In short, every member of the lobbying group equivocated. Then when the Church experienced enough pushback, enough questions from the press to undermine its effectiveness, the committee meetings were discontinued. It probably rankled Church

8. *Salt Lake Tribune*, Apr. 12–14, 1896.

9. *Salt Lake Herald*, Apr. 13, 16, 18, 1896; Hardy, *Solemn Covenant*, 363–88; Penrose journal, Apr. 3, 12, 13, 1896.

10. *Salt Lake Herald*, Apr. 1, 16, 1896.

leaders to see their influence diminished. President Cannon expressed frustration in a general conference sermon, sharing what one confident legislator had told him. "I don't care how much you know, you may have all the experience in the world," the legislator said, "but I don't want to talk to you, you are an officer in the church and I don't want any ecclesiastical interference with me."[11] Cannon thought this showed how ludicrous the legislator's position was. What it actually signaled to those in the know was that elected representatives were learning to stand on their own two feet.

It is difficult today to comprehend what it must have been like for Cannon, who had usually been treated like royalty, at home and abroad, to find he could no longer easily pull the levers of government. For forty years he had been one of the masterminds behind the bids for statehood. To permanently back away from what had been a preoccupation for so many years must have been most difficult. It was the same for some of the others. It would be unreasonable to think they could suddenly move from such full involvement to total abstinence from politics, especially where Church interests were involved. According to political scientist Frank H. Jonas, an expert on Utah politics, Church leaders backed off during the first half of the twentieth century, occasionally getting involved with state government, with mixed success. In the last half of the century, Utah voters became more politically conservative and Church authorities felt emboldened to become more involved.[12] No one could deny their hand in quashing the government's attempt to place MX missiles in Utah or other well-publicized incidents, and most people can probably guess that for every time Church involvement became known, there have been many, many more examples of Church leaders "advising" the legislature in a way that concealed their hand from the public.

The legislature's independence played out in another way as state officials pushed back against directives from the national Republican

11. White, "Utah State Elections: 1895–1899," 241.
12. Jonas, "Utah," 332–38; Alexander, *Utah*, 415–16.

leadership as well.[13] President William McKinley's chief political strategist, Mark Hanna, took over from Clarkson in seeking to re-establish a power base in the West.[14] But at the national Republican convention in 1896, Frank J. Cannon and others marched out of the hall in protest of the party's abandonment of silver. That kind of factionalism would persist in Utah, assuring that Democrat William Jennings Bryan would receive a significant number of votes in Utah. Even so, most Utahns who had voted Republican remained loyal to the party, and that caught the attention of the national leadership, including the fact that apostle John Henry Smith was a McKinley promoter.[15] By contrast, Democrats such as Bryan were shocked to hear of new plural marriages among the Latter-day Saints. The 1904 Democratic platform denounced polygamy in wording reminiscent of the Republican platform from the previous century. It stands as such a dramatic reversal of political positions that it fits what Paul Kleppner analyzed as the intersection of affiliations, or "cross of culture," Bryan the moralistic torchbearer guaranteeing that Utah would remain in the arms of the Republicans.[16]

During that same time, some members of the Church hierarchy would have been doubtless even more disappointed at the governor's firmness on the issue of plural marriage. He was the son of a polygamist, but would not tolerate a resumption of plural marriages. This was appalling to many at Church headquarters, for whom the very objective of statehood had been to obtain a more lenient application of anti-polygamy laws.[17] Already in Wells's inaugural address, he drew a line in the sand by misquoting the manifesto, so that instead of promising that no plural marriages would be *contracted*, he

13. Lyman, *Political Deliverance*, 232–42, 245–48, 277–80.

14. John Henry Smith to Mark Hanna, Nov. 16, 1896; Hanna to Smith, Dec. 29, 1896, John Henry Smith Papers; Hanna to Heber M. Wells, Apr. 2, 1896, Wells Papers.

15. Redfield Proctor to James S. Clarkson, Nov. 21, 1896, Clarkson Papers; Proctor to Henry Payne, Nov. 20, 1896, Proctor Papers.

16. Kleppner, *Cross of Culture*, 369–75. The "cross" referred to the two parties changing moral positions, Bryan's people adopting the old "Stalwart" Republican position on plural marriage.

17. Penrose and Franklin S. Richards to John Taylor, Feb. 16, 1887; Taylor and George Q. Cannon to Penrose and Richards, Feb. 19, 1887, Taylor Papers.

stated that no plural marriages would be *continued*. To outsiders that may have seemed like a slight distinction, but to the hierarchy it was threatening. The ever-vigilant Charles W. Penrose investigated the typographical error and found it in the governor's original draft, rather than being an error in the reporters' accounts.[18] The Church presidency authorized Penrose to set the record straight by reprinting the full manifesto in the *Deseret News*.

Governor Wells was not unsympathetic to the dilemma polygamists faced. When the legislature sent him Senate Bill 120 in 1896, allowing children of polygamists to inherit property, he signed it into law.[19] He was spared having to make a decision over a statute Critchlow prevailed on LDS lawmakers to support, Critchlow saying it would show the outside world the state was serious about polygamy. The legislative leader even convinced Abraham O. Smoot, the onetime mayor of Provo and well-known polygamist, to introduce the bill into the lower house. From there it was sent to the judiciary committee, chaired by Critchlow himself. When Penrose reported it to apostles Grant, Lyman, Richards, and Smith, the four responded that they "desire[d] [to see] it suppressed."[20] In this instance, they were able, by some means, to prevent the bill from emerging out of the committee.

One of the legislature's first tasks was to appoint a Utah Code Commission to organize territorial statutes and recent state laws into a unified set. Included in the consolidation was a strict statute against polygamy passed in 1892. Observers both positive and negative have noted the negligence of Churchmen allowing this to become the polygamy law of the state.[21] Five years later, at the end of the 1901 legislative session, a bill sponsored by senate president Abel J. Evans sought to amend the statute so that only members of a polygamist's immediate family could initiate an investigation, not law-enforcement officers. Evans defended this by saying it would

18. Penrose journal, Jan. 7–9, 1896.

19. Utah Legislature, *Senate Journal*, 536, 574.

20. Penrose journal, Apr. 3, 1896. The apostles were Heber J. Grant, Francis M. Lyman, Franklin D. Richards, and John Henry Smith.

21. Allen and Leonard, *Story of the Latter-day Saints*, 439; also Hardy, *Solemn Covenant*, 245.

reduce "public agitation" every time law enforcement tried to ferret out something he claimed was dying of its own accord.

Rather than suppress public agitation, the bill generated strong feelings on all sides. Representative W. G. Van Horne of Salt Lake City argued that if it passed, the bill would extend the antagonism to the national stage, triggering the long-threatened Constitutional amendment on the subject.[22] The governor felt strongly his responsibility as an officer of the state, even though he felt a personal sense of compassion for those who, like his brother and brother-in-law, had several wives. He confessed that "no official act of my life has been approached with a sense of responsibility so profound as is the consideration of [the Evans] bill." He expressed affection for his family, saying he had been taught from infancy that celestial marriage was approved by God. Still, he believed the best thing for Utah was to maintain a strict prohibition. There was the practical consideration of preventing the additional scorn Utah would reap. He struck down the bill, and the legislature tried unsuccessfully to override him.[23] Some observers considered this an impressive act of courage that confirmed his independence but cost him a run for the US Senate, for which he had been the obvious choice. His proven "unreliability" cleared the way for apostle Reed Smoot to claim the seat in less than two years.

Smoot's star temporarily faded the moment he arrived in Washington, as his suitability was challenged by men who felt an LDS apostle, representing a Church that was still rumored to practice polygamy, was unsuited for the office of a US senator. Hearings beginning in 1904 continued for several years, with the most volatile result being the disclosure that members of the Church hierarchy and others had taken additional wives and fathered children by plural wives since the manifesto. After his own testimony, amounting to a *mea culpa*, the now-president Joseph F. Smith returned to Utah and issued what has come to be known as the second manifesto, which put a final stop (almost) to the Church's condoning of plural

22. *New York Times*, Mar. 12, 1901.
23. Utah State Legislature, *Senate Journal*, 1901, 422–24, 429–30.

marriage. Apostles such as Heber J. Grant and Francis M. Lyman, monogamists after two of their three wives had died, became supportive of Smith's fortified ban. George Q. Cannon, by contrast, persisted in his advocacy of plural marriage until his death.[24]

Showing remarkable fealty to their leaders, LDS people nevertheless felt themselves to be in a tight spot, having believed that polygamy had been jettisoned and now learning otherwise, and the same regarding politics. This paradox probably helped instill in young Utahns the inclination to think for themselves in more than one area of their lives. As Carmon Hardy stated about polygamy, "Although the principle was [thereafter] surreptitiously kept alive by hundreds of stalwarts, thousands more believed the public statements of their leaders."[25] For their part, the hierarchy was stunned, and doubtless angered, by the members' willingness to defy instructions in political matters and some areas of faith.

Although nationally the Republicans were behind the Reed Smoot hearings, they declined to place an anti-polygamy plank into their 1904 platform. James Clarkson had by then regained some prominence within the relatively new administration of Theodore Roosevelt and sought to acquaint the president with the Mormon question. After the storm of the Smoot hearings, Latter-day Saints would enjoy increasingly cordial relations within the Republican Party for most of the next three decades. In the long term, it would be the better relationship Church people established with the leadership of both parties that would be most important for the Church's future, even more than statehood.[26]

The political odyssey of the Church on the run-up to statehood shows its attempt to be accepted into society while simultaneously shunning it. The actions of its leaders may be judged as heroic, defiant, courageous, or desperate, but in essence they were struggling to preserve a way of life and in whatever way necessary, including pulling the levers of the territorial legislature and stalking the halls of

24. Merrill, *Reed Smoot*, 11–104; Alexander, *Mormonism in Transition*, 16–73; Paulos, *Mormon Church on Trial*, 19–142, 177–95; Hardy, "Polygamy, Mormonism and Me," 94.

25. Hardy, *Solemn Covenant*, 244–338.

26. Alexander, *Utah*, 261–63, 292, 313–32.

power in Washington as their right to defend a God-directed morality. However, other government operators acted on their sense of duty, necessity, and entitlement and often proved more adept at the game. Eventually it was not just the harsh legislation and judicial hammer that doomed the territory's theocratic rule, it was a good number of the Mormon people themselves, determined to no longer persist in defiance of the government for the benefit of a shrinking number of advocates of plural marriage. General John A. McClernand, one of the Utah Commission, recognized this trend in the late 1880s in his prediction that "the more often the Mormons commit themselves, whether regularly or irregularly, against polygamy, the more they will have increased the obstacles to a retreat from the path of reform."[27] Many Church members were sufficiently attracted by monogamy, after having made their test-oath concessions, they were disinclined to fully back those who persisted in the old way. Church members were among the most alarmed when they heard about broken promises by the Church. Young Latter-day Saints were becoming more inclined to want to be full-fledged Americans and be done with the drama over marriage.

Statehood brought about a democratization of the social and political landscape for people who previously had been among the most deferential to the commands of their spiritual leaders, until the day came that the harder the leaders leaned in favor of autocratic rule, the more many, particularly of the younger generation, pulled in the opposite direction. They proved able to carve out a space where they trusted their own judgment, not just in politics or faith, but in family life, business, education, and pastimes, so that they gravitated more toward the mainstream of American life, yet still remaining one of the more distinctive demographics in the multi-cultured patchwork of the republic.[28]

---

27. John A. McClernand to Grover Cleveland, June 30, July 5, 9, 1887, Cleveland Papers.

28. Mauss, *Angel and the Beehive*; Alexander, *Mormonism in Transition*; Peterson and Cannon, *Awkward State of Utah*.

"MY DEAR SIR"

James S. Clarkson to Wilford Woodruff, July 11, 1894

The same day Congress passed the Utah Enabling Act, putting the territory on a two-year path to becoming a state, a member of the Republican National Committee, James S. Clarkson, wrote to LDS President Wilford Woodruff. Clarkson rehearsed what he and others had done behind the scenes to make this happen after more than forty years on the part of Latter-day Saint leaders and their Democratic friends in Congress. Clarkson mostly wanted to call in a favor, expressed on page 26 of his lengthy missive:

> Very much of the action taken by others has been taken on my assurance of honor that I was not being misled, that yours were a people in whom faith could safely be placed, and that your destiny as a people and a State ran in the same grooves with Republican policies, Republican patriotism and Republican interest. I shall feel that I am on the bond, that my honor stands for guaranty, and therefore that I am at liberty, and indeed constrained by the highest sense of duty that can actuate an honorable man, to make known to you the obligations which rest upon you in these sacred regards.

What Clarkson wanted was a guarantee that the state would elect two Republican senators. In particular, he wanted Isaac Trumbo, a railroad lobbyist with ties to Utah, and Woodruff's counselor George Q. Cannon or son Frank to be elected to those positions. An additional incentive, on condition that Woodruff would continue to fund the cost of paying newspapers for favorable coverage (a "delicate matter," the "means [being used] … for purely honorable purposes and yet … necessary … without [which] success could not possibly have been achieved"), was Clarkson's "assurance" that the *Salt Lake Tribune* would be put out of business. "The men who control it are actuated only by mercenary interests and therefore are open to negotiation and arrangement," in which case "there ought to be no trouble in securing it" and making the "annoyance" disappear.

The 33-page typed letter is in the Albert T. Volwiler Papers, Lilly Library, Indiana University–Bloomington. Years ago I wondered about the possible existence of the letter when I saw Woodruff's reply to it, and later in seeing passing reference to it in a thesis written under the direction of the late history professor Albert Volwiler, who had taught at Ohio University. The professor's son led me to his father's papers at Indiana University, where the Benjamin Harrison scholar had taught for a year. The collection includes boxes of correspondence and memorabilia, including a large envelope marked 134b with the "Woodruff–Clarkson letter of July 11, 1894." I secured a copy from librarian Virginia Mauck and donated it to the LDS Church History Library in Salt Lake City.

The Shoreham
Washington, D.C.
July 11, 1894.

My dear Sir:

Having at last reached success in the passage through Congress of the bill admitting Utah to Statehood, it is due to you to know something of the more important details of the long and difficult contest. The victory which has been reached has come only through the help of friends whose services can never be forgotten, and through a patience and persistence of effort which I have never seen equaled. Indeed, in this contest have been found nearly all the experiences of effort and resistance, of fidelity as against conspiracy, of loyalty to friends as against temptation, and truly all the experiences nearly that make up the struggles in human life and effort. Coming into it at a comparatively late stage, and having passed through before many noted contests, and not having the intense feeling of the struggle for home and independence that you and your people have felt after so many long and weary years of waiting, I have naturally been able to judge more impartially of the struggle, of the work of the people who have figured in it, of the unworthiness of those who have failed in fidelity, and of the debt of gratitude that all of you must forever owe to those who have stood in the storm, and through the stress and trial of years overcoming every obstacle, foiling every treachery, have brought you triumph at last. In my observation of your people and my analysis of their character I should judge that they are peculiarly endowed with the qualities of appreciation and gratitude. It has been a long and bitter school in which they have been taught the value of friendship, and the withering, bitter, unrelenting force of enmity. It is difficult even now to see, as in a few years it will be impossible for any fair man to see, how remorselessly and persistently prejudice and malice have followed you and your people in the crusade of over a generation against you. As intelligent and Christian people, however, you have that quality which is the most divine in human nature, the quality of forgiveness; and as I have watched this struggle year after year and seen how strangely things have come out, how your enemies [page 2:] have melted away before you, and how unanimously at last has come the victory after so many years of injustice and oppression, I have been forced to feel that the spirit of a higher power than that of man has been controlling in the movements and destiny of your people and in the final judgment toward them of the whole American people. All of us as we grow older learn to value more and more highly the gifts that come to us through discipline, and it is a strange part of human life that nearly everything that is dearest to us, most to be treasured, and most preservative of our liberty, comes to us dearly bought by suffering, sacrifice, and often longtime oppression. Nearly everything dear to human life has been gained along these high lines, where human endurance has been tested, where character and patience have been put to bitter test, and where all that is good and noble in a people has been developed under storm and trial. Neither in this generation nor in any soon to come will the strange blessing of final independence which has come to you and your people be fully understood. But for the spirit that drove you into the wilderness to combat with the savage elements among men and the more savage elements of nature, but for the necessity of industry, courage and patience, made necessary by your battle for life in a country so wild and unfruitful at first as to be unfriendly, but for the strange experiences through which practically the first two generations of your people have passed, your Church would never have been rooted and grounded in the everlasting strength which I believe it now holds, and the strong men you have developed would never have been discovered to you. So it may come out at last that a Providence has been in it all, a Providence apparently unfriendly for many years, but with the final proof that it was a loving Providence in the care of you all the time. Yours will be a very fortunate people as time shall come and different generations shall follow, if those who come after you shall prove as worthy, as true to everything that is right in human life and aspiration, as courageous in the performance of duty, as the strong and fearless men and women who first set up the standard of your Church in Utah and who so loyally and fearlessly upheld it in the first generations of your experience in the Rocky mountains:

While I never was among the American people who are intolerant toward the [page 3:] Mormon Church, being of a liberal and tolerant mind, and having acquaintances with the section of the Mormon Church located in Iowa, made up of as good people as we had in that State, of course I never knew or had opportunity to know fully and distinctly all the facts in regard to the career of your Church and people in Utah and the contiguous western States. It was some ten years ago that in connection with [Republican presidential candidate] Mr. [James G.] Blaine, when we were studying the elements of voters in the United States to try to secure a majority for the political principles in which we believed, I first learned of the magnitude of the Mormon people, the greatness of their development in many States besides Utah, and the large part that they were sure to bear for good or evil in the destiny of this republic. Mr.

Blaine and I were both surprised to see with what far-seeing wisdom the pioneers of your people had looked into the future and had laid the lines along which your descendants were to play a large part in the affairs of this country. Ever after that both of us realized both how unjustly you had been dealt with in the past and what a strong call there was upon the conscience of every lover of his country to endeavor to see that you were dealt with more justly in the future. It was in this way, led by my natural sense of justice and by my knowledge and by my realization of the wisdom necessary to deal with all the composite elements making up the people of our country, and my early recognition of the industry, patience, and good purpose of your people, that I came to take so much interest in your welfare and became so willing to aid in relieving you as much as possible of the wrongs inflicted on you in the past and to secure to you a full share of rights as American citizens in the future.

It was in 1889 that the matter was projected before me so prominently, and at a time when I was in such position as to have some official power in addition to my personal influence, and fortunate enough to be near Mr. Blaine with his almost omnipotent influence, that I took up in zealous manner the effort to serve you to the extent of my ability. It was in this time that Colonel [Isaac] Trumbo, who has proved such a friend to your people as I have never known any people to have, came upon the scene, and gave to Mr. Blaine and to me such a practical and accurate knowledge of your exact situation as to wrongs in the past and rights in the future, that we were enabled thereafter to [page 4:] organize and conduct a contest in your behalf on lines that we knew were absolutely right and as absolutely sure to win for you in the end. Of course, I need not say to you, or to any of your people, how devotedly and wisely Colonel Trumbo over several years has subordinated his own interests in life and made your interests the ambition and aspiration of his every effort, and how with apparently more than human energy he has devoted every day and every thought of his life to your service. It has been almost entirely through his influence, through the genius of his persistence in carrying the story of your wrongs and rights to the door of nearly every influential man in the nation, of his energy in assembling all these influences, and making friends for you wherever there were good hearts to make friends with, that success has finally come to you. I have been much in politics, and in many struggles, I have seen many successful men, gifted with masterful and even peculiar powers in human affairs; but, as Mr. Blaine and I have often talked and discussed, such a character as Colonel Trumbo, with his ability to make friends, his ability to make people listen as to your wrongs and his power to convince them of your rights, and his singular quality of assembling all these forces together, whether represented in the public press, or in the organizations of the different churches, or the more powerful influences of the most powerful corporations, and finally in the seat of supreme power in the United States Congress, has never before appeared on the scene of American politics. It is not in my nature as a devout man and a believer in higher powers, to reject the idea that he has been given for this work even more than the strength of a man. It is refreshing in this age of cynicism and indifference in the world to find friendship of this higher sort sacrificing personal interest and ambition to a good cause and putting the success of that cause above everything else. Equally marked and equally beautiful and worthy of admiration as Colonel Trumbo's persistent and remarkable efforts in your behalf has been the unselfishness of his actions, the subordination of self with no expectation of reward except the great joy of seeing justice brought to you and your people at last. That you and all your people will appreciate this, that you have no confidence too sacred to be given to him, that there is no honor within your control too high to be offered him, that your children after you [page 5:] shall be taught to know the value of his services, I am sure from what I know of the Mormon character will be true.

The story of the struggle of your people, as a people, and the later story of the struggle of your Territory for Statehood, are both so interesting and absorbing that it is hard to confine any analysis of it to anything like the proper limits and space of a letter. But I feel it is due to you, who have been remote from nearly all the phases of these struggles in the eastern States and out of your own Territory, to be told by someone who has known of them and who can make the recital impartial something of the details, to be left in your records in a form that will endure as a part of the history of your Church and people. I take it up here with the attempt to disfranchise your people in Congress in 1889, when a bill was introduced to add this further indignity to the cruelties and wrongs of the Poland Act. It was then that Colonel Trumbo appealed to me for help, feeling that I as a western man, as a man who had tolerance of opinion, and especially as a man who was then in an official position of power, could help him in resisting this further visitation of wrong upon you. He and I craved of Mr. Blaine the use of his far greater power in your protection, and with his help we went before the committee of Congress having this proposition of further wrong before it, and were able to defeat it. If you could have the words, which seemed almost to be the words of inspiration, as they fell from the lips of Mr. Blaine, protesting against this further wrong to you, protesting against such an outrage upon any portion of a free people, asserting that no republic of free men could tolerate such a wrong and live. I am certain that they would be treasured in the affections of your Church and people as being only second in comfort and power to the words of divine speech. I have always regretted that no report was ever made of his appeal to that committee. It came up suddenly, was very informal, no one thought of anything but what Mr. Blaine was saying, and he spoke so deeply from the heart and from the best thoughts that ever arise from the human soul, that his words came almost unconsciously to him and he was never able to repeat them. I asked him afterwards if he could not, and he said that they seemed to come to him as if on wings at a great and critical time, and they had passed away as suddenly and com [page 6:] pletely, and there was left to him only the memory of his indignation at the wrong proposed and of his duty to resist to the highest limit of his power such wrong and encroachment. Of course, your people know something of the courage and loyalty of Mr. Blaine towards you in oppression; but the summit and sublimity of it all was reached when he stood in this small committee room and smote down with the giant strength of his indignant wrath this further attempt in a free government to degrade still further a people already wronged too much. If you but knew the burning words with which he spoke, the spirit with which he spoke, I am sure that the name of Blaine would never pass Mormon lips without the blessing of a prayer following the spoken word or the unspoken thought.

This marked the limit of the high tide against the Mormon people in Congress. Wrong had gone as far as it was possible for it in its malice to go. From that day[,] it receded. Having curbed it in Congress, then it became necessary to spread out the feeling represented by Mr. Blaine over this wide nation and mollify all the great elements into something of the same feeling—nearly all of which, sharing in a prejudice and a hatred which were the more intense because of their ignorance of the facts, were almost implacable at the mere mention of the name of Mormon. Religious intolerance far outruns political intolerance, as you know; and, having checked the highest tide of this feeling in political circles, it then became necessary in a government of the people to go back to the sources of all the powers of Congress and mollify all the great elements toward the final end which has now come. In surveying the field Mr. Blaine, Colonel Trumbo, and myself felt that the next step was to secure, first a larger tolerance in the Republican party, and finally the active friendship of that party in behalf of justice to your people and Statehood for your Territory. It had been the fate of this party, driven forward by the crusade of the churches against your Church, to be in possession of the government and therefore to enact and enforce the laws that public sentiment coerced from Congress in enactment against your people in some of your practices as a church. The first practical step to be taken along this line was to take away from the so-called Liberal party in Utah, which had always been [page 7:] more an engine of injustice and oppression toward you than a representative party of just sentiment, and which had finally become simply a means of persecution and money-making, the apparent sanction of acting in the name of the Republican party of the nation. To do this efficiently it was necessary to dispossess this Utah Liberal party of its membership in the Republican National Committee, and to give admission instead to the Republican party in Utah, and thus to gain entrance of the national party on the local ground, where it could deal in justice and fairness with your people and take up with intelligence the preliminaries of the final settlement which has now come in fairness to you. To those of you who were remote and who know little of the national prejudice and of the difficulty of assembling the support of every State in a National Committee, this may have seemed a trivial matter. I happened to be Chairman of the Republican National Committee at the time, and even I, who knew much of this prejudice, was surprised to find how obstinately most of the members of the Committee held to the old-time prejudice and how timid nearly all of them were as against the reproaches of their people for rejecting the Liberal party in Utah and admitting to membership in the National Committee a party that proposed tolerance and fair play to the Mormons the same as all other Americans. It took a year of patient effort, of direct personal appeal to almost every member of the National Committee, and more than that of systematic work to reach the influences back of these men personally, to give them the courage to act along the line that we proposed. It happened that the meeting of the National Committee where Utah for the first time was admitted to fair-play representation in any National Committee was held in Washington, where all the allied influences against your people had their representatives on the ground for action. These influences stormed at the Committee, frightened away all but the most resolute men, and made it extremely difficult to carry the matter successfully through the Committee. But it was finally done, and when it was done the Liberal party of Utah was <u>for the first time</u> cut off from connection with the supreme sources of national power. Colonel Trumbo may sometime when he is with you, in the confidence that exists between you and in the great affection in which he holds you, give you many of the details of that first struggle, [page 8:] which may seem trivial now but which was the first necessary step toward success at all.

In thus helping to strike down the Liberal party by the hand of the official national power of the Republican party, I gave assurance to almost every Republican of influence and prominence in the nation, and to everyone whose help I finally succeeded in gaining, that despite of the past when Republicanism and Mormonism were made to stand as deadly elements of opposition, the future would be one of fair play and one in which your people would act on the lines of the future and not of the past. There was the natural fear, of course, after the Republican party had enacted and enforced the severe laws against Utah, that there would be treasured up in the hearts of your people the natural feelings of enmity and revenge common to human nature. Utilizing all the facts Colonel Trumbo had given me, and nearly always having him with me to bear testimony to what I was saying and to answer every question that might be asked, I succeeded in convincing enough Republican leaders to control the majority of the party that the future Mormons, all of them instilled with patriotism and love of country, all of them believing in protection to American interests and industries, and all of them animated by the common purpose of all Americans to serve the republic in its government of freedom faithfully, would be found and indeed would be forced by their own destiny as a people to gravitate toward the underlying principles of Republicanism and Americanism. The question was a mighty one, and nearly every prominent man to whom I talked when I revealed to him the fact that this was not merely a Utah question but that the Mormon people were spread through the valleys of eight or ten western States, and that sooner or later they would hold the balance of power in the election of every Senator and of every electoral vote for President in these States, was ap[p]alled at the fact and afraid to trust to the forbearance of a people who had been so severely dealt with as a people by the Republican party. I mention these things, which were the foundations on which I laid our efforts to change the Republican party from being a party of opposition to your people to one of friendship and support, that you may know how deeply the foundations have been laid and that you may understand the expectation and confidence with which the Republican party has come up so bravely at last to the line of doing justice [page 9:] toward you all.

After this step in the National Committee, the next important chapter was to overcome the prejudice existing with President Harrison and the influences almost universally exerted upon him, a man of peculiar religious prejudices and particularly open to the appeals of the more intolerant Churches, and induce him to follow out the permission of the law and the demands of justice and issue amnesty to all your people. This was not dealing with one man, as may appear on the surface. If it had been, and that man of the tenacious and obstinate character of this President, even that would have been a great struggle. But we had to go back of him, and reach all the more intolerant Churches, all the church papers, and lay a mollifying hand upon them and their prejudices, and take upon our lips the words of Christian peace and gospel and appeal to them that, even granting all they said against your people, there was everything in the teaching of the Christian religion, when you had turned away from all things to which they objected, had conformed to the law, and had as a Church under the revelation of the higher power to which you conformed put away all these things, they should take you by the hand even according to their own teaching and make you welcome with them and to equal rights in the republic. We had to see and bring influence to bear on all the church papers; we had to see the bishops and controlling men in all the strong Churches, especially the Catholic and the Methodist. The Catholic, it is only just to say, was more inclined to the new rule of fair play to you, while the Methodist Church was most tenaciously against it. I was sent by the National Committee during the campaign of 1892 to renew the talk I had already had at several times with the President in appealing to him to issue the proclamation of amnesty. He said that amnesty meant so much that for him to issue it was to make an end of all the contest, that if it were done at all it should be an amnesty complete and final and reaching all people who had come under the offense of the law, and that to do this during a campaign, when he was a candidate for reelection, would be considered by the prejudiced people among the Churches as an act influenced more by his needs and ambition as a candidate than by his sense of justice and duty as a President. He said that he feared all the church papers would oppose the act and condemn the pro [page 10:] clamation, and he required that I should have all the editors of these papers seen, and that I should test all the sources of power among the leading religious denominations. When you realize how many there are of these papers and how numerous are the sources of religious power and authority, you can imagine something of the task that he laid upon me. It was then that Colonel Trumbo came on to help in this work, and we were fortunate enough also to have the benefit of the wise counsel and suggestion of President [George Q.] Cannon and [Nauvoo Legion] General [Hiram B.] Clawson, who about this time came to New York and remained several weeks, a fact which in itself was peculiarly fortunate and almost providential in the line of success to our efforts. Difficult as this work was, we took it up, employing the help of many people, and finally secured a favorable expression from all the church papers in favor of showing confidence toward your people in their changed attitudes, and quite a favorable expression from leading church authorities in favor of the President's immediate and favorable action. The amnesty therefore would have been issued in October except for the affliction that fell upon the President in the illness and final death of his wife, when to the credit of his heart be it said everything else, even the campaign for his reelection, was made subordinate to his duties toward his dying wife. Influences counter to our wishes intruded on this effort from Mr. [Stephen] Elkins, then Secretary of War, and for some strange reason from General [Benjamin] Tracy, then Secretary of the Navy, the latter being influenced, I think, through some unrelenting leading men in his Church, the Presbyterian. Mr. Elkins I think wanted to reach some understanding with the authorities of your Church in behalf of some friends and interests he has in New Mexico. As you know, the amnesty was finally issued after the election, and this act of a Republican President following the sanction and permission of the laws of a Republican Congress put great power in our hands to influence all Republican elements in the contest to follow.

Then followed the contest for Statehood, in the winter of 1892–3. In preparing for this we reached out and with systematic effort organized into friendly influences still more all the powerful elements of every State, by reaching the State Committees of our party, getting them in active line of friendship in their influence on Congress, together with the members for each State of the National Committee. We also kept up through the summer of 1892 our active efforts in mollifying all the strong ele [page 11:] ments of the party and of the Churches, and especially of the newspapers, the latter being the power that men in Congress fear more than any other, for they depend on their home papers to keep them right before their people and in public favor. I should not omit to state somewhere in this letter, and here may do as well, the constant efforts of Colonel Trumbo while all these things were going on, and his success in assembling strong influences to accomplish it, in securing favorable action toward your people and Church in the Department of Justice and the other Departments here where confiscation of property and other outrages had been perpetrated or attempted. One of these was the debts imposed by the Poland Act, amounting to nearly a million of dollars, which he was thus able to save you from. Of course, these things you know as well as I; only I have felt that reference should be made to them in this letter, which perhaps, with the paper accompanying it, will be the most detailed statement put into written form of the struggles of your people to emerge from the outrages of Congressional law, to escape penalties laid upon you with so much injustice, and the final struggle of the Territory into Statehood. Of course, I commit this letter to such purpose through you in the confidence that grows up between men who heart to heart have made a struggle against the mightiest of opposition in a common desire for success. I deal frankly with men, revealing to you friends who are worthy of your remembrance and gratitude and also under a sense of duty mentioning those who failed in the time of your need to support you with friendship and met you with enmity and opposition instead. I do not believe in treasuring up even a sense of wrong, nor nursing resentment, nor entailing revenge. Human nature is too weak, the grave too near, the necessity for forgiveness too apparent, for these things to be. They only dwarf those who entertain and exercise them, and make them appear in something of competition and likeness with those from whose meanness they have suffered. But I do believe that every man and every people should know and should remember through time and generation the difference between those who win friends and those who win enemies.

There are some facts in connection with the struggle here in the winter of 1892–3 that should be made known to you in the deep confidence of this letter, and for [page 12:] you to use your judgment in making known to others in authority with you, and the actual facts of friendship and enmity. I very much coveted and so did Colonel Trumbo the admission of Utah to Statehood through a Republican Congress. Through our system of effort, through the assembling of influences reaching into every State of the Union and almost every neighborhood, reaching into the Churches, into business elements and corporations, we succeeded in getting the bill through the House and in gaining practically a unanimous vote in the Senate, and were defeated only by the persistence of the Chairman of the Territorial Committee, who, finding himself finally almost if not entirely alone in his Committee in opposition to Utah, appealed to that thing called courtesy in the Senate in order to defeat what had become practically the unanimous desire of the Senate, and appeal in which he went so fare [sic] as to threaten to resign as Chairman if the majority of the Committee should overrule him and favorably report the bill. We have never fully ascertained, although we are satisfied that we know, the influences that acted upon him. They came from Utah, from the Liberal party, whose leaders never abated any of their efforts to defeat our endeavors, and who I am satisfied have never relinquished their secret opposition up to the present hour. As you have already been informed, we went so far and came so near success that through Senator Allison, who was Chairman of the Committee on Appropriations and who has been, I may say here, one of our most faithful and powerful friends throughout the contest, as to succeed in getting the gate open on the floor for Utah to be called in from the Committee at two different times in the Senate during the absence of Mr. Platt. Colonel Trumbo and I had arranged with Senator Allison in his committee room to go down and give the floor to Senator Carey. Each time the Senator left us he said, "When I come back I will bring you the news that Utah is a State." He did get the chance, but for some reason Senator Carey did not get in in time and when the gap was opened other men jumped in and utilized the opportunity. I have studied over this matter and investigated it a great deal, and I am satisfied finally that Senator Carey erred in these matters only from lack of quickness of action. He is a loyal man, and I am now satisfied has intended to be true to your people, and has failed only where celerity of movement, quickness of brain and a lateness of attention were [page 13:] needed. We are pretty well satisfied now, after a whole year of investigation, that the influences that acted upon Senator [Orville] Platt [R–Connecticut] to hold him in opposition, even after we had secured every Church and political element who had acted with him before to appeal to him to be favorable then, came from Utah, from [*Salt Lake Tribune* co-owner] [Patrick] Lannan, [former Utah Commissioner] [Arthur] Thomas, and [*Tribune* co-owner] [Charles] Goodwin, and that it was secretly exerted through Senator [Fred] Dubois of Idaho. We shall finally discover all the facts, for it is well enough to know even after a campaign has been fought, in guarding against similar occurrences in the future, all the facts in regard to treachery as well as fidelity. I am fully satisfied that Utah would have been admitted by the Republican Congress in February of 1893, except for the influence exerted upon Senator Platt, who alone defeated it then through Senator Dubois. This impression has been confirmed by the indifference and lack of earnestness of the same Senator in the contest of this winter and spring. There can be no possible reason to excuse Senator Dubois against this act of [in]justice toward Utah and its people. He had lived in a Territory where the wrongs against the people were merely a tithe of those against your people, and had suffered from them and knew what they were. He had also received, even after he had been your open and violent enemy, the strange and disarming thing of forgiveness and magnanimity and support. He was bound by all reasons of honor that govern in the hearts of good men to forget a past where your people had never wronged him, and after you had forgiven and forgotten it to become a faithful friend. We have means by which we shall finally ascertain the exact truths in regard to his action and his certain attitude. Meantime I would not wish you and your people to go so far as to share my positive impression that he was the successful enemy against you last year, and that he has been, if not an active enemy this year, at least an indifferent friend. You are making history, and with that high sense of justice which animates all your actions as a Church and a people you will insist upon knowing the whole truth before expressing judgment. We shall be able within a year to give you these facts.

This winter and summer Senator Platt proved to be one of our best friends, wisest counsellers, and most potential influences.

I should have stated earlier in this communication more of the names of the men [page 14:] among the leaders in the Republican party who early identified themselves with this movement and have as constantly served in it loyally ever since. Among the most prominent I may mention Senator [Matthew S.] Quay [R–Pennsylvania], who until we took the matter up with him and caused him to see the truth was amongst your most persistent opponents. For two years, however, he has used all his great power and influence in your behalf. Ex-Senator Thomas C. Platt of New York, who is in many respects the most powerful man in the Republican party and who wields an unusual power in the business elements of the country, was among the earliest, and has not only served with friendship and influence but helped the Colonel and me in raising the means necessary to pay the expenses of the many difficult works and systems we had to carry out—works which required the employment of very many people, all for purely honorable purposes and yet for purposes which required personal visits to every considerable community in the nation. Mr. [Joseph] Manley, of the National Committee, Mr.

[Samuel] Fessenden of Connecticut, Mr. [Garrett] Hobart of New Jersey, all also of the National Committee and among its most powerful members[;] Mr. [Henry] Payne, the Wisconsin member of the Committee[;] Mr. [Richard] Kerens, the Missouri member[;] Mr. L[eigh] S. J. Hunt of the State of Washington, who brought into line nearly all the elements of that portion of the country[;] Secretary [of Agriculture] [Jeremiah] Rusk, now dead, who was always active and always friendly[;] Archbishop [John] Ireland of St. Paul, of the Catholic Church[;] Cardinal [James] Gibbons of Baltimore[;] Ex-Governor [Henry] Warmoth of Louisiana, who has helped us very greatly in dealing with Southern elements[;] [manufacturer] Mr. George M. Pullman, and Mr. [John] Runnells, his General Counsel, who helped us very much with the large business elements and corporations[;] Hon. [industrialist] B[enjamin] F. Jones of Pittsburgh, Ex-Chairman of the National Committee[;] [Union Army] General Russell A. Alger of Michigan, who has been exceedingly active among great corporations and in church circles as well as political[;] Governor [William] McKinley and Ex-Governor [Joseph] Foraker of Ohio, who have proved friendly at all times and active in their friendship[;] William A. Russell of Boston, one of the wealthiest men in New England, who has been both active in help and liberal in means and has drawn into it in help many of the strongest and wealthiest men of New England[;] Hon. F[rancis] W. Palmer, late Public Printer in Washington, [D.C.][,] who has served us with peculiar ability and fidelity[;] Hon. [businessman] Thomas Lowry of Minnesota[;] and many others I might name and perhaps ought to name, have been as devoted friends as any [page 15:] people ever had. These are elements, as you will notice, outside of Congress. In Congress we had at the start the powerful help of Senator [William] Allison [R–Iowa], who was then the most influential Republican in the United States Senate, and Speaker [Thomas] Reed [R–Maine] of the House, these two men furnishing out the most of the power we have utilized on the Republican side in Congress. When Congress was Republican these were our leaders and main helpers.

This brings us down to the expiration of the Republican Congress on the 4th of March, It is well enough to express again, with sufficient emphasis to make it endure, that it was in the heart and intention of that Republican Congress to make Utah a State. Ninety-nine out of every hundred of the Republicans in Congress favored this, the Republican President desired it, the Republicans in the House did their part towards it, the Republicans in the Senate stood ready to do it, and the whole gracious act of Republican intention was defeated only by the strange influence exerted upon the Republican Chairman of the Senate Territorial Committee, an influence exerted from your enemies in Utah in some strange and secret and yet sufficient manner. It is well enough, and I think fair enough, that you and all your people should understand that the Republican party as a party in Congress and in executive power desired and intended to give you Statehood. It was only through that strange thing and its stranger power called courtesy in the Senate that your disappearing enemies in Utah were able through the exercise of peculiar power over one Senator holding a place of peculiar advantage, that this Republican intention was defeated. Let me say here clearly and plainly that this influence, whatever it was, was not one of corrupt character, for no man ever lived who was further above corrupt things than Senator Platt. In some way I think this malign influence in Utah exercised through some Republican Senators from that region an influence on Senator Platt, making him believe that it was necessary to defeat Statehood and that the sole reliance for this necessity was on him.

This brings us to March, 1893. During the summer of '93 we kept in constant motion all the influences through the organizations of friends we had perfected in every State in the Union, not only to hold the turning tide toward friendship for you among all the controlling elements of the nation, but if possible to increase this feeling into friendship. We had able and strong and controlling friends at every influential church gathering, all the Methodist conferences, and all the synods and associations of the dif [page 16:] ferent Churches held during the summer. All the time we had felt that the coercion of church sentiment over men in Congress was the thing to be feared, for religious intolerance is always last to release its grasp. We succeeded well and increased our chances among these controlling elements during the summer; and this brings us to the assembling of the Democratic Congress in December. During the extra session in the summer, called by the President to meet the financial situation, our question played no part. And when Congress met in December, Democratic in both branches, with a Democratic President, our situation had become irritated against us with the Democrats by the results of the various State elections held in that year, including the one in Utah, where your people had elected a Republican Legislature. Nothing during the whole time in which I had been engaged in this movement has made the difficulty of it so plain as when it was demonstrated that we had to go to a Democratic Congress, with the traditional intolerance of the Democratic party against Republican communities and Republican interests, and ask it to make a State of a Republican Territory. [blank half page]

[page 17:] This danger was heightened by the fact that the Democrats held their power in the Senate by a slight majority, a majority sure to be decreased in some of the States electing Senators this year and in especial peril against the probability of Republicanism when Utah is admitted. It was our fortune and salvation in this dilemma that we had been able in five years of constant effort to gain the friendship of the Republican party generally, and to have it mobilized in such hearty manner that it was willing to play any part of honor necessary to success. But it became necessary, of course, not only to gain Democratic support for Utah, which had gone Republican, but to make the Republican friendship and support as unobjectionable to the Democrats as possible and as unobtrusive as possible. The Democratic party is wise always in its generation. They were not deceived as to the Republican Legislature in Utah, nor could they be deceived, with the Wilson Bill taking the profit of protection from everything raised on Utah ground or from under Utah ground, of the tendency its people would naturally have in politics hereafter. There is no doubt that it was the settled

Democratic program in December not to admit Utah, but it is also just as certain that as a party it intended to shirk the responsibility for this and by tactics leave the responsibility on the Republicans. It was then that the wisdom of our organized Republican strength was made apparent. The Utah bill was brought into the House in December from the Democratic Committee, not with the intention of passing it, but with the expectation and settled belief that it could be used in tactics to Democratic advantage on the confident faith that the Republicans would oppose and filibuster against it. It was brought in with the evident intention to shut out and occupy the time desired by Republicans to defeat other Democratic measures. However, when it did come this expectation was disappointed. The Republicans by following a splendid strategy under the leadership of Mr. Reed politely informed the confident Democracy that instead of opposing Utah or filibustering against it they were friendly to the people of Utah and in favor of admitting the Territory to Statehood. The Democrats had gone too far, they could not recede, and therefore the bill passed—another strange evidence in this unanimity of both political powers that something higher than [page 18:] human power and wisdom has been in this matter for its guidance from the first. No one could have believed that in the same House where for so many years the name of Utah and the word Mormon had been used to excite bitter contests, and where the Democrats always stood to challenge the Republicans for their course towards Utah, the time had come when both parties would act together as one man to admit it as a State. There is a blessing in this for the State and its people, I am sure. Before leaving the question of its passage in the House, I should say that in addition to Mr. Reed, whose powerful friendship was so valuable, we had also the benefit of the almost equally powerful influence of Mr. [Julius] Burrows of Michigan, Mr. [Jonathan] Dolliver of Iowa, Mr. [Warren] Hooker of New York, Mr. Babcock of Wisconsin, Messrs. [William] Hepburn, [John] Hull, and [John] Lacey, of Iowa, and indeed of every one of the stronger men among the Republican leaders. The only speeches made in opposition were by Mr. [Elijah] Morse, Republican, the stove-polish [manufacturing] man of Massachusetts whose [uninformed] opposition was a help, and [Michael] Harter, Democrat, of Ohio, whose intolerance of speech simply emphasized the need for national sense and action.

The bill therefore went from the House to the Senate bearing the invincible approval of unanimous passage. Here the Democrats were placed in a dilemma. They still professed to hold in cordial degree the same friendship that they undoubtedly had toward Utah and its people in previous years, notably such men as Senator [Charles] Faulkner of West Virginia, Senator [George] Vest of Missouri, and Senator [Richard] Coke of Texas. They assured us, since they saw no chance of escaping and since they plainly saw they could not defeat Utah without putting it on the ground of objection to the Mormons and without thereby forfeiting the friendship of the Mormon balance of power in several States, that they would pass it and give you Statehood for the holidays. But they did not mean it. They intended to hide it away in the Committee, to keep it in the background, claiming that they were still interested in it but that the absorbing question of the tariff bill had relegated that and everything else of comparatively minor importance to the rear. Thus 1893 was concluded and 1894 began. We saw very plainly that unless we could use in some way the passing chances of the current contests in the Senate and be of service to one faction in the Democratic party as against the other, we could not win. For it was both the party in [page 19:] tention and interest not to admit to Statehood a Territory whose two Senators would be Republican and change the balance of power in the Senate. In addition to this, some of the most powerful men in the Senate were opposed personally to the admission of Utah or any other western States. I should have said further back in this letter that all the time one of the most powerful elements we have had to contend against was the eastern prejudice against the admission of any more western States, and especially of any more silver States. The gold people of the East realize the danger to them of more power going to the West and to the silver States. We have had constantly to combat this influence, especially amongst all New

England Members of Congress, both House and Senate, and all the New York Members and all the Pennsylvania[ns]. Senator [David] Hill of New York, the most powerful Democrat in the Senate, came here in deadly hostility to the admission of Utah or any more western States, and sought a place on the Territorial Committee in order to make his opposition effective and in order more securely to guard the East against what they considered the danger of the admission of more silver States and Senators. In furtherance of this program of Senator Hill's he also had himself placed upon the subcommittee of the Territorial Committee, together with Chairman Faulkner and Senator Platt, Faulkner a former undoubted friend but changed into secret opposition by the secret orders of his party, and the latter the longtime enemy of Utah who the Democrats supposed would continue that enmity and who could be used as a public scapegoat for the secret Democratic opposition. Senator Gorman, the most influential Democratic member of the Senate and the guardian of the party's interest, was also actuated by this fear and belief that Utah would be Republican, and also by the eastern prejudice against western or silver States. We found also as events developed not only this prejudice amongst the eastern or gold States, but also a still more dangerous prejudice in the southern States against the admission of any more western Territories on the ground that they would become northern States and therefore help to decrease the power of the South. Thus we had the dangerous opposition of the mercenary interests of all the eastern States and of the political ambition of all the southern States, which, as you know, are so covetous of power for the South in the government. In the face of the develop [page 20:] ment of these powerful adverse influences, supplementing the plain interest of the Democratic party not to admit a Republican Territory, our cause in January seemed to nearly everybody to be hopeless, and it was in this time that the indomitable will and fertile resources of Colonel Trumbo came forward for your salvation. He did not seem to feel that anything could defeat us. He seemed driven on by some higher power than his own, and he held resolutely to this course and said we must not slacken our efforts a single minute or keep from increasing our chances a single hour. In this emergency the contest over Cleveland's appointments to the Supreme Bench of the United States came up most opportunely. Our most powerful enemies, Senators Hill and Gorman, those who would never have consented to the admission of Utah by this Congress, found their position in politics imperiled so gravely as to threaten the extinction of their public lives. Aggrieved at the President, and finding him unwilling to act in their interest or even to grant them their conceded rights as Senators in their own States and determined to ignore them in all the national politics of their party, they found themselves face to face with a struggle for self preservation, and found that they had to oppose and defeat the President in order to maintain their leadership in the party. No Democratic leader in the Senate had ever before been able to defeat a Democratic President. These men set up to accomplish this undertaking. It was impossible for them to do it without Republican help. For any Democratic Senator to vote against the President's appointment of a Supreme Judge was to exile himself from the favor of the White House and to imperil his chances of party approval in his own State. Consequently Hill and Gorman could find but six Democrats ready to take the risks with them. To defeat the nominations of the Judges they had to have five or six times as many Republicans as they could muster Democrats. This gave us our opportunity. We were able through the powerful help of Senators Allison, Quay, Cameron and others to give to them what they were not able to gain for themselves. In this matter Senator Carey performed especially valuable service, and in your interest directly opposed some of his most powerful eastern friends and no doubt alienated friendships which were exceedingly valuable to him. This should be remembered. We were able to organize a sufficient number of votes [page 21:] to defeat the nomination of Mr. [William] Hornblower [to the Supreme Court]. Before doing so we secured the pledges of honor of [Senators] [Arthur] Gorman [D–Maryland] and Mr. [David] Hill [D–New York] that they would favor the admission of Utah. But for this opportunity we should have stood no show whatever, despite of all the powerful influences we had assembled, to pass Utah into

Statehood in this Congress. On the second fight, over the nomination of [Wheeler] Peckham, these gentlemen again appealed to us and we again organized a line and gave them success. This increased their gratitude. Mr. Hill from the first day changed about and has been our active, willing friend at any call on our part and at every opportunity he could see himself to serve us. Mr. Gorman did not come so promptly up to the fulfilment of his promise and kept wishing to postpone fulfilment until after the tariff bill. Indeed, it is certain that he went so far with his power as Chairman of the Caucus Committee of the Senate, and therefore the dictator of his party in the Senate, to instruct Senator Faulkner, Chairman of the Territorial Committee, to keep the bill in that Committee and out of the Senate. Meantime we had been organizing our forces, and found a splendid ally in Senator [Stephen] White of California, who has been from the first everything as loyal and helpful and vigilant in your interest as he could have been if he had been a citizen of Utah and one of your own people. He has had not only this friendship but he is a man of remarkable resources, of experience in legislation, of determination in purpose, and peculiar facility for such work. He had rendered you a service your people can never fully repay. While waiting on Senator Faulkner's movements, who kept delaying even a meeting of the Committee to consider Utah and who kept going to West Virginia on days that had been appointed for that purpose, and who employed every sort of tactics to keep us defeated and yet in a good humor, we kept strengthening our lines in the Senate and also in the Committee. After they exhausted all their excuses for the non-action of the Committee they began to lay the whole blame on Senator Platt, who was the principal Republican on the Committee. Senator Platt had still retained his opposition up to this time, despite of our bringing to bear upon him the united influence of the party and many powerful influences in New England and his own State. Finally he resented the idea of being made responsible for what was in reality the secret Democratic program of non-action, [page 22:] and he also found that he could not help to discriminate against Utah because it was a western State without alienating from the support of the protectionists in the Senate such western men as Senator [William] Stewart [R–Nevada] and some others. He was too manly to bear off the sins of the secret Democratic purpose, and was too mindful of the interests of the East to help break the protection line or let any Republican Senator vote for the Wilson or free-trade bill. Finally he came out flat-footed, declared himself for Utah's admission, and wrote Senator Faulkner a letter that he was in favor of admission and that as a member of the sub-committee of the Territorial Committee for Utah he was ready to report favorably. This broke the line, and with Senators White, Hill and Call, Democratic members of the Committee, favorable, and under the leadership of Se[na]tor Hansbrough, a Republican member of the Committee whose services I should have mentioned earlier, we were able to stampede a favorable report from the Committee to the Senate. This surprised the Democratic line[,] again by tactics[,] the same as we had [been] surprised [by] it[,] by the passage of the bill in the House. After it was out of the Committee and on the calendar of the Senate it was not longer possible for the Democrats to defeat it except by open opposition. I should have said[,] at the outset of our program in the Senate we found in Senator Hansbrough of North Dakota as valuable and helpful a friend as we have found any place in this contest. In conjunction with Senator Allison, who as an older Senator had that acquired power which is peculiar to the Senate, and acting on his suggestions, he has been our active and working friend and reliance in the Senate. A member of the Committee, a western man who had lived in California and other western States, exceedingly popular in manner and influential and respected by all who know him, he [h]as labored day by day and constantly in our behalf, not only in the Senate and in the Committee, but coming almost every night to our rooms to help lay our plans and programs. Many of the most valuable suggestions have come from him in making the fight. I want you and your people to know that you never can owe more to any man outside of your own people than to Senator Hansbrough. He is a young man, in his first term in the Senate, but sure to be returned and to become one of the most powerful members of this exalted body, so that his friendship in the future will be as valuable as it has [page 23:] been in the past.

The contest in the Senate has been one of such detail, changing every day and frequently every hour in such strange manner, that it is impossible for me to recite it to you with anything like fidelity here. Suffice it to say that it has been such a peculiar situation that we have never been able to leave the ground. Colonel Trumbo and I have remained here since November and devoted ourselves entirely to an alert, vigilant, constant watchfulness of the situation, ready to detect danger at the first moment or to utilize an advantage at every opportunity. We have had to enter into nearly every contest[,] unknown to the public[,] to serve this or that friend or to gain the friendship of this or that element. We have built up our work as a stonemason a wall, stone by stone, laying our hopes in solid mortar and rearing a solid structure on which we felt, despite of the opinion of nearly everybody else and indeed of all the experienced men in Congress, that we should win at last. We have had in Senators Allison and Hansbrough and in other Senators in less degree, constant watchfulness and service. On the Democratic side Senators White and Hill have been supreme in help. It has taken the wisdom of many men to win this difficult fight. Among others I should mention that Mr. R. C. Kerens, whom I have already mentioned, member of the National Committee from Missouri, has come on and spent weeks of his time in our service. He is a friend to remember, for he has been both useful and faithful. I wish I might give you too the names of all our faithful friends. Indeed, you can take the Republican roll call, and I may say of it that two thirds of the names represent loyal and active friends and the other third men who have been brought to friendship through influence and conscience. The same may be said of the mass of the Democratic Senators, who when the situation had to be faced[,] faced it on the side of manliness and justice and voted on the right side despite of their party's interest and their own secret party desire to keep the Territory out because it was Republican.

There is another and more delicate matter, which I have confided to General Clawson, who has been here with us and whose counsel and vigilance have been in the highest degree valuable, and whose courage and cheerfulness have furnished strength and confidence to both of us; and he will confide it to you. These means, used for [page 24:] purely honorable purposes and yet for necessary things, were raised entirely from Republican sources because of friendship for your Territory and your people and because of confident faith that the Territory was to be identified with Republican policies and ambitions. This help has come freely, has been used wisely, and without it success could not possibly have been achieved. It has been used with as much honor and to as good results as conscience could suggest or honesty require.

In closing this letter, which is so long that I fear it may weary you but yet which I could not make shorter and which indeed I might have made longer under my sense of fidelity to all the friends we have found, I am constrained by such a sense of appreciation as I have never been called upon to feel before, to refer again to the strangely loyal and successful and splendid service which over long years and in the face of every obstacle and against impediments which would have dismayed any other man I have ever known, Colonel Trumbo has served you and your people. It has been beautiful to me to see such a friendship possible in the human heart. His ambition for your people, his determination to lift them up out of wrong into victory, to compensate them for the injustice they have suffered, to make them known to all the American people for their honesty of character and their purity of good intentions, and the dedication of his life to the end of making the Mormon name as honorable and as accepted in honor in the sight of every high minded American, have renewed my faith in human nature. It has inspired my own heart to see how he has been actuated also by loving friendship and devotion to you. No son whom I have ever known could be more loyal, and no son I have ever known has served a father as well as he has served you. It has been, as he has constantly said to me, not only his ambition to accomplish this desired vindication for your people, but also to accomplish it in your time and under your Presidency, while you were still the shepherd of your people and the hope of all our hearts.

Whatever appreciation you shall show to him, whatever honor you may offer to him, it will be deserved. In addition to the gratitude you shall forever owe him, I feel it as a sense of duty to you as well as to myself, and to the pledges I have everywhere made, to say that I think he should be sent on your own motion as one of the men [page 25:] to represent you in the United States Senate. No other man could possibly represent you to your benefit and to your vindication as he can. No dozen men nor any hundred men among you are as well known as he is to the powerful and controlling men not only in Congress in this later time, but throughout the country. You know, and this is realized probably more by President Cannon than any other member of your people, that experience and acquaintance are necessary in a Congressman or Senator to serve his people fully and faithfully. If Colonel Trumbo had been a member of the Senate ten years he could not have gained more acquaintance and friendship to your advantage than he has gained now. Universally the people of the country and the people in Congress look to him as representative of Utah. This fact of itself is sufficient for my position. The friendships he has formed, the acquaintance he has gained with the most powerful elements of the country, will all be in your service. Besides, no one else will ever know and therefore no one else could ever redeem as he can, the thousands and thousands of obligations that we have incurred in this long contest in your behalf. He knows many things that none of you will ever know, and yet things that a people or a State can no more afford to forget or fail to fulfill than any man of honor. I feel my own honor involved in the representation of the State of Utah in Congress. This whole matter has been on my conscience as nothing in my public life has ever been. I was the first to take up in detail the position taken by Mr. Blaine, and the first to carry it to the attention of the Republican leaders in detail, and the first to organize and assemble all the party influences in your behalf. Very much of the action taken by others has been taken on my assurance of honor that I was not being misled, that yours were a people in whom faith could safely be placed, and that your destiny as a people and a State ran in the same grooves with Republican policies, Republican patriotism and Republican interest.

I shall feel that I am on the bond, that my honor stands for guaranty, and therefore that I am at liberty, and indeed constrained by the highest sense of duty that can actuate an honorable man, to make known to you the obligations which rest upon you in these sacred regards.

I ought to say also, and will say in brief, that we have carried in parallel with our contest for Statehood the material interests of Utah, that we have never forgotten the industrial and social ambitions of your people, that we have brought to the [page 26:] attention of everybody with whom we have come in contact the empire of natural wealth and resources and industrial possibilities in your borders, and your ambition as a people and a Church to develop a community which will be an example of American intelligence and merit and conservative of the highest average good to every citizen, and always regardful of all true interests of the republic. The railroad enterprise has been in some degree a backbone in our endeavors. This enterprise can be carried forward and can be made the means not only of fulfilling many obligations that we have incurred to many prominent men whose help has been vital, but also of gaining to your State their personal interest and valuable friendship. It is the destiny of your State to parallel the career of the most prosperous States in the Union, prosperous in a material sense and ranking highest in the noblest senses. Since I have become identified in sympathy with your people and your ambition[,] the possibilities of Utah have constantly grown upon me, and I shall find much of my future life[,] I am sure[,] involved with your people and your ambitions. Here occurs to me something I ought to have said earlier, and that is that in securing the help of many of the most powerful elements which have come to our assistance I have not only given assurance that there will be no cause for dissatisfaction with the men who shall come to represent the State of Utah in Congress, but that the elements of discord in your Territory will be pacified or removed. I know it is in your ambition as a people to make your ways by peaceful methods, and this is the high duty of all leaders of men and of all associations of Christian people. The arch enemy of your Territory and your people has been a newspaper, ably edited, almost satanic in its ingenuity for mischief, relentless and cruel, and ever sure to remain an element of harm and injury if left to its present control. I have given the assurance that this will be changed, and I have done this confident in the action I represented faithfully[,] the wisdom and fidelity of your intentions. I think this property should be purchased, and I have pledged that it shall be representative of Republican policies, and I am willing to take it up in connection with such people as you may assign and help to organize it or do anything in the matter which the common interest may suggest or your people desire. The necessity for control of this engine of good or [page 27:] evil is heightened by the fact that such people after defeat are capable of nothing but bitterness and desire for revenge. While it can never control again, it can always make mischief, it can always be a subject of annoyance and an element of discontent. There ought to be no trouble in securing it, for the men who control it are actuated only by mercenary interests and therefore are open to negotiation and arrangement.

There is another suggestion that I feel that I ought to make to you in view of correcting evil impressions in regard to Mormonism and its people in all that wider world outside of Utah, and that is that either in Chicago or New York, and in both would be better still, should you in some way secure the friendship of an influent[ia]l newspaper in each of the great political parties of the country. To me, while I have been in five or six years canvassing this subject with the people of every State in the Union and with people of all shades of opinion and degrees of intelligence, it has been simply astonishing that such dense ignorance as well as such malicious prejudice exists everywhere in regard to the real fiber and actual character and purpose of your people. We have been exceedingly fortunate in our general arrangements and in our effort to systematize and mobilize all the strong and controlling elements in your favor, in reaching the influential newspapers of the political parties, as well as of the Churches. After this I fear many of these publications will naturally lapse into the old-time feeling, and offer nothing by way of resistance to the prevailing prejudice against you, nor by way of enlightenment of the public in regard to your actual merits and ambitions as a community and a people. Undoubtedly the plowing that we have done in every influential community of the nation will yield good things to you constantly hereafter; but it is very important in my judgment that you have in one or both of the great commercial centers of the country such friendship on the part of one or two strong newspapers as will at all times, without appearing to be special pleaders for or special champions of you, defend you against false accusation, and gradually give to all the American people the actual facts in regard to the Mormon Church and its good purposes, to the Mormon people with their refinement and education, their love of gentle things in life, their artistic development, their ambition to rear their children and their State in all the [page 28:] finer things of life, and their aspiration indeed to make themselves fully the equal of any American in every test and accomplishment of civilization and refinement, as well as of Christianity. I shall find it my pleasure, as I have already done in large measure, to keep supplying to the magazines, to the houses printing syndicate letters, and all other diffusive agents, such information as will tend to correct the false impressions existing in this country in regard to the degree of intelligence and the measures of ambition of our your people. In the magazines you will have a hearing that will be international as well, and along these high lines of publications read by all the more intelligent people of the world constant effort to render to you all actual justice on your merits will be advisable. As I have before suggested, I think, in a letter to President Cannon, a book written in comprehensive manner by someone having the historical quality of analysis and the judicial quality of fairness and some one not a Mormon, ought to be written and printed, giving to the world the facts as to the Mormons of today and what they are and aim to be in every feature and respect.

In reading over my letter after having progressed this far, I notice that I have omitted any mention, in the hurry of writing, of the one man who through the long period of your years of trial has stood by you more faithfully than any other public man outside of your own people. I refer to Senator [Henry] Teller of Colorado, who has been a tower of strength to you in all the crises of your career, and who has stood in the Senate and acted throughout the nation whenever called upon to do so with all his power in your sufficient defense. No public man of today stands higher in the respect of the American people than Senator Teller, and his record for sincerity, his approved statesmanship, which has stood the test of manly contests, have all been of wonderful and saving help to you in the last year, and especially in these nervous months of the contest before the present Democratic Congress. I need not multiply to you, however, any words of commendation of this splendid man, for he was deep in your hearts and affections even before you knew of me, and once there will always remain with abiding appreciation.

Neither do I wish to leave the impression that I fear I might have done if I left this letter with no further reference to the good work done in your behalf by influ [page 29:] ential Democrats in this Congress. Mr. [Joseph] Rawlins, your Delegate, has been faithful, capable earnest and vigilant, and has done all that could have been expected of him, and is entitled to your gratitude and praise. In the House, such Democrats as Mr. [Thomas] Geary of California, Mr. [Joseph] Washington of Tennessee, Speaker [Charles] Crisp [of Georgia], Mr. [Joseph] Wheeler [of New York], Chairman of the Territorial Committee, and many others who might be mentioned, and in the Senate such Democratic leaders as [Joseph] Blackburn [of Kentucky], and finally Senator [James] Jones of Arkansas, have constantly rendered good and very valuable service. I am satisfied that if the settled purpose of the Democratic leaders at one time to deny Statehood in some secret manner or in such way as to leave the blame on the Republicans had been carried into the field of open attempt, leaving us to call upon the Republican leaders to force the bill to a passage, we could have carried a solid Republican line in both houses, and enough Democrats of good faith and fairness would have voted with us to carry the bill. Indeed, if it should come that President Cleveland should veto the bill, I have faith that we could pass it over him with a solid Republican line and enough from the Democratic side to give us the necessary two thirds. But so far as we can learn up to this time, President Cleveland is ready to sign the bill.

His expressions have been favorable, his views are very broad, and his own intentions I have no doubt are all favorable to the measure. The only danger in that source lies in the secret influence that may be exerted upon him from the eastern States and the gold people of the eastern States, to which influences he is peculiarly susceptible, and to the influence of Democratic leaders from Southern States, who are opposed to any more northern States. Yet Colonel Trumbo is confident that through the President's favorable disposition, and with the help of Attorney General [Richard] Olney and Secretary [of the Treasury] [John] Carlisle and Secretary [of Agriculture] [Julius] Morton, he can gain the coveted Presidential approval.

The delay put upon you by the terms of the bill, in postponing the realizations of Statehood practically until 1896, were unavoidable. Without these provisions it would not have been possible to pass the bill without endangering it at the White House. The solid Republican line in the Senate wanted to amend these features, and we could have passed the bill as they desired it, but it was not advisable to give any partisan color to it nor afford any partisan reason for Mr. Cleveland to disapprove it. We have carried [page 30:] things from the first along the line of the aspiration to make it unanimous, to tranquilize all the elements, and to bring Utah into the Union a welcome member of the family and welcomed by all elements. Things have moved in a mysterious way to this end, and the devout may well think that the hand of God has controlled in it, bringing a blessing for all time with it.

I hope to visit Utah within a short time, and renew with you and your people the pleasant acquaintance of heretofore, and in the freedom of such interview talk over this great struggle and bring to your attention and knowledge many things which no doubt you and your colleagues will be glad to know. In conclusion I wish to express my own great personal sense of satisfaction that I was permitted to bear a part in this difficult struggle in a noble cause. It has been with increasing pleasure that I have found in every year, and almost in the developments of every day, my faith in your people confirmed and my good opinion increased. It has gradually grown, beginning with 1889, to be an absorbing question in my life, and it has been a pleasure for me since that period to subordinate my own interests to the one aspiration I had come to share with you to make Statehood certain to you, and to make it certain in such a way as would by the testimony of the American Congress vindicate you and your people from the obloquy of the past. I am also glad that the shepherd star of Utah, symbolizing as no other star has ever done an ambition to serve the common people, and the solidarity and destiny of all your people, has appeared in all its sovereignty and beauty upon the flag of our country during the time of your faithful and loving administration as President of your Church. I shall always account it an honor and a pleasure, to be treasured by my children and held by them in sacred memory, to have been associated with yourself, with Presidents [George Q.] Cannon and [Joseph F.] Smith, General [Hiram B.] Clawson, and the other good men of your membership, in this praiseworthy enterprise of gaining justice to a noble Territory and a worthy people. I believe that in the blessing coming to you with Statehood, a blessing to the spirit and the pride of your people, this long contest, ending successfully, will also be the means of bringing to your State countless material blessings. It has made your resources known to all the intelligent people of the republic, to nearly every community, and this information will bring to [page 31:] you speedily and in vast volume the capital necessary to develop your natural wealth, to create your factories, to build your cities, and to make you splendid in everything that commercial ambition and political aspiration may desire.

Hoping you may be spared many years to continue your gentle rule over the people you love so much, and invoking for you and all your people the highest prosperity and God's blessing always, I am,

Sincerely yours,
[James S. Clarkson]

[to:]
President Wilford Woodruff,
Salt Lake City, Utah.

[page 32:] P.S. It has occurred to me, as I have read this letter over that it would not be just to let it go to you, and into the records of your people, without referring to the early, continuous, and remarkably influential and valuable services of the Hon. M[orris] M. Estee, [former Speaker of the State Assembly] of California. It may seem superfluous in me to do it, since you and all of your co-laborers know in far larger degree than I of the fact and measure of his important and devoted services. In the dignity of his strength, and with the profound respect for him in the nation, his early testimony to your honor and merit as a people and a Church, his ceaseless efforts to correct the wrong and false impressions of the Mormon character and purpose, and his loyalty in attesting your good-citizenship and your patriotism and love of the Republic in common with all American citizens, all served you to great results, and helped potentially in changing the opinions of many leaders of public thought and party action. I have heard him in many social and political gatherings in Washington, New York, and Chicago, speak of these subjects; and always he convinced the most of his hearers of the truth and justice of his opinion of the good faith and merit of the people of Utah. You will need some great lawyer, versed in constitutional law and profound in legal wisdom, to draft your Constitution. Judge Estee, I understand, was largely the author of the original and also the revised Constitution of California—an instrument which might well be taken as the model for your Constitution, as it was taken for North Dakota and other Western States. It would be a graceful act of remembering friendship to commit to Judge Estee the work of framing a draft for the Constitution of Utah.

In writing this whole letter I have been keenly conscious of omitting reference to the many good works done, in line with the general effort in the nation by men of your own fold and faith. I have fully appreciated the great value of their service, and yet I felt that I was not entitled to try and tell you of the great work done in the nation by your own people—from President Cannon, with his almost unrivalled abilities and fidelity, of which I have often heard Mr. Blaine [page 33:] speak in words of cordial estimate and admiration, down through many others. But I did not feel I had any commission or indeed excuse to tell you what you already knew of your own faithful men. As I have referred to it, I cannot refrain from speaking from my own knowledge of the especially admirable and capable work accomplished by Mr. Frank J. Cannon, one of the younger of your influential brethren, but who, like Aaron, is noted among his brothers for the eloquence and grace of the speech. Before Committees of Congressmen, before Committees of Republicans, and before popular gatherings, including a Republican National Convention, he has held up your standards and proclaimed your noble ambition as a people, with a persuasive force and enkindling fervor that have wrought great things in placating prejudice and winning the good will of good people throughout the nation. I have seen so much of his good and faithful work, in places remote from you, and in acts unknown to you, that I cannot gain the consent of my own heart to close this letter without at least speaking of the marked fidelity and value of his services.

[signed] J. S. C.

PHOTOGRAPHS

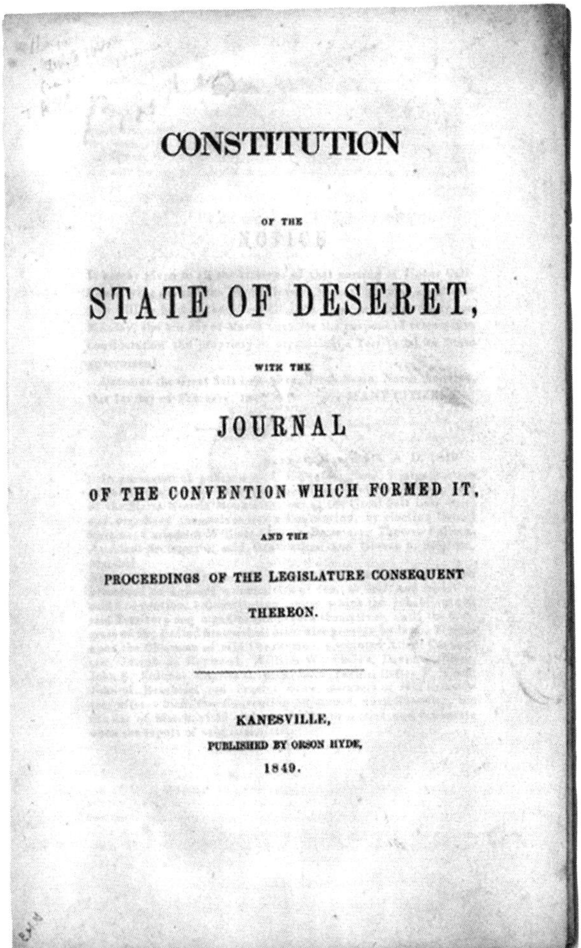

CONSTITUTION

OF THE

STATE OF DESERET,

WITH THE

JOURNAL

OF THE CONVENTION WHICH FORMED IT,

AND THE

PROCEEDINGS OF THE LEGISLATURE CONSEQUENT THEREON.

KANESVILLE,
PUBLISHED BY ORSON HYDE,
1849.

Proposed state constitution, 1849. *BYU Special Collections, Harold B. Lee Library*

In 1849 US President Zachary Taylor proposed the establishment of a state, "East California," extending from the Sierra Nevada Mountains to the Continental Divide midway into what is now Colorado—or alternately one large state incorporating California's population of 126,000 and Utah's 15,000 inhabitants. *Daguerreotype by Mathew Brady, ca. 1847, Library of Congress*

In 1850 US President Millard Fillmore appointed the de facto administrator of the Great Basin, Brigham Young, to be the new territory's first governor. Young considered it a lifetime appointment and had to be removed by force in 1858. *Photo by Charles R. Savage, ca. 1870, Harold B. Lee Library, BYU*

John M. Bernhisel was an LDS negotiator who was caught between two worlds in January 1857 when Brigham Young and the Utah Territorial Legislature sent US President James Buchanan seemingly threatening messages. As the territory's representative, Bernhisel was compelled to deliver them to Buchanan and the Secretary of State, and the experience left Bernhisel too traumatized to appear in public for two months. *Utah State Historical Society*

Robert N. Baskin, an attorney who became mayor of Salt Lake City, stated that the allegiances of the LDS people were incompatible with self-government. *Photo ca. 1890, Utah Historical Society*

Senator George Edmunds (R–Vermont) sponsored the key anti-polygamy legislation. *Portrait ca. 1880, Brady–Handy Collection, US Library of Congress*

Charles C. Goodwin, editor of the *Salt Lake Tribune*, was an aggressive opponent of the LDS Church and Utah statehood. *Photo ca. 1880, Utah Historical Society*

John T. Caine was the Utah terrritorial delegate to Congress for six terms, 1881–93, shown here with his wife, Margaret. *Portrait ca. 1870, Utah Historical Society*

George Q. Cannon came to be a most respected delegate to Congress, 1873–82, while simultaneously serving in the LDS First Presidency. *Orson F. Whitney, History of Utah, vol. 3, 1898*

Utah's suffrage leaders in 1875 had led the LDS-sponsored Ladies' Cooperative Retrenchment Association and served in leadership positions in the LDS Relief Society: Emily S. Richards, Sarah M. Kimball, and Phoebe Beatie. *Susa Young Gates Collection, Utah Historical Society*

Alexander Badlam Jr., a lobbyist for the Central Pacific Railroad, put his lobbying talent to work in behalf of the Latter-day Saints. *Photo ca. 1870, California State Library.*

Lobbyist and delegate to Congress Thomas Fitch wanted to use polygamy as a bargaining chip. *Photo ca. 1883, History of Arizona Territory, with Illustrations, 1884*

Lobbyist John W. Young was a counselor in the First Presidency for only one year, 1876–77. *Photo ca. 1890, Utah Historical Society*

In 1898 Church President Wilford Woodruff died in Isaac Trumbo's home in San Francisco. The house still stands today. *Photo ca. 1960, Joseph H. Lyman*

The aspiration of Colonel Isaac Trumbo of California to become one of Utah's first US senators was never realized. His mother was a member of the LDS Church and he was raised in Nevada and Utah. Professionally he had been an officer in the California National Guard and was the main lobbyist delivering Utah statehood. *Utah Historical Society*

A hard-boiled executive, President Ulysses S. Grant was not fond of Mormons or their civil disobedience, but his opinion was later tempered somewhat when he and his wife, Julia, visited the territory in 1875. *Portrait ca. 1880, Brady–Handy Collection, Library of Congress*

Dignitaries from Washington, DC, traveled to Utah Territory by rail in the comfort of a private Pullman car, and the LDS president had his own car as well, probably looking something like this. *Photo 1902, Ullstein Bild Collection, Getty Images*

Regimental Colonel James B. McKean was appointed and served as an oppressive chief justice of the Utah Supreme Court in 1870. In that position he arrested Brigham Young, but mishandled the case so badly that President Grant asked him to resign. *Portrait ca. 1865, Civil War Photographs, Library of Congress*

Territorial officials (l–r): Supreme Court Justice Orlando W. Powers, US Marshal Elwin A. Ireland, Governor Eli H. Murray, Chief Justice Charles S. Zane, US Attorney William H. Dickson, and Justice Jacob S. Boreman. *Photo created in 1884, Utah Historical Society*

Men convicted of cohabitation with plural wives, and some of the plural wives, were sent to the penitentiary at the edge of the city, the Sugar House neighborhood today. *An 1887 scene, Utah Historical Society*

Third president of the LDS Church, John Taylor spent his last three years running from federal marshals. He was nevertheless kept informed by his nephew George Q. Cannon of activities by Church lobbyists in Washington, DC. *Photo ca. 1875, Utah Historical Society*

Lydia Spencer Clawson was placed in the territorial penitentiary when she refused to confirm in court that she was married to Rudger Clawson. Rudger soon replaced her in prison and was kept there for over three years. *Photograph 1911, Judy Grange-Schmitt*

Utahns cheered the election of the President Grover Cleveland until he denounced polygamy in his inaugural address and allowed passage of the Edmunds–Tucker Act. Later he agreed to more compromise. *C. M. Bell Collection, Library of Congress*

As chair of the Republican National Committee, James S. Clarkson played a pivotal role in bringing the Republicans and Latter-day Saints together and selling President Cleveland on the compromise that resulted in Utah becoming a state. *Mitchell C. Harrison, New York State's Prominent and Progressive Men, vol. 2, 1900*

The Utah Commission in the mid-1880s (l–r): Republicans Algernon Sidney Paddock, Arthur Lloyd Thomas (territorial secretary), Alexander Ramsay, and George L. Godfrey, and Democrats Ambrose B. Carlton, and James R. Pettigrew. *Harper's Weekly, June 20, 1885*

James G. Blaine was a most influential congressman and Secretary of State, who was persuaded by James Clarkson that LDS people were not so much a threat as an electoral opportunity. *Photo by Frances Benjamin Johnston, 1890, Library of Congress*

As a Republican, US President Benjamin Harrison remained cool toward the LDS people while others in his party changed their opinion. *C. M. Bell Collection, Library of Congress*

Since Grover Cleveland was a bachelor, his sister Rose acted as the White House host during his administration. *Prints and Photographs Division, Library of Congress*

Emmeline B. Wells was editor of the *Woman's Exponent* at the time she visited the White House in 1886. *Orson F. Whitney, History of Utah, vol. 3, 1898*

Two years after issuing the manifesto ending polygamy, the First Presidency posed for this photo: George Q. Cannon (left), Wilford Woodruff (standing), and Joseph F. Smith. *Photo by Charles R. Savage, 1892, Utah Historical Society*

The Senate chamber in the US Capitol in 1891. *Photo by Robert K. Bonine, Library of Congress*

One of the first two senators from Utah was Republican Frank J. Cannon.
Autobiographies and Portraits of the President, Cabinet, Supreme Court, and Fifty-fifth Congress, 1899

During the brief interregnum between Wilford Woodruff's death September 2, 1898, and the formation of the First Presidency under Lorenzo Snow eleven days later, the fourteen apostles posing for this photo were (back row, l–r) Matthias F. Cowley, Abraham O. Woodruff, George Teasdale, Francis M. Lyman, John Henry Smith, Heber J. Grant, John W. Taylor, and Marriner W. Merrill; and (front row) Brigham Young Jr., Franklin D. Richards, Lorenzo Snow, George Q. Cannon, Joseph F. Smith, and Anthon H. Lund. *Photo from 1898, Utah Historical Society*

BIBLIOGRAPHY

A handful of sources cited here are currently unavailable. For copies and summaries from the 1970s when I was granted access to them at the LDS Historical Department, see my papers, listed below.

Acts, Resolutions, and Memorials, Passed by the Annual, and Special Sessions, of the Legislative Assembly .... Great Salt Lake City: Brigham Young, Printer, 1852–1870.

Admission of Utah: Report of the Committee on Territories on the Admission of Utah as a State, to the House of Representatives, Second Session, Fiftieth Congress. Washington: Government Printing Office, 1889.

Alexander, Thomas G. "Charles S. Zane ... Apostle of the New Era." *Utah Historical Quarterly* 34, no. 4 (Fall 1966): 290–314.

———. "Conflict and Fraud: Utah Public Land Surveys in the 1850s, the Subsequent Investigation and Problems with the Land Disposal System." *Utah Historical Quarterly* 80, no. 2 (Spring 2012): 108–31.

———. "Federal Authority versus Polygamic Theocracy: James B. McKean and the Mormons, 1870–1875." *Dialogue: A Journal of Mormon Thought* 1, no. 3 (Autumn 1966): 85–100.

———. *Mormonism in Transition: A History of the Latter-day Saints, 1890–1930.* Urbana: University of Illinois Press, 1986.

———. *Things in Heaven and Earth: The Life and Times of Wilford Woodruff, a Mormon Prophet.* Salt Lake City: Signature Books, 1991.

———. "The Utah Federal Courts and the Areas of Conflict, 1856–1896." Master's thesis, Utah State University, 1961.

———. *Utah, the Right Place: The Official Centennial History.* Salt Lake City: Gibbs Smith Publisher, 1995.

Allen, James B. "'Good Guys' vs. 'Good Guys': Rudger Clawson, John Sharp, and Civil Disobedience in Nineteenth-Century Utah." *Utah Historical Quarterly* 48, no. 2 (Spring 1980): 148–74.

———. "The Unusual Jurisdiction of County Probate Courts in the Territory of Utah." *Utah Historical Quarterly* 36, no. 2 (Spring 1968): 132–42.

Allen, James B., and Glen M. Leonard. *The Story of the Latter-day Saints.* Salt Lake City: Deseret Book, 1986.

Allen, James B., Ronald W. Walker, and David J. Whitaker, eds. *Studies in Mormon History, 1830–1997: An Indexed Bibliography.* Urbana: University of Illinois Press, 2000.

Allison, William B. Papers, 1862–1916. C–304. Special Collections, University of Iowa, Iowa City.

Alter, J. Cecil. *Early Utah Journalism.* Salt Lake City: Utah State Historical Society, 1938.

Alford, Kenneth L., ed. *Civil War Saints.* Provo: BYU Religious Studies Center and Deseret Book, 2012.

Anderson, Robert D. "History of the *Provo Times and Enquirer*, 1873–1897." Master's thesis, Brigham Young University, 1951.

Annual Report of the Department of the Interior. Washington, DC: Government Printing Office, 1882–1890.

Arrington, Leonard J. *Brigham Young: American Moses.* New York: Alfred A. Knopf, 1985.

———. *Great Basin Kingdom: An Economic History of the Latter-day Saints, 1830–1900.* Cambridge: Harvard University Press, 1958.

Bagley, Will. *Blood of the Prophets: Brigham Young and the Massacre at Mountain Meadows.* Norman: University of Oklahoma Press, 2002.

Bancroft, Hubert H. *History of California.* 7 vols. San Francisco: History Company, 1884–86.

———. *History of Utah.* San Francisco: History Company, 1889.

Barrett, Gwynn W. "Dr. John M. Bernhisel: Mormon Elder in Congress." *Utah Historical Quarterly* 36, no. 2 (Spring 1968): 143–67.

———. "John M. Bernhisel: Mormon Elder in Congress." PhD diss., University of Utah, 1968.

Baskin, Robert N. *Reminiscences of Early Utah.* Salt Lake City: By the author, 1914.

Bass, Herbert J. *"I Am Democrat": The Political Career of David Bennett Hill.* Syracuse: Syracuse University Press, 1961.

Beeton, Beverly. "Woman Suffrage in the American West, 1869–1896." PhD diss., University of Utah, 1976.

Benedict, Michael L. *A Compromise of Principle: Congressional Republicans and Reconstruction, 1863–1869.* New York: W. W. Norton, 1974.

Bennett, Richard E. *Mormons at the Missouri: Winter Quarters, 1846–1852.* Norman: University of Oklahoma Press, 1987.

———. "A Samaritan Has Passed By: George Miller—Mormon Bishop, Trailblazer, and Brigham Young Antagonist." *Illinois Historical Journal* 82, no. 1 (Spring 1989): 2–16.

———. *We'll Find the Place: The Mormon Exodus, 1846–1848.* Salt Lake City: Deseret Book, 1997.

Bennion, Lowell "Ben". "The Incidence of Mormon Polygamy in 1880: 'Dixie' versus Davis County." *Journal of Mormon History* 11 (1984): 27–42.

Bergera, Gary James. *Conflict in the Quorum: Orson Pratt, Brigham Young, Joseph Smith.* Salt Lake City: Signature Books, 2002.

Bernhisel, John M. Papers, 1818–1872. MS 370. LDS Church History Library, Salt Lake City.

Bernstein, Jerome. "A History of the Constitutional Conventions of the Territory of Utah from 1849–95." Master's thesis, Utah State University, 1961.

Bigler, David L. *Forgotten Kingdom: The Mormon Theocracy in the American West, 1847–1896.* Logan: Utah State University Press, 1998.

Bitton, Davis. *George Q. Cannon: A Biography.* Salt Lake City: Deseret Book, 1999.

———. "Mormons in Texas: The Ill-Fated Lyman Wight Colony, 1844–1858." *Arizona and the West* 11, no. 1 (Spring 1969): 5–26.

———. "The B. H. Roberts Case of 1898–1900." *Utah Historical Quarterly* 25, no. 1 (Jan. 1957): 27–46.

Boreman, Jacob S. "Crusade against Theocracy: The Reminiscences of Judge Jacob Smith Boreman of Utah, 1872–1877." Edited by Leonard J. Arrington. *Huntington Library Quarterly* 24, no. 1 (Nov. 1960): 1–45.

Bowles, Samuel. *From across the Continent: A Summer's Journey to the Rocky Mountains, the Mormons, and the Pacific States, with Speaker Colfax.* New York: Hurd & Houghton, 1866.

———. *Our New West: Records of Travel between the Mississippi River and the Pacific Ocean.* Hartford: Hartford Publishing Company, 1869.

Bringhurst, Newell G. *Saints, Slaves, and Blacks: The Changing Place of Black People within Mormonism.* Draper, UT: Greg Kofford Books, 2018.

Brooks, Juanita. *The Mountain Meadows Massacre.* Norman: University of Oklahoma Press, 1962.

Brown, J. Ross. *Report of the Debates in the Convention of California on the Formation of the State Constitution in September and October 1849.* Washington, DC: John T. Towers, 1850.

Buice, David. "A Stench in the Nostrils of Honest Men: Southern Democrats and the Edmunds Act of 1882." *Dialogue: A Journal of Mormon Thought* 21, no. 3 (Autumn 1988): 100–13.

Bullard, Frederick L. "Abraham Lincoln and the Statehood of Nevada." *American Bar Association Journal* 26, no. 4 (April 1940): 313–17.

Caine, John T. Letters, 1891–1895. MS 8577, LDS Church History Library.

———. *The Mormon Problem, Speech of Hon. John T. Caine ... in Opposition to the So-Called Edmunds–Tucker Anti-Polygamy Bill.* Washington, DC: Government Printing Office, 1887.

———. Papers, 1855–1864. MS 16877, LDS Church History Library.

Caldwell, Gaylon L. "Mormon Conception of Individual Rights and Political Obligations." PhD diss., Stanford University, 1952.

Campbell, Eugene E. *Establishing Zion: The Mormon Church in the American West, 1847–1869.* Salt Lake City: Signature Books, 1988.

———. "Government Beginnings." In Poll, et al., *Utah's History*, 153–57.

Cannon, Abraham H. Diaries, 1879–1895. Vault MSS 62, L. Tom Perry Special Collections, Harold B. Lee Library, Brigham Young University, Provo. For published edition, see Lyman, ed., *Candid Insights.*

Cannon, Frank J., and Harvey J. O'Higgins. *Under the Prophet in Utah: The National Menace of a Political Priestcraft.* Boston: C. M. Clark, 1911.

Cannon, George Q. Journal, transcript available at www.churchhistorianspress.org.

———. "Utah and Its People." *North American Review* 132 (May 1881): 451–66.

Cannon, Kenneth L. "Wives and Other Women: Love, Sex, and Marriage in the Lives of John Q. Cannon, Frank J. Cannon, and Abraham H. Cannon." *Dialogue: A Journal of Mormon Thought,* 43 no. 4 (Winter 2010): 71–130.

Cannon, Mark W. "The Mormon Issue in Congress, 1872–1882, Drawing on the Experience of Territorial Delegate George Q. Cannon." PhD diss., Harvard University, 1960.

Carlton, Ambrose B. *The Wonderlands of the Wild West, with Sketches of the Mormons.* Salt Lake City: George Q. Cannon and Sons, 1891.

Church Historian's Office Journal, 1844–1879. CR 100 1, Church History Library.

Cihak, Herbert E. "Bryan, Populism, and Utah." Master's thesis, Brigham Young University, 1975.

Clawson, Hiram B. Papers, 1850–1862. MS 14296, Church History Library.

Clayton, William. *An Intimate Chronicle: The Journals of William Clayton.* Edited by George D. Smith. Salt Lake City: Signature Books, 1995.

Clements, Louis J., ed. *Fred T. Dubois: The Making of a State.* Rexburg: Eastern Idaho Publishing, 1971.

Cleveland, Grover. Papers, 1743–1945. MSS16188, Manuscript Division, Library of Congress, Washington, DC.

Codman, John. *The Mormon Country: A Summer with the "Latter-day Saints."* New York: United States Publishing, 1874.

Colfax, Schuyler. "Hon. Schuyler Colfax's Journey from the Missouri River to California in 1865, from His Journal." *Western Galaxy* 1, nos. 1–4 (1888): 32–41, 233–51, 347–51.

Compton, Todd. "John Willard Young, Brigham Young, and the Development of Presidential Succession in the LDS Church." *Dialogue: A Journal of Mormon Thought* 35, no. 4 (Winter 2002): 112–34.

Cooley, Everett L. "Carpetbag Rule: Territorial Government in Utah." *Utah Historical Quarterly* 26, no. 2 (Apr. 1958): 107–29.

———. "The Utah War." Master's thesis, University of Utah, 1947.

Coolidge, Louis A. *Orville H. Platt: An Old Fashioned Senator.* 2 vols. Port Washington, NY: The Knickerbocker Press, 1910.

Crane, Charles. *To the Members of the Utah Legislature and the General Public.* Np: Republican Party of Utah, ca. 1895.

Crawley, Peter. "The Constitution of the State of Deseret." *BYU Studies* 29, no. 4 (Fall 1989): 7–22.

Creer, Leland H. *Utah and the Nation.* Seattle: University of Washington Press, 1929.

Culmer, Frederick A. "'General' John Wilson, Signer of the Deseret Petition, Including Letters from the Leonard Collection." *California Historical Society Quarterly* 26, no. 4 (Dec. 1947): 321–48.

Curtis, George Ticknor. Papers, 1863–1892. MSS 7176. Clifton Waller Barrett Library, University of Virginia, Charlottesville.

———. *A Plea for Religious Liberty and the Rights of Conscience: An Argument Delivered in the Supreme Court of the United States, April 28, 1886.* Washington, DC: By the author, 1886.

Davis, Ray J. "Plural Marriage and Religious Freedom: The Impact of *Reynolds v. United States.*" *Arizona Law Review* 15 (1973): 287–306.

Daynes, Kathryn M. *More Wives than One: Transformation of the Mormon Marriage System, 1840–1910.* Urbana: University of Illinois Press, 2008.

DeSantis, Vincent P. *Republicans Face the Southern Question: The New Departure Years, 1877–1897.* New York: Greenwood Press, 1969.

Dix, Fae Decker. "Unwilling Martyr: The Death of Young Ed Dalton." *Utah Historical Quarterly* 41, no. 2 (Spring 1973): 162–77.

Doctrine and Covenants of the Church of Jesus Christ of Latter-day Saints. Salt Lake City: LDS Church, 1981 edition.

Dubois, Fred T. Collection, 1880–1930. MC004, Special Collections, Eli M. Oboler Library, Idaho State University.

Durham, G. Homer, ed. *The Discourses of Wilford Woodruff.* Salt Lake City: Bookcraft, 1946.

Edmunds, George F. "Political Aspects of Mormonism." *Harper's New Monthly Magazine* 64 (Jan. 1882): 285–88.

Eldredge, Alma. Diaries, 1869–1924. MS 1618, LDS Church History Library.

Elliott, Russell R. *History of Nevada.* Lincoln: University of Nebraska Press, 1973.

———. *Servant of Power: A Political Biography of Senator William M. Stewart.* Reno: University of Nevada Press, 1983.

The Facts in the Utah Case. Salt Lake City: [Joseph Cohen, Frederick Kiesel, Orlando Powers, and Michael Tarpey], 1892.

Fales, Susan L., and Chad J. Flake. *Mormons and Mormonism in US Government Documents: A Bibliography.* Salt Lake City: University of Utah Press, 1989.

Farnham, Wallace D. "The Weakened Spring of Government: A Study in Nineteenth-Century American History." *American Historical Review* 68, no. 3 (Apr. 1963): 662–80.

Firmage, Edwin B., and Richard C. Mangrum. *Zion in the Courts: A Legal History of the Church of Jesus Christ of Latter-day Saints, 1830–1900.* Urbana: University of Illinois Press, 1988.

First Presidency Collection. Political and Contractual Papers, 1856–1914. Church History Library. This collection, which no longer exists, is what I consulted during the time I conducted research for this book. See instead Taylor Correspondence and Woodruff General Correspondence.

Foner, Eric. *Free Soil, Free Labor, Free Men: The Ideology of the Republican Party before the Civil War.* New York: Oxford University Press, 1995.

Furniss, Norman F. *The Mormon Conflict, 1850–1859.* New Haven: Yale University Press, 1960.

Gibbs, Josiah F. *Lights and Shadows of Mormonism.* Salt Lake City: Salt Lake Tribune Publishing Company, 1909.

Goodwin, Charles C. "The Political Attitude of the Mormons." *North American Review* 132 (Mar. 1881): 276–86.

Gordon, Sarah Barringer. *The Mormon Question: Polygamy and Constitutional Conflict in Nineteenth Century America.* Chapel Hill: University of North Carolina Press, 2002.

———. "'The Twin Relic of Barbarism': A Legal History of Anti-Polygamy in Nineteenth Century America." PhD diss., Princeton University, 1995.

Gould, Lewis L. *Wyoming: A Political History, 1868–1896.* New Haven: Yale University Press, 1968.

Grant, Heber J. *The Diaries of Heber J. Grant, 1880–1945, Abridged.* Salt Lake City: Privately published, 2013. The original (MS 1233), LDS Church History Library, is currently "closed to research."

———. *Speech of Hon. H. J. Grant: A Ringing Appeal to the Voters of Utah Territory. Patriotism and Gratitude Demand That Voters Support Hon. J. L. Rawlins.* Salt Lake City: Democratic Territorial Convention, Sept. 1894.

Grow, Matthew J. *"Liberty to the Downtrodden": Thomas L. Kane, Romantic Reformer.* New Haven: Yale University Press, 2009.

Grow, Stewart L. "A Study of the Utah Commission, 1882–1896." PhD diss., University of Utah, 1954.

Hafen, LeRoy R., and Ann W. Hafen, eds. *The Utah Expedition, 1857–1858: A Documentary Account of the United States Military Movement under Colonel Albert Sidney Johnston, and the Resistance by Brigham Young and the Mormon Nauvoo Legion.* Glendale, CA: Arthur H. Clark, 1958.

Hale, William H. *Horace Greeley: Nineteenth-Century Voice of the People.* New York: Harper and Brothers, 1950.

Hallwas, John E., and Roger D. Launius. *Cultures in Conflict: A Documentary History of the Mormon War in Illinois.* Logan: Utah State University, 1995.

Hamilton, Gail [Abigail Dodge]. *Biography of James G. Blaine.* Norwich, CT: Henry Bill, 1895.

Hamilton, Holman. *Prologue to Conflict: The Crisis and Compromise of 1850.* Lexington: University of Kentucky Press, 1964.

Hammond, Francis A. Journals, 1852–57, 1864–67, 1883–93. MS 1430. LDS Church History Library.

Hansen, Klaus J. *Quest for Empire: The Political Kingdom of God and the Council of Fifty in Mormon History.* Lansing: Michigan State University Press, 1967.

Hardy, B. Carmon, ed. *Doing the Works of Abraham: Mormon Polygamy, Its Origin, Practice, and Demise.* Norman, OK: Arthur H. Clark, 2007.

———. "Polygamy, Mormonism, and Me." *Dialogue: A Journal of Mormon Thought* 41, no. 2 (Summer 2008): 85–101.

———. *Solemn Covenant: The Mormon Polygamous Passage.* Urbana: University of Illinois Press, 1992.

Harlow, Neal. *California Conquered: The Annexation of a Mexican Province, 1846–1850.* Berkeley: University of California Press, 1982.

Harrison, Benjamin. Papers, 1780–1948. MSS25064, Library of Congress.

Harrow, Joan R. "Joseph L. Rawlins: Father of Utah Statehood." Master's thesis, University of Utah, 1973.

Hearings before the [Senate] Committee on Territories in Relation to the Exercise of the Elective Franchise in the Territory of Utah. Washington, DC: Government Printing Office, 1890.

Hill, David B. Papers, 1886–1910. MssCol 1396, Archives and Manuscripts, New York State Library.

Hirshson, Stanley P. *Farewell to the Bloody Shirt: Northern Republicans and the Southern Negro, 1877–1893.* Bloomington: Indiana University Press, 1962.

Hittell, Theodore H. *History of California.* 4 vols. San Francisco: Pacific Press Publishing and M. J. Stone and Company, 1885, 1897.

Hooper, William H. *"Vindication of the People of Utah," Remarks of Hon. William H. Hooper of Utah in the House of Representatives, January 29, 1873.* Washington, DC: Congressional Globe Office, 1873.

Hoopes, David S., and Roy Hoopes. *Mormon Apostle: The Story of Rudger Clawson.* Lanham, MD: Madison Books, 1990.

Hulse, James W. "C. C. Goodwin and the Taming of the *Tribune.*" *Utah Historical Quarterly* 61, no. 2 (Spring 1993): 164–81.

Huntington, Henry E. Papers, 1794–1970. MssHEH, Huntington Library and Art Gallery, San Marino.

Ivins, Stanley S. "A Constitution for Utah." *Utah Historical Quarterly* 25, no. 2 (Apr. 1957): 94–116.

Jack, James. Papers. LDS Church History Library. This collection is no longer open for research.

Jensen, Alta R. *The Unfavored Few: The Autobiography of Joseph L. Rawlins*. Monterey: Privately printed, 1965.

Jensen, Richard J. *The Winning of the Midwest: Social and Political Conflict, 1888–96.* Chicago: University of Chicago Press, 1971.

Jensen, Therald N. "Mormon Theory of Church and State." PhD diss., University of Chicago, 1938.

Jenson, Andrew. *Latter-day Saint Biographical Encyclopedia*. 4 vols. Salt Lake City: Andrew Jenson History Company, 1901–36.

Jonas, Frank H. "Utah: The Different State." In *Politics in the American West*, edited by Frank H. Jonas, 332–38. Salt Lake City: University of Utah Press, 1969.

Jonathan [pseud.]. *Joseph F. Smith Answered: His Plain Talk Shown to be Full of Errors … Read it Carefully*. Np: np, ca. 1892.

Jorgensen, Victor W., and B. Carmon Hardy, "The Taylor–Cowley Affair and the Watershed of Mormon History." *Utah Historical Quarterly* 48, no. 1 (Winter 1980): 4–36.

Journal of Discourses. 26 vols. Liverpool: Latter-day Saint Book Depot, 1854–86.

Journal History. Multi-volume daily scrapbook prepared by the LDS Church Historian's Office, 1830–present. CR 100 137 (index at CR 100 142), LDS Church History Library.

Journal of the Proceedings of the House of Assembly of the State of California, at Its First Session. San Jose: J. Winchester, State Printer, 1850.

Journal of the Senate of the State of California, at Their First Session. San Jose: J. Winchester, State Printer, 1850.

Juergens, George. *Joseph Pulitzer and the New York World.* Princeton: Princeton University Press, 1966.

Kane, Thomas L. Collection, 1762–1982. MS 16717, LDS Church History Library.

———. Papers, 1845–1884. MS 8184, LDS Church History Library.

Kenner, S. A. *The Practical Politician.* Salt Lake City: Self published, 1892.

Kenner, Scipio A. *Utah as It Is: With a Comprehensive Statement of Utah as It Was.* Salt Lake City: Deseret News Press, 1902.

Kenney, Scott G. Collection, 1820–1984. Ms0587, Special Collections, J. Willard Marriott Library, University of Utah, Salt Lake City

———, ed. *Wilford Woodruff's Journal, 1833–1898*. 9 vols. Midvale, Utah: Signature Books, 1983–85.

Kinzer, Donald L. *An Episode in Anti-Catholicism: The American Protective Association*. Seattle: University of Washington Press, 1964.

Kleppner, Paul. *Cross of Culture: A Social Analysis of Midwestern Politics, 1850–1900*. New York: Free Press, 1970.

———. *The Third Electoral System, 1853–1892: Parties, Voters, and Political Changes*. Chapel Hill: University of North Carolina Press, 1979.

Kotter, Richard E. "An Examination of Mormon and Non-Mormon Influences in Ogden City Politics, 1847–1896." Master's thesis, Utah State University, 1967.

Lambert, John R. *Arthur Pue Gorman*. Baton Rouge: Louisiana State University Press, 1953.

Lamar, Howard R. *Dakota Territory, 1861–1889: A Study of Frontier Politics*. New Haven: Yale University Press, 1956.

———. *The Far Southwest: A Territorial History, 1846–1912*. New Haven: Yale University Press, 1966.

Larson, Gustive O. *The Americanization of Utah for Statehood*. San Marino: Huntington Library, 1971.

———. "Land Contest in Early Utah." *Utah Historical Quarterly* 29, no. 4 (Oct. 1961): 308–26.

———. "The Mormon Reformation." *Utah Historical Quarterly* 26, no. 1 (Jan. 1958): 45–63.

Larson, Robert W. *New Mexico's Quest for Statehood, 1846–1912*. Albuquerque: University of New Mexico Press, 1968.

Lavender, David. *The Great Persuader*. New York: Doubleday, 1970.

Legislative Assembly, Territorial Records. Series 3150, reel 3, Utah State Archives, Utah Division of Archives and Records Service, Salt Lake City.

Lincoln, Robert Todd. Family papers, 1864–1938. MSS85376, Library of Congress.

Linford, Lawrence L. "Establishing and Maintaining Land Ownership in Utah Prior to 1869." *Utah Historical Quarterly* 42, no. 2 (Spring 1974): 126–43.

Linford, Orma. "The Mormons and the Law: The Polygamy Cases." *Utah Law Review* 9, nos. 2–3 (Winter/Summer 1964): 308–70, 543–91.

Lund, Anthon H. *Danish Apostle: The Diaries of Anthon H. Lund, 1890–1921*. Edited by John P. Hatch. Salt Lake City: Signature Books, 2006.

Lund, Anthon H. Journals, 1860–1921. MS 5375, Church History Library. For published edition, see Lund, *Danish Apostle.*

Lyman, Amasa M. Collection, 1832–1877. MS 829, Church History Library.

Lyman, Amasa M. *Thirteenth Apostle: The Diaries of Amasa M. Lyman, 1832–1877.* Edited by Scott H. Partridge. Salt Lake City: Signature Books, 2016.

Lyman, Edward L. "The Alienation of an Apostle from His Quorum: The Moses Thatcher Case." *Dialogue: A Journal of Mormon Thought* 18, no. 2 (Summer 1985): 67–91.

———. *Amasa Mason Lyman, Mormon Apostle and Apostate: A Study in Dedication.* Salt Lake City: University of Utah Press, 2009.

———, ed. *Candid Insights of a Mormon Apostle: The Diaries of Abraham H. Cannon, 1889–1895.* Salt Lake City: Signature Books, 2010.

———. "Elimination of the Mormon Issue from Arizona Politics, 1889–1894." *Arizona and the West* 24, no. 3 (Autumn 1982): 205–28.

———. "Heber M. Wells and the Beginnings of Utah's Statehood." Master's thesis, University of Utah, 1967.

———. "Isaac Trumbo and the Politics of Utah Statehood." *Utah Historical Quarterly* 41, no. 2 (Spring 1973): 128–49.

———. "Larger than Texas: Proposals to Combine California and Mormon Deseret as One State." *California History: The Magazine of the California Historical Society* 80, no. 1 (Spring 2001): 18–33.

———. "Mormon Leaders in Politics: The Transition to Statehood in 1896." *Journal of Mormon History* 24, no. 2 (Fall 1998): 30–54.

———. "The Mormon Quest for Utah Statehood." PhD diss., University of California–Riverside, 1981.

———. "A Mormon Transition in Idaho Politics." *Idaho Yesterdays* 20, no. 4 (Winter 1977): 2–11, 24–29.

———. *The Overland Journey from Utah to California: Wagon Travel from the City of Saints to the City of Angels.* Reno: University of Nevada Press, 2004.

———. Papers. Special Collections, Gerald R. Sherratt Library, Southern Utah University, Cedar City.

———. "The Political Background of the Woodruff Manifesto." *Dialogue: A Journal of Mormon Thought* 24, no. 3 (Fall 1991): 21–39.

———. *Political Deliverance: The Mormon Quest for Utah Statehood.* Urbana: University of Illinois Press, 1986.

———. "Politicians' Perceptions of the Western Political Situation and Their Implications for State-making, 1887–1894." Paper presented to the Western History Association, Oct. 17, 1980, Kansas City.

———. *San Bernardino: The Rise and Fall of a California Community.* Salt Lake City: Signature Books, 1996.

———. "Statehood, Political Allegiance, and Utah's First U.S. Senate Seats: Prizes for the National Parties and Local Factions." *Utah Historical Quarterly* 63, no. 4 (Fall 1995): 341–56.

———. "Succession by Seniority: The Development of Procedural Precedents in the LDS Church." *Journal of Mormon History* 40, no. 2 (Spring 2014): 92–158.

Lyman, Francis M. Journals, 1891–95. LDS Church History Library. Currently only his 1884–85 diary (MS 8292) is open for research.

———. Papers, 1849–1974. MS 14514, LDS Church History Library.

MacKinnon, William P. "'Like Splitting a Man Up His Backbone:' The Territorial Dismemberment of Utah, 1850–1896." *Utah Historical Quarterly* 71, no. 2 (Spring 2003): 100–24.

———. *At Sword's Point: A Documentary History of the Utah War.* 2 vols. Norman: Arthur H. Clark/University of Oklahoma Press, Part 1 to 1858 (2008); Part 2, 1858–1859 (2016).

———. "And the War Came: James Buchanan, The Utah War, and the Decision to Intervene." *Utah Historical Quarterly* 76, no. 1 (Winter 2008): 22–37.

Madsen, Carol C. *Battle for the Ballot: Essays on Woman Suffrage in Utah, 1870–1895.* Logan: Utah State University Press, 1997.

———. "'At Their Peril': Utah Law and the Case of Plural Wives, 1850–1900." *Western Historical Quarterly* 21, no. 4 (Nov. 1990): 425–43.

Madsen, Truman G. *B. H. Roberts: Defender of the Faith.* Salt Lake City: Bookcraft, 1980.

Malmquist, Orvin N. *The First 100 Years: A History of the Salt Lake Tribune, 1871–1971.* Salt Lake City: Utah Historical Society, 1971.

Manuscript History of the Church, 1839–1882 (also known as the Documentary History). CR 100 102 (drafts available as CR 100 92), LDS Church History Library.

Marcus, Robert D. *Grand Old Party: Political Structure in the Gilded Age, 1880–1896.* New York: Oxford University Press, 1971.

Mauss, Armand L. *The Angel and the Beehive: The Mormon Struggle with Assimilation.* Urbana: University of Illinois Press, 1994.

Maxwell, John G. *Gettysburg to Great Salt Lake: George R. Maxwell, Civil War Hero and Federal Marshal among the Mormons.* Norman: University of Oklahoma Press, 2010.

———. *Robert N. Baskin and the Making of Modern Utah.* Norman, OK: Arthur H. Clark, 2013.

McFeely, William S. *Grant: A Biography.* New York: W. W. Norton, 1982.

McKee, Thomas H. *The National Conventions and Platforms of All Political Parties, 1789 to 1905.* Baltimore: Friedenwald, 1906.

McClernand, John Alexander. Papers, 1823–1919. Abraham Lincoln Presidential Library and Museum, Springfield, Illinois.

"Memorials of William B. Hornblower: Data Bearing on His Nomination for US Supreme Court." Cleveland Papers.

Merrill, Marriner W. Journals, 1889–1906. MS 107, Church History Library.

———. Journal and Reminiscences, 1888–1904. MS 1785, Church History Library.

Merrill, Milton R. *Reed Smoot: Apostle in Politics.* Logan: Utah State University Press, 1990.

Message of His Excellency Governor Caleb W. West and Accompanying Documents. Salt Lake City: Legislative Assembly of the Territory of Utah, 1888.

Middleton, Henry J. "The Life of Charles Franklin Middleton: A Man and His Times." Master's thesis, Utah State University, 1965.

Miller, William H. H. Collection, 1862–1919. L108, Indiana State Library, Indianapolis.

———. Letterbooks, 1873–1911. V101, Indiana State Library.

Minority Report of the Utah Commission. Salt Lake City: Np, 1887.

Minutes of the Apostles of the Church of Jesus Christ of Latter-day Saints, 1835–1951. 4 vols. Salt Lake City: Privately published, 2013.

Moody, Eric N., ed. *The Extraordinary Memoirs of "Senator" Thomas Fitch.* Reno: University of Nevada Press, 1978.

———. "Nevada's Anti-Mormon Legislation of 1887 and Southern Idaho Annexation." *Nevada Historical Society Quarterly* 22, no. 1 (Spring 1979): 21–32.

Moorman, Donald R., with Gene A. Sessions. *Camp Floyd and the Mormons: The Utah War.* Salt Lake City: University of Utah Press, 1992.

Morgan, Dale L. *The State of Deseret.* Salt Lake City: Utah State Historical Society, 1940.

Morgan, H. Wayne. *From Hayes to McKinley: National Party Politics, 1877–1896.* Syracuse: Syracuse University Press, 1969.

———. "Populism and the Decline of Agriculture." In *The Gilded Age*, edited by H. Wayne Morgan, 149–70. Syracuse, New York: Syracuse University Press, 1970.

Morgan, John. Journals, 1875–1892. MS 1479, LDS Church History Library.

Mowery, George E. *The Age of Theodore Roosevelt and the Birth of Modern America, 1900–1912.* New York: Harper Torchbooks, 1962.

Muzzey, David S. *James G. Blaine: A Political Idol of Other Days.* New York: Dodd, Meade, 1934.

Neff, Andrew L. *History of Utah, 1847–1869.* Salt Lake City: Deseret News Press, 1940.

Nevins, Allan. *The Emergence of Lincoln: Douglas, Buchanan, and Party Chaos, 1857–1859.* 2 vols. New York: Charles Scribners' Sons, 1950.

———. *Grover Cleveland: A Study in Courage.* New York: Dodd, Mead, 1932.

———. *Hamilton Fish: The Inner History of the Grant Administration.* New York, Dodd, Mead, 1937.

———, ed. *Letters of Grover Cleveland, 1850–1908.* Boston: Houghton Mifflin, 1933.

———. *Ordeal of the Union.* 2 vols. New York: Charles Scribners' Sons, 1947.

———. Papers, 1912–1992. NYCR89–A647, Rare Books and Manuscripts, Butler Library, Columbia University, New York City.

Nichols, Roy Franklin. *The Disruption of American Democracy.* New York: Free Press, 1967.

Nuggets of Truth: Hear Ye the Whole Truth, as to Joseph Smith's Political Views. [Salt Lake City: Utah Democratic Party], 1892. Available in the B. H. Roberts Papers, LDS Church Archives.

Nuggets of Truth and Gems from the Speeches and Letters of the Leading Minds of Utah (Past and Present). [Salt Lake City: Utah Republican Committee], 1892. Available from the Utah State Historical Society Archives.

Official Report of the Proceedings and Debates of the Convention Assembled at Salt Lake City on the Fourth Day of March 1895, to Adopt a Constitution for the State of Utah. 2 vols. Salt Lake City: Star Printing, 1898.

Partridge, Edward Jr. Journals, 1854–1899. MSS B 79, Utah State Archives, Salt Lake City.

Paschal, Joel. *Mr. Justice Sutherland: A Man against the State.* Princeton: Princeton University Press, 1951.

Paulos, Michael H., ed. *The Mormon Church on Trial: Transcripts of the Reed Smoot Hearings.* Salt Lake City: Signature Books, 2008.

Penrose, Charles W. *C. W. Penrose Replies to Joseph F. Smith … Reply to a Republican's Attempt at Criticism.* Np: np, 1892.

———. Collection, 1851–1956. MS 21330, LDS Church History Library.

———. Journals, 1854–1911. MS 8911, LDS Church History Library.

Peterson, Charles S., and Brian Q. Cannon. *The Awkward State of Utah: Coming of Age in the Nation, 1896–1945.* Salt Lake City: University of Utah Press, 2015.

Peterson, Paul H. "The Mormon Reformation." PhD diss., Brigham Young University, 1981. Rpt. Provo: BYU Studies/JFS Institute, 2002.

Poll, Richard D. Papers, 1844–1994. Ms 674, Special Collections, Marriott Library.

———. "The Political Reconstruction of Utah Territory, 1866–1890." *Pacific Historical Review* 27, no. 2 (May 1958): 111–26.

———. Review of Dale L. Morgan, *The State of Deseret. John Whitmer Historical Association Newsletter* 25 (July 1989): 3–4.

———. "The Twin Relic: A Study of Mormon Polygamy and the Campaign by the Government of the United States for Its Abolition, 1852–1890." Master's thesis, Texas Christian University, 1939.

———, Thomas G. Alexander, Eugene E. Campbell, and David E. Miller. *Utah's History.* Provo: Brigham Young University Press, 1978.

Porter, Kirk H., and Donald B. Johnson, comps. *National Party Platforms, 1840–1972.* Urbana: University of Illinois Press, 1973.

Pringle, Henry F. *Theodore Roosevelt: A Biography.* New York: Harcourt, Brace and World, 1956.

Pusey, Merlo J. *Builders of the Kingdom: George A. Smith, John Henry Smith, George Albert.* Provo: Brigham Young University Press, 1981.

Quinn, D. Michael. "LDS Church Authority and New Plural Marriages, 1890–1904." *Dialogue: A Journal of Mormon Thought* 18, no. 1 (Spring 1985): 9–105.

———. "The Mormon Hierarchy, 1832–1932: An American Elite." PhD diss., Yale University, 1976.

———. *The Mormon Hierarchy: Extensions of Power.* Salt Lake City: Signature Books, 1997.

———. *The Mormon Hierarchy: Origins of Power*. Salt Lake City: Signature Books, 1994.

Rawlins, Joseph L. "Reminiscences of Joseph L. Rawlins." In Joseph L. Rawlins Papers, 1885–1964. MS 189, box 1, fd. 1, Special Collections, Marriott Library.

Rawls, James J., and Walton Bean. *California: An Interpretive History*. 7th ed. Boston: McGraw–Hill, 1998.

Report of the Governor of Utah to the Secretary of the Interior, 1888. Washington: Government Printing Office, 1888.

Richardson, Arthur M. *The Life and Ministry of John Morgan: For a Wise and Glorious Purpose*. Salt Lake City: Privately published, 1965.

Richardson, James D., ed. *A Compilation of the Messages and Papers of the Presidents*. 10 vols. New York: Bureau of National Literature, 1896.

Ricketts, Norma B. *The Mormon Battalion: U.S. Army of the West, 1846–1848*. Logan: Utah State University Press, 1996.

Rice, Richard B., William A. Bullough, and Richard J. Orsi. *The Elusive Eden: A New History of California*. 3rd ed. Boston: McGraw–Hill, 2002.

Rich, Charles C. Collection, 1832–1908. MS 889, LDS Church History Library.

Richards, Franklin D. Journals, letterbooks, and papers, 1837–1900. In Richards Family Collection, MS 1215, LDS Church History Library.

Richards, Franklin S. Correspondence, 1867–1932. MS 2459, LDS Church History Library.

Roberts, B. H. *A Comprehensive History of the Church of Jesus Christ of Latter-day Saints, Century I*. 6 vols. Salt Lake City: Deseret News Press, 1930.

———. *The Life of John Taylor: Third President of the Church of Jesus Christ of Latter-day Saints*. Salt Lake City: George Q. Cannon and Sons, 1892.

———. "Life Story of B. H. Roberts." In Papers, 1825–1976. Ms0106, box 1, fds. 1–2, Special Collections, Marriott Library.

———. Papers, 1880–1965. MS 2729, LDS Church History Library.

Robinson, Phil. *Sinners and Saints: A Tour across the States, and round Them, with Three Months among the Mormons*. Boston: Roberts Brothers, 1883.

Roderick, Judith Ann. "A Historical Study of the Congressional Career of John T. Caine." Master's thesis, Brigham Young University, 1959.

Rogers, Jedediah S. *The Council of Fifty: A Documentary History*. Salt Lake City: Signature Books, 2014.

———, ed. *In the President's Office: The Diaries of L. John Nuttall, 1879–1892*. Salt Lake City: Signature Books, 2007.

Roosevelt, Theodore. Papers, 1759–1993. MSS 38299, Library of Congress.

Rothman, David J. *Politics and Power: The United States Senate, 1869–1901*. Cambridge: Harvard University Press, 1966.

Scott, William Lawrence. "Anti Polygamy Bill." Broadsheet, ca. 1887. BX 8608.A1 no. 38, L. Tom Perry Special Collections, Harold B. Lee Library.

Sessions, Gene A. *Mormon Thunder: A Documentary History of Jedediah M. Grant*. Urbana: University of Illinois Press, 1982.

Shipps, Jan. "The Mormons in Politics: The First Hundred Years." PhD diss., University of Colorado, 1965.

———. "The Principle Revoked: A Closer Look at the Demise of Plural Marriage." *Journal of Mormon History* 11 (1984): 65–77.

Sievers, Harry J. *Benjamin Harrison: Hoosier President*. Indianapolis: Bobbs–Merrill, 1968.

Smith, Elbert B. *The Presidencies of Zachary Taylor & Millard Fillmore*. Lawrence: University Press of Kansas, 1988.

Smith, George A. Papers, 1834–1877. MS 1322, LDS Church History Library.

Smith, Helen H. *War on Powder River: The Johnson County War*. Lincoln: University of Nebraska Press, 1966.

Smith, John Henry. Papers, 1852–1921. In George A. Smith Family Papers, 1731–1969. Ms0036, boxes 7–15, Special Collections, Marriott Library.

Smith, Joseph, Jr. *History of the Church of Jesus Christ of Latter-day Saints*. See also Vogel, *History of Joseph Smith*.

Smith, Joseph F. *Another Plain Talk: Reasons Why the People of Utah Should Be Republicans*. Salt Lake City: Republican Central Committee, 1892.

———. Papers, 1854–1918. MS 1325, LDS Church History Library.

Stampp, Kenneth M. *America in 1857: A Nation on the Brink*. New York: Oxford University Press, 1990.

Standage, Henry. *The March of the Mormon Battalion from Council Bluffs to California, Taken from the Journal of Henry Standage*. Edited by Frank A. Golder. New York: Century Company, 1928.

Stegner, Wallace. *The Uneasy Chair: A Biography of Bernard DeVoto.* Salt Lake City: Peregrine Smith Books, 1988.

Stenhouse, T.B.H. *The Rocky Mountain Saints.* New York City: D. Appleton and Company, 1873.

Stewart, William M. Papers. MS/NC 5, Nevada Historical Society, Reno.

Stott, Clifford L. *Search for Sanctuary: Brigham Young and the White Mountain Expedition.* Salt Lake City: University of Utah Press, 1984.

Stout, Hosea. *On the Mormon Frontier: The Diary of Hosea Stout, 1844–1861.* Edited by Juanita Brooks. 2 vols. Salt Lake City: University of Utah Press, 1964.

Taylor, John. Correspondence. CR1 180, First Presidency (John Taylor) Correspondence, 1877–1887, Church History Library.

Taylor, Samuel W. *Rocky Mountain Empire: The Latter-day Saints Today.* New York: MacMillan, 1978.

Thatcher, Linda. "The 'Gentile Polygamist': Arthur Brown, Ex-Senator from Utah." *Utah Historical Quarterly* 52, no. 3 (Summer 1984): 231–45.

Thomasson, Gordon C. "The Manifesto Was a Victory!" *Dialogue: A Journal of Mormon Thought* 6, no. 1 (Spring 1971): 37–45.

Thompson, Margaret. "The Spider Web: Congressional Lobbying in the Age of Grant." PhD diss., University of Wisconsin, 1979; rpt. Ithaca: Cornell University Press, 1985.

To the People of Utah. Salt Lake City: Republican Party of Utah, 1895.

Tolton, John F. "Memories of the Life of John Franklin Tolton." In Tolton Journals and Reminiscences, 1887–1894, MS 4922, box 1, fd. 1, LDS Church History Library.

Trumbo, Isaac. Scrapbook, 1895–1896. MIC A 1960, Utah State Archives, Salt Lake City.

Tucker, John Randolph. *Polygamy: Speech of Hon. John Randolph Tucker of Virginia, in the House of Representatives.* Washington, DC: Franklin Printing House, 1887.

Tullidge, Edward W. *History of Salt Lake City and Its Founders.* Salt Lake City: Star Printing, 1886.

———. *Tullidge's Histories: Containing the History of All the Northern, Eastern, and Western Counties of Utah, also the Counties of Southern Idaho.* Salt Lake City: Juvenile Instructor Press, 1889.

Turner, John G. *Brigham Young: Pioneer Prophet.* Cambridge: Harvard University Press, 2012.

Ulrich, Laurel Thatcher. *A House Full of Females: Plural Marriage and Women's Rights in Early Mormonism, 1835–1870*. New York: Knopf, 2017.

US Senate Committee on Territories. *The Admission of Utah: Report of a Hearing*. Washington, DC: Government Printing Office, 1888.

Utah Commission. Minute Books A–E, Utah State Archives, Salt Lake City.

Van Deusen, Glyndon G. *Horace Greeley: Nineteenth-Century Crusader*. Philadelphia: University of Pennsylvania Press, 1953.

Van Orden, Bruce A. *A Prisoner for Conscience' Sake: The Life of George Reynolds*. Salt Lake City: Deseret Book, 1992.

Van Wagenen, Lola. "In Their Own Behalf: The Politicization of Mormon Women and the 1870 Franchise." *Dialogue: A Journal of Mormon Thought* 24, no. 4 (Winter 1991): 31–43.

———. *Sister-Wives and Suffragists: Polygamy and the Politics of Woman Suffrage, 1870–1896*. Provo: BYU JFS Institute, 1994.

Vogel, Dan, ed. *History of Joseph Smith and the Church of Jesus Christ of Latter-day Saints: A Source- and Text-Critical Edition*. 8 vols. Salt Lake City: Smith–Pettit Foundation, 2015.

Volwiler, Albert T. Papers, 1898–1958. LMC 2425, Lilly Library, Indiana University.

Voters of Utah, Beware! [Salt Lake City]: Republican Party of Utah, 1894.

Walker, Ronald W. "Thomas L. Kane and Utah's Quest for Self-Government, 1846–51." *Utah Historical Quarterly* 69, no. 2 (Spring 2001): 100–19.

———. *Wayward Saints: The Godbeites and Brigham Young*. Urbana: University of Illinois Press, 1998.

———, Richard E. Turley Jr., and Glen M. Leonard. *Massacre at Mountain Meadows: An American Tragedy*. New York: Oxford University Press, 2008.

Warren, Francis E. Papers, 1867–1974. CN 00013, American Heritage Center, University of Wyoming Library.

Weinheimer, John L., comp. *New York Daily Tribune: Index*. New York: Tribune Association, 1881–90.

Wells, Emmeline B. "The History of Woman Suffrage in Utah, 1870–1900." In *Battle for the Ballot: Essays on Woman Suffrage in Utah, 1870–1896*, edited by Carol Cornwall Madsen, 33–51. Logan: Utah State University Press, 1997.

Wells, Heber M. Correspondence, 1895–1904. Series 235, Utah State Archives, Salt Lake City.

Wells, Merle W. *Anti-Mormonism in Idaho, 1872–92.* Provo: Brigham Young University Press, 1978.

West, Franklin L. *Life of Franklin D. Richards: President of the Council of the Twelve Apostles.* Salt Lake City: Deseret News Press, 1924.

White, Jean Bickmore. *Charter for Statehood: The Story of Utah's State Constitution.* Salt Lake City: University of Utah Press, 1996.

———, ed. *Church, State, and Politics: The Diaries of John Henry Smith.* Salt Lake City: Signature Books, 1990.

———. "Utah State Elections: 1895–1899." PhD diss., University of Utah, 1968.

———. "The Woman's Place Is in the Constitution: The Struggle for Equal Rights in Utah in 1895." *Utah Historical Quarterly* 42, no. 4 (Fall 1974): 344–69.

Whitney, Orson F. *History of Utah.* 4 vols. Salt Lake City: George Q. Cannon and Sons: 1892–1904.

Willey, Norman B. Gubernatorial Papers. AR0002.0002. Idaho State Historical Society/State Archives, Boise.

Williams, J. D. "The Separation of Church and State in Mormon Theory and Practice." *Dialogue: A Journal of Mormon Thought* 1, no. 2 (Summer 1966): 30–54.

Williams, R. Hal. *Years of Decision: American Politics in the 1890s.* John Wiley and Sons: New York, 1978.

Wolfinger, Henry J. "A Reexamination of the Woodruff Manifesto in the Light of Utah Constitutional History." *Utah Historical Quarterly* 39, no. 4 (Fall 1971): 328–49.

Woodruff, Wilford. *The Discourses of Wilford Woodruff.* Edited by G. Homer Durham. Salt Lake City: Bookcraft, 1946.

———. General Correspondence. CR1 171, First Presidency (Wilford Woodruff) General Correspondence, 1887–1898, Church History Library.

———. Journals and papers, 1828–1898. MS 1352, Church History Library. For published edition, see Kenney, ed., *Wilford Woodruff's Journal.*

———. Letterbooks, Sept. 1887–Dec. 1893. MS 3923, LDS Church History Library.

Young, Brigham. Papers, 1837–1893. Ms 0566, Special Collections, Marriott Library.

———. Office Files, 1832–1878. CR 1234, LDS Church History Library.

Young, Brigham, Jr. Diaries, 1862–1902. MS 1236, LDS Church History Library. For excerpts, see *Minutes of the Apostles*.
———. Diary, Oct. 1900–July 1902. MS 8575, LDS Church History Library.
———. Papers, 1865–1894. MS 7879, LDS Church History Library.
Young, John W. Papers, 1864–1878. MS 2184, LDS Church History Library.
Zane, Charles S., Diaries. Illinois State Library, Springfield, Illinois.

INDEX

Y

Z

PRAISE FOR FINALLY STATEHOOD!

"Lyman ably details the long historical arc that made Utah the forty-fifth state. Before achieving statehood, Utah faced federal legislation that increasingly threatened the territory's LDS majority. Accustomed to unquestioned obedience, Latter-day Saint leaders took decades to learn how their defiance of federal authority impeded their dream of statehood. After confronting the labyrinthine Gilded Age realities of Washington, DC, LDS officials eventually learned how to avoid political conflict, adapt to national pressure, moderate their image, hire lobbyists, embrace bribery, and disavow polygamy (publicly, if not privately). This is the behind-the-scenes story of how that all came to be."

—**John W. Quist**, Professor of History, Shippensburg University of Pennsylvania; author of *James Buchanan and the Coming of the Civil War*

"Why did it take a half century for Utah Territory to gain statehood, through what maneuvering and by whom was this accomplished, what role did polygamy play, and why is Utah's constitution unique? For answers (many surprising), Lyman's *Finally Statehood!* is a comprehensive study that chronicles the agonizing transformation of the "kingdom in the West" to a conventional yet exciting American state. Fortunately, among the senior lions guarding the waterhole of truth about Utah's turbulent political history, one finds Lyman still on duty."

—**William P. MacKinnon**, past president, Mormon History Association; editor, *At Sword's Point: A Documentary History of the Utah War*

"Leo Lyman offers an insightful, fast-paced, page-turning narrative that should be required reading for anyone seeking to understand Utah. He reminds us of the actual tortured path of Utah's struggle for statehood. Diving deeply into fifty critical years of nineteenth-century primary documents, he produces a compelling history of conflict and grudging progress. It is a fascinating journey into the *realpolitik* of how a raw, emergent nation tried to control a "unique people" who, for their part, did their best to retain their own political aspirations."

—**Ken Verdoia**, co-producer of the documentary film *Utah: The Struggle for Statehood*; former director of production, KUED TV; recipient of twenty-nine regional Emmy Awards